The Unheralded

Men and Women of the Berlin Blockade and Airlift

Edwin Gere

Cover design by Dayna Thacker
Cover photograph by Richard Gere
Index by Betty Steinfeld
Interior design, editing, and production by Claudia Gere

National Library of Canada Cataloguing in Publication

Gere, Edwin A. (Edwin Andrus), Jr.
  The unheralded: men and women of the Berlin blockade and airlift / Edwin Gere.

Includes bibliographical references and index.
ISBN 1-55369-885-1

  1. Berlin (Germany)—History—Blockade, 1948-1949. I. Title.

DD881.G47 2002   943'.155408'0922   C2002-904019-1

 *Printed in Victoria, Canada*

This book was published on-demand in cooperation with Trafford Publishing.
On-demand publishing is a unique process and service of making a book available for retail sale to the public taking advantage of on-demand manufacturing and Internet marketing. On-demand publishing includes promotions, retail sales, manufacturing, order fulfillment, accounting and collecting royalties on behalf of the author.

Suite6E, 2333 Government St., Victoria, B.C. V8T 4P4, CANADA
Phone 250-383-6864   Toll-free 188-232-4444 (Canada & US
Fax 250-383-6804   E-mail sales @trafford.com
Web site www.trafford.com   TRAFFORD PUBLISHING IS A DIVIDIOSN OF TRAFFORD HOLDINGS LTD.
Trafford Catalogue # 02-0698   www.trafford.com/robots/02-0698.html

10   9   8   7   6   5   4   3   2   1

Table of Contents

Table of Contents   iii

Foreword   vii

Preface   xi

Part One   1

1 War and Berlin: The Early Years   3
The Howley Incident   6
Moving Into Berlin   7
The Soviets Plunder Berlin   11
Continued Soviet Intransigence   13
The Road to Potsdam   14
A Fragile Big Three Relationship   15
Teheran   17
Yalta   18
Potsdam   20
Soviet Finesse in Berlin   25

2 The Intermediate Years: 1946-1948   29
An American Airman's Story   32
The British Approach   33
Stuttgart 1946   33
Elections: October 1946   35
The Currency Issue   35

Four Stars for Clay   37
The Marshall Plan   37
An American Soldier's Story   39
The Final CFM Meeting   39
CIA Concerns   40
Three-Power Meeting: 1948   41
Pinpricks   42
Russian Walkout: March 20, 1948   43
April Tensions   44
Blockade   45

3 Blockade and the Western Response: 1948-1949   47
The French Attitude   48
Moving to the Airlift Decision   49
Support for Clay and Robertson   52
Implementing the Airlift Decision   53
French Participation   53
General Tunner Takes Over   54
An Airlift Pilot Remembers   55
Airlift Growing Pains   56
Airlift Housing Problems   58
Public Opinion and the Airlift   61
Those Wonderful Flying Boats   62
A Young Berliner's Outlook   64
Skymasters Needed   65
November 30, 1948: Airlift Nadir   65
Connie Bennett the Morale Builder   67
Christmas 1948: Operation Santa Claus   70
Flynn's Inn   71
1949: Tonnage and Determination   73
April 16, 1949: The Easter Parade   73
Blockade's End   74

Part Two   79

4 Airlift Personalities: Americans   81
Air Police   82
Airways and Air Communications Service   84
Line Mechanics and Technicians   88
The Constabulary Forces   98
Base Support Specialists   102

Flight Engineers and Radio Operators 110

Commissioned Air Crews 117

5 Airlift Personalities: British and Commonwealth Forces 129

Noncommissioned Forces 131

Commissioned Forces 149

Civilian Contract Flyers 153

6 Berlin and the Berliners 161

Historic Berlin 162

The Berliners of 1948-1949 165

Berliners at Heart: West Germans and the Airlift 183

7 Full Measure of Devotion: Commonwealth and German Casualties 187

British and Commonwealth Casualties 188

German Casualties 196

8 Full Measure of Devotion: American Casualties 201

American Casualties 202

9 Airlift Veteran Groups and Reunions 225

The Thirtieth Anniversary 226

The Fortieth Anniversary 226

The Fiftieth Anniversary 229

Airlift Gratitude Foundation 234

Berlin Airlift Historical Foundation 234

Airlift/Tanker Association 236

Berlin Airlift Veterans Association 236

British Berlin Airlift Association 237

South African Air Force Berlin Airlift Reunion Committee 238

10 Perspectives 241

Berlin, July 19, 1949 241

July 19, 1950. What Was Gained? 242

July 19, 2002 244

Appendix 245

Veteran Respondents 247

American Veterans 247

British and Commonwealth Veterans 251

German Veterans 254

Abbreviations 257

Acknowledgments and Sources 259
    Documents 261
    Books 261
    Monographs 263
    Periodicals 264

Notes 265

Index 273

Foreword

THE BLOCKADE OF SURFACE and water supply routes into Berlin by the Soviet Union in the summer of 1948 was an act of war. As a generalization, societies and their historians are quick to identify the architects and managers of war. Societies, however, are equally slow to point out the individuals who must make the personal sacrifices and provide the motivation needed to successfully overcome the struggle.

The Berlin airlift was no exception to this rule. The statesmen and generals who made the decision that led to the airlift have been given substantial press. The Berliners, however, who fought to survive the blockade for eleven months, and the allied personnel who undertook the almost impossible task of feeding, clothing, and providing heat along with medication for the 2.24 million Berliners, have been left alongside the autobahns of history.

Now comes Ed Gere, airlift pilot, author, and political scientist, who tells the story of the Berliners and other nameless groups who made the Berlin airlift a pivotal hinge in history. These were the people who put the welfare of others ahead of self-aggrandizement and provided the needed motivation for success. Ed's work, *The Unheralded: Men and Women of the Berlin Blockade and Airlift,* tells the story of those who have been forgotten in the grand sweep of history. *The Unheralded* brings into graphic relief the personal experiences and motivations of the Brits and their compatriots from the far reaches of the empire who came to relieve the suffering, the Yanks from small towns and cities of America who answered the clarion call to supply Berlin, and the more than two million Berliners who chose to fight for their devastated city rather than suffer under the Russian yoke. *The Unheralded* is a composite of the forgotten in the greatest humanitarian adventure in history.

Who paved the road to the blockade of Berlin? A careful reading of history will show that diplomats and military decision-makers had the most profound influence. The optimistic meeting at Yalta in early 1945 produced a draft protocol that would be used to govern a conquered Germany. At Yalta there was cause to be optimistic as three massive armies converged on the heart of Germany: those of Marshals Zhukov and Konev from the east and General Eisenhower from the west. As these three land forces moved toward Berlin, the strategic and tactical air forces of the allies were reducing the city to four hundred square miles of rubble. The end of the war was imminent. The struggle for peace was at hand.

In July 1945, allied diplomats and decision-makers convened at Potsdam to make the concrete decisions on the governance of defeated Germany. At this historic meeting, the allies signed a utopian agreement designed to provide a structure for governing both a divided Germany and Berlin. In the heady aftermath of victory, this abstract document ignored the fundamental cultural, historic, and philosophical differences that existed between the western allies and the Russians. In addition, the western allies overlooked the fact that Berlin was isolated with no access guaranteed by the treaty.

A great fault line separated the ideology of West from East. This line would create a hinge that sealed the future of Germany. On the one hand, the East was vindictive and wanted Germany and Berlin reduced to a pastoral nation with no manufacturing. The West, on the other hand, was more benevolent and would nurture democratic institutions, allowing Germany to return to the community of nations.

As the seasons passed, it became increasingly clear that the plans laid at Yalta and Potsdam would not satisfy both East and West. Ideological clashes in the Allied Control Council, an economy that had sunk to using cigarettes as currency, and other differences and disagreements between the member nations failed to rebuild a broken nation and city.

By spring 1948, with one exception, all land between the Elbe River in the west and Vladivostok in the east lay under the boot of the Red Army. The historic nations of central and eastern Europe were now in the Soviet orbit, along with vast reaches beyond the Urals. The one exception was a small parcel of land in the western sectors of Berlin. In terms of political geography, the Soviet Union seemed on the verge of capturing control of western Europe. In order to achieve this objective, the Russians imposed a blockade on the supply routes to the western allied enclaves in Berlin. It looked like the dream of the czars was about to come true.

When the blockade began, there was no consensus among the allied military commanders and diplomats as to a solution. General Lucius Clay, the military governor of Germany, had successfully used the air corridors during a mini-airlift in April 1948; there was, however, no protocol covering their use by the western allies. And the standard refrains were heard throughout the land: negotiate with the Soviets, wait for a break, supplying Berlin by air is pie-in-the-sky, this has never been done, and so on.

The military hierarchy and diplomats had failed, but there were two individuals who could recognize the importance of Berlin in the grand design of Europe. The prime minister of Great Britain and the president of the United States said, with a unified voice, "We stay in Berlin!" General Clay, in concert with British General Sir Bernard Robertson, took the initiative to stay in Berlin and launched a full-scale airlift. From this inauspicious beginning evolved one of the greatest humanitarian adventures of all time.

In order to assist General Clay, three men emerged who could put the strategic interest of the western allies and the day-to-day operations of the airlift into high gear. In Washington, two generals, Hoyt Vandenberg and Albert Wedemeyer, promoted the talents of another general, William Tunner, who, following appointment as airlift commander, arrived in Wiesbaden to a very cold reception. In late summer 1948, General Tunner, along with a disparate group that included Aussies, Brits, French, Kiwis, South Africans, Yanks, and the hopes of over two million Berliners, began a stepped-up airlift.

The Berlin airlift was more than a test of national resolve. The Berlin airlift was a defining moment in the struggle for the heart of Europe. A city half again as large as Philadelphia would depend on air power for survival. All food, medical services, and other necessities for survival would come by *die Luftbrücke,* the airlift. For 462 days, the future of Berliners and Germany would hang in the balance.

Between June 1948 and September 1949, this staggering feat became a reality. It is an impossible task to determine who or which group played the ultimate role in the success of this great Homeric effort. As someone in antiquity remarked, "Success has a thousand fathers and failure is an orphan." Success in the Berlin airlift goes to the nameless and faceless individuals who made superhuman efforts as the days passed into months. Each individual and group contributed to the success of this epic event. If there is to be an assignment of failure, it should be reserved for some of those in the military command and the diplomats. These folks failed to understand the strategic value of Berlin and the indomitable spirit of the common person against all odds.

As a group, the people of Berlin showed inordinate perseverance. Those hardy individuals, who had suffered three years under the ever-tightening Soviet yoke, refused to abandon their city. Warmed by twig fires and subsisting on starvation caloric intake, the Berliners stayed the course. Hope returned as they listened to the constant drone of aircraft flying into and out of the city. The epitome of success occurred on Easter Sunday 1949. On this day, with aircraft flying at one-minute intervals, record tonnages of supplies were moved into Berlin in a 24-hour period. The little people had won and they had not fired a shot. The Soviet Union had lost, *and the voice of the turtle was heard in the land!*

The Berlin airlift produced thousands of individuals who made heroic contributions: women who repaired the hot runways during operations, with a York or a C-54 coming their way every three minutes; hundreds of displaced persons on the loading crews who could move ten tons of coal in five minutes—by hand; airmen and sailors who deiced the wings of the planes with swabs and buckets during freezing rain and sleet; sentries on lonely nights walking their posts; aircraft service crews with fuel and cargo always on schedule; air crews who delivered supplies; and lest we forget, the more than two million Berliners who elected to stay and face illness and starvation rather than submit to Soviet tyranny.

The Unheralded remembers those who were not accorded recognition, who have never seen their story told, and yet were the very backbone of the airlift. Ed Gere weaves a rich mosaic of triumph and tragedy as he spins a sample of these experiences into a seamless story. The author also reminds the reader of the casualties suffered. The stories will make you laugh, make you cry, make you angry, make you happy, pinch you in the soft spots of the heart, but they will always make you proud.

The thousands of allied personnel who worked the airlift, and the 2.24 million Berliners who endured the blockade, do not consider themselves heroes. These groups bet everything on a roll of the dice and won the jackpot in the cold war. Their actions permitted Berlin, like the *Phoenix,* to rise from the ashes and once again become the beautiful city on the Spree. A dynamic and industrious people were given the opportunity of self-determination by *die Luftbrücke.*

The lime trees are back on the Unter den Linden, the animals entertain the children of Berlin at the Tiergarten Zoo, a unified Federal Republic of Germany sends a popularly elected Parliament back to a renovated Reichstag. Germany has rejoined the community of nations, thanks to a cohort that included two visionary politicians, four thinking generals, almost two and a quarter million Berlin *burghers,* an assortment of Brits and their compatriots from the empire, and Yanks from the cities, towns, villages, and open spaces of the United States. They manned the ramparts for 462 days back in 1948 and 1949 and are now scattered to the four corners of the earth.

Chuck Powell
Professor of Political Science, University of Nebraska at Omaha
Enlisted navy airlift pilot

Preface

IN MAY 1999, AT THE FIFTIETH anniversary Berlin ceremonies marking the end of the blockade, imposed by the Soviet Union on Berlin's western sectors from June 1948 to May 1949, I became more emotionally linked to the magnitude and significance of the Berlin airlift, the western allies' response to the blockade, than at any time during the preceding half century. I had attended the 1989 fortieth anniversary observances in Frankfurt, Wiesbaden, Fassberg, and Berlin, and certainly had enjoyed and appreciated the full panorama of reunion events.

Nothing, however, equaled in my mind the drama of the fiftieth anniversary ceremonies, with veterans from all participating nations present, and, as I was pleased to learn, Berliners who had worked as civil laborers during the blockade and had performed countless menial, unsung tasks, also present as invited guests of the city and the German federal government. Also attending the reunion ceremonies were family members of those who lost their lives in airlift operations. Upon returning home, I realized that my understanding and appreciation of this stirring moment in cold war history would not be complete until I had written my own account.

Commencing my venture with a review of airlift literature, which seemed to have emerged at approximate ten-year intervals coincident with anniversary observances, I found running through it a persistent strain glorifying those most visible in airlift operations: the pilots, navigators, signallers, and flight engineers; in short, the air crews. This was a natural point of emphasis, it seemed to me then. My own airlift time was served as a C-47 and C-54 copilot, then first pilot, initially at Wiesbaden but for a much lengthier time at Fassberg, in the British zone of occupation in northern Germany, and following the blockade's end, at Tempelhof air base in Berlin. Hence, it was easy for me to appreciate a writer's tendency to focus on the air crews who hauled the supplies, endured the foul flying weather, and took most of the risks associated with mounting the massive air support operation to Germany's historic capital city.

Yet as I studied the airlift literature, an old lesson from my training and combat days in World War II kept coming to mind: it takes ten persons on the ground to keep one in the air. If this remains at least somewhat true today, I thought, then why have those ten persons not been accorded equal billing in the airlift literature? With this question in mind, I decided it was time to pay proper homage to those whose deeds had gone largely unheralded.

This, then, is a story of the allied forces that made the Berlin airlift a success. They came from seven nations—Australia, Canada, France, Great Britain, New Zealand, South Africa, and the United States. While the pilots, navigators, and signallers who flew the all-important coal, food, medicines, and supplies to Berlin form a small part of this chronicle—even junior-grade officers must be considered low on the totem pole of rank, prestige, and recognition—the primary focus of this book rests on the ground forces, those enlisted soldiers, sailors, and airmen, men and women both, and noncommissioned air crew members, all largely unheralded in airlift literature, without whose contributions the airlift would never have succeeded. They are the airplane and engine mechanics (fitters, in British Royal Air Force language), truck and lorry drivers, air and military policemen, supply clerks, constabulary troops, medical personnel, finance specialists, loaders and unloaders, weather forecasters, special services workers, tower, airways, and Ground Controlled Approach (GCA) operators, welders and sheet metal workers, radio technicians, flight engineers, cooks, dining hall attendants, and many, many others who performed endless tasks vital to airlift operations.

Together with the air crews, they saved a city of 2.24 million inhabitants and won the gratitude and respect not only of Berliners but also of the free world. Their stories, some of which are woven into the ongoing text while others appear in chapters earmarked for American and Commonwealth forces, are told as eyewitnesses and participants in that massive, historic, military and political event. These stories are overwhelmingly modest in tone; no one whose personal experiences are described here fancied herself or himself a hero. In their view, they were simply ordinary guys and gals living in extraordinary times. But heroes they were, nonetheless—unheralded heroes.

Equally important, this is very much a story of the courageous men and women of Berlin who, during the years immediately preceding the blockade, rallied in the streets to demonstrate against the Soviets, and firmly resisted their efforts to extend the Russian influence throughout the city. Then, when the blockade was imposed, they steeled themselves against a meager daily food ration and hunkered down in their dimly lighted and under heated dwellings to stand fast against a cold, harsh winter.

For thousands there were no jobs during the eleven months of the blockade, but the lucky ones found employment at the Gatow and

Tempelhof airfields, unloading coal and supplies from the airplanes, filling in runway holes between aircraft landings, and keeping the runways clear of snow and ice. In the late summer and fall of 1948, almost 17,000 Berliners, forty per cent of them women, labored tirelessly on long work shifts to construct in record time, by hand, an additional airfield in Tegel, a district of the French occupation sector, so as to provide a third landing facility for airlift supplies. During those long eleven months of the blockade, all Berliners were too busy trying to survive to consider themselves heroes, yet without their courage and resolve, it is very questionable if the blockade could have been broken. Their stories, too, are told from their vantage points as eyewitnesses and participants.

Other participants in the airlift drama who must be recognized are the hundreds of displaced persons, largely from overrun countries of eastern Europe, some of whom worked tirelessly and anonymously to load aircraft, others who served as guards at western bases, and still others who performed unloading duties in Berlin alongside Berliners themselves.

I caution, however, that the personal stories set forth in this book about both the airlift forces and the Berliners are anecdotal only and have been selected largely from among those responses voluntarily submitted. As such, there has been no attempt to develop a scientific sample—an accurate microcosm of the aggregate experiences of all participants; they are simply presented, hopefully, as a representative cross section of those thousands who fought the blockade and served the airlift in so many different capacities.

From among the many blockade and airlift veterans, sadly, I was successful in securing information about only a few who have since passed on. Accordingly, this, for the most part, is a story of elderly airlift and blockade survivors. Of the personal stories told, most of which are seen in chapters four, five, and six, some are comical, some are poignant, and some are almost unbelievable. But they are all told from the heart.

Last but clearly not least, those who lost their lives in airlift service are highlighted in two chapters devoted to their memory. Some airlift literature has listed and briefly described the 32 Americans, 39 British and Commonwealth subjects, and the indeterminate number of Germans who lost their lives in airlift-related accidents, but these two chapters represent, to my knowledge, the first presentation of both biographical detail and circumstances surrounding their deaths.

British and American airlift veterans are cited in boldface type in the rank, where possible, in which they entered upon airlift duty. German blockade veterans and British and American civilians are also cited in boldface.

I have an uneasy feeling that this book exhibits an imbalance in coverage of events that occurred at the various airlift bases. In eight months of duty at Fassberg, I came to know more about that base than the others, especially the other British bases that I never knew at all, except for being diverted to some in poor weather. Hence, Fassberg receives more detailed treatment. Hopefully, this apparent imbalance is not bothersome to the reader.

As an airlift veteran, a junior-grade officer and pilot, I run the risk in writing this book of casting myself in the ranks of those whom I seek to honor. However, I *had* to write this book, my own airlift status notwithstanding. This is not an autobiography. Far from it. And even though some junior-grade officers' stories are presented herein, mine is not. The book's primary focus remains on those enlisted soldiers, sailors, airmen, and civil laborers, who, despite their disavowals, were truly the unheralded heroes of the blockade and airlift.

In carrying out the research and writing of this book, I have been privileged to meet and correspond with some of the finest men and women one could hope to know. Having taken part in the greatest humanitarian enterprise in modern history, they are all rightly proud of their roles in this momentous cold war undertaking. Yet modesty has been the overwhelming hallmark of their responses to my queries. A sense of simply having done one's duty pervades my mountainous piles of memos, scribblings, telephone notes, returned questionnaires, personal memoirs, letters, and diaries. To read and learn about the experiences, memories, and dreams of these remarkable men and women, and then to try to catch their moods accurately in writing, has been for me a richly rewarding yet humbling encounter. My payoff is that along the way I have made so many wonderful friends, many of them pen pals whom I shall probably never meet in person. They are the unheralded.

Edwin Gere
Leverett, Massachusetts
February 2003

Part One

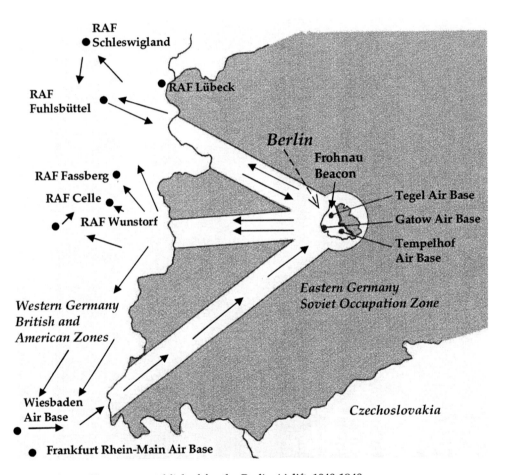

Figure 1. Air traffic routes established for the Berlin Airlift, 1948-1949

One

War and Berlin: The Early Years

I cannot forecast to you the action of Russia. It is a riddle wrapped in a mystery inside an enigma.

Winston Churchill, October 1, 1939

ON TUESDAY, OCTOBER 7, 1947, General Lucius D. Clay, military governor of the United States occupation zone in Germany, landed in Washington aboard his luxury C-54, ready to take part in high-level talks concerning the German economy. An old hand on the Washington political scene, having had several duty assignments in the D.C. area, the general was warmly greeted by President Harry S. Truman as he arrived in the elaborate White House cabinet room for a meeting of the National Security Council (NSC). Accompanying Clay were his close friend and political advisor in Germany, Ambassador Robert Murphy, and General Walter Bedell Smith, Ambassador to Moscow, the latter having traveled to Washington for a brief period of state department consultations. Discussion of financial matters was quickly followed by questioning about relations between the United States and the Soviet Union respecting the German occupation. In their response, Clay and Smith electrified their listeners with a forceful warning that "we must be prepared for Soviet action to force our withdrawal from Berlin and we must remain."

Their shocking announcement marked the first time, a full nine months before the actual blockade of Berlin was imposed, that those on the firing line in Germany had voiced such an alarming view before the assembled NSC officials, and it staggered those in the cabinet room, who since the end of the war had accorded rather low priority to occupation affairs. Would Truman and his Washington advisors now heed Clay and Smith's warning? In the weeks and months prior to the Washington meeting, Clay had clearly harbored growing feelings about Soviet intentions but generally kept his own counsel, particularly on the possibility of being pushed out of Berlin.

For nearly two-and-a-half years following his arrival in Germany, the hard-working, chain-smoking Clay labored long and tenaciously to foster good will among the four victorious World War II powers. Appointed deputy military governor under General Dwight Eisenhower in April 1945, he arrived early in May as a freshly minted lieutenant general to take up his new post, realizing full well that the Soviets had an agenda for Germany of their own design. Yet he was determined to understand their point of view, to reach out for four-power unity, and to keep always in front of him the goal of a democratic and peaceful Germany eventually governing itself under a new constitution. To that end, he toiled ten- and twelve-hour days, demanded the same work commitment from his staff, and sought harmonious official and personal relationships with his English, French, and Russian counterparts, especially the latter. In those two-and-a-half years, virtually nothing deterred him from seeking amity with the Soviets.

On June 8 in Frankfurt, Clay commented to Charles "Chip" Bohlen that the key to getting along with the Russians is that one must give trust to get trust, whereupon the veteran state department diplomat responded, "...within a few months, or certainly within a year, you will become one of the officials in the American government most opposed to the Soviets." Bohlen, fluent in Russian and one of his department's few Soviet experts, knew what he was talking about. Clay was perhaps not in a year's time convinced of Bohlen's view, but as mentioned earlier, he had clearly come around to that position by the fall of 1947. It had to be, then, an immense disillusionment with the Soviets that led him, with Ambassador Smith, to make his blockbuster October declaration before the National Security Council.

Despite Clay's ongoing efforts to stimulate harmony among the four allies, the Russians' behavior with respect to occupation matters triggered increasing alarm among the three western allies, raising more and more questions about their long-range intentions. One of the first incidents to arouse his suspicions occurred in early September 1945, soon after allied settlement of the four zones of occupation and the four occupation sectors of Berlin, and shortly after agreement had been reached by which ten western allied trains per day would move through the Soviet zone. Without warning, the Russians stopped trains moving from the west into Berlin and checked the identity of passengers. In response, Clay threatened to place armed guards on his trains, with orders to shoot if necessary. Clay did the right thing; the Russians backed off. Access to Berlin was viewed by the western allies as a natural right, emanating from previous tripartite agreements over the physical division of defeated Germany.

Lying 175 kilometers inside the new Soviet zone of occupation, Berlin was a virtual island, isolated and incapable of self-support. If the western allies were to supply their garrisons in the capital city, and fuel, goods, medicines, foodstuffs, and other vital necessities of life were to reach the 2.24 million persons living in its western sectors, everything had to cross the Soviet zone. Yet the guarantee of access had not been reduced to writing. On June 29 of 1945, a meeting took place at Marshal Georgi K. Zhukov's headquarters at Karlshorst in Berlin's eastern suburbs, one of its purposes being to conclude various details of the emerging occupation. Present were General Clay as Eisenhower's representative, accompanied by Ambassador Murphy and Major General Floyd Parks, the new U.S. troop commander in Berlin. For the British were Lieutenant General Sir Ronald Weeks and Sir William Strang, a veteran diplomat and advisor to General Weeks. The Soviet Union was represented by General Alexei Antonov, the Red Army chief of staff.

Field Marshal Bernard Law Montgomery, commander of British forces in Germany, was on home leave. Eisenhower, too, was back in the states for a month of leave and vacation. "After addressing a joint session of Congress," wrote Murphy many years later, "Eisenhower began on June 25 a quiet fortnight's golf-playing vacation at [the Greenbrier] White Sulphur Springs, West Virginia. He did not return to Germany until July 10, a week before the opening of the Potsdam conference." He would have had no desire to attend the June 29 meeting at any rate, after being rudely forced to wait for six hours for Zhukov's appearance at their first session on June 5. This time, however, the heavyset Zhukov, Soviet conqueror of Berlin in the last days of World War II, top-heavy with medals draped across his chest, who had himself just returned from Moscow and a round of victory parades and celebrations, was genial and sociable, as was General of the Army Vassily D. Sokolovsky, who would ultimately become Clay's opposite number as the Soviet representative to the Allied Control Council (ACC), the four-power organization designated to govern occupied Germany. Would these two be equally genial about hard business matters over Berlin and Germany soon to arise in the ACC?

At the lengthy June 29 session, Clay took personal notes, including the passage, "It was agreed that all traffic—air, road, and rail...would be free from border search or control by customs or military authorities." His notes tended to confirm two important factors: first, a message from President Truman to Marshal Joseph V. Stalin on June 14 specifying the right of free access to Berlin and, second, Stalin's June 16 general response in which he provided a vague assurance "that all necessary measures would be taken in accordance with the plan agreed upon...." On this basis, then, weak and nonspecific as Stalin's answer was, the Americans felt that sufficient common ground had been reached for maintaining direct and unfettered access to Berlin from the west. General Parks also wrote a rather elaborate account of the meeting, yet both his and Clay's personal notes were just that; no *official* record was made of the meeting. Through the remainder of his duty in Germany, Clay was to rue the fact that no written guarantee of access to the capital city had been secured.

Five years later, however, in his *Decision in Germany*, Clay had changed his mind about guarantee of access to Berlin. "I doubt very much if anything in writing would have done any more to prevent the events which took place than the verbal agreement which we made," wrote the former commander. He then went on to point out that the Soviets always seemed to find technical reasons for ignoring agreements, verbal or written.

The Howley Incident

During the first two postwar years, additional incidents occurring in Berlin and throughout occupied Germany heightened tensions between the western allies and the Soviet Union. In the early summer of 1945, even before the September train incidents, the first distressing episode occurred as the British, French, and Americans moved to take possession of their designated sectors in the capital city. Colonel Frank Howley, recently appointed deputy commandant in the American sector of Berlin, encountered Soviet resistance as he prepared to lead a reconnaissance contingent of troops through the Russian zone to assume their positions in the city's western districts.

To Howley's great delight, one of his aides had found a Horsch roadster, once the prized possession of a Nazi officer, hidden under a haystack at a farm near Halle, where his reconnaissance unit was temporarily encamped. Howley immediately took a keen liking to the vehicle, and it was hauled to the unit garage to be made ready for his use as a command car. "At daybreak on June 17 [actually June 23], we started for the German capital," wrote Howley. "I led the column in my Horsch, which was the only piece of non-American equipment. The Stars and Stripes flapped from the right fender of my car, as from the other command cars, and every windshield bore identifying American stickers."

Howley led his force of about 500 men and 120 vehicles, many of them half-tracks armed with machine guns, from Halle, situated about 33 kilometers northwest from Leipzig, on to Dessau at the Elbe River. There they bivouacked overnight and waited for clearance to continue to Berlin, some eighty kilometers to the northeast. The following morning the convoy crossed the Elbe on an American-built pontoon bridge and immediately made contact with the Russians on the east side of the river. Overhead at the end of the bridge rose a giant arch supporting huge portraits of Lenin and Stalin. A Russian WAC whipped small, red and yellow signal flags at the convoy in some sort of indecipherable greeting. Anxious to move on to Berlin, Howley was impatient to secure the necessary papers and proceed. The Russians had other plans.

Moving up the highway under escort by a Soviet officer, Howley's column was suddenly confronted by a roadblock. He was advised by the

Russian to follow him to headquarters, where, after greetings, handshakes, toasts of vodka and wine, and considerable delay, the Russian colonel in charge coolly pointed out that bringing so many men and vehicles violated a prior agreement; only 37 officers, 175 men, and 50 vehicles could be permitted to proceed to Berlin. Howley's quick temper, for which he would later become well known in sessions of the Kommandatura, the planned four-power city governing body, immediately boiled over. He argued the validity of his own orders, demanding to speak with whoever had issued the Russian orders limiting the size of his convoy. This led to an escalation up the ladder of rank from a Colonel Gorelik to an unnamed one star general, until he came face-to-face with a colonel general who gave him the choice of sticking with the number of men and vehicles stipulated by the Russians or returning to Halle. Howley sent word to General Parks in Berlin, describing the problem, and asking his advice.

After a delay of several hours, during which time it became increasingly apparent to Howley that from the beginning he had been on the receiving end of bungled orders, Parks requested Colonel General Sergei Kruglov, Stalin's chief of security in Berlin, to pass only the number of American troops and vehicles previously agreed upon at the diplomatic level. The correct numbers of men and vehicles, however, apparently had not been passed on to Howley in the field. When the dust settled, he was ordered to move on to Berlin with his 37 officers, 150 men, and 50 vehicles and to dispatch the remainder of the contingent back to Halle.

Moving Into Berlin

Colonel Howley would face further surprises in the march to assume his new post, and it was ultimately more than a week before he and his troops took up their stations in Berlin's new American sector. Moving on from the Elbe with his now smaller convoy, he was detained at Babelsberg, twenty kilometers south of Berlin where his contingent met with other American and British troops busy preparing the Cecilienhof Palace at nearby Potsdam for the forthcoming conference of the Big Three—Truman, Churchill, and Stalin. Surrounded by Soviet forces everywhere, Howley's troops found themselves virtual prisoners of the Russians, physically restrained from proceeding on to Berlin, and limited in their movements around Babelsberg. In Berlin itself, a British Royal Air Force advance group moving to assume command of Gatow airfield was forced into a hangar where they were detained for 24 hours, with the freshly appointed station commander virtually imprisoned for two days. Few or no explanations were given by the Soviets for their behavior.

Colonel Howley's detainment, however, provided him with a chance to stop and reflect upon the character and personality of the average Russian soldier—unmoving, absolutely obedient to orders, innately suspicious of the unknown (in this case, the Americans and British), and an inability to exercise any discretion whatsoever. Howley, himself a no-nonsense, bombastic Irishman from Philadelphia, quickly learned that Russian delays meant they were awaiting orders from above, most of which came at a snail's pace. No Russian commander could use any initiative or discretion whatsoever, nor was it likely that any commander might even entertain the notion. Orders were orders, to be strictly obeyed without deviation.

Then, on June 30, 1945, a complete reversal of Soviet attitude occurred. Howley was directed to proceed to Berlin, and the Russians bent over backwards to accommodate the movement of his contingent. Their troops lined the roads leading into the city, shouting encouragement and welcomes, raising their vodka bottles high, and insisting that the Americans stop and share in toasts to allied unity. But not all was sweet and harmonious. At one point in transit an aggressive Soviet officer, his behavior hardened by an overdose of vodka, sought to halt Howley's convoy at a certain bridge along the route, whereupon an American officer whose name, in Howley's words, "I have forgotten but whose deed I will cherish always," alighted from his vehicle and forcefully knocked the Russian into a ditch along the roadside.

Before Howley's convoy reached its final goal of West Berlin, his troops became witness to some of the most terrible devastation seen in all of the Second World War. By early April 1945, Berlin had been reduced to rubble by two years of allied air attacks. Then, in the early morning hours of April 16, the Red Army had moved westward across the Oder and Neisse Rivers, situated about fifty kilometers east of Berlin. Marshal Zhukov had been waiting, amassing his First Byelorussian Army Front for two and a half months, building up strength for this final, momentous siege of Germany's eastern frontier and its historic capital city.

Marshal Ivan S. Konev's First Ukrainian Army Front was also driving against Berlin in a pincers movement. The actual seizure of Berlin, however, had been granted to Zhukov by Stalin himself as a special reward for having defended Moscow against the Nazi assault earlier in the war. The drive came with brutal force over a 325-kilometer front, supported by over 2.5 million troops equipped with powerful assault weapons—6,250 tanks, 41,600 artillery pieces, unnumbered howitzers, automatic guns, and an air armada of 7,500 fighter aircraft.

Defending German troops, composed largely of the *Volkssturm* home guard, a pitiful assemblage of old men and young boys, fought as bravely as they could, armed meagerly with some old rifles, some hand grenades, and a few hand-held *Panzerfaust* anti-tank rockets. They courageously erected makeshift street barricades from which to mount their defenses but, by May 2, when Berlin's garrison commander, General Karl Weidling, formally surrendered the city, the terrible damage had been done. Russian soldiers climbed atop the Brandenburg Gate to hoist the hammer and sickle on the Quadriga, the fabled statue of a Berlin goddess riding a chariot pulled by four sturdy horses. Berlin lay prostrate, in ugly ruins at the hands of the conquering Soviet forces. And for good measure the Soviets changed all Berlin clocks two hours ahead to Moscow time.

On Sunday, July 1, as Howley and his men entered Berlin to take over the U.S. sector, the scene greeting them was one of stark destruction and devastation everywhere. Seventy-six per cent of the city's 1.5 million dwellings were rendered uninhabitable, while twelve per cent were completely destroyed. The *Reichstag* building was a naked skeleton. Vast areas of the city were smoldering ruins. Almost 3,000 water mains were smashed, electric power was virtually nonexistent, and broken sewage lines allowed raw sewage to spill into the rivers, canals, and the ruptured water mains, thereby contaminating what little drinking water was available in the city. The schools were for the most part closed and faced a monumental task in reopening. All telephone service had been destroyed; transportation facilities had been rendered completely inoperable. It was impossible to move about in the city except on foot or perhaps by bicycle. Since no motorized ambulances were left in working order, transport of the sick, wounded, and dead was accomplished by wagon or cart. Medical services, including hospitals not destroyed, were taxed far beyond normal capacity by the rapid spread of typhus, tuberculosis, and starvation. Everywhere corpses awaited burial in shallow, temporary graves.

When President Truman and his party arrived in Berlin in mid-July for the Potsdam conference, they were aghast at the sight of such overwhelming destruction and human suffering. His chief of staff, Admiral William D. Leahy, a tough old sea dog, wrote five years later about the long lines of old men, women, and children he observed moving along country roads in great numbers, clutching their meager belongings, without hope and presumably without any particular destination, just a fervent wish to escape the Soviets. It was only then, even after his years of harsh World War II naval combat, that the veteran fleet commander realized the "horrible destructiveness of modern conflict."

Shortly after Colonel Howley, his men, and other American units took over the occupation of the new U.S. Berlin sector, the 6th Cavalry Group also moved in. **Private First Class Bob Monasmith** of San Francisco was one of those arriving with this group. He had recently been in combat as a radio operator with the 89th Cavalry Recon Squadron, but with the end of hostilities his unit stopped in Bayreuth, near the Czechoslovakian border, only to be reassigned the next morning to Berlin. Bob states that his unit had to proceed northwesterly to Braunschweig, then easterly to Helmstedt for the autobahn trip to Berlin. They were equipped with M-8 armored cars, jeeps, M-5 Stuart light tanks, and M-24 Chaffee light tanks. The men were armed with M-1 Garand rifles, Thompson submachine guns, M-1 carbines, and .45 caliber automatic pistols.

Moving from the Helmstedt border point eastward along the autobahn into Soviet-occupied territory, they were immediately stopped by the Russians and delayed for several hours. This was a favorite Russian tactic, despite the fact that tentative agreements on access to Berlin had been settled and the western allied forces were moving in to take over their respective Berlin sectors. "We finally arrived in the Lichterfelde-West district of Berlin," Bob remembers. "We immediately garrisoned our unit in the recently evacuated barracks of the 1st SS Panzer Division (Hitler's own), which looked like a battlefield. Machine guns and armaments were scattered all over. In the supply buildings we found stack after stack of black panzer uniforms, crash helmets, and other items of battle." Bob's 6th Cavalry Group stayed there for about a week, following which it made several moves within the U.S. sector before settling into permanent quarters. "I should have confiscated a few of those black SS uniforms," says Bob in retrospect. "They would have been valuable souvenirs."

In the early months of occupation, Bob's unit's mission was to maintain roving liaison patrols along the Russian sector borders. Since movement across and through the four Berlin sectors was unrestricted, Bob's forces frequently encountered Russians, fully armed, traveling through the American sector, yet direct contact with them was infrequent, limited usually to barter and sale of small souvenirs.

Russian obstruction of allied movement into Berlin's western sectors and the subsequent establishment of four-power government had a catch to it. At the June 5 meeting between General Eisenhower, Field Marshal Montgomery, General Jean de Lattre de Tassigny, and Marshal Zhukov, the same meeting at which Zhukov had kept the others waiting for six hours, it became crystal clear that unimpeded allied entry into Berlin was directly linked to the American withdrawal from Saxony, Thuringia, and Pomerania, the rich agricultural provinces slated to be part of the Soviet occupation zone that U.S. forces had overrun in the last days of the war.

When Zhukov was reminded by the American commander Eisenhower that it was time to install the Allied Control Council in Berlin, the Marshal responded, "No, not until your troops will have been evacuated from the areas in the Soviet Zone they now illegally occupy." Zhukov was insistent that nothing further would be done until such time as all occupation forces were settled in their respective zones. Once more, here was an example of a high ranking Soviet officer being unable to exercise discretion on his own authority on matters for which his opposite number, General Eisenhower, clearly possessed adequate power.

Stalin's reins on his senior commanders were tight; he reportedly told Harry Hopkins, the legendary former close advisor to President Roosevelt and later President Truman, that Zhukov would not have much authority concerning affairs in Germany. It was Andrei Y. Vishinsky, Stalin's vice-minister for foreign affairs and chief prosecutor for the Soviet Union in the notorious Moscow "purge" trials of 1936–1938, in whom the dictator placed his greater trust.

As a result, until an agreement was reached on exactly when the Soviets would take over those fertile lands designated to be in their occupation zone, they politely but firmly resisted allied entry into Berlin's western sectors and any move to install either the Allied Control Council, which would govern occupied Germany, or the allied Kommandatura, which was to be the governing body for the city. It would not be until July

30 that the ACC was formally convened, with headquarters in the Schöneberg district in the newly formed American sector. The four-power Kommandatura assembled for its first meeting on July 11, 1945.

The Soviets Plunder Berlin

Coupled with the stubborn Soviet posture on withholding allied access to Berlin was the fact that having reached and conquered it while the American and British forces were still far to the west, the Soviets were busy plundering and looting the entire city, including those districts marked for occupation by the western allies. Ever mindful of a victor's virtual right to ravage the conquered land, Russian troops were viciously intent upon stripping it of anything of value: raw materials, machinery, consumer goods, rolling stock, food supplies, and even livestock. Hence, they were not ready to turn over to the western allies their allocated sectors in Berlin until, so to speak, the bird had been plucked. The Soviet command had even issued orders to its troops vacating the western sectors not to leave "even a pisspot" behind.

In February, at the Yalta conference in the Crimea, Stalin had demanded $10 billion in reparations for the Soviet Union out of a possible $20 billion used as a figure for discussion. Again at the Potsdam conference in July, Stalin pressed the issue, making it clear that reparations were uppermost in his mind. By that time it was no secret that the Soviets had plundered all German territory they had overrun, including Berlin, hauling away everything they could seize with complete disregard for accountability to the western allies. Hence, by the time occupation forces were settled in their respective zones and in their designated Berlin sectors, millions of dollars worth of railroad cars, machinery, armaments, food stuffs, and most of the existent livestock were long gone in the direction of Moscow. The western allies were simply faced with a *fait accompli* by the Soviets and in poor position to do much about it. Yet ironically, the Russian ability to organize, maintain account of, and transfer items seized as reparations was less than efficient, with the result that months later numerous loaded flatcars stood idly on railroad sidings in eastern Germany and western Poland, their contents unused, undelivered, and rusting in the elements. Could it be that Stalin derived his pleasure from the mere act of plunder?

The Russians had another motive for stalling on giving up Berlin's western sectors. They had a program, and they exercised it, of propagandizing the Berliners against the western allies, seeking to convince the city's residents that they were the good guys and the British and Americans were not to be trusted. At the same time, the Berliners were not told of the four-power agreement by which their city soon would be carved up into four sectors, being led to believe that the entire city would be permanently occupied by Soviet forces.

Such efforts at brainwashing the Berliners were nonetheless doomed to failure by the unconscionable behavior of the Soviet army. Flush with victory and conscious of the terrible destruction perpetrated by Nazi forces on their own homeland, Russian soldiers, particularly the Central Asians, or Mongols, in the Red Army second echelons, set about in Berlin to rape and loot on a ghastly, staggering scale. As they advanced through East Prussia, Silesia, Hungary, and Romania in their march on Germany, they had been psychologically prepared by their own political officers who erected road signs such as those exhorting their soldiers "to take revenge on the Hitlerites." No woman, young or old, was safe from their violence. Maddened by alcoholic binges, the Red Army mop-up troops, many of them conscripted from Soviet prisons, attacked women in their homes, raped them as their children, horrified, looked on, then looted the premises. If a woman's husband protested, the offending soldier pulled out his pistol and shot him. The fabled order, *"Frau, komm,"* became a nightmare to all Berlin women. Historian Norman Naimark reported that, "Even as they entered bunkers and cellars where Germans hid from the fierce fighting, Soviet soldiers brandished weapons and raped women in the presence of children and men. In some cases, soldiers divided up women according to their tastes; in others, women were gang-raped.

Many victims could not recall how many times they had been ravaged, and over 90,000 women sought medical treatment after being raped. A common practice among Berlin women, in addition to hiding out in attics and closets, was to make themselves as unattractive as possible by dressing in rags and smearing their faces with mud or coal dust. Still, the pattern of conduct appeared to have little consistency, for some Russians, particularly officers and the better educated, abhorred what their fellow soldiers were doing to Berlin women and would take no part.

Conquering armies over the course of history have looted, raped, and plundered in a "to the victor belongs the spoils" frame of mind. Even the armies of the western allies in 1945 were no exception, yet the magnitude and savagery of the Russian assaults were without equal. A rationale for the monstrous raping and looting committed in the early weeks of the Berlin occupation ostensibly had its justification in a remark made by Stalin himself when he suggested that his soldiers were just having a little fun after weeks and months in battle. How horribly misguided and insensitive on this matter the Soviet dictator turned out to be. Ann and John Tusa expressed the point succinctly. "The Red Army lost Berlin politically at the moment it captured it militarily." It was for the most part, the savage Russian behavior in raping, looting, kidnapping, and destroying property that turned Berliners against the Soviets; on the other hand, British and American forces came across as friendly, generous almost to a fault, and helpful to the distraught citizens. From then on, despite a gradual return to normalcy and more civilized Russian behavior, Berliners on the whole shunned them and looked to the western powers for protection, security, and eventually, political, social, and economic leadership.

Continued Soviet Intransigence

Following the attempt by Russian guards in September 1945 to board allied trains and check passengers' papers, there were no further transportation difficulties during the remainder of the year or through the occupation years of 1946 and 1947. Allied trains moving through the Soviet zone of occupation to and from Berlin encountered no further delaying tactics or resistance by the Russians. The number of daily trains was even increased from ten to sixteen, and they remained free from any Russian attempts to halt, enter, or inspect them. The late **Corporal Frank Melton**, a native of Hayward, Wisconsin, rode the mail train as an army postal supervisor between the west and Berlin on a regular basis in the years prior to imposition of the blockade in June 1948. Armed with M-1 rifles and hand revolvers, Melton, who served 28 years in the army, retiring as a sergeant major, developed a fixed procedure with others in his detail. Locking themselves inside their mail car, which itself was a veritable fortress with its steel-barred windows and heavily bolted doors, they rode through the Soviet occupation zone, encountering little or no interference until early 1948, when the Russians began anew their harassing tactics against trains and road vehicles passing through their territory.

By implication, however, the Russians reserved what they felt was their right to halt and inspect trains; they simply chose not to exercise it further until early 1948. In the intervening years, 1946 and 1947, they had numerous other means in mind by which confrontations with the allies might be accelerated.

Agreements over water transport access to Berlin were made between the British and the Russians because coal-carrying barges commenced their journey in the Ruhr, situated in the British occupation zone. In this case, the British secured such agreements in writing, yet their existence meant nothing to the Russians, who failed to attach any more importance to a signed document than to a verbal agreement; as a result, troubles over water access continued. "The Russians seldom provided information about traffic movements in their zone," wrote Ann and John Tusa, "and consistently failed to send back empty British zone barges, which they seemed to regard as reparations."

As for access rights to Berlin by air, no guarantees as yet existed in the early occupation months. During the years prior to the blockade, the allies simply flew passengers, mail, and supplies to Tempelhof and Gatow airfields. Except for some air passage agreements made for the Potsdam conference, no formal air corridors were established until later, and few navigational aids existed for guidance. Pilots flew as a habit under visual flight rules, using the tried and true method of pilotage—flying at a low altitude and following clearly visible landmarks such as highways and railroads. Several months into the occupation, however, the Allied Control Council surprisingly reached an agreement formally establishing three air corridors, each 20 miles wide, between Berlin and the west: a southern corridor stretching northeasterly from Frankfurt, a central one pointing due east roughly from Hannover, and the third angling southeasterly from the Hamburg area. They converged over Berlin in a wide circle extending 20 miles in every direction from the ACC headquarters, thereby embracing the existent western sector airfields.

The agreement, formalized in writing in early 1946 following several months of negotiations, placed governance of the air corridors in a Berlin Air Safety Center, to be staffed by technicians from the four occupying powers. Numerous pilots and other air crew members who flew for EATS, the European Air Transport System, in the immediate postwar years were among the first to fly the formally established corridors as they airlifted passengers and cargo to and from Berlin between 1946 and early 1948. The three corridors would then ultimately be used to mount the so-called Little Airlift in April and the airlift itself in June.

The Road to Potsdam

In order to place events leading up to the 1945 Potsdam conference in historical perspective, it is useful to revert to September 1, 1939 when Adolph Hitler unleashed his *Blitzkrieg* forces against a weak, outnumbered Polish army. Two days later Great Britain and France declared war on Germany and World War II became an ugly reality. America was not yet directly involved. Still, the bonds between the two English-speaking nations were strong, and as the ferocity and scope of the war increased, a feeling grew that it would be only a matter of time before the United States would find itself drawn into the conflict.

In early March 1941, Congress enacted the lend-lease program, and President Franklin D. Roosevelt was happy to sign it on the eleventh. Prime Minister Winston L. S. Churchill's long-remembered statement of February 9, 1941, "Give us the tools and we will finish the job," had been answered. Under authority of the new law, supplies needed by Britain for her war efforts would be transported to England by convoys made up of both British and American ships. But the German U-boat campaign against allied shipping was mounting in intensity, with ever-increasing losses in ships, tonnage, and human lives. In this alarming atmosphere Roosevelt directed that the lend-lease program be broadened to include not only supplies but also armaments—tanks, guns, aircraft, and ammunition. Britain ultimately received approximately $31 billion in lend-lease war materiel.

The flurry of communications between Churchill and Roosevelt over implementing lend-lease tended to strengthen their growing friendship. Indeed, in their prolific exchange of cables Churchill became fond of referring to himself as a "former naval person," perhaps because each at one time had maintained naval ties, Roosevelt having been assistant secretary of the navy and a lifelong lover of the sea, and Churchill having been appointed first lord of the admiralty twice, in 1911 and 1939, the second time at the outbreak of World War II. By July 1941, the president felt that the time had come to meet face-to-face and dispatched Harry Hopkins to sound out the prime minister at No. 10 Downing Street. Churchill was immediately agreeable, so arrangements were quickly made for a meeting at sea early the following month.

Churchill proceeded on the battleship H.M.S. *Prince of Wales*, while Roosevelt headed north on the heavy cruiser *Augusta*. They met in Placentia Bay off the coast of Newfoundland for a few days of talks. "I had the keenest desire to meet Mr. Roosevelt, with whom I had now corresponded with increasing intimacy for nearly two years," wrote Churchill nine years later. "...a conference between us would proclaim the ever closer association of Britain and the United States, would cause our enemies concern...and cheer our friends." In the course of their shipboard talks, Roosevelt suggested and Churchill agreed that a joint declaration of broad principles might be in order—principles to guide the two nations, one at war and the other soon to follow, along a common path in pursuit of an eventual peace. Accordingly, Churchill forged the first draft, and following several changes and amendments, they ultimately produced a statement that on August 12, 1941 was signed by the two men, to become known as the Atlantic Charter.

Idealistic in tone and not precisely an official document, the Charter's value lay in serving as a moral compass at a time when the western nations were fervently casting about in search of unity and direction. Couched in glowing terms of freedom, sovereign rights, self-determination, and the pursuit of peace, it became more specific in passages denouncing territorial aggrandizement and the destruction of Nazi tyranny. Before the two western leaders parted company, they sent a message to Premier Stalin assuring him that he would be furnished "the very maximum of supplies that you most urgently need" in the fight against Nazism.

Following America's entry into the war, a move that further strengthened the long-existent bond between Great Britain and the United States, the two nations continued to be guided by the Atlantic Charter principles. But it was a different story when it came to their ally, the Soviet Union. Although the Big Three—Great Britain, the United States, and the Soviet Union—were united against the common enemy, Nazi Germany, the Soviet Union was not a signatory to the Charter. Sadly enough, it would soon become easier for Stalin to ignore the Charter's noble principles than to be guided by them.

A Fragile Big Three Relationship

A few short months after the Atlantic Charter signing, Japan attacked Pearl Harbor. Within days Germany declared war on the United States, and America found itself totally involved in global conflict. Our ally to the east, the Soviet Union, had been added to the lend-lease program in November 1941, a movement that significantly enhanced its ability to wage war against Nazi Germany. By war's end Russia had received over

$11 billion worth of lend-lease equipment from the United States—armaments, trucks, rolling stock, airplanes, and numerous other materials to support its war effort. Yet the grudging manner in which this massive aid was acknowledged by the Soviets should have been, but was not, cause for concern. The Russians desperately needed this aid in their struggle against the German armed might, and they welcomed it, but on only one occasion did Stalin display any outward gratitude or give credit to lend-lease for helping his war effort. At an evening reception during the 1943 Teheran conference, the dictator offered a toast to "American industrial production, particularly of engines." The Soviets' otherwise odd behavior toward the lend-lease program should have touched off alarm bells among American and British officials as to their eastern ally's intentions in a postwar world; on the contrary, it was largely overlooked in the rush to achieve unity against a common enemy.

Despite early warning signals from the Soviet Union that a warm and genuine friendship with Great Britain and the United States was not in the cards, the relationship nonetheless continued to grow by necessity since the three nations were allied in common cause against the Axis powers, Germany and Italy. As the armed conflict against them progressed, it became necessary for Churchill, Roosevelt, and Stalin to reach various high-level decisions about the war effort. What would be the allied goals in the Pacific, and would the USSR enter the war against Japan? If so, when? Would the western allies enter upon a second front in the European war, thus easing the burden on the Soviets in the east? What should be the terms of surrender by each enemy, a negotiated peace in one theater, then another, or a total and unconditional surrender? And how would a defeated Germany be occupied and governed?

Churchill and Roosevelt, in a series of summit conferences following the Atlantic Charter event, moved ahead with resolutions to these and related war issues, meeting in far-flung corners of the world in order to map out clear strategies for bringing the war to a swift, decisive conclusion. Their combined military chiefs also met frequently, at summit conferences and on occasion by themselves, to iron out military problems bearing on specific theaters of operations.

From January 14–24, 1943, Churchill, Roosevelt, and the combined chiefs of staff met at Casablanca in French Morocco to grapple with issues of the North African campaign, launched in November of the preceding year. The two leaders had hoped that this would be their first session with Marshal Stalin since he had been expressly invited to attend. Whether from an innate reservation about his opposite numbers, or from his habitual reluctance to travel beyond his home borders, the wily dictator declined. He seized the occasion, nevertheless, to toss a barb about the promised second front in western Europe. "Allow me to express my confidence," he cabled, "that the promises about the opening of the second front in Europe given by you, Mr. President, and by Mr. Churchill in regard to 1942, and in any case in regard to the spring of 1943, will be fulfilled." The major accomplishment at Casablanca was not, unfortunately for Stalin, resolution of the second front question. It was the announcement of the unconditional surrender doctrine for which this conference is best remembered.

A second front, with allied landings to be carried out in France, was agreed upon several months later at Quebec, where Churchill and Roosevelt met again, together with Prime Minister William Mackenzie King of Canada and Foreign Minister T. V. Soong of China, who attended to establish the China-Burma-India theater of operations. Limited recognition of Charles de Gaulle's French Committee of National Liberation, of vital importance to both France and Britain, was also granted on Churchill's recommendation at the August conference. Having no love for de Gaulle, Roosevelt was cool to this move but reluctantly acceded to Churchill's persuasions.

Despite later French intransigence in the Allied Control Council, even to the extent of using the veto frequently, the decision at Quebec would have ultimate significance for later western allied relations with the Soviet Union, particularly those bearing on the East-West conflict over administering German occupation affairs. The canny Churchill knew intrinsically, as Roosevelt did not, that a strong, rejuvenated France on the continent could form an appropriate bulwark against any future Soviet plans of aggression. Chip Bohlen, writing about his role at the 1943 Teheran conference, held much the same view. "Given my experience in Soviet affairs, I could not help feeling suspicious, as I listened to Stalin, that he was also thinking a little bit along other lines. He foresaw in the revival of a strong and healthy France an obstacle to Soviet ambitions in Europe."

Teheran

Churchill and Roosevelt met again in late November 1943 in Teheran, the capital of Iran, this time with Joseph Stalin— the first meeting of the wartime Big Three. Situated just over the border from the Soviet Union's southern reaches, Teheran was a convenient site for Stalin, close to his homeland and quite secure. British and Soviet troops had jointly occupied it since August 1941 because pro-Nazi forces were active in the country. The site won out over the port city of Basra, Iraq when Stalin reacted coolly to this suggestion on the grounds that he could not effectively direct his war effort from there. Roosevelt flew to Teheran from Cairo where he, Churchill, and Chiang Kai-shek had been meeting to work out questions of the Asian war with Japan.

Upon meeting Stalin, the president faced a small, graying person, modest in bearing and quietly polite. His unassuming demeanor, nevertheless, masked an inner toughness that usually worked in his favor as the three leaders debated and resolved crucial war and postwar related issues, not only at Teheran but later at Yalta and Potsdam. As their acquaintance developed in social company, the dictator, being a native of wine-producing Georgia, showed a preference for wine over vodka, the traditional Russian beverage, and he also displayed himself as a heavy cigarette smoker. Despite the ever-present occupation forces, security fears abounded due to alleged Nazi plots to assassinate the conference leaders. Accordingly, Roosevelt was housed inside a heavily guarded Soviet compound where the conference itself would convene. Churchill stayed at the British Embassy, securely guarded by a regiment of Sikhs.

Few major decisions were made at Teheran. The conference was, rather, a getting-to-know-you session between the principals in their first ever meeting, a chance to size up one another, although Churchill and Stalin had met previously. The four-day conference, in session from November 28 to December 1, served as a warmup for Yalta and later, Potsdam, with the three leaders engaging in considerable discussion but not much more. Since it had been cast as a meeting primarily concerned with military matters, the Big Three foreign ministers were not present, except for Anthony Eden with whose presence Churchill felt more comfortable. Discussions ranged widely over India, China, Syria, Indo-China, the role of France, and the general question of some type of world organization.

Stalin pressed for a definite date for an invasion of France across the channel and was rewarded with a positive decision from Churchill and Roosevelt on the day before the conference adjourned. He voiced reservations about the unconditional surrender doctrine proclaimed at Casablanca the preceding January, and both he and Churchill vigorously discussed the fate of a postwar Poland, raising questions about its ultimate borders. Curiously, Roosevelt proceeded carefully in discussions on Poland, explaining to Stalin that should he run again for reelection in 1944 he did not wish to alienate any of the six to seven million American voters of Polish extraction. The question of Poland's borders was more political than military, yet Churchill and Stalin, despite their awareness, proceeded to draw lines on various maps, with Churchill generally agreeing to Stalin's point of view. The dictator knew very clearly what he wanted for Poland. At Yalta, the question of a Polish government would touch off bitter debate, while a few months later at Potsdam, Stalin would present the entire Polish issue as a *fait accompli*.

Yalta

Marshal Stalin not only had a fear of flying; he was fearful, most likely for security reasons, of traveling at all, unless such travel were confined to the Soviet Union or territory close to it, as with the conference at Teheran. On the other hand, the other leaders of the Big Three, Churchill and Roosevelt, had always felt a certain exhilaration in travel. As a consequence of these divergent feelings, the latter two agreed to meet in February 1945 at Yalta, a picturesque resort city on the Black Sea in the Soviet Crimea, for talks about numerous postwar matters but chiefly the question of a defeated Germany. By that time Roosevelt, reelected in November 1944 to an historic fourth term, was a mere shadow of his former self. He was in fact dying, despite official denials and protestations that he was merely tired. His stout courage was about the only force that kept him going.

The President traveled from the United States to Malta aboard the cruiser *Quincy*, arriving in Valletta harbor on February 2 to the cheers and salutes of British seamen and other spectators lining the piers. Prime Minister Churchill was already in Malta, having arrived three days earlier. From Malta the two men proceeded over a 2,250-kilometer route in separate aircraft to a hastily restored airfield at Saki, in the Crimea. Roosevelt's airplane was escorted from Athens to Saki by five American P-38 Lightning fighter aircraft, but from there it was still a 130-kilometer drive over the mountains to Yalta. Riding in Russian vehicles driven by Russian drivers, the president's party, which included his daughter, Anne Boettiger, was well-protected by Soviet troops guarding the entire distance from Saki to Yalta.

At Yalta, following a round of greetings by Soviet foreign minister Vyacheslav Molotov and a lavish reception with sumptuous Russian food and drink, Roosevelt and his American contingent were escorted to their quarters in the Livadiya Palace, a white granite, fifty-room mansion constructed in 1911 in Italian Renaissance style, and once the summer home of the czars. The British were housed about nineteen kilometers further along the coast in the Vorontzov Villa, while the Russians settled into the Koreis Villa, about ten kilometers from the Livadiya Palace. The Russians had gone to extreme lengths to prepare all living quarters and conference facilities for everyone's comfort.

Why Yalta? Two reasons. First was Stalin's reluctance to travel outside his own country. Next, Yalta is the French Riviera of the Soviet Union. This comfortable seaside resort, playground of the wealthy in the czarist era and in the 1940s a favorite vacation spa for high-ranking Soviet officials, was sheltered from the bitterly cold Russian winters by the Crimean mountains to the north. In February 1945, it was about the only warm location in the Soviet Union for a summit conference. The weather, in fact, was to the Russians very pleasant—about 40 degrees Fahrenheit. They called it "Roosevelt weather."

At the Yalta conference, the three leaders, knowing that victory was close at hand, sought to establish a postwar allied strategy embodying the noble ideals of self-determination, destruction of the Nazi menace voiced in the Atlantic Charter, and the goal of unconditional surrender emanating from the Casablanca conference in 1943. The Big Three continued in an idealistic tone at this vital meeting on the Black Sea shores, expressing a general view that German militarism must be destroyed and that Germany must never again be a threat to peace.

They became more specific, however, when they worked out plans to bring war criminals to justice, to exact reparations from a defeated Germany, and to ratify recommendations of the European Advisory Commission (EAC), established in London in late 1943 to deal with a number of questions, among them the formation of occupation zones for the victorious powers. The EAC, composed of the American ambassador to London John Winant, Sir William Strang for Britain, and the Russian ambassador to England Feodor T. Gusev, delivered its proposals for the German occupation zones on September 12, 1944, in time for consideration and approval at Yalta. Its work had been preceded by an *ad hoc* British committee headed by Clement Attlee.

France, after considerable opposition by Stalin, was granted its own occupation zone when Roosevelt, who himself was cool to France playing a major postwar role, at length persuaded Stalin that there could be no permanent resolution of the German question without France. The zone was ultimately established, however, from territory initially planned for the British and American zones. At Yalta, they further decided to divide Berlin into occupation sectors, but no actual occupation plans for the city were made, or even discussed.

Churchill, Roosevelt, and Stalin also agreed to invite China and France to join in sponsoring the San Francisco conference in April for the formation of the United Nations. Agreement was reached, as well, to establish allied control councils to administer the occupations of Germany and Austria. Considerable time at the conference was also devoted to Poland and the nature of its future government. Churchill and Stalin had decided on the new Polish borders at Teheran, but at Yalta they debated, along with Roosevelt, whether the puppet Lublin government, installed by the Soviets the previous year, or Poland's government-in-exile in London should form a new provisional government. A compromise inevitably followed whereby the Lublin government would be reorganized on a more democratic basis to include representatives from elsewhere in Poland as well as the exiled government, with free elections founded on universal suffrage. Following Potsdam, however, this seemingly equitable arrangement never materialized. Since the Red Army occupied Poland in its entirety, Stalin held all the cards. He could simply ignore the accord and therefore he did. The agreement ended on the scrap heap, with Russia thereafter transforming Poland into a Soviet satellite, thus giving the western allies a clear preview of what Stalin had in mind for postwar Germany.

Potsdam

Late on July 6, 1945, Harry S. Truman, not quite three months in office as the 33rd President of the United States, boarded a train at Union Station and departed Washington in utmost secrecy, bound for Newport News, Virginia, where he embarked on the heavy cruiser *Augusta* for his lengthy journey to Germany and the crucial first postwar European meeting of the Big Three, scheduled to take place at Potsdam, a once affluent suburban community some twenty kilometers southwest of Berlin. As his ship departed the huge naval facility, lavish arrangements for the forthcoming conference were being made by the Americans, British, and particularly the Russians at the Potsdam site, which had been chosen by the Russians late in May because Berlin was virtually destroyed and Potsdam had suffered relatively little war damage. Roosevelt, too, had favored a meeting in the Berlin area. At the close of the Yalta conference, he reportedly said to Stalin, "We will meet again soon—in Berlin!" The president never got there, but the Potsdam venue would most likely have met with his approval.

Following Roosevelt's death in April, it fell to Truman to carry on with general agreements made at the first Big Three meeting in Teheran in late November 1943, and the more specific agreements on postwar Germany made at Yalta in February 1945. Such being the case, he called in Harry Hopkins, Roosevelt's former loyal and personal advisor, and requested that he make a special trip to Moscow to sound out Premier Stalin as to a time and place for an early meeting with Churchill and himself. Hopkins, with whom Stalin was comfortable, made the journey despite his chronic poor health and on May 28 reported to Truman by cable that the Soviet leader had agreed to a July 15 date for a meeting in Babelsburg, a Potsdam suburb.

Truman knew that high on the agenda for the meeting would be such matters as the necessity of bringing war criminals to justice, doing away with the Nazi party, settling the victorious powers in their respective zones of occupation, and resolving the thorny issue of reparations. The new president also knew full well that his negotiating skills would be tested at this meeting, hence he chose travel by sea in order to have adequate study and consultation time with his large accompanying staff. "I decided to make the journey aboard a naval vessel," wrote Truman in his memoirs ten years later, "since I felt I would be better able aboard ship to study the many documents that had been assembled for my information. There would be an opportunity as well to consult with my advisers...." It was vitally necessary, felt the President, to prepare fully for this initial confrontation with Stalin, to him an as yet unknown quantity. Much was said about the decision to travel by sea after it became public; it was well-known that Truman had little love for flying, although he flew when he considered it necessary. After the *Augusta* docked at Antwerp on July 15, he flew, for security reasons, on the presidential C-54 *Sacred Cow* to Gatow airfield in Berlin, although he would have preferred to proceed by automobile or train.

As he assumed the presidency when death came to Franklin Roosevelt on April 12, 1945, Truman appeared terribly miscast for the awesome role so suddenly thrust upon him. In his modest life prior to election to the U.S. Senate in 1934, he had worked on the family farm, served in France during World War I as a captain in the field artillery, co-owned a haberdashery in Kansas City, and later worked his way through the labyrinth of local party politics with the strong support of Thomas J. Pendergast, boss of the Kansas City Democratic machine. He never went to college, a fact that gnawed at his sense of adequacy as he rose steadily higher in the political arena. Chosen as FDR's running mate in 1944, he was thereafter virtually ignored by Roosevelt as he struggled through the 82 days he was to serve as vice-president. As a consequence, the suddenly new President Truman found himself woefully ignorant of much that had taken place in both domestic and foreign affairs.

Soon after the inauguration in January, Roosevelt left for the Yalta conference, not to return for a month. In March he and Truman met twice but on each occasion only briefly and without reference to the war or any plans for the peace to follow. Since his predecessor never confided in him, Truman had to learn after Roosevelt's death from Admiral Leahy, who had attended all of Roosevelt's major international meetings, and other Washington insiders, about the many wartime decisions that had been taken. But he was a good learner. In classic Truman fashion, he prepared for Potsdam with his habitual self-discipline and attention to detail, directing that position papers be prepared on every topic slated to arise on the conference agenda.

Meanwhile, Winston Churchill concluded a relaxing vacation on the French Riviera and on July 15 flew directly to Berlin. He would not know the results of the recent parliamentary elections in Britain until absentee ballots had been counted, but having led his nation through the war and to victory, he was confident of yet another successful outcome for his Conservative Party. Stalin arrived at the Potsdam conference a bit late, having traveled from Moscow by train. Truman may not have enjoyed air travel, but Stalin was terrified of it, reportedly having flown only once.

The Big Three world leaders convened in Potsdam in July largely due to Churchill's pressure for an early date. Through the final months of the war, the prime minister had harbored suspicions about Soviet postwar intentions as its armies advanced westward, and given his choice, the conference would have begun much sooner than mid-July. Each passing day in May and June, in Churchill's view, afforded the Red Army more opportunity to strengthen Stalin's hand, through plunder, looting, and propaganda, particularly in the western sectors of Berlin that the western allies were slated to occupy.

Unlike Truman, however, Churchill was almost cavalier in his approach to the Potsdam negotiations, having committed little or nothing to writing in advance of the meeting. When they first met at Potsdam, Truman asked Churchill if he had an agenda to present at the meetings. "No, I don't need one," responded the prime minister, waving his ever-present Royal Jamaican cigar at no one in particular. His style was, rather, more verbal. He was prone to brood about the fundamental difficulties he saw in dealing with the Soviets, to urge caution on every issue, and to admonish the west to negotiate from a position of strength. In brief, he viewed the East-West relationship in adversarial, political terms rather than military, and he therefore approached the Potsdam deliberations in that frame of mind.

In the final weeks of the war, Churchill felt so strongly that the western allies should push on to Berlin that he loudly and repeatedly urged

Truman and Eisenhower to do so. Short of reaching Berlin before the Russians, the American and British forces, he insisted, should not retreat from the territories they had already taken until they were firmly established in Berlin, and prior agreements about its occupation and administration were actually in force. To no avail, he begged his American allies to follow his views. Truman was determined to honor agreements reached at Yalta establishing occupation zones and zonal occupation lines, while Eisenhower agreed with Truman's thinking in his own military terms. In the final analysis, it was Eisenhower's decision to make. He prevailed over Churchill's pleas, the Americans stopped at the Elbe, and the western allies suffered the ensuing consequences of getting settled in Berlin. Reflecting many years later on the verdict not to take Berlin, Robert Murphy regarded it as "...a decision of such international significance that no Army chief should have been required to make it."

At the Potsdam site, the Russians outdid themselves in preparing the historic Cecilienhof Palace for the coming sessions. Constructed in the years 1913–1917 for the odd, peculiar Crown Prince Wilhelm, Kaiser Wilhelm's only son, and his wife the Duchess Cecile, the palace was clearly not the most elegant of palatial structures. Composed of brownstone and stucco on a two-story wooden frame, it spread outward in four wings from a central courtyard. Its chief advantage was perhaps that it was undamaged and large; it boasted of 176 rooms. Potsdam as a whole escaped allied bombing and remained relatively unscathed, as did neighboring Babelsberg, where Truman, Churchill, and Stalin were to be housed. Brightened by new paint, new furniture and carpeting shipped in from Moscow, and a general cleaning throughout after having served as a hospital during the war, the Cecilienhof was given a final touch with the addition of a huge red star of geraniums in the palace gardens.

In contrast to the Yalta conference, which met for seven days from February 4–11 and was attended by only a small support staff, the Potsdam meeting opened on July 17 and continued through many sessions, closing on August 2. The Big Three leaders were surrounded by large contingents headed by their foreign secretaries, with support from their military and staff aides, security personnel, and interpreters. One such support staff member was **First Lieutenant Dean W. Terlinden** from Waukesha, Wisconsin, who during the blockade three years later would be assigned to Burtonwood as a weather forecaster. Dean arrived in Berlin well in advance of the Potsdam opening date, so as to set up the necessary weather services for VIP aircraft arriving at Tempelhof and Gatow for the conference. "On July 15, 1945 I was Officer of the Day," writes Dean, "so I had a better than usual chance to see the arriving dignitaries such as Truman, Marshall, Eisenhower, Churchill, Eden, and General [Henry] Arnold."

Britain's Clement Richard Attlee of the opposition Labour Party was in attendance as a matter of courtesy at Churchill's behest, and on July 28 he returned as prime minister when the Conservative Party lost in the July 5 elections. Churchill's somber foreign minister, Anthony Eden, was retired in favor of Ernest Bevin, a rough, coarse-voiced veteran of the trade union movement, and one who added color to the conference proceedings, especially in contrast to his boss, the quiet Attlee. Secretary of State James F. Byrnes, an old Senate ally of the president, was at Truman's side throughout the conference.

As the only head of state among the Big Three, President Truman was nominated by Marshal Stalin, as Churchill and Stalin had done for Roosevelt at Teheran, to be conference chairman, and this courteous gesture was unanimously accepted. As the conference proceedings moved ahead and the inevitable photo sessions took place, Truman's habitual double-breasted attire at the conference placed him in stark contrast with Churchill and Stalin, each of whom was resplendent in uniform, the British leader garbed as an officer of the Royal Navy while Stalin was prominent in his customary marshal's regalia.

It was the purpose at Potsdam to confirm and expand on decisions made at Yalta in February when general agreements were made to be fleshed out later. Following three weeks of steady Big Three meetings, as well as foreign minister sessions, agreements were ultimately hammered out, often only after extensive study, debate, and considerable give and take. Throughout the conference days a tone of cordiality prevailed; still, a subtle undertone of tension was apparent to all. Allies in the recently ended European conflict, Truman, Churchill, and Stalin found it difficult to preserve a genuine sense of unity in this first postwar conference. Nonetheless, when it came to swift punishment for the defeated enemy and the abolition of national socialism, they had no problem determining what to do. Full agreement was also reached to transfer the administration of Germany to the military commanders in each occupation zone. This would be accomplished through the Allied Control Council, composed of the four zonal commanders. Decisions were reached to ensure that Germany would never again mount a threat to world peace and that specific disarmament procedures would be followed. A four-power Council of Foreign Ministers (CFM) was established to meet at least quarterly in formal session, to draw up peace treaties with Germany, Italy, and Austria, and to point the way to eventual constitutions for each country

Dear to Stalin's heart, the reparations question was pursued vigorously. Each of the allies would take reparations from its own occupation zone; Russia, however, because it had suffered so extensively at the hands of the Nazi war machine, would be permitted a share of the reparations taken from the three other zones as well. Stalin persisted with his Yalta claim to $10 billion out of a total $20 billion figure originally used only as a basis for discussion, yet the precise amounts allotted were destined to become bogged down in numerous post-Potsdam haggling sessions, with the result that the Soviet Union received an extra margin of reparations based on its widespread war damage and suffering, but in no way equal to the $10 billion originally demanded by Stalin.

The overall reparations issue required a resolution that considered the prostrate German economy and the need to permit Germany to grow to economic self-sufficiency, thus reducing the financial burden on the occupation forces. Wide differences were voiced over exactly what to do with the German economy, ranging from reducing the country to an agricultural, vassal state to encouraging full industrial development. But the die had already been cast. Each zone was destined to receive the treatment that its military commander decreed, despite the four-power agreement that Germany would be treated as a single economic unit.

Was the Potsdam conference a success? It was clearly a social success, with numerous rounds of receptions, formal dinners, and courtesy calls by the Big Three leaders on one another. In this environment, politeness and even outward displays of camaraderie were in evidence, but they never bubbled over into sincere friendship between Stalin and the western leaders. In terms of political gain, Stalin went home quite satisfied with having forced the French occupation zone to be taken from the other western zones, not his. He had to be somewhat pleased with the reparations settlements and the western allies' promise to turn over to him supplemental booty from their zones. And prior to the conference he had already finessed a large portion of eastern Germany for Poland, to which Truman and Attlee quietly acquiesced.

The United States, Britain, and France were happy over the creation of four occupation zones, establishment of the Allied Control Council, and formation of the Council of Foreign Ministers, but agreement that the four powers must act in unison in matters respecting all of Germany was a big win for the Soviet Union. In effect, it established the veto that the Soviet Union, and to a considerable extent France, used many times over the occupation years to gain its own advantage by blocking western proposals. Robert Murphy summed it up by remarking, "...Stalin and his group either obtained the settlements they sought, or managed to sweep ticklish questions under the rug." The Potsdam conference came to its end, and the allies moved ahead with the occupation of Germany. Clearly, they faced an uncertain future, for within some decisions reached at Potsdam lay the seeds for the breakdown of allied unity, the veto in both the Allied Control Council and the Kommandatura chief among them. From Potsdam on through the occupation years, diametrically opposed ideologies would drive the western allies and the Soviet Union further and further apart, with a divided Berlin suffering the consequences.

Soviet Finesse in Berlin

Having conquered Berlin while the armies of the western allies were still sixty to seventy kilometers to the west, the Soviets took every advantage of being there first. As they entered the devastated and ruined city, a Moscow-trained German communist arrived with them. Walter Ulbricht, captured in battle by the Russians, spent his remaining war years in the Soviet Union organizing a cadre of communists to prepare for the seizure of Berlin and the formation of a citywide municipal government. Slight, bald, and cursed with a squeaky voice, the 51-year-old member of the prewar Reichstag turned out to be the ideal functionary to carry out the Soviet plan for the city.

In late April, a few short days before the city fell, Ulbricht and his small group of subordinates flew from Moscow to Frankfurt on Oder, about fifty kilometers east of Berlin. Following Berlin's final gasp, they moved in and deftly established a *magistrat*, a city governing body, grasping in the process control over all of the city's technical and public functions by placing trusted persons in every strategic city office. Although Ulbricht and his Russian superiors selected Arthur Werner, an elderly, retired, non-communist architect as the lord mayor, effective communist control was guaranteed through the communist deputy mayor, Karl Maron and the personnel administrators in eighteen of the twenty city boroughs, who were either communists or communist sympathizers.

No element of the city's governmental life was left untouched by the Soviet plan. Vital service departments such as police, schools, public utilities, traffic, finance, health, and social welfare, were placed under persons trained and brought in by Ulbricht, or under those Berliners whose loyalty was unquestioned. The other German political parties—the Social Democrats, the Christian Democrats, and the Liberal Democrats—were accorded formal recognition but used merely for window dressing. While their members were given visible posts in the city administration, the communists unerringly retained the offices of deputy mayor, police chief, personnel director, and director of education. Named to lead the police department, always a vital force in developing a Soviet style urban administration, was Paul Markgraf, a former Nazi colonel, who also was captured and trained for many months in the Soviet Union,

Ulbricht, who one day would become secretary-general of the Socialist Unity Party (SED) in the new German Democratic Republic, insisted that his Berlin city administration should appear democratic in every way but that his communist group must be in absolute control. Hence, when the allied Kommandatura, the four-power group slated to administer the city, convened in July to commence its work, the British, French, and American commandants quickly realized that the communists under Ulbricht had been directing urban affairs on a citywide basis for over two months. One document innocently accepted by the western commandants was a general order requiring that all ordinances and rules already established by the Soviet Military Administration (SMA) remain in force until further notice. In short, the western allies rubber-stamped the citywide Soviet government organized prior to their arrival in Berlin! Although each western commandant directed matters in his own sector, it would not be until after the elections in 1946 that the political balance in citywide administration would tip in favor of the western allies.

As the year 1945 came to a close, the western allies had for some time concluded that the wartime unity they had enjoyed with the Soviet Union was now over. Events occurring throughout the now defeated and occupied

Germany, particularly in Berlin, bore stark witness to this change in viewpoint. Since the onset of the occupation in May, the Soviets had demonstrated at every turn a coolness and arrogance toward the United States, Great Britain, and to some extent France, manifested first in their beastly behavior upon reaching Berlin, then in their delaying tactics over settling into the agreed occupation zones and sectors, and next in an intransigence and reluctance to cooperate thereafter in the ACC and Kommandatura. Additionally, they signaled a clear intention to turn every facet of the occupation to their advantage. The cold war was in full bloom. What, if anything, would the coming occupation years hold for allied unity? Would the Soviets achieve their apparent goal of dominating all of Germany? In mid-1945 did Stalin have in mind a blockade of Berlin three years down the road? Would Berlin be the first of the Soviet targets to fall, or would the western allies stand firm in a show of determination to check the Russian bear?

Two

The Intermediate Years: 1946-1948

More than an end to war, we want an end to the beginnings of all wars.

Franklin D. Roosevelt, speech prepared for April 13, 1945, the day after his death.

AS THE WESTERN ALLIES TOOK OVER their respective occupation zones in the summer of 1945, each military governor understood how crucial it was to be guided by his nation's formal policy concerning postwar Germany. For the Americans, General Eisenhower's marching orders were contained in a rather mysterious document known as JCS 1067 that emanated from the office of the Joint Chiefs of Staff in Washington, and that spelled out the Roosevelt administration's thinking. By the time that JCS 1067 was issued on May 15, 1945, only a week after VE Day, Franklin Roosevelt was dead, Harry Truman had assumed the mantle of leadership, and the American role in the occupation of Germany was about to commence. Because the document bore a top secret classification, General Clay, who was effectively in command of the American occupation, although formally he was only the deputy commander, was not free to explain publicly how the occupation would be guided.

Involved early on in the development of JCS 1067 were the war and state departments, and strangely, the treasury department. It was only natural that the first two agencies should be concerned with postwar Germany, but treasury's involvement was an oddity. Treasury Secretary Henry Morgenthau, intent upon reducing Germany from the industrial giant it had become before and during the war to a simple agrarian nation that never again could pose a threat to its European neighbors, virtually pushed his way into the postwar planning process. Being Roosevelt's neighbor in Dutchess County and a political ally when FDR was governor of New York did not hurt, and the president's own instincts about how to treat the Germans after the war inclined him toward Morgenthau's approach. While the final version of JCS 1067 incorporated the combined, but often at odds, thinking of the war and state departments, Morgenthau's views had become clearly evident as well.

At the second Quebec conference, which met September 11-16, 1944, President Roosevelt embraced the so-called Morgenthau plan without really thinking it through, perhaps because Morgenthau was on hand to press for its acceptance. Later in the month, moved by the judgments of others, he reversed himself and in a memorandum to Secretary of State Cordell Hull, declared that "No one wants to make Germany a wholly agricultural nation again," and "no one wants 'complete eradication of German industrial productive capacity in the Ruhr and Saar.' " When Harry Truman assumed the presidency, he advised Secretary of War Henry L. Stimson of his own views as to how Germany should be treated. "I made it clear...that I was opposed to what was then loosely called the Morgenthau plan...I thought it was proper to disarm Germany, to dismantle her military might, to punish war criminals, and to put her under an overall allied control until we could restore the peace. But I did not approve of reducing Germany to an agrarian state." By that time, however, JCS 1067 had been distributed through channels in classified form, and Morgenthau's views were somehow retained in the document.

The president later dealt with Morgenthau in classic Truman fashion. "When he found out I was going to Potsdam in July, Secretary Morgenthau came in to ask if he could go with me," wrote Truman in his memoirs. "I told him I thought the secretary of the treasury was badly needed in the United States—much more so than in Potsdam. He replied that it was necessary for him to go and that if he could not he would have to quit." The president shot back that if that was the way he felt, he would accept his resignation then and there. "And I did," concluded Truman. "That was the end of the conversation and the end of the Morgenthau plan." Harry Truman, a veteran poker player, had forced Morgenthau to fold his hand.

Additionally, JCS 1067 was very stringent in its instructions for the day-to-day occupation in Germany: seek out and try war criminals, eliminate Nazism, dismantle war factories, disperse political and governmental machinery, do nothing to elevate Germany's standard of living above that of her neighbors, take no action to forestall inflation, and do not fraternize.

General Clay and his subordinates found many of the restrictions contained in JCS 1067 intolerable and unworkable. His financial advisor, Lewis W. Douglas, a former Arizona congressman and later ambassador to the United Kingdom, was as much disgusted as Clay who wrote in his memoirs, "[Lewis and I] were shocked—not at its punitive provisions but at its failure to grasp the realities of the financial and economic conditions which confronted us." In assessing the full document, Douglas loudly declared, "This thing was assembled by economic idiots!" The document had been drafted prior to Germany's surrender; hence, those who wrote it had no knowledge of what conditions would be found in postwar Germany.

Other JCS 1067 features were equally as offensive, particularly its ban on fraternization. How could one carry on the business of military government, hire German employees, and work with them daily in a formal, reserved, business only manner? How could one prevent the naturally friendly Americans from having informal contact with the German people? Impossible. American GIs were not about to live a cloistered life on occupation duty, with so many thousands of attractive German fräuleins anxious to be friends. JCS 1067 was doomed to failure from the start, but its terms were not officially softened or amended until more than two years later, in July 1947, when JCS 1779, embracing a more liberal approach to occupation matters, was issued.

In the interim, many features of JCS 1067, including the Morgenthau-inspired requirement to force an agrarian economy upon postwar Germany, were either ignored or loosely interpreted, and official Washington passively permitted General Clay to interpret and administer the document's provisions as he saw fit.

The French and British were in effect invited to embrace the spirit of JCS 1067 and, in the interest of overall allied occupation unity, also to be guided by its terms. Not wishing to become locked in to American handiwork, each politely declined, despite the fact that each later approached the occupation of its ancient enemy in rather harsh terms, thus largely emulating JCS 1067 without the need to adopt it as a policy guide. The Soviets were also encouraged to adopt the American-inspired document, but predictably they had already carved out their own agenda for Germany.

France was determined to avenge the humiliation of Germany's occupation of its homeland during the recent war, and it virtually equaled the Soviet Union in its demands for reparations, having suffered billions of dollars worth of damage and ruin at the hands of the Nazis. Further, its leaders strenuously resisted any notion of new, centralized German administrative units for conducting the occupation, favoring instead a vastly decentralized system that would pose little threat of resurgent German power. To the French, Germany's condition at the end of the war—prostrate, defeated, and in ruins—was just fine. In the Allied Control Council, France's behavior toward Germany reflected this view; French leaders ranked second to the Russians in using the veto power to thwart any action that might threaten their nation's security.

An American Airman's Story

A young American soldier who experienced at close hand the French attitude in four-power relations was **Staff Sergeant Charles K. Church.** Charles was an army infantryman during World War II, serving in the Pacific theater, and only eighteen years old when first shipped overseas. After V-J Day, he transferred to the army air corps, volunteered for duty in Germany, and arrived in Bremerhaven in January 1946 as the occupation was assuming some semblance of stability and order. Assigned to Fürstenfeldbruck, then Erlangen, and later Erding, he quickly learned the intricacies of C-47 flight line maintenance and found this specialty to his liking.

Later in the year, Charles and his fellow aircraft maintenance workers suddenly found themselves driving trucks to France to comply with General Charles de Gaulle's dictum that the Americans remove all of their military equipment from French soil *toute de suite*. It mattered not what a person's job specialty might be; truck drivers, experienced or otherwise, were needed to move tanks, jeeps, and armaments from France to Germany. "The French citizens were not very nice to us," remembers Charles, a native of Rainelle, West Virginia. "As we drove through the villages, they threw rocks at our trucks that were loaded with bombs and armaments. We always tried, on each trip, to reach the German border before stopping for the night." Clearly, the French behavior was a far cry from their excitement and gratitude two years earlier at being liberated by the Americans from the German yoke. Memories can be short.

While stationed at Erding, a massive air depot in Bavaria, Charles and others received instructions to destroy German military equipment that had a potential for further use as weapons. In carrying out those orders, they had to bulldoze deep trenches in which they buried such items as the revolutionary ME-262 twin-jet fighter that, had it been on-line earlier, might well have changed the tide of the war. As a lover of airplanes, regardless of their national origin, Charles found that a difficult task to carry out.

When the airlift commenced, Charles moved on temporary duty (TDY) from Erding to Rhein-Main, where he was initially assigned to vehicle and ground power equipment maintenance. But he eventually succeeded in returning to his first love—general flight line maintenance on C-47s—a skill he simply picked up on the job as he went about his hands-on training. His airlift duty at Rhein-Main, which he found pleasant and satisfying, continued for six months, following which he returned to the United States. He then saw service in Korea and Vietnam. Altogether, Charles served 28 years on active duty, retiring as a chief master sergeant. "Of all my military service," he points out, "I am most proud of my time on the Berlin airlift. It was the most outstanding military and humanitarian achievement of this century, and most Americans don't even know about it."

The British Approach

Ann and John Tusa reported that the British approach to the occupation had its own distinctive air. "The British occupiers in Germany behaved less as conquerors, more like conscientious colonial civil servants," they wrote. In doing so, the British created a large bureaucracy, composed of many more workers than the American administrative corps. "There were 22,000 British in the zone by 1946 to administer a population of 22.3 million," continued the Tusas. By comparison, there were only 5,000 American civil servants by 1947 to administer 17.1 million Germans in their own zone.

The British, too, long noted for their pioneering achievements in local government, focused on rebuilding the German political and economic system in their zone from the bottom up, in traditional colonial fashion. Whatever differences in administrative styles and approaches there were between the western allies, they did not prevent Britain and the United States from moving their zones more closely together economically. The result, ultimately, was the creation of Bizonia in 1946, whereby the two zones were merged economically, much to the alarm of both France and the Soviet Union.

Stuttgart 1946

By the end of the summer months in 1946, the allies were about a year into the occupation, and each nation had settled into distinctive patterns of behavior for administering its respective zone. In the American zone, General Eisenhower had been succeeded the previous November as military governor by General Joseph T. McNarney, yet General Clay continued as de facto commander for civil affairs by virtue of his position as head of the Office of Military Government, United States (OMGUS). The Americans continued to labor under the restrictions of JCS 1067, with on-site modifications made by Clay and little opposition from official Washington.

Clay held to his widely publicized position of seeking to get along with the Russians, in both the governance of Berlin and Germany as a whole. In brief, Clay sought to carry out to the letter his country's policy of a cooperative quadripartite occupation respecting Germany. General Sir Brian Robertson, as British military governor in Germany, continued to shape policy in the British zone, directing a plan of action toward the occupied nation generally consistent with that of the United States. In England, however, an economy severely weakened by the war effort was still in the throes of recovery. Shortages of food and consumer goods at home rendered the nation rather ill-equipped to support the occupation effort. On that account, Prime Minister Clement Attlee, anxious to put Germany on a self-supporting basis, favored the restoration of civil government and the rebuilding of its industrial, manufacturing, and agricultural capabilities as quickly as possible.

General Pierre Koenig, a veteran brigade commander in the 1942 fighting in North Africa, a prominent figure of French resistance on the continent following the Normandy landings, and his country's commander in Germany, was a strong supporter of General de Gaulle and his classic hostility toward France's historic enemy. In the Allied Control Council Koenig adhered closely to the French policy of limiting Germany's capacity to recover, and his vetoes in this body, especially in 1945 and 1946, served as convenient vehicles for carrying out this policy.

In the year since the occupation had begun, the Russians had made it plain by their actions, both militarily and in the Allied Control Council, that their intent was not only to disarm Germany according to the Yalta and Potsdam agreements, but also to force the defeated nation into economic prostration, a position surprisingly similar to Morgenthau's plan, but more severe in application. In carrying out this policy, they drained their occupation zone of so many of its resources—for their own benefit, of course—that it was rendered economically prostrate. Additionally, they administered their zone in virtual secrecy as a separate enclave, thereby thwarting the Potsdam goal of treating Germany as a single economic and political unit. It was becoming increasingly clear that Stalin was trying to lay the groundwork for disaster in the west, a move that would further his ultimate goal of driving out the western allies and taking over not only Berlin but all of Germany.

As an American countermeasure, General Clay, with the help of Senators Tom Connally and Arthur Vandenberg, foreign policy leaders on Capitol Hill, urged Secretary of State James F. Byrnes to deliver a major foreign policy speech in Germany, setting forth in strong terms the United States position respecting the German occupation, with the intent of rebutting the Soviet thrust. Byrnes quickly agreed, Stuttgart was picked as the site, and on September 6, 1946 the secretary delivered a memorable speech in the city's Opera House before a large audience, many of whom were German civil government officials, including all of the minister-presidents of the German states.

The diminutive Byrnes, former congressman, former U.S. senator from South Carolina, former associate justice of the U.S. Supreme Court, director of war mobilization and reconversion during World War II, and future governor of his state, reconfirmed America's determination to demilitarize and de-Nazify Germany, to punish war criminals, and to exact reparations. But these points were not his major purpose in traveling to Stuttgart. In a direct, clear voice he stated unequivocally, "As long as an occupation force is required in Germany, the army of the United States will be a part of that occupation force." General Clay had expressed the same sentiment many times since arriving in Germany, and now he had urged Byrnes to include the statement in his speech. This bold declaration, following more than a year of increasing Russian intransigence in the

Allied Control Council, marked the first announcement by the United States at the highest level that it intended to remain in Germany, and especially in Berlin, come what may. Unfortunately for Byrnes, he delivered his speech without clearing it in advance with Truman, a move that helped to hasten his departure as secretary of state early in the following year.

Elections: October 1946

By the time that the three western powers had settled into their respective occupation sectors in July 1945, Berlin city officials had already been appointed and placed in office. This had been accomplished by German communists, led by Walter Ulbricht, all of whom acted under Soviet orders.

Throughout the remainder of the year and in the early 1946 months, western leaders in Berlin, particularly the British and Americans, pressed in the Kommandatura, the city's four-power governing body, for fresh city elections so that candidates freely chosen by Berlin voters could fill the elective offices. Their efforts were realized for the first time on October 20 when the Soviet puppet Socialist Unity Party (SED) was roundly defeated at the polls by the other competing parties. Social Democrats (SPD) drew almost one-half of the votes by garnering 48.7 per cent of the total. Christian Democrats (CDU) won 22 per cent, while a minor party, the Liberal Democrats (LPD), received nine per cent of the vote. And the SED? Its candidates drew 19.8 per cent, less than one-fifth of the citywide vote. Even in East Berlin the SED managed only an embarrassing 21.9 per cent of the vote! Election results translated into 26 seats for the SED in the city assembly, 29 seats for the CDU, twelve seats for the LPD, and the greatest number, 63 seats, for the SPD.

Upon appraising the results of the election, disastrous enough for the Soviet command, Russian leaders concluded that free elections were too risky and that they would need to employ more extreme and controlling measures to put across their government's policies.

The Currency Issue

As the allied powers settled into their respective occupation zones in the summer of 1945, it became glaringly evident, to the western allies at least, that drastic measures would be necessary to restore the shattered German economy. By war's end, inflation had rendered the Reichsmark, the nation's currency, virtually worthless. Germany's financial condition was one of sheer chaos; money circulating throughout the country had risen from five billion to seventy billion Reichsmarks during the war years. Rampant inflation, the result of the Nazis having freely printed vast amounts of new paper currency, had so robbed consumers of their purchasing power that farmers withheld their crops from market and merchants hoarded their goods rather than sell them for the vastly inflated currency then circulating. Personal bank savings had lost approximately eighty per cent of their original value. Small wonder, then, that cigarettes and other material items quickly became the real medium of exchange.

When Lewis Douglas, General Clay's financial advisor, returned to the United States early in the occupation, he was succeeded by Dr. Joseph Dodge, a friend and banker from Detroit. Shortly thereafter, Clay commissioned him to study Germany's financial crisis and develop a plan for currency reform. So important was the currency issue, in fact, that it ultimately would become one of the two measures on which quadripartite government broke down, resulting in an irreparable division of Germany. The other, the creation of a West German government, was well in its planning stages by 1948 and would become a reality a year later.

Dodge and the commission he organized were immediately faced with numerous considerations, not the least of which was that the western allies had naively, at the beginning of the occupation, turned over to the Russians a set of plates for printing allied occupation currency. With the plates in their possession, they freely turned out mountains of new notes, gave their troops back pay with the fresh currency, and aggravated existing inflation by ostensibly inundating the western zones with the new money. Following ten weeks of discussions, however, with Russian, French, and British financial experts, Dodge and his staff recommended a sweeping move to devalue the Reichsmark as the major step necessary to return the economy to health. The heart of his plan was the issuance of one new Deutsche mark for ten old Reichsmarks, a profound devaluation intended to restore the mark's purchasing power.

Upon submission of the Dodge report to the Allied Control Council in August 1946, American hopes ran high that true four-power cooperation would prevail in this most critical of allied endeavors. The Soviets seemed favorable but immediately commenced to stall. Suddenly, they insisted that rather than have all the new currency printed in the state printing works, located in the American sector of Berlin, they should print their zonal share in Leipzig. This step, for Clay, was too fraught with the danger once again of the Soviets printing new money without restraint, thereby inciting further inflation. General Robertson was hesitant but inclined to go along with the Russian proposal. Clay remained opposed.

By early December of the following year, amazingly, no progress had been made on currency reform, despite the fact that the Dodge report a year and a half earlier had stated that the need for reform was urgent. Clay reported to Washington that "no decision has been made to undertake currency reform or to issue new currency in [the] U.S. zone or jointly with any other zone. In fact, we are trying hard here in Germany to obtain quadripartite agreement for currency reform and new currency." Down the road, however, agreement was not to be. When the Soviets walked out from the Allied Control Council on March 20, 1948, quadripartite government came to a sudden, final halt, and full four-power currency reform was at once a dead issue. The western allies, with France slowly and reluctantly coming around, ultimately concluded that currency reform in their three zones alone was the only feasible procedure.

Four Stars for Clay

When General McNarney was reassigned to a stateside post in March 1947, General Clay succeeded him as U.S. military commander in Europe. Since the occupation's start in 1945, Clay had served as head of OMGUS, and thereby had been recognized unofficially as the actual military governor, although McNarney retained the official title. Now, on March 15, upon formally assuming the office, Clay was awarded a fourth star, the first general officer of that rank who never had served in combat. No matter. He now became free to conduct the occupation more in keeping with his personal outlook. As one manifestation of promotion and advancement in position, he moved toward a much more flexible interpretation of the JCS 1067 document, which conveniently for him was replaced on July 11 by JCS 1779, reflecting a clearly more liberal approach to occupation affairs.

Clay also reorganized his command structure so that military government was elevated to a par with the military combat forces. With his new authority, he became the first American commander-in-chief in Europe (CINCEUR), and from that point on, he felt for the first time completely unfettered by all of the previous constraints imposed on his office. He had become, in the words of some grudging admirers, the "American Proconsul" in Europe, with almost absolute power. To his supporters Clay was skillful and decisive; to his critics he was overbearing, somewhat imperious, and unbending in negotiations. He was committed, nonetheless, to pursuing the four-power goal articulated at Potsdam—the goal of a united Germany acting under a new democratic constitution. Time and circumstances would ultimately change his outlook toward this goal, but at the moment, in early 1947, he exerted all of his energy in that direction.

The Marshall Plan

James Byrnes was Harry Truman's first appointment as secretary of state, and he took office shortly after Truman became president upon Roosevelt's death in April 1945. Byrnes served well, was at Truman's side throughout the Potsdam conference, delivered his powerful speech at Stuttgart in September 1946 emphasizing to Soviet leaders and the German people America's intent to remain as an occupation force and, very importantly, was responsible for General Clay being named military governor in

Germany when pressure was mounting in Washington for a civilian high commissioner to be appointed.

Byrnes' personal style, however, was much too independent for Truman. The South Carolinian established a small inner circle of confidants, largely ignored his department's professionals, and decided early in his watch when and when not to report to the president, a decision that, unfortunately for his tenure, was not often enough for Truman. Their relationship cooled, and by February 1947 sufficient instances of Byrnes acting independently and failing to keep his boss informed had clashed with Truman's own brisk style and his determination not to allow his presidency to be undermined. Byrnes voluntarily resigned, yet subtle presidential pressure for him to do so surely hastened the day.

Truman's choice as Byrnes' successor was the venerable General George C. Marshall, army chief of staff and one of the nation's small, elite group of five-star generals. He accepted the nomination readily and very quickly established a new image and new style of American diplomacy. Byrnes's Stuttgart message had been right for the time; now it was the moment, under Marshall, for a broader direction in American foreign policy. The ancient capitals of eastern Europe—Bucharest, Warsaw, Sofia, and Budapest—had fallen within the Russian orbit, as Winston Churchill so vividly described in his famous "Iron Curtain" speech at Westminster College in Fulton, Missouri in 1946. Prague would fall, too, early in 1948. Clearly, America needed to look beyond its responsibilities in Germany and generate a firm response to the Soviet Union's bald pattern of widespread aggression.

Unless the Russian expansionist threat, and Stalin's apparent willingness to permit continued poverty, sickness, unemployment, and devastation, were halted, their reach would extend throughout Europe. Early in his term of office, George Marshall proposed that the economies of all European nations might be strengthened to the point where they could all be, whatever their political ideology, self-sufficient. And if they could be self-sufficient, by implication they would be strong enough to resist the Soviet grasp. In a well-remembered speech at Harvard University in June 1947, the new secretary set forth his plan for the rebuilding of European economies, with European nations helping themselves as well as accepting American aid. By the following April, after the necessary public discussions, congressional committee deliberations, and spirited debate in Congress, Marshall's plan was enacted into law. To manage the plan, an Economic Cooperation Administration (ECA) was established that in the next three years distributed over $13 billion in aid, most of it designed to foster domestic production and stabilize national currencies.

Marshall Plan aid was offered not only to western European nations but also to Czechoslovakia and other countries of the eastern bloc. Predictably, the Soviet Union lashed out at the plan as a device to split east and west, and Stalin refused to permit participation by his satellite countries. Czechoslovakia announced its willingness to take part but was quickly rebuffed by the Soviet leader. "For Stalin the Marshall Plan was a watershed," wrote Zubok and Pleshakov in 1996. It was, from his point of view, "a large-scale attempt by the United States to gain lasting and preeminent influence in Europe—again, contrary to all expectations of the Soviet wartime planners." Stalin was right. The Marshall Plan was a huge success and contributed immensely to the economic recovery of Europe. Funds distributed under the plan enabled Great Britain, France, Italy, West Germany, and other recipient countries to restore their war-shattered economies and in the process to resist further Soviet overtures. Yet in the three years of ECA administration, as Stalin predicted, lines between east and west hardened. The Potsdam goal of a united Germany was becoming less and less of a possibility.

An American Soldier's Story

One young American on station in Berlin in 1947 was seventeen-year-old **Corporal Louis R. Schuerholz,** a native of Ocean City, Maryland. Arriving as a ranger with the 82nd Airborne Division in November, following airborne training at Fort Bragg, North Carolina, and ranger training at Fort Lewis, Washington, he was assigned to the unit motor pool. Lou felt that, being so heavily outnumbered in the city by the Russians, he and his colleagues were surely going to die. Even at that time, almost two years beyond Potsdam, he observed the Russians still causing strife and contention, and stealing anything they could grab in the western sectors. Slowly, nonetheless, he and his fellow rangers became cautiously friendly with a few Red Army occupation troops, communicating in German, playing chess together, drinking vodka with them during the Christmas holidays, yet always maintaining a healthy suspicion.

But once the blockade was imposed, all bets were off. "We were assigned to neighborhoods to deliver food to German homes," Lou recalls. "On one occasion, we drove into East Berlin, approached a Russian fuel dump, got the guards drunk on Four Roses, backed up our trucks to the tanks, and took 5,000 gallons of fuel oil which we then delivered to German households in our assigned neighborhoods."

Lou saw blockade duty through March 1949 and later served in Korea, where he was wounded, won the Silver Star and also a battlefield commission. Years later he served in Vietnam where he was awarded the *Croix de Guerre* for pulling a French general out of the line of fire. In 1982, after 35 years of army duty, he retired in the rank of colonel. Louis served four terms as commander of his Dundee, New York, Veterans of Foreign Wars (VFW) chapter until his death in July 2001.

The Final CFM Meeting

On November 25, 1947, the Council of Foreign Ministers (CFM), met for the fifth and what would be the last time until May 1949. Formation of the

CFM had been proposed by Truman, with ultimate approval by the Big Three, at the 1945 Potsdam conference. They also made provision for ultimate French membership. Its goals were to clean up the problems brought on by World War II, including reviving the German economy and constructing peace treaties with the defeated nations.

Following its establishment, the CFM met at least quarterly as per Potsdam directive, rotating the site of its gatherings. The Council held its first meeting in London in the fall of 1945, Paris in the summer of 1946, and New York that winter, followed by a session in Moscow in March and April 1947. Disunity marked the CFM meetings from the very beginning. The French, insecure as always, took a firm stand against any move to restore Germany economically, preferring stubbornly to hold the defeated nation prostrate and splintered. Foreign Minister Georges Bidault pressed constantly for internationalization of the industrial Ruhr, economic integration of the Saar with France, and decentralized administration throughout the western occupation zones of Germany.

Now, shortly more than two years later, the meeting site was the Lancaster House in London, the organization's headquarters. By this time the rift between the western powers and the Soviets had grown deep, the Soviets committed to forging their occupation zone in the socialist mold and the west, with continued reservations by the French, determined to establish a democratic climate in their territories. Up to this point, nonetheless, official western policy was still quadripartite in nature, with the United States and Great Britain firmly committed to a whole, united Germany, if that could be achieved with Russian and French cooperation. Matters of Germany and Austria were the topics before the ministers at this CFM meeting, which continued until December 15. The mood among them, however, became so frosty that there was no real expectation that any progress would emerge from these talks. And none occurred. It became clear at the end that four-power unity, if it had ever existed, was now finished.

Throughout seventeen sessions of the Council, Molotov, normally cordial and proper, yet always aggressive in stressing his nation's views, was obdurate and abusive to his colleagues, hurling insulting accusations at them. With this, Secretary of State Marshall, seeing no further point to continuing the abuse, brought the three-week long meeting to adjournment. It would not be until May 23, 1949 that the CFM would meet again, this time in Paris.

CIA Concerns

Apprehension over the failure of the CFM talks spread through numerous channels of government in Washington as Soviet intentions with respect to Germany came under increasing scrutiny. The Russian-controlled press in Berlin and the Soviet zone stepped up its criticism of four-power government, raising the question of whether such an arrangement would ever be successful. At the same time, General Bedell Smith, the American ambassador to Moscow, cabled the state department that the Soviet press there was engaged in a vigorous campaign to frighten the western allies out of Berlin. Then, on December 22, Admiral Roscoe Hillenkoetter, the director of central intelligence (CIA), reported to President Truman the clear "possibility of steps being taken in Berlin by Soviet authorities to force the other occupying powers to remove [their presence] from Berlin." General Clay and Ambassador Murphy's October 7 admonition to President Truman and the National Security Council about the likelihood of being forced out of Berlin now loomed larger than ever.

By the end of the year the western allies, with the possible exception of the French, had come to the realization that a showdown with the Russians was drawing near. Even the vaunted social times among the four occupation powers, which had been so much in evidence in the immediate preceding years, had slowed to a trickle. Behavior on informal, social occasions was often an indicator of underlying official feelings, so when Soviet representatives declined to take part in the annual Christmas party that had become almost a tradition in the preceding years, the western allies took notice. Although it was not yet clearly in evidence, the stage was being set by the Soviets for an ultimate push against Berlin. It might be an attempt to take over the city; it might be a total blockade. No one in the west could be certain at the time, but something was going to happen in the new year, 1948.

Sensing the Soviet mood early in January 1948, the army general staff went to work and produced a contingency study, setting forth necessary steps to take should the Russians actually try to force the western allies out of Berlin. Much later, in July, with the blockade imposed, the airlift building force, and the threat of war very real, Generals Robertson, Koenig, and Clay worked out emergency plans for a withdrawal of military forces to the Rhine. They maintained a confident mood, however, that the airlift would prevail and that few, if any, emergency steps would actually be required.

Three-Power Meeting: 1948

"By late 1947," reported Chip Bohlen, the state department's Soviet expert, "positions on both sides [the Soviet Union and the western allies] had hardened. There seemed to be no basis for compromise, no common ground, and each side set about to make its half of Germany work as a separate entity." Beginning in February 1948, the foreign ministers of the three western powers commenced a series of meetings in London. Relations between their governments and the Soviet Union had become so strained that the representatives of France, Great Britain, and the United States felt they must themselves decide about the future of western Germany. Consequently, the three foreign ministers recommended to their governments that the three occupation zones be combined as a step preparatory to forming a West German government. They also moved ahead with long-standing plans to revalue the mark as a necessary companion piece.

Pinpricks

The push commenced almost immediately in the new year. On January 23, Soviet guards halted a British military passenger train at Marienborn, close to the West German zonal border, and demanded to board it in order to inspect the papers of German passengers. The British officer in charge refused, whereupon the train was moved to a siding, left standing for twelve hours, and finally permitted to move on, minus the two coaches in which the Germans were riding. The two coaches were later returned to Berlin. Approximately two weeks later an American train was stopped, and German passengers were once more harassed by Russian inspectors who insisted on entering the cars to conduct searches. In each instance, the German passengers were employees of the respective allied governments and were fully authorized to travel.

Geoff Smith remembers it well. In March, the young RAF airman was on the way to his new post in Berlin. "We were traveling in a motor convoy on the autobahn," recalls Geoff, who began his RAF service in June 1947, with training at Padgate and Luffenhan. "Suddenly, we were halted by the Soviets and required to show our travel documents." Geoff and others in his convoy were required to present their papers four times during the transit along the autobahn to Berlin. Once the convoy reached Berlin and Geoff was safely ensconced in his unit at Gatow, he settled in to his military assignment as an electrician, working with a leading electrician, eight other electricians, four RAF (WRAF) women, two instrument mechanics, and a German instrument repairman. During the remainder of his airlift tour in Berlin, Geoff and his compatriots worked long duty hours keeping aircraft starter batteries in working order and making minor electrical repairs on such items as aircraft position lights.

Freight trains were also stopped, with the Russians demanding to inspect the cargoes for contraband. Vehicles on the autobahn were halted, too, usually for "bridge repairs" or some similar trumped up reason. These so-called pinpricks continued into the spring months, but what made them unusually significant was that they represented the first instances of harassment and intimidation on access routes to and from Berlin since September 1945, well over two years earlier. The Russians were unmistakably embarked on a renewed offensive.

During the same early months of 1948, the Russians mounted a propaganda campaign that quickly spread throughout the entire city. With clever use of east sector newspapers and radio stations, bolstered by ubiquitous street-corner loudspeakers, they boldly proclaimed that the western allies were preparing to withdraw from Berlin. This psychological effort to intimidate the citizenry, in a growing atmosphere of uncertainty about the future, was highly effective and meshed conveniently with the physical harassment of trains and autobahn traffic.

Russian Walkout: March 20, 1948

In late 1945 and the ensuing early years of the occupation, 1946 and 1947, relations among the four military governors of the occupation were warm, genuine, and friendly. They enjoyed each other's company on social occasions and often extended little courtesies to one another. General Clay reported that on the occasion of his son's wedding in Berlin in January 1946, General of the Army Vassily Sokolovsky remained after the reception to join a group of young officers in singing American military songs. Numerous other instances of warm, social relations prevailed. Field Marshal Sir Bernard Montgomery hosted a dinner on one occasion at which British soldiers performed a highland dance "to the tune of bagpipes." On Washington's birthday, the Americans traditionally held a large party with representatives of the other occupying powers in attendance; the Russians did likewise on Red Army Day. General Sokolovsky was one Russian with whom General Clay developed a genuine friendship, and in addition to large social functions, the two and their wives often dined together.

During those early years, debates in the Allied Control Council were spirited but polite, with each representative firmly, but without rancor, advancing his nation's formal policy positions. But in early January 1948 the mood in the ACC commenced to harden, largely on the Soviet lead. At the January 20 ACC meeting, all pretenses of past friendly relations disappeared as Marshal Sokolovsky with a vengeance accused the western powers of seeking to establish a German government from Bizonia, the American and British occupation zones in the west. At the council's next session on February 11, Sokolovsky made the charges once more but added a military dimension to the equation.

In March, the Soviets assumed the ACC chair on the standard monthly rotational basis, and a meeting was called for the 20th. Sokolovsky had been called to Moscow on March 9 and returned in time for the scheduled meeting, apparently, as it became clear, with orders to scuttle the ACC. The meeting turned out to be the council's swan song. As hosts for this monthly session, the Russians had laid out their usual lavish buffet spread for the postmeeting social activities. About halfway through the business session of the council, Sokolovsky, without warning, demanded to know the details of the western allies' three-power conferences in February and March when they had met without the Russians present. Both Clay and Robertson acknowledged to Sokolovsky that they would need to confer with their respective governments before responding, because they had neither been present nor involved in any decision-making. The Soviet, hardly waiting for the translation to come through, launched into a prepared tirade "which repeated all of the old charges against the western powers in more aggravating language." Almost on cue, Sokolovsky and his delegation arose and stalked out of the conference room as the marshal exclaimed, "I see no sense in continuing this meeting, and I declare it adjourned." The caviar, vodka, and other delicacies prepared for the postsession remained on the table. Sokolovsky never returned.

Years later, Clay was asked if he had expected Sokolovsky to walk out of the March 20 meeting of the ACC. "I certainly did not expect him to walk out at that meeting, but I can't say that it took me by surprise. It was quite obvious to me that the Control Council was dead, and the question was who was going to walk out first. I was pretty well determined that it was not going to be me."

But with this Soviet action, tensions and uncertainties increased severely. The friendly times of old were gone forever. War could very well be on the horizon, but one thing was certain: by the Soviet walkout, Germany had become irreparably divided.

April Tensions

On April 1, Russian harassment of traffic increased in intensity. Once more claiming the right to board western trains and inspect individual papers as well as cargo, Soviet guards stopped five military trains dispatched deliberately to test Russian firmness. Four trains, two American and two British, were forced after delays to detach passenger cars carrying Germans. The cars were then backed embarrassingly out of the Soviet zone; a third American train was permitted to proceed when the commander allowed Russian inspectors to board it and examine papers of German passengers.

Air Commodore Reginald N. Waite, riding one of the two British trains west from Berlin to the British zone, revealed many years later that squirreled away on his train were five German spies, British agents, who were being secreted to the British zone because their identities had become known to the Russians in Berlin. At Helmstedt, the border station where the trains were halted for inspection, British soldiers and passengers created a noisy diversion while the German spies were hustled from the rear of the train forward to the British cars. The forward half of the train then proceeded through the checkpoint, the five agents safely aboard, while the rear portion with German passengers was forced to return to Berlin.

Determined not to acquiesce to Soviet demands, Generals Robertson and Clay then canceled all train traffic and mounted a so-called Little Airlift to provide supplies for their military garrisons but with no plans or expectations of provisioning the population of Berlin by air. USAFE C-47s hauled 327 tons of cargo to Berlin in ten days, and the Soviets ceased stoppage of western surface traffic soon thereafter, thus permitting the Little Airlift to be called off. In those ten days, however, western leaders were encouraged as they realized that the military garrisons, at least, could be adequately supplied by air.

Despite the resumption of surface traffic to and from the west, Soviet pinpricks increased during the remainder of April and into May as new permit and documentation requirements for barges on the waterways and freight and passenger traffic on the railways were imposed. These actions, while not bringing traffic to a halt, resulted in numerous frustrating delays, all designed to demonstrate to the west that the Soviets were in control of access routes and could manipulate the western allies at will.

As discords between east and west increased in early April, pressures grew in Washington to evacuate American dependents from Berlin. Some members of Congress, sensitive to constituent views, urged army leaders in the Pentagon to bring dependents home. These requests resulted in General Omar Bradley asking Clay's opinion. Clay responded that such a move would play into the Soviets' hands and would demoralize the citizens of Berlin. He urged that a firm stand be taken in Berlin and that those dependents who were nervous be permitted to pack up and return home. Clay, however, had one caveat. He told his officers and men that anyone who was stressed about his family was free to send them home but on one condition—they would have to go with them. No one did.

General Bradley's air force son-in-law was stationed in Berlin with his family, and the general, a prominent World War II veteran and chief of staff of the United States army, was highly apprehensive of their fate should the Russians overrun the city. On this account, he made a formal request to air force leaders to reassign his son-in-law to Pentagon duty, which they did. Bradley was happy, but his son-in-law, having had nothing to do with the decision, was quite displeased. Bradley's action, nonetheless, unfortunately reflected official Washington's lack of resolve toward the impending Berlin crisis, and tended to weaken General Clay's position as American military governor.

Blockade

On June 18 the three western military governors, Generals Robertson, Koenig, and Clay, advised General Sokolovsky that due to the failure of all attempts at quadripartite agreement, currency reform would take place on June 20 in their zones of occupation. They were quick to point out, however, that in the hope for an agreement on a single currency for Berlin, the reform would not extend to its western sectors. Sokolovsky retaliated on June 22 by announcing a currency reform in the Soviet zone *and* Berlin. Caught by surprise, the three western military governors had little time to react and little choice but to extend their own currency reform to Berlin. They did so, with the new Deutsche marks slated for circulation in the city hurriedly stamped with a "B."

Under the western currency reform plan, German citizens in the end received 6.5 new Deutsche marks for 100 of the old Reichsmarks. As if by

magic, farm produce and consumer goods quickly reappeared in the
marketplaces and shops. A new confidence in the value of their currency
ultimately transformed the people and the economy, laying the foundation
for what in later years would be called Germany's *Wirtschaft Wunder*, its
"Economic Miracle."

On June 24, the Soviet Military Administration (SMA) closed traffic
between West Berlin and western Germany and cut off electricity in the
western sectors. A complete blockade of Berlin's western sectors was in
effect; 2.24 million residents in those sectors were now cut off and isolated.
Was the Soviet action a direct response to the western allies' currency
reform? General Clay, years later, was not at all certain. In his view, the
blockade was generally blamed on the reform, yet it might have been the
establishment of Bizonia, or the breakdown of the London conference of
foreign ministers in December of the previous year, or perhaps a combination of factors. Conceivably, the Soviets could see their German occupation
policy failing, and the blockade, therefore, represented their final desperate attempt to balance the equation by driving the western allies out in
humiliation and defeat. One thing was clear. Soviet communism and
western democracy were on a collision course.

Three

Blockade and the Western Response: 1948-1949

And in the average man is curled the hero stuff that rules the world.

Samuel Walter Foss, In Memoriam

BY JUNE 24 AT 6:00 A.M., WITH THE BLOCKADE of Berlin fully imposed by the Soviets, the immediate question for the western allies was, Do we take a firm stand and resolve to stay in the now isolated capital city, or do we pull out our troops, abandoning it to the forces of Russian aggression? To Generals Clay and Robertson, the choice was no choice at all. Their innermost feelings dictated that they must remain in Berlin. But how? Highway, rail, and water access was now completely cut off. The Russians had demonstrated in April that, with respect to rail access, they need only halt a train—in that case a train loaded with armed soldiers deliberately dispatched by Clay as a test—shunt it off to a siding for a few days, and then send it unceremoniously back to its point of origin.

They employed the same tactic again on June 20, holding an allied train on a siding before forcing it to return to the west. Now, late in June, General Clay felt so strongly about forcing through an armed convoy of trucks and supporting military vehicles that he requested authority from Washington to move ahead with this alternative. Ambassador Robert Murphy firmly sided with Clay, but there were too many opposed to such an idea, including Secretary of State Marshall and others at the policy level in the state department. Secretary of the Army Kenneth Royall and the Joint Chiefs of Staff (JCS), especially General Omar Bradley, who felt that American armed forces, vastly weakened by hasty demobilization at the end of the war, would now be no match for the Red Army, were equally opposed. Despite his position that the allies should stand fast in Berlin, General Robertson was also averse to any notion to force through a surface convoy. President Truman, however, impressed by Clay's view that the Russians would not risk war, pointed out that if the JCS would approve an armed convoy, he would sign the necessary papers. They did not.

Harry Truman and Omar Bradley, both Missourians, were old friends, and the president had great respect for Bradley's views. With Bradley, Marshall and the JCS firmly opposed to Clay's proposal for an armed convoy, the idea was shoved to the back burner. But there were other concerns as well. Murphy worried about the larger issue of the west remaining in Berlin by whatever means. On June 26 he dispatched a cable to Secretary Marshall, making it clear that the presence in Berlin of the western allies was a measure of U.S. prestige in central and eastern Europe, and for Germany a test of American ability in Europe. "If we docilely withdraw now," he wired, "Germans and other Europeans would conclude that our retreat from western Germany is just a question of time. The U.S. position in Europe would be much weakened, 'like a cat on a sloping tin roof.' " Ambassador Murphy conjectured that a possible western retreat from Berlin would be the "Munich of 1948."

At this point, no one could see further ahead than a day or two. Most western leaders felt that the newly imposed blockade might last a week, certainly not longer than a few weeks. The Soviets might simply be testing western resolve, fully intending to reopen access to Berlin within a short time.

The French Attitude

Nor was it too difficult to observe pessimism from other quarters. On June 24, Jefferson Caffery, the U.S. ambassador to France, briefed Secretary Marshall with a report on the French attitude. According to Caffery, an unnamed official in the French foreign office advised that his country's leaders believed the United States was wrong to place so much importance on remaining in Berlin at all costs. Given the west's untenable position, Berlin could easily be overrun by the Soviets and incorporated into their zone. "Moreover," continued Caffery in paraphrasing the French official, "feeding the city and maintaining its economic life would be virtually impossible."

French fears and hesitancy about remaining in Berlin, however, were not uppermost in the minds of Clay and Robertson. Their ally's pessimism was bothersome but failed to deter them; they had to figure out a way to provision the blockaded city and its 2.24 million inhabitants. Food stockpiled there since April was enough to last for about a month, coal stocks for about a month and a half. If not by rail, highway, or canals, then the city would have to be supplied by air, impossible as that option might appear. "These stocks had been built up with considerable difficulty as our transportation into Berlin was never adequate," explained General Clay. "We could sustain a minimum economy with an average daily airlift of 4,000 tons for the German population and 500 tons for the allied occupation forces." Yet he had little faith at the time that such a tonnage delivery could be accomplished.

Moving to the Airlift Decision

A key to supplying Berlin by air was the availability of transport aircraft. Within the United States Air Forces in Europe (USAFE) command there were about seventy aging C-47s, each of which could lift three tons maximum. At Rhein-Main, there were about 25 attached to the 61st Troop Carrier Group, while about 45 were assigned to the 60th Troop Carrier Group at Kaufbeuren in Bavaria. These veteran workhorses required a high level of daily maintenance; many had seen service on D-Day and still retained their invasion marking stripes. Also available were a few four-engine C-54s, with a ten-ton lifting capacity, yet the need for more was dire. But in order to mount a full-scale, if even temporary, airlift to supply the three western sectors of Berlin, the military commanders, Clay and Robertson, needed precise, quality information. Were there actually enough flyable aircraft, replacement parts, and air and maintenance crews to do the job? Was there sufficient fuel at hand? Could a supply network be developed for the delivery of goods to the departure airfields in both the American and British zones?

Their answers came from Air Commodore Reginald N. Waite, cited in chapter two. A 47-year-old flying boat veteran and the senior RAF officer at the Control Commission for Germany (CCG) in Berlin, Waite served during World War II on General Eisenhower's planning staff for the D-Day invasion, and after the surrender he was charged with disarming the German Luftwaffe in the British zone of occupation. "It was Air Commodore Waite who made the vital calculations for the logistics of supplying the western sectors of Berlin by air," reports **Aircraftsman First Class David Edwards** of St. Albans, Hertfordshire, a teleprinter operator assigned in 1948 to the signals office of Waite's Air Branch, Combined Services Division (ABCSD), "and it was he who, armed with this information, was able to persuade the British Military Governor, General Sir Brian Robertson...of the feasibility of the operation." Robertson, in turn, presented Waite's findings to General Clay, but the American was not immediately convinced. Although he was willing to consider a trial airlift on a stopgap basis, especially for the Berlin garrison, he still harbored an uncertainty that a city of 2.24 million inhabitants could actually be provisioned by air alone, and for an indeterminate period of time.

Despite lack of support at higher levels, Clay clung to his faith that an armored column moving down the autobahn from Helmstedt, the western zonal border point, could force the Soviets to back down. In fact, he had already made advance preparations for such a column in Heidelberg, where he had named Brigadier General Arthur Trudeau, commanding the First Constabulary Brigade in Wiesbaden, to equip and lead a 6,000 man provisional combat team. General Curtis LeMay, who in 1948 was USAFE commander in Wiesbaden, reported in his 1965 memoirs that Trudeau had his column assembled and ready to go. He (Trudeau) would have to determine, once the column was advancing, whether he had mere token or genuine resistance on his hands. If it turned out to be a real fight, LeMay was prepared to put his fighters in the air to wipe out Russian fighters and other aircraft parked in neat rows on their airfields, and his B-29s would also be at the ready. "If you do that," claimed General Robertson, "it'll be war—it's as simple as that. I am sure that [General Pierre] Koenig will feel the same."

Clay was undeterred. "I am still convinced that a determined move-ment of convoys with troop protection would reach Berlin," he reported confidently to his Washington superiors. Nonetheless, he realized pain-fully that what little support prevailed in official Washington for his armored column proposal had eroded, so he simultaneously moved on with the airlift option, in concert with General Robertson, each of them sus-tained by Waite's careful estimates. The two leaders hoped desperately that somehow enough life-supporting supplies might be transported by air to maintain not only the military garrisons but also the civilian population of the now besieged city.

David Edwards and his signals office operated from the Commission's Lancaster House in Berlin's Fehrbelliner Platz. The small group of about twenty persons included five teleprinter operators: two air force, two army, and one navy. Working in shifts, they maintained a constant 24-hour watch. During one of the early days after the blockade was imposed, members of this group were ushered into Air Commodore Waite's office to hear his announcement that there was going to be an airlift. "About fifteen people were present," writes David, who trained at Compton Bassett, arrived in Berlin on May 6 and ultimately served on the airlift until late in April 1949. "Air Commodore Waite confirmed to us that all attempts at negotiating a solution [to the blockade] with the Russians had failed and that it was the intention of the British, together with the Americans and French, to supply the city by air."

Pondering his options as to exactly how to mount an airlift, Lucius Clay got on the telephone to General LeMay, asking if he could haul some coal to Berlin. "Sure. We can haul anything. How much coal do you want us to haul?" responded LeMay. "All you can haul," was Clay's startling answer. "You'd better start doing it," he added. "I want you to take every airplane you have and make it available for the movement of coal and food to Berlin." LeMay's trademark cigar dropped from his mouth. Recovering quickly and correctly believing that Clay's request was to provide a temporary, stopgap measure, he went ahead and ordered the available C-47 crews to commence the Berlin run.

Meanwhile, General Robertson ordered Dakota sorties out of Wunstorf. In what the British called Operation Knicker, three RAF Dakotas flew their initial missions to Berlin on June 25, hauling six-and-a-half tons of supplies for the British garrison. On June 27, sixteen Dakotas moved from their home base in the United Kingdom to Wunstorf, followed soon after by 42 more Dakotas, then forty Yorks. By the end of the month the RAF fleet was airlifting more than 1,000 tons daily to Berlin. The entire British operation was given a new name, Carter Paterson, and the mission was broadened to supply the civilian population of West Berlin.

Reasonably secure in the knowledge that enough serviceable aircraft were available, Clay then made perhaps his most important move in deciding whether or not to mount a full-scale air effort. He summoned Ernst Reuter, the Berliners' moral leader whose election as mayor a year earlier had been vetoed by the Soviets in the Kommandatura. Reuter appeared, sporting his distinctive beret and accompanied by his young assistant, Willy Brandt, who would himself in 1957 become mayor of West Berlin and twelve years later chancellor of the new federal republic. Clay's close friend and political advisor, Bob Murphy, was also present. "I want you to know this," said the military governor to Reuter. "No matter what we may do, the Berliners are going to be short of fuel. They are going to be short of electricity. I don't believe they are going to be short of food. But I am sure there are going to be times when they are going to be very cold, and feel very miserable. Unless they are willing to take this and stay with us, we can't win this. If we are subjecting them to a type and kind of treatment which they are unwilling to stand and they break on us, our whole lift will have failed. And I don't want to go into it unless you understand that fully, unless you are convinced that the Berliners will take it."

Tough, courageous, and a veteran of many clashes with the Soviets and Berlin communists, Reuter had been a prisoner of war in Russia in 1916, returned to Germany as a communist, rose to be secretary general of the German communist party, but became soured on communism not only by Moscow's brutality but also by the radical, communist-inspired, 1919 Spartacus uprising in Berlin. He was arrested by the Nazis in 1933, was twice condemned to a concentration camp, fled to Turkey in 1935, and returned to Germany in 1947 as a socialist, thoroughly disillusioned with Soviet communist tactics. In June 1947 he was elected lord mayor of Berlin with 89 of 108 votes in the city assembly, but the Soviets, fully aware of his rejection of communism and his turn to socialism, vetoed his election. The quiet, diminutive, yet very tough deputy mayor Louise Schroeder was chosen to serve as acting mayor in his place.

Reuter had fully supported Clay's plan for pushing an armored column down the autobahn, feeling that the Russians were bluffing. Fluent in English, his response to Clay's airlift proposal, nonetheless, was quick, direct, and supportive when the military governor called him in. "General, I can assure you, and I do assure you, that the Berliners will take it." With that, Clay moved ahead with the fateful decision to mount an airlift, not really certain of what the outcome might be.

Many years later, Clay was asked about Washington's response to his airlift decision. "I never asked," he responded. "I never asked permission or approval to begin the airlift. I asked permission to go in on the ground with the combat team, because if we were stopped we'd have to start shooting. But we didn't have to start fighting to get through in the air, so I never asked permission." By late July, when asked by the press corps to comment on reports that he advocated busting the land blockade with an armed column, Clay replied, "It is my duty not to carry us into war. That decision would have to be made by the Government if it is ever necessary."

Support for Clay and Robertson

Since General Clay became military governor, he had been granted wide latitude in decision-making by his superiors in Washington, who realized, albeit reluctantly, that many vital judgments on occupation matters had to be made by him on the spot. His momentous airlift decision became the most visible example. Still, it needed the stamp of legitimacy in the form of solid support from the White House. Harry Truman, who had great confidence in Clay, provided it at once. "On June 26, the day after I discussed the Berlin crisis with the Cabinet," he wrote in 1956, "I directed that this improvised 'airlift' be put on a full-scale organized basis and that every plane available to our European Command be impressed into service." Clay now had the green light to shape the American side of the airlift as he saw fit.

In England, Foreign Minister Ernest Bevin furnished confirmation that his country would stand firmly behind General Sir Brian Robertson, the British military governor in Germany. On June 25, the Cabinet met to discuss the Berlin situation, but most members were in a pessimistic mood. Bevin would have none of it. The sturdy veteran of many political and labor battles stood in common cause with Ernst Reuter and "demanded the biggest possible force of transport aircraft to be made available at once" to supply Berlin by air.

The next day Bevin issued a press statement that Britain was determined to stay in Berlin. The day after that, Bevin also proposed that B-29s be placed on temporary duty in the United Kingdom as a show of force to the Soviets. General Clay and General Hoyt Vandenberg, USAF chief of staff, both quickly agreed, and within a few weeks two B-29 groups from South Dakota and Florida had made their way to British air bases. Much has been made of the fact that the B-29s at that time were not configured to carry nuclear weapons. Questions were raised: Was it general knowledge at the time about the B-29s, and did the Soviets realize this? What if they did or did not? The simple fact that B-29s, armed only with conventional bombs, were on call in England, posed a mighty deterrent threat itself.

Implementing the Airlift Decision

With the airlift decision now a matter of public policy, Curt LeMay moved to organize a task force to implement it. He called on Brigadier General Joseph Smith, commander of the Wiesbaden military post, to be the task force commander of the upstart airlift, which no one expected to last more than a few weeks. Smith moved quickly. Altogether, the RAF had enough Dakotas on hand, as well as about forty Avro Yorks, the four-engine transport version of the World War II Lancaster bomber, capable of lifting eight-and-a-half to nine tons. USAFE had a sufficient number of C-47s, but clearly not enough of the larger C-54 Skymasters. On June 26, C-47s flying out of Rhein-Main hauled eighty tons of food and medicine to Tempelhof in 32 flights.

When asked what his newly formed operation was called, Smith retorted, "Hell, we're hauling grub. Let's call it Operation Vittles." By July 19, the British had labeled their side of the airlift Operation Plainfare, and so the names stuck. Thirty days later, the hastily initiated airlift operation was so glaringly improvisational in nature that it was aptly dubbed in a German publication, *Eine Cowboy-Operation mit einem Dummen Vogel* (A Cowboy Operation with a Gooney Bird).

To meet the glaring need for more C-54s and their ten-ton capacity, USAF ordered 45 Skymasters moved at once from Alaska, Hawaii, and the Panama Canal Zone to Germany. Air and ground crews quickly stuffed their duffel bags, said hasty farewells to their families, and boarded their aircraft for the lengthy over-water flight to the European continent. Departure was so hurried for some that they had to leave personal automobiles in care of friends and their dry cleaning still in the shop. By mid-July the requested additional C-54s were on site in Germany.

French Participation

Despite France's negative mood about standing up to the Soviets in Berlin, her leaders slowly acquiesced and came about-face to support the airlift in principle. Her actual airlift role, however, was limited in both time and scope. First, the language barrier worked against any sizeable involvement. Next, French officials argued that their air force was too deeply involved in the Indo-China conflict to permit a strong airlift role. Finally, French aircraft were too few in number and too slow.

In the weeks immediately prior to imposition of the blockade and for a few weeks thereafter, the French air force flew a small number of German JU-52s, manufactured in France, into Berlin, but mostly to supply its own garrison. The French also flew a B-17 in on a weekly basis, this too for provisioning their own Berlin forces. Too slow and capable of lifting only a ton-and-a-half, the JU-52s actually got in the way of the RAF and USAF aircraft attempting to build a firm, smooth operation, and they were politely requested to bow out. "The French air force participated in the

Berlin airlift for psychological and political reasons," wrote Christienne and Lissarague. "It must be admitted that French participation proved rather troublesome for the organizers because of the slowness of the JU-52s, their small capacity, the language difficulty...and the inadequacy of French radio equipment."

General Tunner Takes Over

General Smith had every desire to lead the hastily improvised airlift on a permanent basis. He performed extremely well in his unenviable position and made numerous important early decisions designed to put the operation on a sound footing. USAF chief of staff General Hoyt Vandenberg and General Albert Wedemeyer, of the army general staff, clearly recognized, nonetheless, that if Berlin were to be sufficiently supplied by air on a long-term basis, someone with air transport expertise would be needed to lead the charge.

Such an expert happened to be available. Major General William H. Tunner, at the time a deputy commander of the Military Air Transport Service (MATS), was noted for having led the Hump airlift in the China-Burma-India theater during World War II. Tunner himself, vividly aware of the start-up airlift in Germany, wanted the job badly and immediately lobbied in Washington for MATS (meaning Tunner) to take it over. "I knew both General LeMay and the actual commander of the airlift, Joe Smith, and admired and respected them both as combat officers," he wrote in 1964. "But this was not combat. In air transport everything is different— rules, methods, attitudes, procedures, results." Vandenberg and Wede-meyer felt likewise; Vandenberg was even thinking of Tunner for the post without the latter's lobbying efforts. But first, he and Wedemeyer consulted General Clay, who was cool to the idea on the grounds that things were going fine and tonnage was increasing daily. In the end, Vandenberg made his decision. Tunner was named to command the airlift, yet he realized that the chief of staff's decision would not be unanimously supported by all.

"So I was relieved," ruminated General Smith in a 1976 interview. "I just was relieved because General LeMay was offered Tunner, who was an experienced transport commander. I am frank to say that I felt hurt. I would have liked to have kept it; I was doing a good job on it." Later, Smith commented that "He [Tunner] didn't create this MATS [airlift] command for anybody except himself, for his own glorification."

On July 28, at the controls of his personal C-54, number 5549, Tunner touched down at Wiesbaden, ready to go to work and put the airlift on a streamlined, transport footing. A hand-picked staff of Hump veterans as well as **Katie Gibson**, his secretary, had accompanied him on the lengthy transatlantic flight. Checking in with LeMay upon arrival, he found the USAFE commander cordial but businesslike; as Tunner suspected. LeMay, like Clay, was not overly pleased to have him as the new airlift commander. Despite this mood, the two worked reasonably well together in the ensuing months until LeMay departed in mid-October to replace General George C. Kenney as head of the Strategic Air Command. To replace LeMay in Europe, Lieutenant General John K. Cannon, of fighter command tradition, was named to lead USAFE.

A short three weeks after Bill Tunner assumed command of the Airlift Task Force (Provisional), three squadrons of C-54s began to arrive at Fassberg RAF station, situated about 120 kilometers north of Hannover in the British zone of occupation. USAFE historian Daniel Harrington points out that in late July, as he settled in to take over American airlift operations, Tunner poured over the route maps between Frankfurt and Berlin. Warming to an idea initially raised by General Smith, he realized immediately that aircraft based further north in Germany would have a much shorter run, thereby saving time and fuel, but most importantly, they would increase deliveries. "Two planes based at Fassberg, for example, could do the work of three based at Wiesbaden," he wrote fifteen years later.

Negotiations with the British for acquisition of northern bases were quickly concluded, even though the RAF had only on July 19 transferred their Dakotas to Fassberg from Wunstorf to alleviate crowding at the latter. By August 27, all RAF Dakotas were moved again, after little more than a month at Fassberg, and consolidated at Lübeck, commencing operations from that base, located even further north than Fassberg.

For the remainder of August and into September, C-54s continued to arrive at Fassberg; the three original squadrons turned into four, all organized under the 313th Troop Carrier Group. General Tunner—and General Smith, too—proved to be right about acquiring northern bases, for by the end of August the Americans had set a new daily record of 3,124 tons delivered to Berlin. And on Air Force Day, September 18, 1948, a record 6,987 tons of coal were flown in. In celebration, a special bonus of coal was declared for Berliners. During the summer months following his arrival, General Tunner had not only secured the northern British bases of Celle and Fassberg for the American C-54s, but also had labored mightily to streamline procedures, shorten turnaround times, issue new flight regulations, secure better food and living quarters for airmen, and generally make himself available as a sounding board to air and ground forces. His dream was of a giant conveyor belt in the sky, with loaded aircraft moving in clockwork precision to deliver their cargoes and return expeditiously to their bases.

An Airlift Pilot Remembers

A pleasant, affable, native of Bergoo, West Virginia is **Albert Lowe,** who remembers well his Fassberg time as a young airlift pilot. During World War II, Al flew an impressive fifty B-24 missions against Germany's heartland, only to find himself three years later hauling coal to blockaded

Berlin. Assigned to the 313th Group's 29th Troop Carrier Squadron, First Lieutenant Lowe served on the airlift from December 1948 through the following September when Operation Vittles came to an end. Air crews, like the ground support forces, endured long work shifts, from 0600 to 1800 hours, then rotated after several days to an 1800 to 0600 hours cycle. An aircraft commander and instructor pilot as well, Al flew 267 Vittles missions in his nine months of airlift service.

"The weather was very rough from December through March," he recalls. "Amazingly, I had only three missed approaches due to bad weather." Nobody liked a missed approach, for it meant that they had to return to the home base with their full ten-ton load intended for Berlin. "But the weather was in my favor on December 24, 1948," remembers Al as if it were yesterday. "A snowstorm closed down Tegel and allowed me to spend Christmas Eve in Berlin."

In Al's opinion, the air crews blazed a trail in all kinds of weather, night or day. His memories clearly include the sounds and sights of rain, snow, noisy C-54 engines, red hot exhaust stacks, and the labor and strain of lifting heavy loads into the air. Those memories also include an unpleasant experience one overcast night at Tegel. While preparing to board his Skymaster for the return trip to Fassberg, Al was approached by a displaced person who had been mingling with the unloading crew in the rear of the airplane. He offered Al $10,000 to fly him and a woman companion to the west. The young pilot would have nothing to do with the proposal. "Get off my airplane!" thundered Al, normally soft-spoken and mild mannered. The couple beat a hasty retreat. Fifty years later, Al told me that it very well could have been an army Criminal Investigation Division (CID) setup, a trap. Whether it was or not, Al would never know, but in any case he was not about to enter into such a shady arrangement.

Al went on to complete an air force career, retiring as a lieutenant colonel. Now living in Charleston, South Carolina with his wife and childhood sweetheart, Glendine, he looks back to the airlift as a most unforgettable career experience, and in gratitude he has donated pictures and other airlift memorabilia to the Allied Museum in Berlin. "For those of us who participated and still survive," says this modest veteran, "we can hold our heads high and be extremely proud that we were a part of the greatest humanitarian undertaking the world has ever known."

Airlift Growing Pains

As quickly as they arrived at Wiesbaden or Rhein-Main, air crews were sent out on their first missions to Berlin, whether they were ready or not, and whether they were fully trained or not. Shortly after his early September arrival at Wiesbaden's so-called Y-80 airfield, **Lieutenant Frank Zamboni's** operations officer singled him out. "Hop aboard, buddy. We're going to Berlin." Frank, a native of St. Louis who ultimately served 28 years on active duty and retired as a colonel, was suddenly a copilot on a

C-47, in service around the world since the 1930s and now the aging workhorse of the U.S. Air Force, the Royal Air Force, a few banana republics, and some civilian contract carriers. Fondly dubbed the Gooney Bird by the Americans and the Dakota by the British, it could lift three tons of cargo.

Frank's first flight to Berlin is locked forever in his memory. For him, the airlift was a new flying situation, in a strange land. Radio procedures were new and different, terrain and navigation routes were different, and the moment was different. Additionally, visions of Yak-2 fighters in the corridor were ever-present in his mind.

A hardy veteran of the treacherous Hump flying during World War II in the China-Burma-India theater of operations, Frank had accumulated plenty of C-46 and C-47 cockpit time. "Those of us who had flown on the Hump were quickly upgraded because of our instrument experience and our time in C-46s and C-47s," remembers Frank. "Flying the airlift became a piece of cake by comparison." Despite such confidence, minor apprehensions were inevitable, but they soon passed, and the rhythm of flying easily reappeared as it did for all those getting back into the cockpit. Sure enough, in a very short time, Frank's valuable experience flying the Hump was recognized, and he was upgraded to first pilot.

From June through September when they were withdrawn from airlift duty, the C-47s chugged their way up the southern corridor in concert with their big brother C-54s, spaced by time blocks to accommodate differences in cruising speeds. In this time period the RAF Dakotas made their regular return trips to Gatow from Wunstorf, Fassberg, Bückeburg, and Lübeck. The British never did abandon the Dakota, using it steadily throughout the long months of the airlift. Another point about the Dakota: RAF crews flew it with only one pilot plus a signaller, and a navigator who was qualified to double as a pilot. This was very much in the tradition of several British multi-engine military aircraft whereby the cockpit was configured for only one pilot.

The RAF airlift role was significantly augmented in the autumn months of 1948 by the arrival of Commonwealth Dakota crews. In mid-September, ten crews of the Royal Australian Air Force checked in at Lübeck. By October 16, ten South African Air Force crews had arrived at that northern German air base, and by November 3, three crews of the Royal New Zealand Air Force were on duty at Lübeck, where all RAF Dakotas were ultimately based for airlift duty. These air crews brought no aircraft; they were assigned instead to Dakotas already in service at Lübeck, and their record of airlift performance was exemplary.

On November 9, the U.S. Navy also became an airlift participant. On that date the first of 24 R5Ds, the navy designation for the C-54, arrived at Rhein-Main, the vanguard of two squadrons, VR-6 and VR-8, that comprised the navy contingent.

During the autumn months of 1948, the earlier practice of rushing pilots and flight engineers into the cockpit, albeit necessary at the airlift's onset, gradually changed to a more deliberate approach marked by increased attention to systematic training. Air crews and numerous entire units continued to arrive in Germany, but now many of them were fresh from the newly established training facility at Great Falls, Montana that had been quickly set up to prepare air and ground crews for airlift duty through establishment of an exact replica of radio frequencies, radar facilities, and air corridors from western Germany into Berlin. "The three-week course provided preflight and flight training for all crew members," wrote USAF historian Roger Miller, emphasizing that the trainees were mostly reservists recalled to active duty. Needless to say, they had not flown or serviced heavy aircraft since the end of the second world war, and prior experience in C-54s was almost nil. Hence, the three-week Great Falls "prep" course proved to be precisely what was needed for airlift replacement purposes.

Upon arrival in Germany, the graduates were immediately subjected to further training and flight checks as they became indoctrinated to actual airlift procedures directed by **Captain Thomas A. Williams** of Oak Grove, Louisiana and eight other check pilots of the 60th Troop Carrier Group at Wiesbaden. No more of the hasty, crisis-filled early moments of the airlift when air crews and airplanes were hurried into service, ready or not. By late 1948 and early 1949 many airlift practices had become nicely standardized, and the entire airlift operation was taking on the appearance of a smoothly oiled machine. Improvisation had been replaced by organization and disciplined procedures.

A little airlift within Operation Plainfare quickly sprang up on the British side. Known as the "Plumber Flight," it was composed of six Dakota freighters, plus their air and ground crews. Plainfare aircraft were maintained at their own bases in Germany, but the Plumber's job was to fly in engines, wheel assemblies, instruments, and other aircraft parts for the Yorks, Hastings, and Dakotas on duty at Wunstorf, Lübeck, and other RAF Plainfare bases. One air crew member on duty with the Plumber Flight was **Flight Lieutenant Michael Downes,** from Southend-on-Sea, Essex, who flew as navigator on several missions. A suboperation of the airlift, the Plumber Flight was responsible for servicing all British aircraft assigned to Plainfare. Its crews hauled 400-500 tons of parts monthly and flew about 100,000 miles during its life. It proved to be a vitally important component of the airlift effort.

Airlift Housing Problems

Fassberg's vast military airfield, established in 1933 as a Luftwaffe technical training base and after the end of World War II occupied by the RAF, virtually engulfs the tiny village from which it takes its name. In August 1948, following negotiations with the British, USAF forces assumed command of most of its facilities, ideally suited for the American C-54s with its new railroad spur, access road, and loading accommodations constructed earlier in the year by the British. At the same time, RAF Dakotas moved from Fassberg to Lübeck in a regrouping designed to bring more efficiency to overall airlift efforts.

As the Americans moved in to take over the air base, those few on permanent change of station (PCS) and therefore authorized to bring their dependents, could find little or no housing in the tiny Fassberg community. Apparently, very few private German homes had been requisitioned by the British prior to the Americans' arrival, and for the remainder of 1948 and into 1949 the Americans took over only a small number. Since there were no family quarters on the air base itself, the housing problem had become acute by early 1949.

Many air and ground crews ordered to Germany from far-flung bases in Hawaii, Japan, Guam, Alaska, and the Caribbean, as well as reservists recalled to active duty from civilian life, arrived in Wiesbaden and Frankfurt on temporary duty status (TDY) and therefore had no authorization to bring along their dependents. Their TDY status was initially for ninety days, later extended to six months and in some cases, for even lengthier periods. From these disagreeable circumstances arose widespread morale problems, both among airmen in Germany and their dependents back home. Others arrived in Germany PCS but quickly found themselves in a TDY fiasco. Orders of some recalled reservists directed them, for example, to the 60th Troop Carrier Group at Kaufbeuren air base in Bavaria on a PCS basis, yet in reality they never saw Kaufbeuren since the 60th, by the time of their arrival in Germany, had already moved north to Wiesbaden in the early weeks of the airlift in response to an immediate need for transport aircraft and supporting air and ground crews.

Whether airmen came with their units from other corners of the earth or were recalled from civilian life, most of them converged in the first instance on the Marburg reception center, located about eighty kilometers north of Frankfurt. After a week or two of processing and orientation at Marburg, many were then further assigned to the Wiesbaden Y-80 air base, or the Rhein-Main base at Frankfurt, immediately generating a huge crunch in living facilities for themselves alone, considerations of dependent quarters aside.

Air crews and ground crews alike had to cope by cleaning out bombed buildings and old barns to serve as temporary sleeping quarters until something better could be requisitioned or constructed. Some were assigned, upon first arriving at Rhein-Main, to tar paper barracks from which displaced laborers had been hastily evacuated. Even those barracks were too ugly for some airlift crews. They took a quick look, rebelled, moved to nearby barns, and settled into their new homes for the foreseeable future.

With a steady influx of air crews, maintenance and supply personnel, and others skilled in the everyday needs of airlift operations, housing problems continued to mount. Fassberg was fully taken over by the Americans on October 1, with numerous air and support personnel transferred from Wiesbaden and Rhein-Main to flesh out the 313th Troop Carrier Group settling in at this northern air base in the British occupation zone. Early in October, **Captain Harry Schiele**, a liquor salesman from Nashville; **Major Eliot Tobin,** a Yankee from Vermont, who later would become one of the pilots of the renowned Fassberg Flyer; **Frank Zamboni**; and **Lieutenant Larry Kemp,** a happy-go-lucky, free-spirited bachelor from Detroit, rode bucket-seat style in a C-54 from Wiesbaden to Fassberg, their new destination, still on TDY status. During World War II, Larry was forced to bail out over Soviet territory on a shuttle bombing mission from England and was interned in Poltava, in the Ukrainian S.S.R. Given Larry's nature, he wasn't too concerned about the flight northward, but the others, being more serious-minded air crew members, remained keenly sensitive, as the Skymaster droned along, to the skills of the guy occupying the left seat up front, never quite confident that he would deliver them safely.

Married men on that flight, together with many others later assigned to Fassberg, and to Celle in December, were immediately despondent over the lack of dependent housing at their respective bases. All were anxiously looking forward to the time when their families would join them in Germany.

Because Fassberg was originally constructed as a permanent Luftwaffe base, many bachelor quarters were of good quality. Both officers and airmen were assigned, to the extent possible, to comfortable rooms in two-story concrete and brick barracks with maid service. Herman Göring had taken good care of his airmen. There was inevitable overcrowding, but the facilities per se were good. Yet with little or no dependent housing available, hopes for an early reunion of airmen with their families remained dim as the weeks of autumn passed into the grim cold of winter.

With Fassberg fully operational in the early autumn, pressure mounted to make the Celle base ready for airlift service at the earliest possible moment. Work on a new runway sturdy enough to accommodate the C-54s continued at a steady pace. When Celle opened on December 15, 1948, the progression of men moving north from bases at Wiesbaden and Rhein-Main was repeated, as the 317th Troop Carrier Group, recently uprooted from Tachikawa, Japan, settled in at this former Luftwaffe base north of Hannover and a few kilometers south of Fassberg. Dependent housing facilities at this newly opened base were also in short supply, and morale sagged as the new arrivals learned of this nagging problem, seemingly incapable of solution.

Although GI grousing over lack of dependent housing tended to unite those based at Celle and Fassberg, airlift pressures to supply Berlin separated them as ground and air crews developed a friendly rivalry in the race to deliver increasing daily tonnages. Cries of "Beat Celle" and "Beat Fassberg" echoed throughout the respective mess halls, maintenance shacks, administrative offices, and flight lines, to the very moment in autumn 1949 when these bases ceased operations.

Public Opinion and the Airlift

From its very beginning the airlift, as previously noted, had the firm support of President Truman, Prime Minister Attlee, and many high-ranking government officials in each country. Further, despite harsh working conditions, separation from families, and uncertainty as to the ultimate outcome, those assigned to airlift operations were extremely proud and supportive of their overall mission. Beyond this, however, the airlift strongly needed another kind of support: the broad support of public opinion, in both the United States, the United Kingdom, and Germany. If messages received by Truman in the airlift's early months were any indication of the mood of Americans, they firmly supported a tough stand in Berlin and the June decision to mount the airlift. On June 25, as Clay and others deliberated, a telegram from Alfred Bingham, chairman, American Association for a Democratic Germany, and several other leaders of liberal causes, arrived at the White House. It read in part, "We urge you make this country's position unmistakable by declaring that under all circumstances short of war, we will remain in Berlin and maintain supplies for the civilian population."

Additional messages of support continued to arrive during the summer months, indicating that a large majority of Americans were in favor of the action taken. Representatives of the labor movement, chambers of commerce, individual congressmen, and the old socialist warhorse, Norman Thomas himself, voiced their agreement with the airlift decision.

Throughout Germany in particular, public opinion polls conducted by the U. S. military government revealed that 98 per cent of the populace was in favor of the western allies remaining. And at home, perhaps the most unique expression of public opinion was offered by Richard Wallace, an eight-year-old schoolboy in St. Louis, who in autumn 1948 wrote a short note to President Truman in his own handwriting, as follows: "Dear President Truman, I think we should have more farms in [B]berlin, Germany. So the people could raise there [sic] own food. That way we can use all our planes to fly fuel and coal."

Public support was not, however, unanimous. On September 12, a disgruntled Philip Johnston of Los Angeles sent a letter to Truman, in which he wrote in part, "The so-called 'Berlin Crisis' is entirely an outgrowth of your own incredible stupidity. When you attended the Potsdam confrence [sic] to arrange final details for the occupation of Germany, it was your duty to...insist upon the establishment of a corridor to the American zone...I am inclined to think that you were just too dumb to know that such a corridor was necessary."

In Philadelphia at the Progressive party's July convention, Henry Wallace won the nomination for the presidency, declaring in his acceptance speech his fervent support for American withdrawal from Berlin "in a search for peace" with the Soviet Union. Truman received other communications, more civil in tone, from those in favor of withdrawal or a negotiated settlement, but on balance, his mail was clearly supportive of the decision to remain in Berlin and supply it by air. Perhaps most important, eighty per cent of Americans, in public opinion polls, stood firmly in support of the airlift.

Those Wonderful Flying Boats

In addition to coal, flour, dried eggs and beans, Berlin needed salt. But how to get it there? Salt filtered from its containers and through aircraft flooring, corroding aircraft control cables and otherwise making its menacing presence known. Over time, obviously, conventional aircraft were at risk if loaded with a salt cargo. The solution was found in the RAF Coastal Command's Short Sunderland flying boat, a charming, if not really beautiful, craft. With its control cables installed high in the fuselage ceiling, away from the damaging effects of salt, and with its aluminum frame treated against the corrosive effects of salt water, it was the ideal bird to carry this product.

Early in July, ten Sunderlands, operating from Finkenwerder, the former Blohm and Voss seaplane facility on the Elbe River near Hamburg, joined the airlift forces with their first salt deliveries. Their assignment was very much the work of Air Commodore Waite, instrumental in the basic airlift decision and a veteran of flying boat operations. A civilian contractor, Aquila Airways, also joined the salt delivery efforts in August with two Hythe flying boats. Both the Hythes and Sunderlands had a relatively direct course through the northern corridor into Berlin, where they landed on the *Havelsee,* moored in the lake's quiet waters off the *Schwanenwerder* Peninsula, and were unloaded by German workers supervised by British army troops. The Sunderlands created so much excitement, even among the military forces in Berlin, that many airmen hoped for a ride. One of the lucky ones was **Aircraftsman S. Michael Williams**, from East Sussex, who, while stationed at Gatow, made a duty flight one fine day from the Havel to Finkenwerder in Hamburg. All of Mike's friends were understandably jealous of his good fortune.

In early September, **Second Lieutenant Courtenay A. Latimer** of the Royal Army Service Corps (RASO) was posted to Gatow to command its Water Base Unit. What was so special about this unit? It was a small group of British soldiers and German workers assigned to handle flying boat deliveries as they arrived on the *Havelsee.* "To unload the flying boats a ramshackle fleet had been gathered—a personnel launch, two diesel tugs—noisy, smelly little steel bathtubs—an elegant little cabin cruiser, and 26 army pontoons," explains Courtenay. His unit was composed of a subaltern, a lance corporal, and two sergeants; the others, Germans, were the foreman **Karl-Heinz Heinig,** an interpreter-clerk, two policemen, three tug drivers, and 32 stevedores.

Courtenay's office was a tiny hut perched on the deck of a derelict barge, which in turn rested on a quiet sandy beach at the edge of the

Havelsee. Stationed also on the British side of the lake were two RAF flight lieutenants who, armed with two-way radios, acted as "tower operators" for the arriving and departing Sunderlands. There was no night flying to the *Havel,* so the first flying boats arrived at 0500 to take advantage of every daylight hour. "As they touched down and skimmed across the water, fans of spray flying," continues Courtenay, "our tugs would roar out with pontoons lashed alongside and go in under the wings. The doors would open, and the stevedores would fling themselves on the salt bags. Speed was essential. A boat could be turned around in twelve minutes."

As for the Berliners who worked with the unit, Courtenay slowly came to know them reasonably well. "I thought I knew about Germans— that they were obedient to authority, with little sense of humour, hard-working and dull," he muses. "These fellows were half starved, yet cheerful, and crackling with repartee. I never understood the quick *Berliner deutsch,* or the reasons for the gusts of laughter that erupted from the stevedores as they toiled over the salt bags." But he says that as he learned more about Berlin and the unique Berlin personality, the jolly manner in which those in his tiny unit behaved soon made more sense to him.

Flying Officer Ian Bergh, a 21-year-old South African Air Force navigator, flew on Sunderlands with No. 230 squadron for the few short autumn months in which they operated. Cruising down the northern corridor, approaching the blockaded city, and setting down smoothly on the *Havelsee* with five tons of salt was a highly enjoyable experience to Ian. "On one trip we were confronted by a Russian biplane performing aerobatics ahead of us," he remembers. "Suddenly the Russian pilot saw the great flying boat approaching; he panicked and momentarily lost coordination, causing his aircraft to spin out of control. We could only laugh at his embarrassment."

Ian spent 42 years in military service, alternating several times between the SAAF and the RAF, and in 1986, following a rich and varied career, he retired as a colonel in the SAAF. "Anyone who has been to Berlin," concludes Ian, "and has listened to the citizens who were there in 1948-1949 will learn how vital the airlift supplies were to them—their very lifeblood."

With the onset of winter and formation of ice on Berlin's lakes, the colorful flying boat parade came to an end in mid-December. Berliners, especially children, who had watched those magnificent machines come and go since the preceding July, were now saddened by their departure. Yet everyone could take immense pride in the fact that they had delivered 5,000 tons of much needed salt, as well as a small amount of other commodities, to their beleaguered city. The Sunderlands also flew 1,113 Berlin children and many cartons of electric light bulbs, manufactured in Berlin, to the west. During the remaining months of the airlift, salt was carried by civilian contract Haltons in panniers slung beneath their fuselage. The flying boats, however, had stolen the show during those memorable autumn weeks. The excitement they had created would now be autumn weeks. The excitement they had created would now be keenly missed!

A Young Berliner's Outlook

As the airlift matured and grew to adulthood in the autumn months of 1948, Berliners, airlift leaders, air crews, and ground support people commenced to steel themselves for the long winter haul. Gone were the earlier hopes for a quick resolution of the impasse between the western allies and the Soviets. The people of Berlin's western sectors, bracing themselves for the oncoming cold season, went about their bleak, tension-filled daily lives. Increasingly greater tonnages were delivered each day, but families still were forced, as they had been since June 24, to get by on a tiny coal ration. Electricity was still limited to four hours a day, two hours at a time. Food supplies remained stark and meager. Neighborhood "warming centers" were set up so that economical use could be made of the little heating fuel available.

Dietmar Kurnoth was a nine-year-old during that autumn, living with his family in Reinickendorf, slightly northeast of the new Tegel airfield under construction. They remained there throughout the entire blockade, conserving their food and fuel, fearful of the oncoming winter and what it might mean in terms of survival, for themselves and for the city, too. But for young Dietmar and his friends the tensions were much less than for their parents. The schools remained open, thereby giving the children of Berlin a constant in their lives.

"We children had no fear," he is quick to explain. The blockade was not so real to him and his playmates as it surely was to their parents. It was more of a game to the city's youngsters, part of their daily lifestyle as they watched the giant airplanes roar overhead. "I hoped everyday that a C-54 would make an emergency landing and that lots of candy would fall out," says Dietmar with a twinkle in his eye.

During the blockade many thousands of Berlin children and elderly persons were flown out of the city to the west, for reasons of health and well-being. Young Dietmar was one of those lucky children. "On the recommendation of my teacher and my doctor, I was chosen to go," he recalled as we sipped coffee in a Berlin cafe. "We were taken to Gatow airfield, loaded on a Dakota, and flown to Lübeck. From there we were driven in a British military truck to a nearby hospital. We were royally entertained with so much meat and bread in rolls that we all got stuffed and sick. It was all recorded on newsreel. The next day we children were scattered to all points of the compass; I went by train to my grandparents' home in Münster, and everybody aboard gave me apples and other fruits. My grandfather was so upset at my tattered clothing that he bought me a new jacket, new trousers, and new canvas shoes with wooden soles."

With the end of the blockade, Dietmar's sojourn in the west also came to an end, and he returned to his home city. Today, married and in his early sixties, he is the manager of a successful insurance business in downtown Berlin. During all of the years since the airlift, however, he must have retained vivid memories, for he now lives with his family only a short distance from Tempelhof airfield. Is it possible that the noise of those ancient, propeller-driven aircraft can still be heard throughout the city by those who remember them?

Skymasters Needed

Lucius Clay made perhaps the fastest round trip to Washington from Germany that has ever been accomplished. He was there for less than 24 hours. The date was October 21, 1948. The occasion was a meeting with the National Security Council where he made his case for more C-54s. By that time Clay already had about 200 aircraft working the airlift, 157 of which were C-54s, with a ten-ton load capacity. His staff had calculated that with 66 more Skymasters, the lift could be sustained through the winter with the combination of RAF Yorks, Dakotas, various British civil aircraft, and the C-54s, together delivering the daily minimum 4,500 tons required to sustain the city and the military garrisons.

"The National Security Council approved my recommendation," reported Clay, "and...when I reported to President Truman, he advised me directly that the additional planes would be forthcoming. This made it a very happy visit for me." The NSC's action was a direct about-face from its position when the blockade was imposed; at that time, USAF chief of staff General Hoyt Vandenberg had argued that the assignment of so many C-54s to the airlift would seriously detract from the air force ability to carry out transport duties in other world areas. Nonetheless, Truman's action brought the total number of C-54s assigned to the airlift to 223, and by early January 1949 the total topped out at 225.

November 30, 1948: Airlift Nadir

On Sunday, November 28, 1948, one of Europe's classic dense fogs engulfed the continent, stretching from Finland to Italy and from Ireland to Czechoslovakia. For 99 hours it gripped that vast area as a blanket covers a bed. It was so widespread and pervasive that it closed down practically every airport in northern Europe and many in the southern regions. In England, one of the worst transportation tie-ups in British history occurred. An ugly train crash killed one and injured 21 persons in Manchester when one train, whose engineer's visibility was sharply reduced by the fog, slammed into the rear of another.

Other wrecks occurred in London, which was shrouded in thick fog for a thirty-mile radius from Charing Cross and in Birmingham, but fortunately there were no injuries. Croydon and Northolt airports were both shut down due to near zero visibility. In Berlin, the airlift was brought to a complete halt at Gatow, while Tempelhof saw limited activity. Addition-ally, fog and reduced visibility were the causes of ship collisions in Har-wich. At the same time, nine small ships ran aground off the Norwegian coast. Further south in France, one person was killed and three were injured in automobile accidents.

The winter of 1948-1949 was not so severe in terms of low tempera-tures and snow cover as the memorable winter of 1946-1947, but with respect to heavy fog it was a match for the winter of 1944-1945 when in mid-December German armored forces moved their tanks and heavy guns into the Ardennes in their last great offensive of World War II, the Battle of the Bulge. The Germans attacked under a protective fog cover that prevented the allies from countering with air power until a clearing in the weather on December 22.

By Tuesday, November 30, 1948, the airlift had come to a virtual halt; only ten aircraft reached Berlin during the 24-hour period ending at noon on that date. Altogether, those airplanes, seven of which were British, were able to deliver only 83.2 tons of supplies to the beleaguered city. By December 1, despite the continuing dense fog, 465 tons were flown into the city in 54 flights, most of them from Fassberg and Wunstorf to the British airfield at Gatow. This represented a small improvement in deliveries, and by mid-December, with most of the fog swept away, deliveries returned to the normal tonnages of 4,500-5,000 daily.

November 30, however, is the date remembered as the airlift's gloomiest, least productive day. To the Soviets, that almost four days of crushing fog should play havoc with airlift deliveries was sweet music to their ears, indeed, given their hopes and expectations that the onset of a harsh, severe winter would somehow force the western allies to abandon the airlift and Berlin itself. It was certainly clear, too, that in some western circles lingering doubts about the airlift's capabilities persisted.

Despite such doubts, Major General William H. Tunner, the Com-bined Airlift Task Force commander, felt otherwise. On the afternoon of November 29, he telephoned his crew chief, **Technical Sergeant Earl Morrison**, and asked him to report to base operations at Wiesbaden where Tunner was headquartered. He asked the veteran airman what he thought about flying to Berlin through the dense, soupy fog. "General," responded Morrison, an Oklahoma native who served 22 years in the air force and retired as a chief master sergeant, "you know that I flew a lot out of Hamilton Field in the San Francisco bay area, and the fog there was just as bad as it is here." "Then you will fly with me?" queried the task force commander. "Naturally, sir," replied Morrison.

Tunner had other business matters to complete prior to departure for Berlin, so preparations for the intended trip did not get fully underway until some hours later. By the time that Tunner, Morrison, and the rest of the crew were ready for their flight, it was evening, darkness had fallen, and the Follow Me jeep guiding Tunner's C-54 along the taxiway and out to the active runway had to be guided itself by two men walking ahead and carrying flashlights. Rhein-Main air base, where air traffic control for both Frankfurt and Wiesbaden was centered, had been shut down by fog since Sunday, the 28th. Lying in bottom land at the confluence of the Rhein and Main rivers, it was quite likely the most susceptible to fog formation of all the airlift bases. Air traffic controllers, nevertheless, were on duty and Tunner's flight was quickly cleared for departure. After all, the commanding general of the Combined Airlift Task Force was at the controls of his coal-laden aircraft, and if he wanted to fly in weather that had even the birds walking, no one was going to deny him.

The trip up the southern corridor via the Fulda range and across Soviet-occupied territory was uneventful. The Russians didn't even know how to fly instruments, so they were clearly not expected to harass any flights during those 99 hours of pea soup fog. Upon reaching the Berlin area, Tunner entered the prescribed traffic pattern, turned at the Frohnau beacon, and was cleared to the Tempelhof Ground Controlled Approach (GCA) system whose operators guided him expertly through the letdown procedure, while Morrison handled the landing gear, engine power settings, and flap controls. Following the prescribed flight pattern, Tunner turned onto final approach, spotted the runway threshold lights at approximately 100 feet of altitude, and set the heavily laden Skymaster smoothly down on the pierced steel planking runway surface. Of the aforementioned ten aircraft that reached Berlin that day, Tunner's C-54 was number eight. As Sergeant Morrison remarked to me 51 years later, "the general certainly earned his 'Fog and Smog Club' certificate with his precision approach and landing that night." His remark was in reference to an honorary group founded during the airlift to reward pilots who made at least one landing at below minimum weather conditions.

Following taxi to the unloading area and engine shutdown, Morrison timed the off-load, a habit with Tunner, while the general checked weather reports and the GCA unit. Due to the continuance of submarginal weather conditions in the Frankfurt area, they were unable to return to Wiesbaden that evening. Socked in at Tempelhof, General Tunner and his crew reluctantly spent the night in Berlin. But he made a statement with that flight; the story of his daring run into the blockaded city at the lowest point in five months of airlift operations spread rapidly throughout the task force air bases, resulting in a much needed morale boost and a renewed confidence and resolve among air and ground crews alike that the airlift was there to stay, the vagaries of a harsh, forbidding winter notwithstanding.

Connie Bennett the Morale Builder

Frequently seen making the rounds at Fassberg were the air base commander, Colonel Theron (Jack) Coulter and his wife, the glamorous movie actress Constance Bennett. Discovered by movie magnate Sam Goldwyn, she was best known for her starring roles in the "Topper" series in which she played a sultry, bewitching ghost. In the first "Topper" film in 1937, she played opposite one of the most popular actors of the day, Cary Grant.

Colonel and Mrs. Coulter had found suitable quarters in the Fassberg area for themselves and Adrienne Morrison, Connie's mother, a movie actress in her own right. Coulter had been selected for the Fassberg post because of his ability to work well with the British, and he set about at once to ease American-British relations which had been somewhat fractured by the American invasion of this heretofore British air base. Of the previous two American base commanders at Fassberg, each had displayed a singular inability to get along with the British. Coulter turned out to be the right choice. Both he and Lieutenant Colonel Paul Jones, commander of the 313th Troop Carrier Group, exhibited a flair for doing the right thing in relation to their English counterparts.

Connie knew how to do the right thing as a commander's wife, although her track record didn't reflect any particular marital skills, since her marriage to Colonel Coulter was her fifth. Aware, however, that she had a job to do as the base commander's wife, and concerned about the shortage of both wives and housing at the Fassberg and Celle bases, Connie threw herself immediately into the task of making the Americans more comfortable, both at Fassberg and on occasion, in the Celle social whirl. Responding to persistent gripes about Brussels sprouts, pickled herring, tea, and poor recreational facilities, she threw herself into the task of improving the dining hall menus, and even dressed up the dining rooms themselves in colorful new drapes. She prowled the flight line along with the few American wives then present, serving coffee and doughnuts, talking with ground crews, line chiefs, and common laborers, and making herself easily available to them as a sounding board.

One airlift veteran who remembers Connie Bennett well is **Staff Sergeant Calvin R. Haynes**, who enlisted in the air force from South Carolina and served 28 years on active duty, retiring to Biloxi, Mississippi as a senior master sergeant. When the airlift commenced, young Cal was stationed at Erding air depot in Bavaria but was transferred to Fassberg as soon as the base was opened to American forces in the summer of 1948.

Cal, who was assigned as a crew chief to flight line duty at Fassberg, clearly remembers one occasion in the early autumn of 1948 when a C-54 pilot aborted his impending flight to Berlin after he had started engines, muttering something about inoperative warning lights. When Colonel Coulter heard about it, he and Connie hurried to the flight line to determine what might be wrong with the aircraft, parked at an odd angle, out of line with other C-54s neatly arrayed on the tarmac. After carefully looking over the Skymaster, Coulter exclaimed, "Why this bird is all right; I can fly it to Berlin right now." Sergeant Haynes was pressed into service as fire guard, Colonel Coulter climbed into the left seat to take the controls, Connie slipped into the right seat, Coulter said to the flight engineer, "Let's go," and together the three hauled ten tons of coal to the blockaded city. This act of derring-do was not lost upon the base personnel; they loved it, and in turn they loved Connie.

Herta Tiede, a native *Berlinerin,* remembers Colonel and Mrs. Coulter well. As secretary at the Fassberg officers mess during the airlift, Frau Tiede pedaled her bicycle two kilometers daily to her job on the air base, and she knew the comings and goings of many British and American officers at that RAF station. "The Colonel [Colonel Coulter] occupied the so-called general's suite on the second floor of the officers mess," recalls Frau Tiede, who migrated to Fassberg in 1937 with her German air force husband. The two were divorced several years later, but she remained in the area and secured the secretarial position at the officer's mess. With the blockade's end she continued her employment on the air base for many years but finally returned to Berlin where she lives today. Once a Berliner, always a Berliner.

When Connie arrived in Fassberg to be with her husband, new furnishings were moved into the suite to accommodate the two, plus their dog. "Later the Coulters and Connie's mother moved to a double house in town," continues Frau Tiede. "Early in 1949 the Americans commenced to take over local homes to provide housing for dependent families arriving at the air base." The German families forced to vacate their Fassberg homes for the Americans were provided with Nissen huts in nearby Munster, whereupon the Fassberg mayor negotiated with the Hannover government for a huge sum of money to finance 84 new single-family homes for the displaced citizens.

Connie had a soft spot in her heart for airmen and noncommissioned officers (NCOs). Always ready for a good time, she and her husband organized a party one autumn evening in 1948 at the *Sudbahnhof* in Celle with a large group of NCOs, airmen, and a few wives who arrived in town aboard a special train that had been set up to transport the party goers. The *Sudbahnhof* was a favorite haunt of both RAF and USAF airmen, and on that particular evening the gaiety was enlivened by a noisy oompah band.

The few wives present with their husbands were happy, but many bachelor airmen attending the party were alone, so a **Lieutenant Brodie** and Sergeant Calvin Haynes were dispatched in an army truck to the *Ratskeller* to round up some German fräuleins to help balance out matters. In short order about two dozen arrived, and the party picked up speed. Sergeant Haynes was sitting at a table with his good friend, **Sergeant Bill Korndorfer** and other noncommissioned officers when Connie approached to ask Sergeant Bill for a dance. As they went off to the dance floor Mrs. James Hayes, the wife of Sergeant Haynes' squadron commander, asked Cal for a dance. Meanwhile, Connie and Sergeant Bill staggered under the increasing tempo of the oompah band and fell down. Moments later Sergeant Cal and Mrs. Hayes slipped and almost fell but kept their balance. Connie's apt retort was "Copycats!"

Connie's biggest contribution to airlift morale stemmed from her wide circle of Hollywood friends in the movie industry who responded enthusiastically to her requests to come to Germany and entertain the troops. Among those celebrities who traveled to Europe for this purpose were Bob

Hope, Jinx Falkenburg, and the renowned songwriter Irving Berlin. Their presence in Germany might not be attributed solely to Connie's influence since basic arrangements were made by the United Services Organization (USO) back in the states. Yet she was instrumental in persuading special friends from the entertainment world to take part, to come to Germany, and to help honor the men and women of the airlift and the airlift itself.

Hope and his group arrived in Germany during the week before Christmas on a VIP aircraft piloted by **Captain Clifford Dwinell,** whose future wife, **Elizabeth "Libby" O'Neal**, served in Wiesbaden as a civilian secretary in airlift task force headquarters. The troupe performed its first shows in Wiesbaden on December 22, then repeated in Frankfurt the next day. By Christmas they were in Berlin where they gave several performances for airmen and occupation soldiers, followed by an evening Christmas party at the home of General and Mrs. Clay, and attended by then Vice-President-elect Alben Barkley, the Bob Hopes, and assorted military and civilian dignitaries.

Hope and his troupe also performed at several British bases during the Christmas season. In his many appearances at far-flung military bases all over the world, he used a standard routine of poking fun at local situations that airmen and soldiers were experiencing and could savor. It was the same this time in Germany. Commenting on the early December fog that had shrouded the continent, Hope quipped, "Soup I can take, but this stuff has noodles in it." The knowing airmen roared in appreciation.

But all did not go smoothly. Shows were scheduled at locations far from actual airlift bases, meaning that regular occupation troops would find it convenient to attend but that airlift personnel would be left out. When General Tunner learned of these arrangements, he exploded in fury as only he could. Before he simmered down he had let USAFE headquarters people know that if they went through with their intended schedule for the Hope entourage, then advance publicity should make no mention of the airlift, a possibility that was sure to backfire on air force public relations. Schedules were quickly changed so that the troupe's performances would be at airlift bases where airlift people could attend, including Celle and Fassberg where they appeared immediately after Christmas.

When the airlift ended, Connie moved with her husband to his next post at Rhein-Main, then subsequently back to a stateside assignment. Years later in 1965 she died unexpectedly of a cerebral hemorrhage at the very early age of 59. A noted movie star she was, but to the men and women of the Berlin airlift she was the star of her own show.

Christmas 1948: Operation Santa Claus

In December, cold weather set in, with the fury of winter not far behind. Many Americans and Britons on the airlift began to think of the Berliners, especially the children, for they all knew that airlift aid notwithstanding, those children were cold, undernourished, and faced the prospect of several long, frigid months.

At Fassberg, several groups, thinking the same thoughts at the same time, precipitated action back home that resulted in a banner Christmas for the children of Berlin. Student leaders at Alfred University in western New York, Charley Clark and Kathy Lacakes, assisted by Mary Forrest of the University staff, set out on a gift procurement and wrapping spree by rallying the student body and area merchants to the cause. In a burst of enthusiasm that can only be remembered as nothing short of miraculous, they rounded up several hundred Christmas gifts and shipped them to Fassberg for delivery to Berlin just before Christmas. Imagine the virtual disbelief and wonderment when in mid-December those several hundred gift packages arrived from Alfred at the air base post office!

Another Fassberg group, composed of five airlift pilots, at the same time, independently and unknowing of other efforts, organized and made their own requests back in their home communities. On Long Island, New York, John Green, editor of the *Nassau Review Star*, personally publicized the fliers' pleas, and soon the story spread across the country, with pleasant results in the form of Christmas packages for the children of Berlin. It was truly a joint, yet uncoordinated, effort with each group working in apparent ignorance of the others' endeavors. In the end it all turned out beautifully. By Christmas time an almost unbelievable several thousand gift packages had arrived in Fassberg for delivery to Berlin children. Operation Santa Claus was in full force, and many Berlin *kinder* enjoyed their 1948 Christmas because of it. For many at Fassberg, this was clearly their most memorable and satisfying airlift experience.

Flynn's Inn

By January 1949, the first few American dependents of airmen hastily called to airlift service during the previous summer arrived in Bremerhaven by ship. The *General Maurice Rose*, a transport named after the World War II commander of the Third Armored Division, who was killed in action on the western front on March 31, 1945, delivered American dependents on a regular schedule out of New York, each time bringing wives and families to join with their army, navy, and air force spouses on duty with occupation forces in Germany.

Most airlift wives, as part of the ship's contingent of passengers, were posted on a temporary basis, if their housing arrangements were incomplete, to Bad Mergentheim, a noted European vacation community, situated on the Tauber River in Baden, east of Mannheim and south of Würzburg. Here an armed forces dependent housing center had been established, and the army had requisitioned fifteen hotels in order to alleviate a crunch in family quarters at existing military bases. The location was nicely convenient to bases in the Frankfurt and Wiesbaden areas but well over 300 kilometers from Fassberg and Celle; airmen from the latter two bases had little chance to see their wives regularly No matter. The more enterprising dependents were not to be deterred. Wives from Bad Mergentheim began to appear in the Celle and Fassberg areas as if by magic, searching in the German neighborhoods, contrary to established military rules, for a room, a small apartment, or anything to put a roof over their heads and thereby be reunited with their husbands.

Despite such efforts, the housing situation in the two communities remained tight. In Fassberg the club and billeting officer, **Captain N. C. Flynn,** requisitioned a storied country manor some 35 kilometers east of the town to serve as a hotel and recreation center of sorts for airlift dependents, and he hired Germans to staff it as cooks, waiters, maids, and groundskeepers. A sturdy, three-story stonewalled and granite edifice, the manor loomed stark and forbidding to the eye, yet exuded a quiet charm in its interior of paneled wood walls set off by comfortable drapes and furnishings. On its first floor the inn was nicely furnished with complete kitchen facilities, a bar, a large, handsome dining room, a comfortable study with deep, overstuffed chairs, game rooms, and an extensive living room large enough for parties and dancing.

Legend had it that the inn had once been used by Herman Göring as a hunting lodge. This was only a rumor, yet supported by the manor's inward elegance and the beauty of its grounds, with brilliant flower gardens, some of them sunken, tennis and volleyball courts, a bowling alley, and well-manicured shrubbery and lawns. The numerous bedrooms on the second and third floors gave rise to further rumors that it had once been used in the Nazi era as a high class whorehouse. Whether because of this—American film star Errol Flynn of that era was renowned for his alleged sexual prowess—or in order to honor the base housing officer, it was aptly dubbed by the patrons as Flynn's Inn.

In the early weeks of 1949 a small number of airlift wives at Bad Mergentheim, thoroughly maddened with the daily ritual of awaiting further orders, and clearly wishing to be closer to their husbands, deliberately gravitated northward. A few took up residence at Flynn's Inn. In effect, they went AWOL from their Bad Mergentheim base, yet they were made welcome to move into the upper floors at the inn—for fifty cents a night.

In the weeks and months following their spouses' arrival at the Inn, airmen spent their off-duty hours at this relaxing country house, enjoying the convivial atmosphere while resting up between duty tours. A few men also took up residence there with their wives, although in sum the Inn accommodated no more than twenty to thirty persons. Largely an American operation, Flynn's Inn turned out to be an ideal spot for building US-UK relations, since British army supervisors in charge of displaced persons, civil laborers, and aircraft loading at Fassberg, among them **Jock Hamilton** of London, and **Jack F. London**, from the Australasian Petroleum Co., Ltd. in Port Moresby, New Guinea, were very much in evidence at the many parties that took place.

Captain Flynn worked aggressively to find housing and billeting for officers and airmen on the Fassberg base and in the surrounding community, but he was probably best known as the patron saint and godfather of Flynn's Inn. By the time that he rotated to the states in May 1949, he had not only found housing for many airmen and officers but also had managed to fly more than 100 missions on the airlift.

1949: Tonnage and Determination

As the New Year 1949 dawned, winter wore on with unrelenting fury, causing more aircraft accidents and raising havoc with tonnage deliveries, which despite poor weather had risen to an average of 4,500 tons daily, the minimum Berlin requirement, and then to 5,500 tons in January and February; this despite days of meager deliveries such as February 20 when only 205.5 tons reached Berlin. But a big assist in tonnage efforts was due to an increase of available C-54s; by early January, 225 Skymasters had been assigned to Vittles operations, and with clearing weather total CALTF deliveries reached 8,025 tons on February 22.

In the Soviet sector, Marshal Sokolovsky and his staff, confident for some time that harsh winter conditions would bring down the airlift, now became alarmed as they looked up day after day, only to see endless waves of allied transports arriving and departing on a virtual conveyor belt. The former secretariat officer of the Soviet Military Administration (SMA) in Berlin, Askold Lebedev, reported in 1994 that the magnitude of the airlift as it developed had completely surprised the Soviet leadership. March saw steadily clearing weather conditions, thus permitting a significant improvement in CALTF average weekly deliveries. Berlin and the Berliners were assured of surviving the blockade.

April 16, 1949: The Easter Parade

Ever interested in perfecting airlift procedures to the nth degree, General Tunner looked forward to the day when an airplane might land in Berlin in each of the 1,440 minutes of a 24-hour period. Accordingly, he set in motion preparations for such a day. Easter Sunday, April 16, was the date selected. It was decided that with only a few exceptions, coal would be the airlifted commodity. From Oberpfaffenhofen to Burtonwood, from Rhein-Main to Schleswigland, men and machines were made ready in meticulous preparation for the coming "Easter Parade." Burtonwood mechanics, among them **Sergeant Clarence Durbin,** whose personal story is told in the next chapter, completed periodic inspections, while engine fitters at Wunstorf and Lübeck fine-tuned the power plants on their Yorks and Dakotas. Weather forecasters poured over their charts.

Although secrecy surrounded tonnage goals set for the mission, airlift personnel were made aware of the forthcoming maximum effort. From

General Tunner to the displaced person coal loader, everyone was psyched and ready. On Good Friday, one day prior to the mission's start, Tunner made brief visits to the various airlift bases in order to pass the word and generate a positive mood among all. And on Sunday, the big day, he also visited airlift bases, encouraging friendly tonnage competition from base to base. The results are history. In 24 hours, crews of the Combined Airlift Task Force delivered to Berlin an incredible 12,940 tons of cargo in 1,398 flights, the equivalent of 22 freight trains of fifty cars each. In the aftermath of that achievement, nothing was impossible.

Blockade's End

Contrary to a persistent mood among airlifters that the Easter Parade had broken the back of the blockade, diplomatic negotiations initiated in January with the Soviets ultimately resulted in the gates being lifted on the autobahn. Kingsbury Smith, an American foreign correspondent, had asked Stalin by letter about the importance of the monetary question in Berlin, given that the Soviets at the onset of the blockade had insisted that allied currency reform was the reason for imposing it. Amazingly, Stalin replied, rambling on about general conditions in Germany but saying nothing about the monetary question. This omission led to secret diplomatic talks between UN Ambassador Philip Jessup and his Soviet counterpart, Jacob Malik. Jessup wished to know if Stalin's omission of the currency question was deliberate, for if such were the case, it meant that he was tiring of the blockade and that talks to bring about its end could be pursued.

A month later, Malik, after being gingerly stalked by Jessup outside the men's room at UN headquarters, advised him that Stalin's omission had been deliberate. "Truman and [Secretary of State] Acheson," writes Chip Bohlen, "directed Jessup to sound out Malik on the possibility of arranging a settlement that would permit the lifting of the blockade, the ending of the airlift, and the return of Germany, although still divided, to the relative tranquility it had enjoyed since the end of the war." Following extensive talks, an accord was reached, and on May 4 the four-power UN representatives fixed May 12 as the date for ending the lengthy blockade.

But why had the diplomatic initiative in January occurred in the first place? Precisely because Stalin realized that the well-organized, efficient, and productive airlift was beating him. It wasn't a single April 16 that turned the tide; it was that "steady beat, constant as the jungle drums," in its dramatic daily accomplishments, that gave him second thoughts about the blockade he had imposed. Accordingly, he chose diplomatic channels for bringing it to an end. But airlift participants, in the end, could take heart in knowing that ever-increasing airlift efficiency and tonnage deliveries, particularly through the miserable winter months, had already created a massive psychological effect on the Soviets, thereby steering Stalin to the diplomatic process.

Just past midnight on May 12, 1949 the barriers that had closed off western surface access to Berlin for eleven months were lifted, and normal two-way surface traffic between the city and the west was resumed. Elated that they had proven to themselves and the world that they could be tough and survive the Russians' cruelty, Berliners shouted in unison, *Hoora, wir leben noch!* (Hooray, we have survived!)

Delivery of supplies by air continued, nonetheless, through the summer months, just in case the Soviets decided to reimpose the blockade. The buildup was maintained through the month of September but at a steadily declining pace.

On May 12, 1999, at the fiftieth anniversary ceremonies marking the lifting of the blockade, Berlin's governing mayor Eberhard Diepgen delighted the assembled crowd in the Olympic Stadium with his opening statement, *Hoora, wir leben noch!*, reminiscent of the cries of Berliners a half a century earlier as they realized that they had survived eleven months of cold, hunger, and privation. Berliners not only survived the blockade, but they proved to the world that their freedom is a commodity not lightly to be surrendered.

Figure 2. The Berlin Airlift Historical Foundation's "Spirit of Freedom" at Knoxville, Tennessee, October 2000. This beautifully restored aircraft actually flew on the airlift. Courtesy Richard Gere.

Figure 3. The Berlin Airlift Historical Foundation's "Spirit of Freedom" at Knoxville, October 2000. Crew Members, left to right: Joe Groetsch, Ron Travell, Bill Morrissey—all airlift veterans, Eric Oberst, and Tim Chopp, BAHF president and pilot. Courtesy Richard Gere.

Figure 4. C-54 in a maintenance dock, Rhein-Main, 1949. Courtesy Bill Morrissey.

Figure 5. Post airlift formal review, Celle, 1949. Courtesy Robert VanDervort.

Figure 6. RAF York departing Wunstorf, October 1948. Courtesy Kenneth King.

Figure 7. RAF Dakota at Gatow. The Dakota was heavily used throughout the airlift by the RAF. Courtesy James McCorkle.

Figure 8. Skymaster on final approach to Fassberg, September 1948. Author's photo.

Part Two

Figure 9. Jake Schuffert's final airlift cartoon, the last of many he published to keep up morale during the long months of the blockade. Courtesy Berlin Airlift Veterans Association.

Four

Airlift Personalities: Americans

History does not long entrust the care of freedom to the weak or the timid.

Dwight Eisenhower, First Inaugural Address, January 20, 1953

FROM THE BEGINNING, AMERICAN dominance in the Berlin airlift operations was a foregone conclusion. The United States Air Force, augmented during the airlift by the United States Navy, clearly had the greatest strength in numbers of participating personnel and aircraft. Active duty forces comprised the greatest proportion of all American personnel, supported heavily by individual reservists called up from civilian life. This preponderance of men and materiel also dictated that an American, Major General William H. Tunner, would be named in September 1948 to command the Combined Airlift Task Force, with Air Commodore J.W.F. Merer, Royal Air Force, as deputy commander.

Many military units exercising widely varying duties and specialties of labor provided crucial support to airlift operations, yet the contributions of the men and women of these units to the airlift's success to this day have gone largely unheralded and unsung. This book, with its theme of emphasizing the ground support forces, including German and displaced person civil laborers, as well as noncommissioned air crew members, seeks to redress this oversight by highlighting the soldiers, sailors, and airmen whose contributions to this historic cold war confrontation must not be forgotten. This chapter, then, focuses on a selective but, to the extent possible, representative sample of Americans, who by their skills and dedication, together with their British counterparts and those from nations of the British Commonwealth, molded the airlift mission into a disciplined, regimented operation. As General Tunner pointed out, "It is this beat, this precise rhythmical cadence, which determines the success of an airlift. This steady rhythm," he emphasized, "constant as the jungle drums," became the trademark of the Berlin airlift.

Individual memoirs commence with the air police, then proceed through an array of military specialties, all of which and more were vital to the success of the airlift. Without those portrayed in this chapter, in the next chapter, and throughout the book, as well as the thousands whom those selected here represent, there would have been no airlift, no final victory. Individuals whose personal stories are presented here and in other chapters, as well as those briefly cited, are portrayed in the rank they held when they first commenced airlift duties. Those who during the airlift were civilians, or in the enlisted, noncommissioned, or junior-grade officer ranks, are cited at first mention throughout the book in bold face.

Air Police

Air policemen of the Berlin airlift can trace their origins to General George Washington's orders in 1778 to a newly established corps of light dragoons. The corps commander and his men were charged with camp patrol in order to arrest stragglers, drunkards, deserters, and other disorderly persons, and also to detain all persons, civilians and military alike, who did not have proper papers. Suspected spies were also to be held for further questioning and trial, if so indicated. By those orders, the general obligation to maintain good order and security in and among the Continental forces gradually developed and was implemented. From such a crude beginning over 200 years ago grew a military security organization that became steadily transformed into military police units as the armed forces of our young nation developed over the decades in war and peace.

When the Berlin airlift commenced, the U.S. Air Force was less than a year old; hence, air policemen assigned to the airlift were new to their title. Most of them had recently been known as military police of the Army Air Corps. Regardless of nomenclature, however, unit and individual duties remained largely the same as in the past. Yet the need for added security became paramount during the fifteen-month airlift. Aircraft, supplies, equipment, air base facilities, and perimeters were all accorded extra protection, and it fell to the air police, as well as infantry and constabulary forces, and civilian displaced persons hired as guards, to provide such protection. One air policeman at Rhein-Main who carried out his duties in rain, fog, and less-than-enjoyable conditions was **Private First Class George McClarity** from Boston. Only seventeen when the airlift commenced, George felt certain that the blockade would lead to armed conflict with the Russians. Yet he warmed to his airlift role and even requested extended duty in Germany. Other individuals who follow in this segment tell of their personal air police experiences while serving on airlift duty at other American airlift bases.

Corporal William Trackler, Air Policeman, Fassberg and Wiesbaden. Bill Trackler hails from the mile-high city of Denver, Colorado, and he lives there today in Aurora, a pleasant Denver suburb. During the airlift, Bill was a corporal in the air police, stationed with the 60th Air Police Squadron at Fassberg. Grinning, he reports, "I had a choice of jobs when I enlisted, the cooks or the cops. I chose the cops." After military police training, he left the states shortly after Christmas 1948, arriving on the *USS Sturgis* in Bremerhaven eleven days later. He denies having done anything heroic "My job was base security," affirms Bill, who was only eighteen years of age when he reported for duty in Germany. In great modesty, he shares his view of the airlift. "I was mostly on the outside looking in on a world-class event."

Bill remembers that there were over 200 air policemen stationed at Fassberg. Their chief responsibilities were gate duty, issuing passes, base lockup, hangar security, town patrol, the C-54 loading area, and guarding trains incoming from Bremerhaven to Celle and Fassberg. "We had dogs," he recalls, "but most of them were assigned to the Polish guards, of which there were about 100. The guards performed base perimeter and flight line security. Despite language difficulties, they were superb and could be relied upon to stay awake and alert." They endured the bitter cold of winter, standing in the open under airplanes and guarding the perimeter until their air police supervisors reduced their work shifts from eight hours to four, then to two hours as the bitter cold of winter set in.

With the end of the airlift, Bill was reassigned to the so-called Y-80 air base at Wiesbaden and remained on duty there until 1951. Despite the excitement of airlift involvement, Bill chose not to pursue a career in the military. Returning to civilian life in 1952, he joined the federal treasury department and worked in the computer division of the San Francisco mint, retiring in 1989. Through the years, however, his small band of air police veterans who worked so closely together long ago remains bonded in a cohesive alumni organization, joining forces regularly in reunion celebrations. Bill serves as editor of their *Wiesbaden Air Base* periodic newsletter, an impressive publication featuring reunion news, photos of past reunions, and personal articles written by members. Bill is a member of BAVA and attended the May 1999 fiftieth anniversary reunion in Germany.

A sad note. Mrs. Trackler recently informed me that Bill died on June 11, 2001, following a lengthy illness. He was simply a wonderful human being and will be very much missed by many, especially his fellow air police vets from so many long years ago. In his memory I choose to retain his airlift story in the present tense.

Corporal Ralph H. Hudson, Air Policeman, Oberpfaffenhofen. Not everyone involved in the airlift was stationed in Berlin or at one of the active airlift departure bases. Oberpfaffenhofen, in the Munich area, popularly known by American GIs as Obie, was an important maintenance depot for conducting periodic aircraft inspections as well as engine and radio equipment overhauls. Aircraft constantly came and went at this busy Bavarian air base, once a Luftwaffe *Fliegerhorst,* (air force base). A native of Charleston, South Carolina, Ralph Hudson was slightly older than Bill Trackler when he arrived in Germany, reporting to the 1184th Military Police Co., later changed to the 7294th Air Police Squadron. He was all of nineteen, and his air police squadron was kept very busy throughout the airlift period patrolling the air base and the town, providing on-base security, and furnishing escort services. He and his fellow air policemen worked long hours, usually on around-the-clock shifts. Many airmen in Germany at that time were very young, and most of them had never been very far from home prior to entering military service. As a result, considerable air police time was taken up in town patrol keeping tabs on young GIs who drank too much and got into minor troubles because of it. "Even if the duty [demanded] long hours and a lot of work, I rather enjoyed it," writes Ralph. "I was proud to be part of this historic mission [the airlift]."

In 1949, with his airlift duties coming to an end, Ralph decided to pursue an air force career, and he ultimately served thirty years, attaining the rank of senior master sergeant. At the conclusion of his service years at Charleston AFB, his native South Carolina beckoned once more, and he settled in North Charleston where he lives today. In 1999, he joined hundreds of airlift veterans in attending the fiftieth anniversary Berlin reunion ceremonies. He feels today, as do many, that his airlift service was the defining moment of his lengthy career. "I think it was one of the greatest military missions for a peacetime operation that ever took place, and it was one that will be remembered for many years to come by a lot of people, especially those who benefited the most from that memorable airlift mission."

Airways and Air Communications Service

On February 12, 1921, the first segment of a newly conceived transcontinental airways route was inaugurated between Washington, D.C. and Dayton, Ohio. This event marked the beginning of what would become the Army Airways Communications System (AACS) in 1938, a vital arm of the U.S. military establishment that since that early beginning has developed and maintained a worldwide system of navigation and communications for flights along military airways, guiding and protecting USAF and allied air crews as they have carried out their domestic and global missions. Along the way, its name changed to the Airways and Air Communications Service.

AACS stations are located in all fifty states and have been established in 52 foreign countries; its personnel staff air base control towers, air traffic control centers, radio beacons and other route facilities, ground controlled approach (GCA) systems, and radio ranges. Weather information for flights along AACS routes is transmitted on its lines.

In June 1948, when the Berlin airlift was initiated, AACS was there. Navigational facilities between Frankfurt and Berlin, however, were few. The air corridor linking the two cities was utilized during the early occupation years by a few military and commercial flights making infrequent trips, largely by day and under favorable weather conditions. By contrast, mounting airlift needs for precision navigational facilities in all kinds of weather were staggering: additional route beacons, GCA installations at western bases and Berlin, standardized airways procedures, and addition of more AACS specialists. Yet the demands were met. Soon after his arrival in Germany, General Tunner, facing a severe shortage of experienced GCA operators, combed stateside air traffic control rosters and very quickly had twenty new skilled technicians on hand.

Veteran Celle control tower operator **Bill Morrissey** points out that "During the Berlin airlift, AACS was the parent organization of the GCA units that provided final approach radar guidance, thereby permitting successful landings under adverse weather conditions, chiefly at the four feeder stations: Rhein-Main, Wiesbaden, Fassberg and Celle." A testimony to GCA's vital airlift role was offered by USAFE chief of staff Major General Robert W. Douglas, Jr., who pointed out in 1949 that GCA must be credited with assuring the success of the airlift.

In their detailed account of the airlift, Giangreco and Griffin praised the pioneering accomplishments of AACS, known today as the Air Force Communications Agency. "Although much of the technology used then has been overtaken by revolutionary developments in electronics in the 1960s and 1970s," they wrote, "the procedures developed during the Berlin airlift became a vital building block for the modern air traffic control system as we know it today." Personal stories of a small number of those skilled AACS technicians follow.

Private First Class William E. Morrissey, Control Tower Operator, Celle. A well-known BAVA member, Bill Morrissey, with his charm, ever-present smile, and fierce dedication to the memory of 1948-1949, is the Berlin airlift personified. A native of Tyrone, Pennsylvania, Bill, not yet nineteen years old, joined the air force in April 1948 and was assigned immediately to control tower school. The AACS detachment at Celle was his first duty assignment following graduation. He arrived there in November 1948 as a private first class after having crossed the Atlantic aboard a troop ship. By the time that the 317th Troop Carrier Wing arrived in Celle in December, after its well-publicized, historic forty-day sea voyage from Japan, Bill and his fellow AACS workers, having set up the local air traffic system, were ready for business. He served as an operator in the Celle control tower through the end of the airlift in September 1949, always with a cheerful greeting for incoming and departing air crews. Pilots and other air crew members recorded the number of airlift missions they flew to Berlin, but how about the tower operators? How many successful aircraft departures and returns did they log, if they logged them at all? Bill's accomplishments in this category would be mind-boggling.

"The briefing room at Celle was somewhat different than expected," recalls Bill. "It was small and spartan; there was barely room enough for the charts. American airmen were being briefed at an RAF base in the British occupation zone of Germany, where in the not-too-distant past, Luftwaffe fighters had roared off the runways."

Bill remembers off duty times at Celle well. "Train trips to Hannover. A pretty big city. Free transportation. GIs in the American zone have to pay to ride the trains. We in the British zone get the works free—buses, trolleys, trains. But as with all good things, it soon comes to an end. Celle GIs now will have to pay to ride the trains. But Yankee ingenuity prevails! An airman produces his chow pass and tells the German conductor it is a train pass. It works. The conductor selects the date and punches breakfast, lunch, or dinner for the trip. The conductor is happy; we're happy. Word gets around fast. The trips to Hannover continue unabated."

Working his way up through the ranks while on airlift duty, Bill was a sergeant when the 317th Group closed down at Celle in October 1949. By then he had decided to pursue an air force career, and he ultimately served twenty years as an air traffic controller, retiring in the rank of senior master sergeant. Following that, he worked 24 years as a civilian air traffic controller with the Federal Aviation Administration, finishing with duty at the Purdue University airport.

Today Bill, who lives in Danville, Indiana but is not very often at home, is a roving ambassador for the legacy of the Berlin airlift. Active in the Berlin Airlift Veterans Association, he is also a member of the Berlin Airlift Historical Foundation, the British Berlin Airlift Association, the *Luftbrücke* chapter of the Airlift Association, and of course, his own AACS alumni organization. As a member of the *Spirit of Freedom* crew, he has flown in that beautifully restored C-54 flying airlift museum to many parts of the world, spreading the word about the Berlin blockade and airlift, thus doing his best to keep the memory alive.

Sergeant Donald L. Stensrud, Control Tower Operator, Tempelhof. On the morning of December 16, 1948, Don Stensrud was on duty as senior tower operator at Tegel airfield, directing air traffic in and out of the busy new French sector facility that had welcomed its first Vittles aircraft on November 5 but was not yet quite fully operational. In mid-morning his attention to tower duties was interrupted by a French sergeant who hurriedly mounted the tower stairway to advise Don that he and his fellow operators would have to evacuate at once. "What's the problem?" asked Don. The sergeant replied that General Jean Ganeval, the French commandant, intended to blow up two radio towers situated close to the path of incoming aircraft. Operated by the Russian-controlled Radio Berlin, the towers, one 100 meters high and the other 87 meters, had become a daily hazard, particularly in poor weather conditions, to arriving aircraft.

Despite several pleasant earlier requests from Ganeval to General Alexander Kotikov, the Soviet sector commandant, that the towers be removed, the surly Russian continued to do nothing. "I was in charge of air traffic control operations at Tegel," remembers Don, "so I called Tempelhof tower to divert our incoming aircraft, and I gave instructions to our aircraft on the ground to hold tight. Everything worked out OK. We all got out of the control tower, saw the French grab the Russian guard, prepare the dynamite and blow up the radio towers. Wish I had a camera at the time." An enraged Kotikov protested vigorously the next day, but the deed had been done. The French, who up to that point had contributed little to the airlift except the land on which Tegel was constructed, enjoyed new prestige among British, Americans, and Berliners.

The Russians resumed broadcasting by 10:00 p.m. the same day from Grönau in their sector, with Heinz Schmidt, the station director, making its first statement. The destruction of the towers was an "act of brutality against a cultural wireless station," insisted Schmidt over the air, "unworthy of the French people."

A native of Minneapolis, Don enlisted in the air force in March 1948, trained in control tower operations at Scott AFB, Illinois, and arrived at the 1946th AACS Squadron in Berlin in September. "If there were problems with incoming traffic, problems on the ground, radio problems, weather problems, or other unexpected events, we would make the necessary adjustments," recalls Don. "I was eighteen years old when I began my duties. By the time I left Berlin a year later, I was at least 21. It was a very maturing job," he emphasizes.

In addition to his military skills, Don is an accomplished pianist. Learning of this, his superiors requested his appearance at various social and official events in Berlin, including two airlift variety shows. On the occasion of General Clay's West Point reunion in 1949, which took place at the U. S. Army Berlin headquarters, he was requested by the general to play. "It was real exciting for me, and General Clay had me take off my uniform jacket and tie." recalls Don. "So did the general. Most of the songs I played had familiar melodies, and I could easily pick up the music."

On another occasion, Don was on night duty at Tempelhof, and as it often happened, a few visiting pilots came by to view tower operations. "One pilot in particular was asking quite a few questions. I was rather busy with the arriving block of aircraft and said that if he could wait a few minutes I would be glad to talk with him. He was older than the others and looked somewhat familiar. Later, I looked around and noted that he had left. The task force officer on duty motioned to me to look at the visitors' log. It was signed: Charles A. Lindbergh, Colonel, USAFR."

Don served on active duty 28 years, retiring as a lieutenant colonel in 1976. His airlift years, and his duties as a tower operator in Berlin, however, continue to be the most memorable of a lengthy and exciting career.

Corporal Jack D. Fellman, Tower Operator and Air Traffic Controller, Tempelhof. At BAVA reunions, the airlift veteran smoking a pipe is probably Jack Fellman. Or he may be toting a camera. Or both.

Since those halcyon days in Berlin as a young nineteen-year-old, Jack has been a pipe smoker. "Unlike cigarettes," says Jack, "pipe tobacco had little black market value. The German men didn't like it." And the camera? He has been snapping pictures since boyhood, and from his vantage post in the Tempelhof and Tegel control towers, he took pictures of every type of aircraft arriving at those air bases during the airlift months.

During his time in Berlin, Jack and his colleagues in air traffic control worked long duty shifts, as did all those on airlift assignment. Handling the unprecedented "conveyor belt" of Vittles aircraft was extremely stressful; a mistake in radar directives to pilots could be costly, even fatal. It was necessary for all air traffic controllers to be alert and ever-careful, and to maintain balance in their daily lives. Jack and his fellow workers made the most of off duty time. "We did have a few recreational pastimes," he remembers. "An Olympic pool in the army area, tennis courts, the Skyrider Club at Tempelhof [a Special Services facility], a nice NCO club, and a very good open mess." Jack is still grateful today for "the great gals at Special Services." They kept up our morale and held many special events—costume parties, a Christmas tree event, and many others. **Virginia Reissaus** [an active BAVA member today] was one of our real motivators in that time of extreme stress, and she helped to keep many off the streets." **Diane Day** was another wonderful Special Services girl stationed at Tempelhof. On December 11, 1948, Diane survived the crash of a Navy R5D in which AMM3 Harry R. Crites, Jr. was killed.

At one time Jack and his friends, always in pairs, explored the huge underground areas built by the Germans at Tempelhof but succeeded in reaching only three of the reputed five levels. There they found rooms containing old personnel records, paper gas masks, and various other artifacts left by the Germans in the closing days of the war. When they did go out on the town, however, temptation was everywhere—the black market, love-starved German girls (reputedly nine women for every man in Berlin), and an overabundance of corner bars and taverns. "The streets were very dark," Jack recalls, "and a flashlight was standard equipment if you left Tempelhof at night. We went to only those neat little *Bierstuben* that had a back door for a hasty exit in case the MPs came."

Following the airlift, Jack reached the rank of sergeant but nonetheless decided against military life, choosing instead to join Boeing where he fashioned a civilian career as a buyer and procurement manager. Today, he lives on an island in the northwest near the community of Shelton, Washington and often thinks back on his unforgettable airlift time. "The airlift was an experience I'll never forget," says this popular and well-liked BAVA activist, "but I don't know if I could live it again."

Line Mechanics and Technicians

Line mechanics at airlift bases worked some of the dirtiest jobs of the entire operation, and they performed their duties under the most gruesome conditions possible. At Fassberg and a few other bases, large hangars once used by the German Luftwaffe provided cover and heat for mechanics and other technicians working on Operation Vittles aircraft. At other bases there were few such facilities; the mechanics worked at open-air maintenance docks that were nothing more than crudely erected wooden and sheet metal structures affording only partial protection against the elements.

Even at bases with hangar facilities, there were always more aircraft than could be accommodated indoors. That the men were able to perform necessary maintenance at all under such conditions is a lasting tribute to their courage, perseverance, and ingenuity. Many maintenance teams were short of proper and adequate tools, a predicament forcing them to adapt by using what was available: fashioning usable tools, or scrounging them by whatever means—even purchasing them on the German market with their own money! The shortage of tools and dreadful working conditions contributed to an unenviable assignment that these men bore with a quiet dignity and very little recognition for their dedication. The following are personal stories told by some of these unheralded airlift heroes.

Corporal John E. Ross, Line Mechanic, Gatow. Upon completing airplane and engine mechanics and C-54 schools at Keesler Field, Mississippi in 1947, John Ross was assigned as an eighteen-year-old to Westover Field where mechanics with his skills were very much needed. While there, John volunteered on one occasion for TDY to Greenland, making several ski and jet-assisted takeoff- (JATO) equipped C-47 flights onto the icecap. But on Sunday morning, July 11, 1948, two short weeks after the airlift began, he was abruptly ordered to the Westover flight line for assignment to Rhein-Main. Arriving there three days later, John immediately commenced servicing C-54s until mid-August when he was further assigned to the 7350th Air Base Group at Tempelhof in Berlin. "We were billeted at Tempelhof," recalls John, a native of Little Rock, Arkansas, "but we were bussed daily to Gatow to work on C-54s flying into this British sector airfield." He remembers vividly working twelve-hour shifts with very little maintenance equipment. Only emergency repairs were made at the Berlin air bases, so that aircraft in need of service could be made sufficiently flyable to return to their home bases. "We changed blown nose wheel tires, repaired hydraulic lines, and examined fuel cells for leaks—C-54s were notorious for fuel leaks from their integral wing tanks—and performed general fire-guard duty for engine starts with ice chunks spinning away from the propellers as they turned over," recalls John. "If a starter failed, the engine was windmilled and started on the takeoff run." Those wonderful line mechanics were masters of improvisation; windmilling an engine on takeoff was just one of the many ways by which they kept their aircraft flying.

As John reminisced about his airlift experiences of 51 years earlier he stated, "I can remember off duty times in Berlin. Having walked a considerable distance from the base during daylight hours, after darkness had fallen, with no lighting in the city except as the Russians permitted, I had to thread my way through street rubble back to Tempelhof by following the C-54 landing lights on their final approach." John worked through the cold, fog, ice, and sleet of the 1948 winter, ultimately rotating back to the states by ship from Bremerhaven in late February 1949. Although his airlift experience was in his words, "a real adventure for a nineteen-year-old," he nonetheless decided to return to civilian life at the end of his enlistment in August. Today, following a college education at the University of Arkansas and a lengthy, rewarding career as an industrial engineer, he continues to enjoy life in his hometown of Little Rock.

Private First Class Frederick A. "Joe" Hall, Line Mechanic, Flight Engineer, Rhein-Main. One of the truly unheralded soldiers of the Berlin airlift, Joe Hall continues to live in awe of the massive effort mounted in 1948-1949 to feed and maintain the people of Berlin. Fresh out of airplane and engine mechanic school at Keesler AFB in 1948, he headed for Bremerhaven on a troop ship and was quickly assigned to the 331st Troop Carrier Squadron at Rhein-Main. At this bustling airlift station he commenced his duties as a maintenance mechanic on C-54s, performing troubleshooting procedures and solving a multitude of engineering problems, day after lengthy day.

On his first night of duty at Rhein-Main, Joe was assigned by his engineering officer to Dock No. 2 to help another mechanic replace a Skymaster carburetor. Being from the seaport city of Baltimore, he knew a dock as a place where ships tie up. He commenced searching, therefore, for the water, asking directions from a master sergeant along the way. When questioned by the sergeant, Joe explained his orders to head for Dock No. 2. "There's no chance of me falling in the water in all this fog, is there?" asked Joe. "All we need here is another clown," muttered the sergeant, as he hurriedly directed the still unsuspecting airman toward a huge C-54 whose nose was protruding from between two pieces of corrugated steel, very soon to become known to him as a dock.

After that rude awakening to the easy lingo of the airlift, Joe settled into his work routine, using his top-notch Keesler training as a foundation for the crude daily demands for mechanical ingenuity and perseverance. Working side-by-side with American dock crew members were German mechanics recruited to bolster the engineering work force. Early in the airlift, former Luftwaffe airplane mechanics were sought for employment at the major air bases. Training manuals were translated into German to facilitate the transition, and Joe soon found himself supervising a German crew. One of his workers was an elderly former colonel known to the other mechanics as Pop. "One day," reported Joe, "after I had brought some apples for the crew, Pop drew me aside and in a very serious and confidential tone advised that Hitler was alive and had been seen in California." Going along with what he considered to be a joke, Joe inquired, "What's he doing there?" "Picking apples" was Pop's straight-faced, deadly serious reply. Humor helped all to cope with the long hours of work and less than desirable living conditions.

Midway through the airlift, Joe was offered the opportunity to become a flight engineer, and he jumped at the chance, thereafter making frequent C-54 flights to Berlin but still responsible for maintaining his aircraft. Later, with the airlift in phasedown, he pondered his career options, deciding to serve a few more years on active duty so that he could make the right decision about a military career. In the end, Joe remained in the service until 1952, participating in the Korean airlift from his station at Westover AFB and mustering out as a staff sergeant. In civilian life he worked as a middle management transportation and mechanical maintenance supervisor.

Never one to forget his airlift days, Joe is now an active member of BAVA, serving as the association's director of programs and reunions, in which role he also publishes *The Legacy*, the BAVA newsletter. He also holds membership in the British Berlin Airlift Association, the Berlin Airlift Historical Foundation, and the Tunner chapter, Airlift Tanker Association. Perhaps the crowning event of Joe's total airlift experiences has been his role as crew member of the fabled C-54 *Spirit of Freedom*, the flying airlift museum acquired and restored by BAHF members. In Berlin with the *Spirit* crew in June 1998, Joe was moved to tears by the long lines of Berliners who had lived through the blockade, waiting to greet and embrace the crew members, most of whom were airlift veterans who fifty years earlier had given their all to save the embattled city.

Corporal Fred I. Murtishaw, Line Mechanic, Oberpfaffenhofen and Burtonwood. Another veteran of Oberpfaffenhofen stationed at that active airlift support base was a young nineteen-year-old from Hillsboro, Oregon. Fred Murtishaw arrived on TDY at Obie, as the Bavarian air base was popularly known, in August 1948, fresh from airplane and engine mechanic school at Keesler AFB, with added specialist training on B-29s. His Obie assignment was to the 1421st Maintenance Squadron. The airlift beckoned, however, and Fred, along with many others who had received specialized training on other aircraft, very quickly found himself learning the fine points of C-54 maintenance.

Obie was an active air depot in the Munich area where Skymasters were sent for 200-hour inspections. Fred was very much a part of this vital operation, functioning generally as an airplane and engine mechanic but more specifically as an engine specialist. Working under his supervision were two German civilians named Hans and Gerhard, both former Luftwaffe mechanics who knew their skills well and worked long and hard, grateful to have employment in the devastated German economy. Gerhard, the older of the two, in his forties, was highly skilled; Fred even learned a few tricks of the trade from him. "Gerhard asked me one day if his wife might do my laundry," reports Fred, "and I said 'sure'." Upon returning the clean laundry, for payment Gerhard asked modestly for one or two candy bars, sometimes a pack of cigarettes. Whatever price the German set, Fred always doubled it as the service continued because in Fred's words, "the wife did an excellent job, and they badly needed the work," even though he suspected that they turned the candy and cigarettes into cash on the black market.

When the 200-hour inspection process was transferred to Burtonwood air depot in England, Fred moved there, too, assigned to the 7296th Maintenance Squadron. The pace continued at Burtonwood; C-54s arrived regularly on a stepped-up schedule for their periodic inspections. Somehow, though, life wasn't quite the same at this drab former World War II base where American aircraft shipped to England in sections had been assembled. An avid sportsman, Fred missed the off duty times he had spent in Bavaria hunting wild pigs and deer. When his six-month TDY assignment was completed in February 1949, Fred decided to return to the states. By then he had moved to the rank of sergeant, but his enlistment was about to expire as well. After some thought, he chose to leave the service and use his acquired military skills in civilian life. With this in mind, he signed on with the Federal Aviation Administration and enjoyed a lengthy career as an electronic engineering technician until retirement in 1991.

Technical Sergeant Cloyde C. Pinson, Sr., Maintenance and Supply Sergeant Major, Fassberg. That's correct. The name is *Cloyde* Pinson. Clyde is his twin brother. When the airlift commenced, Cloyde already possessed a virtual storybook lifetime of military service. In February 1941, ten months before Pearl Harbor, he and Clyde enlisted in the army from Ohio and were sent to the infantry at Camp Shelby, Mississippi. Clyde later went to the Philippines while Cloyde was ordered to North Africa. By November he was a sergeant. Moving from Casablanca through Morocco to Oran, Algeria, his unit boarded a French tramp steamer to Naples, Italy. From Naples they fought their way up the Volturno Valley through Anzio, Rome, Leghorn, and Pisa. Cloyde became a platoon leader and first sergeant in that campaign, taking a lot of enemy fire in the process.

Transferring to the air force in 1948, Cloyde was posted to the 313th Troop Carrier Group at Bergstrom AFB, Texas, and assigned immediately as group sergeant major. When the 313th was ordered to Germany and the airlift in October, Pinson reported that "Our group headquarters unit moved through Camp Kilmer, New Jersey, then by ship to Bremerhaven, Germany where no transport awaited. The group commander ordered his staff car off-loaded, then departed at once, leaving 21 officers and 138 enlisted men under his command on ship-board while he arranged transport by train to Fassberg, thereby saving us from spending another night on board ship." There, the 313th designation was preserved for the flying squadrons, but the air base and maintenance and supply groups were established with the 513th identification.

Cloyde and his crew made their office on the second floor of one of the huge hangars on the east side of the runway. For living quarters they moved into the hangar's top floor, so it wasn't a very long commute to work. Work days, however, were long, often 24 hours at a stretch. "We kept personnel records, wrote orders assigning people to squadrons and made duty assignments within the headquarters unit," reports Cloyde. "I had **Staff Sergeant Bob Wallace** helping me and also **Private First Class Rolando Roblejo,** a young man of Cuban heritage and very comical. He was fun to be around."

Following the end of the airlift, Cloyde reenlisted in the states, was promoted to master sergeant, and in 1951 received a direct commission as a second lieutenant. "When people ask me how I got a direct commission, I say that I ordered it out of the catalog." He served 21 years in military service, retiring in 1961, and he then spent 22 years working at General Dynamics in Fort Worth, Texas as a civilian air force representative. Thinking back on his airlift time, Cloyde calls it "a great humanitarian undertaking. It was the sort of decision America would make, and it was effectively executed."

Private First Class James R. "Spat" Spatafora, Hydraulics Specialist, Rhein-Main. Spat is one of those individuals for whom the air force fits like a glove. Totally committed to service, even as a young private first class, he served 29 years, working his way up through the ranks, retiring as a lieutenant colonel. On the airlift, Spat's primary job duty was that of hydraulic specialist with the 61st Troop Carrier Group. "We all changed engines and propellers, replaced wheels, tires, wiring, instruments, and rudders," he reports, while describing his airlift duties. He and his fellow workers also towed airplanes from hardstands to maintenance docks and back. There was no such thing as "That's not my job." But that is only part of the story about this colorful man.

On many occasions Spat worked on one of two "suicide crews"—teams that flew to Berlin to return damaged aircraft that regular flight crews would not fly back to Rhein-Main air base. Such airplanes usually had total hydraulic system failure or perhaps had one or more engines out. It was a risky business, barely noticed in everyday airlift operations, clearly unpublicized, but vitally necessary since maintenance and repair facilities at the three Berlin air bases were minimal.

While flying suicide missions, Spat, who made the grade of corporal during his airlift duty, recalls that radio silence was the watchword in the air corridors. Beyond the Fulda beacon and across Soviet-occupied territory to Berlin there was to be absolute radio silence except in an emergency. "Nonetheless," continues Spat, "we told jokes on the radio waves in order to stay awake. You couldn't hear the guys in the other aircraft laughing, but you knew that they were." One night a British voice suddenly came on the air in the midst of the merrymaking. "This is Wing Commander (name forgotten). You Yanks are to maintain strict radio silence!" Everything went dead, as Spat remembers it, until out of the void came a soft voice saying, "I wonder if the * * * really is a wing commander."

In reflecting on the overall working of the airlift from the vantage point of years, Spat is blunt. "There were no heroes," he emphasizes, "just ordinary guys living in extraordinary times. We may have done a great job, but we didn't think about it at the time. Most of us were cowards who controlled our fears."

In retirement since 1976, Spat resides in Albuquerque and continues to live and think air force. A loyal member of BAVA, he is the air force service representative to the association. He faithfully attends annual reunions with his German-born wife, Elfriede, and their son Jeff, often wears his dress blues, and on special evening occasions sports his formal dress uniform. His well-known handcrafted table-mounted operating model of the Berlin airlift memorial site at Rhein-Main air base is always on regular display at BAVA meetings. Spat also holds life membership in the Berlin Airlift Historical Foundation; the *Luftbrücke* chapter, Airlift Association; and the Tunner chapter, Airlift Tanker Association.

Today Spat continues to live his dream as a new crew member of the *Spirit of Freedom*, thereby extending his link to the past. "I have had a lot of rewarding assignments during my 29 years of active duty," concludes this exceptional man, "but the Berlin airlift is undoubtedly the one I remember most fondly. I am extremely proud and grateful to have been a part of it."

Technical Sergeant Clarence W. Durbin, Line Mechanic, Burtonwood. Clarence Durbin is one of the airlift's "old timers." A veteran of World War II, he enlisted in the Army Air Corps at Lubbock, Texas in November 1940 to avoid being drafted into the infantry. Following indoctrination at Kelly Field, Texas, he was assigned for five months to aircraft and engine mechanic school at Chanute Field, Illinois. After graduating from mechanics school, he moved to successive assignments at New Orleans; Muroc Dry Lake and March Field, California; Las Vegas; Umnak and Adak Islands in the Aleutians where he flew bombing raids against Kiska and Attu; Salt Lake City; and Biggs Field at El Paso, always working in aircraft maintenance. And what a variety of aircraft he was proud to work on! The ancient twin fan B-18, soon rendered obsolete by the B-17; the LB30, the British version of the B-24; as well as the B-17, B-24, and B-29. After World War II began, he also attended gunnery school as part of training for flying mechanics.

Clarence, whose hometown is Savannah, Missouri, spent his airlift time from January through October 1949 at Burtonwood, the air depot in Warrington, Lancaster, England where Skymasters were given 200-hour inspections, following transfer of this function from Oberpfaffenhofen. He was 32 years old during his tour of duty at this English base, one of the more senior Americans in age assigned there. In his words, Burtonwood was "for the most part dreary, wet, muddy and cold. We lived in World War II Nissen huts, ten or twelve men to a hut. Lighting was dim, and there were two small coke heaters for each hut. Toilets and showers were located in separate huts." Living facilities were situated some distance from the hangars, so the men were bussed back and forth to work, often in the dark, since the shifts were twelve hours long, six days a week.

"There were two planes in a hangar at all times," remembers Clarence. "We worked on the first aircraft until inspection and repairs were completed; then it was towed to the flight line for preflight and a test hop. Retraction tests and tire changes were accomplished on the second plane before it was moved into the dock for engine inspection and any necessary engine changes. The worst job, however, was changing deicer boots."

Most memorable to Clarence about the airlift was the time squeeze in April 1949, when all Skymasters at Burtonwood had to be inspected and returned to Germany in time for the renowned Easter Parade, when an all-time tonnage delivery record was set. On that occasion, line mechanics at that vital air depot clearly earned their pay many times over for their role in making April 16 the high water mark of the airlift.

Now enjoying life in Pensacola, Florida, Clarence is proud of a 25 plus year air force career and the satisfaction of retiring as a chief warrant officer. Thinking back, he is reflective. "Being in England, with its drab, foggy weather, as well as distance from Germany, we didn't realize the importance of the airlift at the time. But as the years pass, we can now appreciate what a great humanitarian undertaking it was."

Aviation Electronics Technician Second Class Kinzie K. Cole, Navy Electronics Technician, Rhein-Main. Kinzie Cole is a native of Baltimore who had barely passed his eighteenth birthday when he enlisted in the U.S. Navy. Following one year of training in aviation electronics, he was assigned to San Diego, then to Guam. As an electronics technician (AET) in Navy Squadron VR-6, he worked on R5Ds, the Navy version of the C-54. When the airlift commenced, his squadron was ordered to Germany. "It was a long trip from Guam to Germany," says Kinzie. "We made about nine stops on the way. It took a very long time, and at journey's end everyone was about out of money, most of us having borrowed from the other guy."

At Rhein-Main his squadron's first two electronics shops were tents pitched in the mud. The first tent burned to the ground when someone over stoked the stove. The second tent was hastily strung with two wires running across the field with a German-style electrical connector. "Nothing fit, wrong voltage, no adapters," recalls Kinzie. He and his fellow workers eventually scrounged enough electrical fixtures, however, to get their shop up and running. As working conditions slowly improved, Kinzie and his fellow technicians moved into a semi-trailer—a real step up in comfort. Finally, a Quonset hut with electricity, heat, and a floor!

Kinzie strongly wishes that more credit were given to all of those airlift veterans who shared their goodies from home with German kids. "Parachutes and gum were only starters," he continues. "We all shared CARE packages and other items such as fruit and candy with kids, girl friends, and displaced person (DP) loading crews. Doing such things left us all with a good feeling."

Kinzie finished his airlift duty tour in May 1949, shipped home shortly thereafter, was discharged from active service, and later worked in civilian life as an electronics optic technician. Today he lives in Berwyn Heights, Maryland, just north of Washington, D.C. and thinks back on the massive effort made by all those involved in the airlift. Most memorable to him about the airlift was in being part of a very noble and worthwhile effort.

Sergeant Robert W. VanDervort, Avionics Supervisor, Celle. "Let me out of here!" shouted Bob VanDervort, as he pounded on the trap door over his head. But as the C-54 engines came to life, they made too much noise for him to be heard. The Berlin-bound Skymaster taxied out to the active runway at Celle and was quickly airborne. Bob was unwillingly forced to ride the entire journey in the "hell hole," a tight crawl space under the fuselage floor where he had been replacing one of the C-54's twin ARN-7 radio compasses as it was being loaded with coal. As he lay helplessly, his large, rangy frame pinned in that tiny compartment, the engines droned steadily on, with the crew unaware of his presence. Fortunately for him, the air temperature was mild, a minor factor in his favor. On the ground later at Tempelhof, Bob's persistent pounding and yelling were finally heard by the flight engineer, with the result that he enjoyed a more normal ride back to Celle, sitting on a pile of bags in the near empty cargo bay.

"I joined the newly formed USAF in November 1947," says Bob, a native of Bristol, Tennessee. "I went to Lackland for basic training but never attended any formal, specialized schools. It was on-the-job-training all the way." In March 1949 he joined the 317th Troop Carrier Wing at Celle and was stationed there through the formal airlift wind down in September. The work days were long: twelve-hour shifts, seven days a week. Now and then a weekend off and a chance to indulge in his love: horseback riding. Bob was fortunate in this respect to be stationed at Celle; the town is famous for its horse stud farms and its annual parade of stallions in the autumn. "We lived in Quonset huts with double bunk beds and ate in the RAF noncom mess," recalls Bob. "The food was very British—sometimes good and sometimes very bad. We often had mutton for breakfast and warm milk for our cereal."

His job was that of avionics supervisor, with a crew of about twenty men. Since Celle had limited indoor facilities, Bob and his crew performed most of their work outside. Radio equipment on the C-54s often tested normal on the ground but malfunctioned in flight. To cope with such anomalies, Bob flew Vittles missions about once a month, checking the various onboard radio transmitters and receivers in the air. On later flights he was very careful to stay out of the hell hole.

Following airlift service Bob, who was a sergeant during his tour in Celle, served 21 active duty years, retiring as a senior master sergeant. Today he lives in Murfreesboro, Tennessee, is active in BAVA and is a regular attendant at the annual reunions, proudly sporting a bank of miniaturized medals on his jacket.

Corporal J. D. Batteas, Radio Mechanic, Rhein-Main. While the focus of this book is on allied forces and German and displaced person laborers of the airlift who received little or no recognition for their efforts, it is refreshing to take note of one individual whose work was officially rewarded. The Legion of Merit, one of America's most prestigious military awards, is granted to individuals who in the performance of their duties have rendered "exceptionally meritorious and distinguished service."

In practice, the award is customarily reserved to high-ranking officers, including officers of allied foreign nations. On July 8, 1949, however, Lieutenant General John K. Cannon, commanding general, USAFE, in a ceremony at Rhein-Main air base, presented the Legion of Merit to Corporal J. D. Batteas of the 61st Maintenance Squadron. As he stood in the reviewing ranks with colonels, commanders, lieutenant colonels, and majors who also received this distinguished award on that day, Colonel Lee Herman, USAFE director of personnel, read the citation, as follows: "For exceptionally meritorious service, the Legion of Merit is awarded to Corporal J. D. Batteas, Radio Mechanic, for designing and building an adapter for aerial radio equipment."

Thus one of the airlift's own noncommissioned airmen, serving in a nonflying position, received a well-deserved recognition for applying his creative skills to solving a problem of aircraft maintenance. On July 12, however, *The Task Force Times* featured a front-page picture of seven Rhein-Main officers, ranging in rank from major to colonel, who also were awarded the Legion of Merit. Corporal Batteas was nowhere to be seen in the photo.

Sergeant Larry "Corky" Colegrove, Crew Chief, Rhein-Main. When the airlift began, there were only twelve Douglas C-74 Globemasters in operation. One was assigned for a short period to the airlift run, hauling large items that smaller aircraft could not carry. Ten C-74s transported engines back and forth to the states for overhaul and return to service. The giant aircraft, with a load capacity of 25 tons, could carry sixteen engines in their mammoth hulls, and Corky Colegrove was there with the 1629th MATS Squadron to supervise the process. "As crew chief of the so-called C-74 Turnaround Crew, I had seven American and ten German mechanics, working three shifts," recalls Corky. "Work commenced one-half hour prior to an inbound C-74 touchdown and continued until one hour after departure. But it was common to work ten-to-sixteen-hour shifts and often two to three days straight."

A native of New England, North Dakota, population 700, Corky was early on the airlift, arriving at Rhein-Main on July 11, 1948. "I went to school for two hours a day during the lift," explains this personable fellow who was barely nineteen at the time, "and I earned my airplane and engine mechanic license right there." During his tour of duty at Rhein-Main, he was constantly around the C-54s and C-74s and remembers the incessant, nonstop noise of the engines, running, as Corky remembers, "every minute, every hour of every day, during takeoffs, landings, and mechanics running power checks."

Another inhabitant of the bustling air base was Big John, a huge mascot dog named after **Master Sergeant John Zarkowsky**, also of the 1629th Squadron. "Fat, with brown spots on dirty white, Big John loved to ride in airplanes being taxied by crew chiefs," continues Corky about his airlift remembrances. "As soon as a mechanic picked up a logbook, Big John would climb up the almost vertical ladder into the cockpit, and settle himself in the pilot's seat, ready to go. At the end of the taxi ride to the terminal, he then had to be lifted gently out and carried down the ladder." Dizzie, the squadron's second pet dog, was so named because he loved to stand under a running propeller and bite at the vortex created by the spinning blades, especially when there was water on the ramp. "We always expected his head to fly off," explains Corky, "but luckily it never did."

From time to time, Corky worked other duty, usually on C-54s. He and a fellow worker were taxiing a C-54 from the Rhein-Main passenger terminal across to the military side when they were instructed by the tower to hold for a scheduled block takeoff. Forced to park just off the runway in dense fog, they were trapped for nearly three hours as aircraft after aircraft, only their green right wing lights visible, shot past them every two minutes until the block was completely airborne. "While stuck there, we could not burn out or power up the engines. When we got to the hangar," continues Corky, "we had a lot of spark plugs to change."

Corky departed Rhein-Main in 1950 and left active duty in favor of United Airlines, where he spent the next 35 years as a top mechanic. Now a resident of Fort Lupton, Colorado, he rarely misses a BAVA reunion, always reuniting and reminiscing with his long-time friends, **Sergeant Hugh Tosone** of Gladstone, Missouri, an airplane electrical mechanic and **Sergeant Paul Curtis** from Fort Worth, Texas, a senior aircraft mechanic, both of whom were Rhein-Main squadron colleagues from airlift days. Following the airlift, Hugh moved into civilian life as an aerospace engineer at Boeing while Paul enjoyed a successful career with American Airlines as a senior aircraft mechanic. "If Truman had not beat down Stalin with the Berlin airlift," concludes Corky, "he would have gone to the sea with his 300 divisions, and all of Europe would be speaking Russian right now."

The Constabulary Forces

With the war's end in 1945, Congress and the American people demanded that the troops come home at once. War weary veterans of combat, flush with seniority and accumulated demobilization points, returned to the states in droves, thus decimating the combat-hardened forces that had fought across western Europe and Germany's heartland in the spring of that year. The few veterans who remained, as well as the raw, new, young recruits who weakly replenished the nascent occupation forces ranks, fashioned a wholly undesirable image of the conquering warrior as they caroused the taverns of a defeated Germany, frolicked with its women, dressed in a slovenly fashion, and generally behaved, in the opinion of some, little better than the Russian soldiers who had conquered Berlin.

To correct such an unfavorable image, a decision was made by the war department to establish a 35,000 man U.S. Constabulary force throughout the American occupation zone. The American military commander in Germany, Lieutenant General Joseph McNarney, had recently taken over from General Eisenhower, and he moved quickly. Early in January 1946, he called in Major General Ernest N. Harmon, a hardened combat veteran of the North African and Italian campaigns, as well as the Battle of the Bulge where he commanded the "Hell on Wheels" Second Armored Division, and said to him, "Harmon, you are going to be head of the constabulary." Not exactly a household word, "constabulary" gave General Harmon pause. "What's that?" he exclaimed. He soon learned. With dash, discipline, and imagination he set about to form, equip, and train the new forces to police the 2,200-kilometer zonal frontier as well as Berlin's American sector.

On May 1, 1946, the 16th Constabulary Squadron (Separate) was activated in Berlin from remaining units of the 78th Infantry Division. Training was stern; responsibilities were real. Its job was to police German civilians and American military troops. During the pre-blockade years the new Berlin constabulary forces, known as troopers, achieved a signal renown throughout the city, not only through their exemplary behavior but also for their standout appearance, featuring shining helmet liners, immaculately cleaned and pressed uniforms, yellow neck scarves, highly polished boots, and the constabulary shoulder patch of yellow with a large blue C pierced by a red lightning bolt. Although they were jokingly referred to by some as the "Circle C Cowboys," they looked and acted like the effective soldier/police forces they were. The people of Berlin took notice.

Berlin constabulary troopers patrolled the streets and cafes, regulated traffic, staffed the guard at the ACC and Kommandatura headquarters, patrolled the 175-kilometer autobahn between Berlin and Helmstedt, and generally monitored life in the city's U.S. sector by assisting many Berliners in time of need. With the onset of the airlift in 1948, they also supervised the unloading of aircraft at Tempelhof. A few troopers were even assigned to ride "shotgun" now and then on Vittles airplanes, although no one seemed to know exactly why. **Private First Class Roger Clift**, from Baraboo, Wisconsin, arrived in Berlin in February 1949, riding a Vittles Skymaster through a dense fog, with just enough visibility for him to see Berliners at breakfast, peering through their windows as the giant craft descended through the line of apartment houses on Tempelhof's final approach. Roger commenced his constabulary duties immediately, supervising the unloading of airplanes and performing air base guard watch. Much later, when asked if he had any memorable airlift experiences, he responded, with tongue in cheek, "I'm still living with her after 47 years!"

Here, in addition to **Robert Monasmith's** experiences in chapter one, are the personal stories of two constabulary troopers who served in Berlin before and during the blockade.

Staff Sergeant William C. Strub, Constabulary Trooper, Berlin.
Bill Strub's very first ride in an airplane took place as he departed Berlin

on leave in a drab, drafty, bucket-seated C-47. Stationed with the Berlin constabulary troopers, he had to take some accumulated leave or lose it. Bill landed in Frankfurt two hours later and on an impulse booked a flight to Brussels. "At the end of my leave, when I got back to the Frankfurt airport, I went directly to the MATS [Military Air Transport Service] counter and requested passage to Berlin," recalls Bill. The clerk looked at him as if he were crazy. "Don't you know that Berlin has been blockaded and that there are no flights in or out?" he queried. Having been isolated on leave for almost three weeks, Bill knew nothing of the impasse in Berlin and the onset of the airlift. Yet as good luck would have it, he secured a ride on General Clay's plush, personal C-54, Berlin bound for standby duty at Tempelhof, just in time to avoid being recorded as AWOL.

Born and raised in Brooklyn, Bill was one of the early eighteen-year-old army replacements sent to Germany in 1945. When the 16th Constabulary Squadron was formed, he was ordered to Berlin and assigned to its C Troop. "Barracks life was hard," says Bill today, thinking back on his time there. "Imagine, we had to stand reveille, then do basic training, motor maintenance, motorized city patrols, and guard duty." The only events that broke the routine were periodic ultimatums from the Russians: "You have 72 hours to get out of Berlin, or else." But the young American troopers, undeterred despite being vastly outnumbered by the Soviet forces, maintained a confident mood. "Who do you think you are to tell us to get out of Berlin?" was their response. They were there and were going to stay. "We were all young and bulletproof in those days," Bill notes with a chuckle.

Later in the year, the autobahn patrol from Berlin to the British zone border checkpoint at Helmstedt was added to the constabulary's duties. By Thanksgiving Day the notoriously severe 1946-1947 winter had already set in, and as Bill led his "ice patrol," as the troopers dubbed it, westward in two jeeps and an armored car, the cold permeated their inadequate winter clothing. Upon reaching the British aid station 105 kilometers out, Bill and his fellow troopers were numb from the freezing weather. It had been difficult to hold the steering wheels and to feel the accelerator pedals. The British soldiers had to remove the Americans' frozen clothing and thaw them out in the warmth of the aid station, and as a result they fell behind schedule. Although roundly chastised by their superiors for returning late that day, in the end they were issued warmer clothing, and all key Berlin officers and NCOs were later required to make the autobahn run, just to experience what it was like.

At the onset of the blockade in June 1948, a move that Bill had made earlier during the Little Airlift in April proved to be just the ticket for the constabulary forces. As police operations sergeant, he had rounded up all the city maps he could find for use in each vehicle and had also posted a large operations wall map in the squadron situation room that he had set up. When the blockade was imposed, patrols were increased throughout the U.S. sector to a 24-hour, seven-day basis. Bill's map acquisitions, then, turned out to be a lifesaver for patrolling duty.

Following the blockade and airlift, Bill remained in the army reserve, then was recalled to active duty for the Korean war and the Cuban missile crisis. He retired as a sergeant major, enjoyed a successful civilian career in advertising print production, and today lives in Briarcliff Manor, New York. Active in the U.S. Constabulary Association, the organization of constabulary veterans, as well as BAVA, Bill has been lately in the forefront of an effort to secure issuance of a constabulary commemorative stamp.

Private First Class Samuel Young, Constabulary Trooper, Berlin. Another nattily uniformed trooper of the 16th Constabulary Squadron in Berlin was Sam Young from Columbus, Ohio. Only a few months after his eighteenth birthday, he enlisted in the U.S. Army on June 16, 1948 and was sent directly to Fort Jackson, South Carolina for basic infantry training. Ten days later, with the Berlin blockade imposed, Sam sensed that his first assignment following basic would be Germany, and it turned out to be true. He arrived there early in August, took special constabulary training at Sonthofen in the American occupation zone, and soon thereafter arrived in Berlin with assignment to the 16th Constabulary Squadron. "We supervised the unloading of planes at Tempelhof," remembers Sam. "We also pulled a lot of security duty and patrolled the Allied Kommandatura, the Allied Control Council, General Clay's headquarters, and also his home in Dahlem." An additional duty for the troopers was to keep displaced persons off the streets after dark, since the Russian secret police were in the habit of kidnapping them.

Sam recalls that life in McNair Barracks in West Berlin was good, and that he had "a bunch of nice people with whom to pull duty." They all had to be especially cautious on patrol in the city, however, because the brass did not want any trouble with the Russians. "We had to walk a tightrope because we were told to be awfully careful about causing any incidents. Brigadier General Frank Howley, the Berlin Military Post commander, said in no uncertain terms that we do not want any problems with the Russians, unless they cannot be avoided."

Following fifteen months of airlift duty, young Sam remained on station in Berlin until mid-1952 when he was transferred to Camp Polk, Lousiana for discharge. In February 1952 he married a girl from East Germany whose father, a veterinarian from the Leipzig area, had sent her to school in the west. Today, Sam lives in Salt Lake City, having enjoyed a thirty-year career with General Motors as a skilled tinsmith. Thinking back, he feels that the airlift was the greatest humanitarian effort of all time. He is proud to have been a part of it and wishes that the constabulary would receive more credit for the role it played in this historic event. "If we had not been there on the ground," he concludes, "it could not have been done."

Base Support Specialists

So many different types of skills were necessary for the airlift to operate smoothly, that it is virtually impossible to describe them all. Most airlift literature focuses on flight crews—pilots, copilots, flight engineers, and now and then radio operators and navigators—making it easy to overlook the all-important contributions of those who served the airlift from their ground posts. From truck drivers to cooks to control tower operators, a constant need existed for a wide array of specialties if the airlift were to be successful. So the call went out for supply clerks, sheet metal workers, personnel specialists, loaders, truck drivers, radar and radio technicians, and a host of additional experts in many specialized fields. Some were assigned individually to Germany from stateside bases; others arrived as members of whole units transferred to airlift duty.

The persons whose stories are told in the following pages represent but a sampling of the specialists needed in that massive effort of 1948-1949, yet in the eyewitness accounts of their duties and personal experiences they reveal a rarely disclosed side of airlift life. The long hours of duty and the harshness of working conditions are blended with a clear modesty, yet a certain pride of accomplishment. They were all professionals. They made the airlift hum. Let these unheralded veterans themselves speak.

Corporal Donald R. Neild, Public Information Specialist, Celle. Barely eighteen years of age when he enlisted in the Army Air Corps, Don Neild hopped on a train for the first time and rode from New York City to San Antonio and Lackland Field. It was July 1947. Two cars of enlistees made the trip, playing cards, singing, and getting to know one another. Don was a long way from his hometown of Binghamton, New York, but he endured the basic training, then was assigned to instructor school right at Lackland, graduating as a physical training (PT) instructor.

Having studied German in school for three years, Don volunteered in 1948 for Germany and quickly found himself at Furstenfeldbruck, just north of Munich, assigned to the public information office. The switch to public information, however, was simply one of the mysteries of military life. "When the airlift got under way, I was one of the first to be transferred to Celle," recalls Don of his time at that northern air base that opened on December 15, 1948. But this time, although still assigned to public information, he maneuvered his way back into the sports field for which he had been trained. By the spring of 1949 a Celle baseball team had been organized, and in the tryouts Don won an infielder spot. "Our coach was **Al Goot,** a recalled pilot who had pitched in the Yankee farm system. We had a great season, winning ten of our fifteen games. Our biggest rival, of course, was Fassberg. It was amazing how many games we won. So many of our team members were on flying status, it was never certain who would be present for a game."

With the blockade broken and the airlift winding down in the summer of 1949, 20th Century Fox moved its camera crews to Germany for the filming of the movie *The Big Lift,* starring Montgomery Clift. Don was placed on TDY to Berlin and was given a small role playing the part of radio operator on the same C-54 for which Clift was the flight engineer. "When the last shots had been filmed, the movie moguls held a nice banquet for all of us at a posh German restaurant," Don reports. "It was a terrific experience, to say the least."

Don left the air force in 1950, then spent 23 years with General Motors, working on various management teams that experimented with different types of management approaches. Today he lives in St. Petersburg, Florida, runs a travel agency with his wife, Elaine, and is an active BAVA member.

Sergeant Thomas S. Talty, Finance Clerk, Rhein-Main. The finance office at Rhein-Main where Tom Talty worked was located right on the flight line, in an old machine shop, situated next to the emergency repair sheds. Engine noise from the Skymasters revving up was loud and continuous. "I could see the C-54s lined up, loaded, and ready to go," recalls Tom. "I was terribly impressed with the magnitude of the efforts of all involved and was very proud of them."

From his flight line vantage point, Tom computed and processed payrolls as well as travel vouchers. The finance officer, **Captain F. L. Bachman,** one of the few African-Americans serving on the airlift, supervised an all-white staff, and with his deputy, **First Lieutenant C. C. Davis,** led their multinational team of U.S. Air Force military and civilians, two German nationals, and a Swiss civilian. The Germans worked side by side with the Americans and were highly skilled in the system. **Staff Sergeant Joe Licata** served as cashier, with **Staff Sergeant David Fuller** backing him up. **Sergeant Bill Collett, Sergeant S. Berman, and Corporal Merle Eakins** worked with Tom in the military pay section which was supervised by **Technical Sergeant Ed Czamata**. Working conditions were hard—twelve-hour shifts, often seven days a week, especially during the first and final ten days of the month when demands were the greatest. But Tom relished it all; he was building up valuable experiences that would serve him well as his career progressed.

A native of Buffalo, New York, Tom enlisted in October 1946 at age eighteen. Following basic training at Lackland, he attended a series of specialized schools at which he learned the intricacies of office work and finance administration. Then, in August 1948, while stationed at Brooks AFB, Texas, he received orders for the 61st Finance Disbursing Unit at Rhein-Main and airlift duty. "I was a young man at the time," Tom says, "only twenty. But I was thrilled to be a part of it all. Living accommodations were poor—cold, drafty, wooden barracks with potbellied stoves at each end. The food, however, was great. No complaints there. Mess halls were open 24 hours a day."

As the airlift came to a close in September 1949, Tom was assigned further to USAFE headquarters in Wiesbaden. Then, in an enviable career spanning 23 years, he enjoyed successive assignments in Vienna, where he met his future wife, Texas once more, Turkey, Florida, England, New

York, and back to Germany in 1966, always improving his skills in finance and accounting, and earning a college degree along the way. He retired from the air force in 1969 as a chief master sergeant, then worked as an auditor with the federal government until 1983.

"Today I am a substitute teacher," reports Tom from his home in Rio Rancho, New Mexico. "I am not quite fully retired."

Elizabeth "Libby" O'Neal, Civilian Secretary, Wiesbaden. As soon as the airlift commenced, the involved military units needed civilian staff. One of the first volunteers for secretarial duty in Germany was Libby O'Neal from the small, northwestern Georgia town of LaFayette. At the time, she was an air force civilian secretary at headquarters, Military Air Transport Service (MATS) at Gravelly Point, Virginia, and the prospect of sixty days temporary duty in Germany was enticing. Libby left Westover on July 28, flying by way of the Azores, Paris, and Frankfurt, arriving in Wiesbaden three days later.

She was assigned at once as secretary to Colonel Theodore Milton, recently named by General Tunner as deputy chief of staff for the airlift task force. The secretaries were housed at the Palast Hotel in town. Libby's work during the early days of the airlift, as well as that of other civil servants, was no picnic; they endured the same taxing schedule that others bore: ten hours a day, seven days a week, until the aerial lifeline to Berlin could be ironed out on a smoothly functioning basis. She and her fellow workers organized the headquarters unit, established administrative procedures, and developed effective communication techniques. The sixty days inevitably turned into eight months, but Libby enjoyed her work and performed it in such an exemplary manner that at the end of her airlift duty she received a commendation from General Tunner. Libby had her own thoughts about the magnitude of the airlift. "The German people realize that the airlift is their life line of sustenance and where they once lived in dread of approaching airplanes, they now fear the ceaseless drone of airlift planes will not be heard."

In 1949 Libby returned to her former post at MATS headquarters; two years later she married air force pilot **Cliff Dwinell**, cited in chapter three as pilot for the Bob Hope entourage, and she continued her civil service career in other locations as she moved with her husband to his various air base assignments. When Cliff retired from his air force career, the couple moved to Granby, Massachusetts where Libby continued community activities at home and more civil service work at nearby Westover Air Reserve Base. In all, she compiled twenty years in the civil service. Sadly, Libby died in December 2000 at age 75, but she will be remembered as a bright symbol of those women who proudly and ably made their vital contributions to the success of the Berlin airlift.

Sergeant John L. Zazzera, Aircraft Dispatcher, Rhein-Main. If any airlift pilot or flight engineer from Rhein-Main thinks that his aircraft simply flew a prescribed route to Berlin with only instruments and radio aids to monitor and guide him, let him talk to John Zazzera. From his vantage post in wing operations, John kept tabs on every airplane assigned to the 7497ᵗʰ Airlift Wing. Wherever they were, John "The Shadow Knows," knew. "We tracked the whereabouts and the condition of each aircraft," he points out. "We were in constant touch with the squadrons and groups, base operations, the tower, other departments, and some other bases as to the disposition of every aircraft. Where was it? Arrived at Berlin, on the way back, estimated time of arrival, stacked, gone to Obie for maintenance, and so on."

John was only seventeen when he entered the Army Air Corps in July 1946. After telephone and telegraph school training at Scott Field, Illinois, he moved on to base operations at Goose Bay, Newfoundland, then to flight control at Fairfield-Suisan airfield in California. He arrived for airlift duty early in August 1948 and found himself, in his words, in the middle of "a cowboy atmosphere."

"The development of a routine process, a system that began to work well in all areas of the lift came later," he explains. "One obvious improvement was to paint large aircraft numbers on the tail for easy identification." As airlift procedures became regularized, John settled into a work routine alternating between tower duty in the mornings and operations headquarters time in the afternoons.

Living conditions for John and his colleagues were initially "in the category of messy confusion." They eventually, however, were assigned quarters in the Betts area, a former German army facility, crowded yet favored by airlift personnel. The food was very good, but duty shifts were long—twelve hours on, 24 hours off, seven days. With the arrival of more people from the states, however, working shifts eased off to eight hours. "Off duty time was great," John says. "It was a time for checking out the area, including wine, women, and song. My friends and I frequented the Palmgarden, a favorite spot, but we soon 'graduated' to local German establishments in Offenbach. I met a German girl in one of them and almost married her."

After a bit more than six months of airlift duty, John was reassigned to his California base and discharge, but not before receiving a personal letter of commendation from his wing operations officer, in recognition of his superior performance of duty at Rhein-Main. Civilian life did not last too long; in 1951, as the Korean war heated up, he was recalled to active duty and spent twenty months at Loring AFB, Maine. Following that tour of duty, he attended Boston College night school for eight long years, graduating in 1961. Along the way, he held a part-time job at Raytheon as an engineering assistant. Later, he and his brother established a restaurant and ice cream business that they developed over a thirty-year period. John now lives in Kittery, Maine and wouldn't miss a BAVA annual reunion for anything.

Corporal Lewis Dale Whipple, Supply Clerk, Celle. The Celle air base opened on December 15, 1948. Many support personnel arrived, therefore, during the cold of winter, in need of numerous supply items. Lewis Whipple was there to hand them out. But before he got there, he had to endure, with the 1,100 other officers and enlisted men of his 317th Troop Carrier Wing, a lengthy forty-day sea voyage from Japan to Germany. "The voyage was an unprecedented movement of men and materiel, made in record-breaking time," recalls Lewis. "We moved from Tachikawa air base, Japan, with orders to Rhein-Main, but in midocean they were changed to Celle." The wing arrived at that northern Germany RAF station in early January 1949, by train from the port of Bremerhaven.

At Celle, Lewis was assigned as supply clerk, although he had not received any special training for the job. "We supplied all the uniforms, bedding, and office equipment for wing headquarters," he continues. There were numerous supply shortages on the base because there was no supply depot at either Celle or Bremerhaven. Since Celle was an RAF station, the British loaned the Americans there most of their needed furniture.

A native of Conneaut, Ohio, Lewis joined the air force at age seventeen and was sent immediately to Japan upon completion of thirteen weeks of basic training at Lackland air base. With the phasing down of Celle in August 1949, Lewis returned to a stateside assignment, then left military service in 1952 in the rank of sergeant. Still, his air force experiences served him well during the next thirty years with the Caterpillar Corporation.

Thinking back today on the massive airlift effort, Lewis is reflective. "I firmly believe the airlift saved Berlin, also Germany, and quite possibly all of Europe from falling under Soviet rule," he insists. His feelings were reinforced during a 1992 visit to Celle when a sales lady in a local wine shop, upon learning that he had been stationed there during the airlift, excitedly proclaimed that she had been a little girl at that time, and that the airlift had saved Germany. "To me," says Lewis, "this was a very moving experience. I am always humbled when meeting Germans who remember and are so grateful to this day of our efforts, when actually we were just doing our jobs in the best way we could."

In July 2000 Dale published a memorable monograph on the history of his organization during the airlift years. Entitled *317th Troop Carrier Wing (HVY): The Mission, 1948-1949, Berlin Airlift,* it provides a thrilling account of the wing's movement by sea from Japan to Germany and its vital role in the airlift.

First Lieutenant Dean W. Terlinden, Weather Forecaster, Burtonwood. The air base at Burtonwood was a vital, busy crossroads during the airlift. Heavy air traffic moved through this depot to and from the states as well as to and from airlift bases in Germany. Weather forecasters at Burtonwood, because of its slightly northerly geographical location, were able to provide information for Vittles aircraft flying the corridors. Dean Terlinden whose experiences with the American advance contingent at the 1945 Yalta conference are described in chapter one, was among the small team of weather experts collecting and disseminating such information at Burtonwood, England.

In September 1948, Dean's unit, the 21st Mobile
moved from Tinker AFB, Oklahoma, to Wiesbaden, th
a week of weather indoctrination. Following that,
Burtonwood on 75 days of temporary duty. At Burtonw.
fellow weather men scrounged for furniture and equipm.
Nissen hut quarters as they settled in for what ultimately would .
month stay. "We started with only a barometer, a wind vane, and a rυ
in the control tower," says Dean. "We had communications with British
weather central, and AACS later installed the necessary equipment so we
could deal with the C-54s arriving from Germany for their 200-hour
inspections."

Dean found his forecasting duties to be not too demanding. He pulled
night and weekend duty, as did the others, yet with a full complement of
personnel, everyone was able to have sufficient time off. An avid swimmer,
Dean was fortunate to locate baths in the nearby area where he could
swim almost every day. His colleagues who preferred golf, hunting, or
fishing were not so lucky because winter was just around the corner.

Following his return to the states in the spring of 1949, Dean continued on active duty until he had completed ten years of service, then
remained another twenty years in the reserve, retiring as a lieutenant
colonel. During his reserve time he served 25 years as a substitute high
school teacher and junior college instructor in the Los Angeles basin area.
In final retirement from everything, he and his wife have traveled extensively around the country, visiting numerous military bases. But he found
during his teaching years that his heart was really in the west, and so
today he lives in Long Beach, California.

Corporal George M. Meyer, Army Engineer, Berlin. Much has
been written about the construction of Tegel airfield in the French sector
of Berlin. It has been noted in numerous publications, for example, that
17,000 Berliners, both men and women, toiled long and hard to build the
Tegel runway and other facilities, yet little has been written about the
army engineers who supervised and managed the overall project. Corporal
George Meyer was one of those engineers. "My station immediately prior
to the airlift was at Giessen, in the American occupation zone, with the
502nd Engineer Utilities Company," remembers George. "Five of us from
the 502nd were sent to Berlin in September 1948, and we worked at
Tempelhof for a while. Then we moved to the French sector to build Tegel
airfield."

George and his fellow engineers stayed in the French compound at
Tegel, but they found it to be dirty and unkempt. Fortunately, they had
their own American mess, which they themselves could keep clean. George
was in charge of a rock crusher, and he was kept busy with the mountains
of rubble transported to the airfield site from bombed out sections of the
city. Maintenance was an ongoing problem because the machines were
worked hard and broke down regularly under heavy and constant use. "We
did a lot of fixing," says George. "Working conditions were long and
stressful; the Russians were always watching and the French did nothing."

George enlisted in the army in February 1946 when he was seven-
en. After eight weeks of basic training at Fort Lewis, Washington, he
ttended auto mechanics school for another eight weeks before moving to
regular army assignments and ultimately transferring to Germany. He
served in Berlin through December 1948, putting the final touches on the
new Tegel airfield that would prove to be so vital to the airlift's success.
Tegel went into full operation on December 15, 1948, although the first
C-54 landing actually occurred on November 5. But George remains today
quite disappointed at the manner in which the newly completed airfield
dedication ceremony was carried out. "The U.S. troops who built it were
invited to the dedication," he continues, "but we were not permitted to get
close. There were too many French big wheels up front." George seems to
have had reservations, as did so many others, about the French in Berlin.

George served in the army for six years, including time in the Korean
war, but a lengthy military career was not in his thinking. In February
1952 he was discharged with the rank of sergeant first class, and today he
lives comfortably in his hometown of Columbus, Ohio, spending a lot of
time traveling, including a return trip to Germany that he and his wife
made in 1989 for the fortieth anniversary airlift reunion. At Tempelhof,
"George and I spied a little old white-haired lady," reports George's wife,
Joan. "She looked lost, so we asked if we could help her. She said that she
just wanted to say thank you to someone. Can you imagine waiting forty
years to show gratitude? Her name was Frieda Staab, an 86-year-old
Berlinerin, who had moved to Frankfurt. When it came out in the papers
that the Yanks were returning for the reunion, her friends put her on an
airplane and sent her to Berlin. She stood with tears running down her
cheeks as she told her story. That was the highlight of our trip."

Corporal Albert G. Tindall, Truck Driver, Fassberg and Celle.
Al Tindall is a rare person who doesn't agree with conventional military
wisdom that one should never volunteer for anything. "I arrived at Fassberg in October 1948, and there was no work for me. So I volunteered to
drive a truck," remembers this native of Ira, New York, a small upstate
village northwest of Syracuse. "I also volunteered a friend, **Corporal
Richard I. Howland,** and orders for him came through, too." Al continued in this self-imposed activity for a month, driving supplies to the
airplanes for loading. Then, when Celle opened in December he was
transferred there (he probably volunteered) to the 317th Troop Carrier
Wing where he served as a message center jeep driver for several months
until the expiration of his airlift duty tour.

"I enlisted when I was just two weeks past my seventeenth birthday,"
says Al, thinking back on those youthful days. "The date was August 28,
1947, and I was sent right away to Lackland for basic training." After that,
he attended clerk-typist school at Lowry AFB, Colorado, then took up his
first post-school assignment at Brooks AFB, Texas, later moving to
Orlando army airfield. By then, the airlift was on. Once again the
volunteer, Al willingly signed on for ninety days TDY to Germany. The
ninety days quickly turned into 180, as it did with so many other airlift

participants. By April 1949, however, his tour of duty had come to an end, and he reported back to his old base unit at Orlando.

His airlift experiences in volunteering and driving vehicles in a clearly unsung capacity had been memorable to him, and he pondered the possibility of remaining in the military service. The call of civilian life was stronger, though, so he left the air force on December 19, 1949, after having served for almost two-and-a-half years. In civilian life, he joined the Carrier Corporation in Syracuse, working in a variety of job specialties but devoting most of his efforts to sales. While in the military, Orlando must have appealed to his liking, for he lives there today in retirement. Thinking back on the place of the Berlin airlift in cold war history, Al pauses to reflect. "When I was there doing it, I didn't grasp the enormity of it all. I only realized what we had accomplished when I attended the fiftieth anniversary reunion in Berlin."

Private First Class Malcolm A. McBride, Army Truck Driver, Berlin. Mal McBride didn't arrive in Germany until after the blockade had been lifted, but he was kept very busy during the summer supply buildup that continued through September 30, 1949. A native of Olympia, Washington, Mal grew up on a dairy farm near Fort Lewis. Following high school graduation in 1946, he worked two years for the state department of forestry, then signed on in January 1949 for a three-year army enlistment. He breezed through eight weeks of basic training at Fort Ord, California, and arrived in Berlin in June, assigned to the 16th Infantry Regiment, First Infantry Division (The Big Red One). "I actively worked on the airlift as a truck driver," recalls Mal. "We hauled guards to Tempelhof from our barracks, and between guard runs I hauled supplies. My duty hours were seven days a week, 24 hours a day. This lasted from June 20 to September 30, 1949. We were stationed at Roosevelt Barracks in the *Botanischer Garten* District near Schöneberg. They were large brick buildings, formerly SS barracks, and they housed both our battalion and the 759th Military Police Company. After the airlift, we moved to McNair Barracks where the 16th Constabulary was stationed."

Mal remembers that his airlift duties went smoothly with the exception that he received only one pass during his several months of service. As a result, he didn't see much of the city on his own. The only incident of note while he was on duty, serious enough in the blockaded city, occurred when a German unloader stole a pound of butter from an incoming shipment. "Tempelhof was locked down for two hours," reports Mal, "until the MPs finally caught the thief!" Following the closedown of the airlift, Mal was sent to Oberammergau for a short course in military intelligence, then returned to Berlin for further duty on scout patrols around the city's three allied sectors.

Mal reports good relations between his 16th Infantry Regiment and the 16th Constabulary Squadron in Berlin. "They furnished guards at Tempelhof and Spandau Prison the same as our unit," he continues. "We also worked together on training exercises in the *Grünewald* Forest near Lake *Wannsee*. All of the occupation troops in Berlin actually had great camaraderie. It has carried on all these years, and is now expressed in our recently formed Berlin Veterans Association as well as the Berlin Airlift Veterans Association."

Discharged from the army in 1952 as a corporal, Mal returned to the state forestry department for two more years, then transferred to the state highway department and worked there until retirement in 1982. Today, Mal still lives in Olympia and is a regular at the annual BAVA reunions. "They [BAVA members] all have welcomed me into the group although it is about 98 per cent air force, and I represent one of the few army members," he says. "I just think we have a great group who all put their best efforts into saving a city from the Russkis."

Flight Engineers and Radio Operators

Crucial to the success of any airlift mission were the men who "mothered" the C-54s flying from the various airlift bases. Without a flight engineer, the C-54 was a useless piece of aluminum. Training for their job was intense and demanding. Once on the job, they made certain, in concert with the line chiefs, that their aircraft were ready to fly. Then they made the flight as well. Flight engineers were, in fact, the third pilot; they did it all. They raised and lowered landing gears, controlled power settings, manipulated wing and cowling flaps, monitored engine instruments, carefully watched fuel consumption, served as general managers of their aircraft, and on more than a few occasions, for one reason or another, the person riding the copilot seat was the flight engineer himself. He may never have made the actual takeoff or landing, but he jolly well did everything else. What General Tunner didn't know didn't hurt him.

Some flight engineers suffered injuries or died in airlift crashes. One of them, **Staff Sergeant John L. Hanlon** from Milwaukee, bailed out from his disabled C-54 on March 4, 1949 when an uncontrollable fire developed in the Skymaster's entire right wing while he and his crew were heading eastward for Berlin over the Soviet zone. John, his copilot, **Lieutenant Thomas W. Keating** from Elyria, Ohio, and two hitchhiking control tower operators, **Sergeants W.J. Sakkinen** and **William A. Kinzalow**, all escaped from the burning aircraft, but the pilot, **Lieutenant Royce C. Stephens**, failed to get out and was killed in the crash. The survivors, all from Wiesbaden air base, were taken to a Soviet military hospital, where John's badly cut leg was treated; they were all turned over to U.S. authorities in Berlin the next day. In this segment personal experience stories are told by some of the brave men who served in the vital role of flight engineer.

On the American side of the airlift, radio operators were "as scarce as hens teeth," given that they were not part of the standard C-54 crew. Yet a small number of them played supporting, but no less brave, roles in airlift operations, flying in special capacities as will be seen in **Ken Skoog's** and **Jim Colburn's** stories that follow.

Technical Sergeant William R. Michaels, **Flight Engineer, Celle.** Bill Michaels did it all. A native of Youngstown, Ohio, he joined the army air forces during World War II, flew 174 missions on the Berlin airlift, met a German girl, fell in love and married her, had an exciting post-airlift air force career extending to thirty years, and now looks forward to each BAVA annual reunion. Sadly, he lost his wife, Annie, to cancer in 1986, but the memories of a storybook courtship and 37 happy years of marriage remain with him.

His airlift story commences in Great Falls, Montana, where Bill, as a flight engineer, went through transition training, the so-called airlift prep school, established there for airlift replacement crews. Following the three-week course, he moved to Westover AFB for transportation to Wiesbaden and the beginning of airlift service. "My quarters was the attic space of an old Luftwaffe barracks. The building had suffered war damage, and holes in the roof had been simply covered with canvas—in late November!" he remembers. Fortunately, Bill's stay at Wiesbaden's Y-80 was brief, for his organization moved to Celle when this northern RAF base opened for the Americans the next month. "The sergeants' mess there," continues Bill, "was ruled over with an iron fist by a company sergeant major from a Scottish regiment who always wore kilts and reminded me of Field Marshal Montgomery."

Bill's airlift tour of duty was anything but routine. On one memorable mission his aircraft lost an engine inbound to Berlin over Soviet-occupied territory. The crew followed normal engine shut-down procedures and continued toward Gatow since a three-engine, empty-load takeoff on the return posed no problem. On final approach, however, the Gatow tower operator suddenly warned them that a Lancastrian tanker, with radios out, was hedgehopping and sideslipping onto the runway directly beneath them. Bill's pilot then executed a missed approach and headed for Celle. "Just at that time," says Bill, "we lost a second engine on the same side but amazingly made it safely back home, even with our full load of coal!"

"One night, early in 1949," continues Bill, "we were on a return trip from Berlin. The weather was miserable—turbulence, snow, sleet and rain mixed. We had to use the deicing boots. Suddenly, a brilliant flash, a sharp crack, and the smell of burning rubber caused us concern." Upon landing, an inspection of the C-54's damaged outer skin revealed that it had been struck by lightning.

Perhaps Bill's most telling airlift experience involved a premonition of disaster by his then fiancée, Annie Kirschbaum. Visiting her in Celle one evening after a lengthy twelve-hour duty shift, he found her distraught and crying. She had dreamed that his aircraft had caught fire and crashed, killing the entire crew. She could even recall the airplane tail numbers, 236. "My usual aircraft was 233 which had recently returned to the states for a 1,000-hour inspection," remembers Bill, "but my replacement aircraft had the tail number 236." Soon thereafter, C-54 number 236 departed Celle late at night, caught fire over eastern Germany and crashed, killing all three crew members, including Bill's roommate, **Technical Sergeant**

Herbert Heinig, who had just returned from leave and having slept all day, volunteered for the mission that evening. Bill Michaels was not aboard that flight. He had requested, at Annie's urging, temporary suspension from flight duty. But others in his unit were unaware. "The next morning I returned to my quarters to find my bedding and footlocker gone, my wall locker open and empty," Bill remembers. "In the orderly room the adjutant looked up as I entered, his face turned white, and he exclaimed, 'My God, Sgt. Michaels, you're dead!' "

In January 1950, Bill and Annie were married in Celle in a civil ceremony, then had their church wedding in Youngstown six months later. After Bill's retirement as a senior master sergeant, they made their home in Wichita Falls, Texas, where he still lives today, savoring the memories of the airlift and their happy married years.

Corporal Kenneth Skoog, Radio Operator, Rhein-Main. Ken Skoog should have hired out to the RAF, because radio operators, or signallers, as they were known, were part of the crew on almost all British aircraft. Not so with USAF C-47s and C-54s. Still, he managed to fly on the airlift. How did he do it? "I took my advanced radio training in Germany," explains Ken, a native of Christine, North Dakota. "On training flights, we flew the corridor to Berlin. Skymasters carrying passengers out of Berlin also needed a radio operator; so I was aboard on several of those flights." Ken crewed as well on flights to Burtonwood for 200-hour C-54 inspections and trips to the United States for 1,000-hour overhauls. Crossing international boundaries necessitated permissions and regular position reports; hence, radio operators were needed in such situations. "I crossed the Atlantic fifteen times," he remembers.

Ken's dad would not give written permission for him to enlist while he was still seventeen. So on his eighteenth birthday, Ken signed on. In January 1948, following three months of basic training at Lackland AFB in Texas, he moved to Scott AFB, Illinois and studied radio. By the next autumn, bored with radio maintenance at a Sioux City reserve base, he volunteered for Germany and the airlift. "While processing in at Bremerhaven, a colonel looking over my shoulder noticed that I was a radioman. He asked me if I wanted to fly. I said I would love to. He said the only catch was that I would have to attend a tough radio school at Rhein-Main and that the washout rate was high." Always a high roller, Ken took the chance, beat the odds, and won.

Veteran World War II radiomen still on the job were too slow for new postwar communications techniques, and freshly trained operators were needed. Only a third of his class of 120, including Ken, made it. Then, on the grand test, only one-quarter of the finalists, Ken included, passed. "However, we had to be retested every six months," he continues. "The odds grew slimmer with each retest, but I passed every time." In the final retest, he was the only one out of eleven to pass. Then his airlift service began in earnest.

Following the airlift, Ken flew the air force band around Europe, then moved on to Japan and flew on B-29 missions during the Korean war. The war's high casualty rate eventually required increased hospital flights back to the states, with Ken on board one of them as radio operator. While at McChord AFB, the flight's destination, Ken's discharge papers came through. Turning immediately to civilian goals, he went to work in December 1951 as a brakeman on the Great Northern Railway, eventually worked his way up to conductor, and retired in 1993 after almost 43 years of railroad service. Ken and his wife, Erlys, now enjoy life in Wahpeton, North Dakota (he is a great booster of his home state), and they have attended all of the airlift reunions in Germany. As an active BAVA member, he is also a faithful attendant at the association's annual meetings.

Sergeant Ralph G. Dionne, Flight Engineer, Rhein-Main. "There was always much improvisation on the airlift," states Ralph Dionne. Having served as aircraft mechanic, crew chief, and flight engineer on the big C-54 Skymasters, he witnessed and participated in many such efforts to get the job done, whatever skills and creativity it might take. "Considerable aircraft maintenance, both major and minor, was performed day and night, out in the elements," he continues. "Early during the airlift, and when proper maintenance equipment was not available, air force improvisation prevailed. I recall that on one or more occasions, displaced persons and German workers from the loading trucks crowded into the rear area of the aircraft cargo compartments until the rear skid dropped to the ground. This allowed us to quickly service the nose gear. To remove the rudder, we placed a 55 gallon drum under the nose gear to support the C-54 in a nose-high position to reach the high tail surface more easily."

Ralph grew up in Nashua, New Hampshire, about forty miles northwest of Boston. He enlisted in the Army Air Corps shortly after his high school graduation in June 1946 and completed basic training in San Antonio. His first assignment after that was to C-54 aircraft mechanic school at Keesler Field, Mississippi. "Upon graduation, I was assigned to the Air Transport Command, 14th Air Transport Squadron at Westover Field," recalls Ralph. "I advanced to the grade of sergeant while there."

In late July 1948, with the airlift building momentum and the need for on-the-spot mechanics increasing, he was among those selected from his squadron to prepare for movement to Germany and Rhein-Main air base. It was an exciting time for the young sergeant who by then was almost 21 years of age. As he departed Westover, reclining on a pile of mail sacks in the overcrowded C-54, he took time to ponder the future for both himself and on a larger scale, future relations between the USSR and the west. "As the U.S. coastline disappeared from sight, and as we headed for a confrontation with Russia, it was very sobering to me. I asked myself: How will the ruthless Russian leader Josef Stalin react to our intervention in behalf of blockaded Berlin? Am I looking at the U.S. mainland for the last time? Yes, young sergeant, take a long look!"

Young Ralph served his airlift time with distinction, advancing to flight engineer status and making runs between Rhein-Main and airlift maintenance depots, as well as regular Vittles runs into Tempelhof. In February 1949, he was reassigned to his former squadron at Westover where he commenced work on Lockheed Constellations (Connies), with which the squadron had been newly equipped.

Anxious, however, to further his formal education, Ralph left the air force, earned a civilian pilot rating and graduated from Boston University with a bachelor of science degree. Today he lives with his wife Ellen in Dracut, Massachusetts after a successful 35 year civilian career in pulp machinery manufacturing, specializing in inventory auditing and international customer service and sales. Active in BAVA, Ralph enjoyed tremendously the fiftieth anniversary reunion in Germany in 1999. Once again, as the reunion ceremonies unfolded over the span of several days, his emotions overwhelmed him as they had fifty years earlier, and he found himself thinking back to that greatest humanitarian undertaking of modern history.

Staff Sergeant Orville C. "Sarge" Grams, Flight Engineer, Wiesbaden. Sarge Grams had to wait a year for his mother's permission to join the service, but he knew all along that a military career was what he wanted. A native of Augusta, Wisconsin, he finished high school in 1940 and then worked in the local post office for a year before enlisting in the Army Air Corps. On the way by train to Sheppard Field, Texas for basic training, he suffered a common ill fortune of the raw recruit, losing his food allowance in a crap game. "It was an educational experience that I have retained," says Sarge today. The post office experience at home, however, made him a marked man; upon arrival at Sheppard he was immediately assigned, despite his objections, to the base post office. Permanent party, ugh!

Not to be outsmarted by his superiors, Sarge kept pushing for a life beyond post office work and ultimately landed an assignment to B-17 mechanics school at Amarillo army airfield, graduating in class 8-11-43B. From that time to the war's end, there followed a chain of interesting assignments at several air bases, and a specialization in other types of aircraft such as B-25s, B-26s, C-47s, and C-45s. One of the C-45s he later named for his daughter.

In 1948, with the airlift under way, Sarge volunteered for Germany and very quickly found himself off to Europe on the *General E. D. Patrick*. Assigned to aircraft maintenance at Wiesbaden's Y-80 air base, he served as a flight engineer with the 22nd Troop Carrier Squadron, making regular missions to Berlin. "On one occasion," he reports, "we were diverted from Tempelhof to Tegel, to pick up German children and their mothers to transport them to Wiesbaden. Some of the children were apprehensive and crying, and a few had to use the bucket latrine in the rear of the cargo compartment. As we continued toward our destination, I helped some of the youngsters to the astrodome to view the sunset, which was really impressive. They enjoyed it all, after I convinced them that I was not trying to throw them out of the hatch."

Following the airlift, Sarge continued his air force career, ultimately serving thirty years, one month, and 28 days, retiring in the well-earned rank of chief master sergeant. Today he lives in El Centro, California with his wife, Ollie, and is a regular attendant at BAVA annual reunions. Thinking back on the cold war and how the airlift influenced its course, he points out that "The Soviet plan to achieve world domination was the Kremlin's continuing aim, and therefore it would have been unwise for the United States to permit uncontested Soviet success in their plan to achieve complete control of Berlin."

Sergeant James P. Colburn, Radio Operator, Rhein-Main. An air crew member who had an out-of-the-ordinary airlift assignment was Jim Colburn, a native of Memphis, Tennessee. Following basic training in 1946 at Keesler Field, Mississippi, he attended radio operator and mechanic school at Scott Field, Illinois. The skills he acquired there led to Eglin Field, Florida and a variety of crew assignments as radio operator on flights throughout Central America and the Caribbean, picking up valuable experience in C-47s, C-54s, B-25s, and B-17s.

Since radio operators were not needed on airlift C-47s and C-54s, Jim was not too hopeful, upon his arrival at Rhein-Main, of a regular assignment as an air crew member. But luckily, he was posted to the European Air Transport Service (EATS), with airborne C-47 duty as radio operator and mechanics helper with the 61st Maintenance Squadron. "There I flew test flights, often to Berlin, on C-47s and C-54s being returned to service after maintenance, and I also made several ferry trips on aircraft returning to Westover AFB and then on to Tinker AFB, Oklahoma for major overhauls," recalls Jim.

At Rhein-Main, neither he nor his squadron colleagues had any experience in raising aircraft on pneumatic lifting bags after a gear-up landing. "So I was dispatched to Oberpfaffenhofen to observe and learn this fine art," he continues. It was all part of seemingly endless extra workloads—in addition to testing radio equipment—associated with maintaining aircraft so that they could be returned to airlift service. Rhein-Main was good duty, Jim remembers. Frankfurt was a very interesting place to be stationed, and he had a chance to visit many of the historic sites in the area. Life on the air base was okay, too. "Our quarters were in the Betts area, the best I had seen in the air force. The food was good, too, but then, I will eat almost anything."

Jim stayed on active duty for five years, including Korean service, then entered civilian life, returned to college, worked in sales at Minneapolis Honeywell, and flew 21 years as a pilot for Southern Air Transport. Today he enjoys life in Mulberry, Florida, where he has lived for more than thirty years, and flies his beautifully restored 1952 Cessna 170 as often as he can. He is also busy restoring a 1941 Piper J-5 (his third). Thinking back to 1948-1949, Jim says, "I am glad that I had the opportunity to participate in a small way, but I regret that at the time I didn't have a better understanding of the larger picture. The airlift was, in my opinion, still a political game that had to be played. However, I believe the humanitarian effort was what made it so successful."

Staff Sergeant W. C. "Dub" Southers, Flight Engineer, Celle. Not quite eighteen years of age, Dub Southers enlisted in the military service on August 2, 1946 and attended primary airplane mechanics school at Keesler Field where he also completed the C-54 mechanics course. A series of assignments followed at Bergstrom Field, Texas, and McChord Field, Washington, with TDYs in Alaska and North Carolina, during which he worked on C-54s and C-82s. But he got his hoped for flight engineer ranking, however, soon after returning from the North Carolina operation. He was then called up for the airlift in November 1948, and in the course of eight months flew 196 missions, considerably more than the average. "On the end of the McChord AFB runway awaiting clearance for Alaska, we received instructions to return to base operations," reports Dub. "There I was advised that my orders had been changed and that I was to leave immediately for Germany and the Berlin airlift. Together with others from McChord, I was transported by air to Camp Kilmer, New Jersey for processing, then to the port of embarkation for troop transport to Germany."

Briefly assigned to Wiesbaden upon arrival in Germany, Dub spent most of his airlift time at Celle with the 41st Troop Carrier Squadron of the 317th Troop Carrier Group, following the opening of that northern RAF base in December. "Most of the early landings at Celle were from straight-in approaches because GCA and positive radar control had not yet been fully installed. On one of our landing approaches, we were advised that we were over the end of the runway, but upon breaking out, we saw no runway at all, only bright lights everywhere. The pilot executed a missed approach and fortunately came around again to a safe landing."

Celle was a city that escaped heavy allied bombing during World War II; hence, most buildings in the town had been preserved. It was a nice community to visit. There were a number of good restaurants that featured fancy floor shows, so the Americans stationed there had no shortage of good entertainment. Dub enjoyed his time at Celle, the flight line mess hall was open 24 hours a day, and the food was good, as it was at most flight line mess halls.

Following the airlift, Dub returned to the civilian world and in 1954 graduated from the University of Houston in electrical engineering. After college life, he worked fifteen years for Collins Radio, then formed his own printing company that manufactured award ribbons and badges. Since 1971 he has lived in Duncanville, Texas, a suburb of Dallas, and always busy, is now in the home health care software business.

Recently named BAVA secretary to succeed long-term **Bill Gross**, who served the airlift at Tempelhof as an unloading supervisor, Dub remains a loyal member of BAVA, and seeks to perpetuate the memory of the airlift by speaking to local community groups about it and his own airlift experiences a half century ago.

Commissioned Air Crews

Much has been written about airlift pilots, and considerable glory and recognition have been accorded many of them in the voluminous literature of the airlift era. **First Lieutenant Gail S. Halvorsen** became a popular airlift flyer during its early months with his initiation of parachute candy drops to the children of Berlin. He is perhaps the best known of all airlift veterans, both American and Commonwealth, who took part. Other pilots vied for the honor of having flown the greatest number of Vittles missions, achieving some renown in the process. **Captain Harry D. Immel, Jr.**, became one of this group when he flew his 403ʳᵈ airlift mission on September 30, 1949, making the final C-54 flight into Berlin. A record? Perhaps. But with others also claiming the title, the record holder has never been firmly determined.

Other pilots achieved fame the hard way. On the night of September 14, 1948, **Captain Kenneth Slaker** and **Lieutenant Clarence Steber** were forced to bail out from their disabled C-47 over the Soviet zone. It was their second trip of the night and only Ken's sixth Vittles mission overall. The two pilots barely made it out of the aircraft door at a very low altitude. Clarence was apprehended by Russian soldiers, taken to a Soviet zone hospital for treatment, and U.S. officials were notified of his whereabouts and physical condition. Two Americans from the Potsdam Liaison Committee holding diplomatic status were permitted to visit him, and while there, to avoid the guard posted outside his hospital room, they all quickly sneaked out the window, then clambered into their diplomatic vehicle. Before Soviet authorities could react, they whisked Clarence to safety in West Berlin. Ken also made it safely back to the west, but not before enduring a touch-and-go escapade with the Soviets. He avoided capture through the help of an East German, a former POW of the Americans, who escorted him across the border to his home base. Ken feels that he could not have made it safely to the west were it not for the help of Rudolph Schnabel, the East German, who knew what route to take and how to bribe the border guards. At the same time, Schnabel decided to defect, and he went across the border with Ken.

Yet for the hundreds and hundreds of pilots and other commissioned air crew members who saw service on the airlift, most all of whom were very young junior grade officers, anything approaching lasting recognition and rewards was not to be. Except for air medals awarded to some, but not all, for completing 100 Vittles missions, formal kudos were genuinely difficult to attain, and press publicity was spotty at most. This segment sets forth personal airlift stories and experiences, all but one previously untold, of a small, random group of American pilots and a flight surgeon— young men who, while enjoying the moment tremendously in the classic, carefree fashion of birdmen everywhere, still saw their airlift task as a solemn duty and approached it with great pride and professionalism.

First Lieutenant Johnny Clark, Pilot, Wiesbaden, Fassberg, Berlin. Johnny Clark is one of those airlift veterans who served at three bases and therefore accrued a broad perspective about the total operation that few others shared. In 1948, he was stationed at Hamilton AFB, California when the call went out for pilots with a four-engine military occupational specialty (MOS). They were badly needed on the Berlin airlift. In no time he was assigned to the 60th Troop Carrier Group at Kaufbeuren air base in Bavaria for a three-year tour of duty. But the 60th wasn't there. It had been moved, by the time of Johnny's arrival in Germany, to Wiesbaden, so he reported directly to Wiesbaden. From this air base, known informally as Y-80, "I flew eight trips to Berlin as a C-47 copilot," remembers Johnny. "On one trip we had 2,800 pounds of five-gallon Jerry cans. I asked the crew chief if we were hauling gas, and he replied that their cargo was wine, not gas—red on one side [of the aircraft interior] and white on the other. It seems that we had to provide everything for the French in Berlin, including wine, or they were going to leave!"

From Wiesbaden, Johnny moved north on October 1 to Fassberg, after the C-47s were withdrawn from airlift duty. There he transitioned smoothly to the C-54 and the Fassberg mission of delivering coal exclusively. On one of his return flights from Tegel, the weather was marginal with extremely low visibility. "After receiving instructions to hold in the pattern, we held for the maximum fuel reserve time to reach Munich," he explains. "We were then diverted to Oberpfaffenhofen using the most direct route. Upon landing, two engines quit from fuel starvation and upon dipping the tanks, we found that only one-half an inch remained in the other fuel tanks. It was my lightest landing in 2,500 hours in a C-54."

At Fassberg Johnny was lucky enough to get a couple of ferrying assignments returning C-54s to the states for 1,000-hour inspections. On his first trip, in December 1948, as he landed at Newfoundland for refueling, he met 22 sailors on Christmas leave waiting in the terminal for a ride. "I had the airplane filled with Christmas mail bags and didn't have seats or safety belts for them," he recalls. "So I told them to tie themselves down on the mail bags during takeoff and landing, and they all gratefully rode in that fashion to Westover AFB." On a second ferrying trip the following March, he was able to get back home to Cresco, Iowa and see his new daughter for the first time.

Johnny's third stop on his airlift tour was Tempelhof and the 7350th Air Base Group, with duty as task force officer at Tegel, maintaining a constant check on the flow of arriving and departing aircraft. During this time he deadheaded periodically back to Fassberg in order to keep up his flying status and to fly additional airlift missions. With the end of the airlift in September, he transferred to Chanute AFB, Illinois, served 22 years on active duty while continuing to fly C-54s in a variety of situations, and retired in 1965 in the rank of lieutenant colonel. Following an interesting twenty year civilian career as an industrial development consultant for the natural gas industry, Johnny lives today in Papillion, Nebraska, just south of Omaha, and looks back on the airlift and its place in the cold war. "We should have called the Russians' bluff and made them live by the Potsdam Agreements. If we had stood our ground, there would have been no Korean or Vietnam wars."

Captain Edwin L. Glazener, Flight Surgeon, Wiesbaden. Yes, there were actually flight surgeons assigned to the airlift. Dr. Edwin Glazener, a native of Fairfield, Texas, was one of them, but he was not a pilot. He joined the 60th Troop Carrier Group in early October 1948 following a long flight from Westover AFB. After arrival, he found that there would not be much surgery to perform. "It was mostly sick call, physical exams, and treating air crews for ear troubles," he reports, "and about once a week I made a flight to Berlin on a Vittles aircraft."

Preparing to make one such flight shortly after his arrival in Wiesbaden, Ed picked out a plane and pilot (he had this option) only to discover that the copilot was General Tunner. "I was not smitten with General Tunner, believe me," he remembers. "I could not abide the man, and I really mean it. Not an ounce of friendliness or sociability about him. He asked me if I really wanted to take the flight with them, so I said 'No, General, I think I'll fly later', and I did." Ed was smarting from a dressing down the general had recently given him in the presence of his enlisted medical staff: a no no that all would-be second lieutenants learn in their officer candidate training. Ed takes nothing away from the task force commander for his successful management of the airlift, but in terms of people skills, he feels that Tunner was a washout, and not too knowledgeable about military protocol.

On flights to Berlin, now and then Ed encountered hairy situations, just like other air crew members. "We had flown into Berlin with ten tons of coal, but the landing gear down and locked green signal light did not go on. We were directed back to Wiesbaden. Same thing. No light. We were then sent on to Oberpfaffenhofen where, instead of treating us like we had the plague, they were very nice, got out the emergency vehicles, and foamed the runway. On final approach, much to our surprise, the green light suddenly went on. Our ten tons of coal went on a round robin that day!" Easter Sunday sticks vividly in Ed's memory. He remembers that on that exciting day of maximum effort, with everyone doing his part, they turned around at Tempelhof so quickly that the unloaders were still getting off their airplane as it was taxiing back to the active runway for departure.

As one might imagine, Ed, who graduated from Baylor Medical School at the tender age of 23, was not enamored of air force life and chose to return to the civilian world after his airlift service. He took up residency in anesthesiology at Cleveland Clinic in Ohio, later moving to San Diego where he has since been engaged in anesthesiology practice. But he retains a strong feeling today about the airlift and its place in the cold war. "Those goddam Russians were pushing us, and we pushed back— thanks to Harry Truman."

First Lieutenant Gerald L. Munn, Pilot, Wiesbaden. "Sarge, would you mind going aft and bring forward three boxes of those berries?" The flight engineer responded, "I was waiting for you to ask, Gerry. What took you so long?" It was late June 1949, and Gerry Munn and his crew were headed for Berlin, their C-54 loaded to the hilt with fresh strawberries! As they passed over the Fulda range, the heavenly, mouth-watering aroma wafting forward from the cargo compartment to the cockpit had become so tantalizing that they decided they must sample their wares. After all, they did not wish to deliver a spoiled shipment to Berlin. But by the time the Skymaster reached the Tempelhof area, everyone's fingers were sticky, and the throttles, control yokes, and seat backs were covered with a bright red goo. This was all a pleasant, one-time diversion from the usual cargoes of coal and flour, each with its distinctive, unsavory odor.

A native of Nichols, New York, a small southern tier community near Binghamton, Gerry is one of those who a mere four years earlier had flown heavy bombing missions against Germany. Stationed with the 15th Air Force in Italy, he completed an astounding fifty B-24 missions over enemy territory, his final raid being against Regensburg on May 29, 1944. He still was not twenty years old! It was a rather strange adjustment, therefore, to find himself a few years later flying necessities of life to the people of Berlin.

Returning to civilian life after World War II, Gerry flew in the air reserve, volunteered for active duty after the airlift start up, then completed the airlift prep course at Great Falls, Montana prior to reporting to the 60th Troop Carrier Group at Wiesbaden in February 1949. Following seven months of airlift service at Y-80, Gerry moved to a MATS assignment at Westover AFB until May 1952, then transferred to Tachikawa air base, Japan, from which he flew C-54s into the Korean theater of operations. The airlines were hiring, however, and after only a few months in Japan he opted for a civilian flying career with Mohawk Airlines, amassing an amazing 31,500 hours, military and civilian together, before retiring in 1984 from U.S. Air, Mohawk's successor airline.

Today Gerry lives in Bradenton, Florida, is a loyal BAVA member, and continues to fly as a member of the *Spirit of Freedom* crew. In 1998 he crewed on the *Spirit's* two-month trip to Europe and its triumphal mission to Berlin/Tempelhof to observe the fiftieth anniversary of the airlift's beginning. And what, to Gerry, stands out as the most memorable experience of his lengthy flying years? Here's the answer: "During my entire career—both military and civilian—my small part in the Berlin airlift was the high point. I have never blown my own horn, but I am proud that I made my 121 flights to Berlin, and I would gladly do it again."

First Lieutenant Robert N. Cyzmoure, Pilot, Wiesbaden and Celle. "After each day's last coal-laden flight, I headed for the shower. The coal dust choked my hair and ran down my body. I had to get it washed out," so Bob Cyzmoure reports about his pilot duties hauling coal to Berlin from Celle. Bob commenced his airlift service in September 1948 with the 317th Troop Carrier Group at Wiesbaden, flew out of its Y-80 air base for three months, then moved north with his group when it opened the Celle air base in December. "I was strictly a buck pilot," says this native of Milwaukee. "I had no other duties. My experiences were quite routine." In his six months of airlift duty, Bob flew 139 missions to Berlin. But he enjoyed the Wiesbaden environment better than Celle; there was more to do in one's free time, and living conditions were less austere. He did, however, secure a ferrying trip home during his time at Celle, and that was ample compensation.

During World War II Bob served in the Troop Carrier Command at Bergstrom Field, Texas, with assignment as an instructor pilot. With the end of the war, he moved to the Pacific area and flew hundreds of transport missions from Tachikawa air base to Korea, the Philippines, Guam, Okinawa, Iwo Jima, and Hokkaido.

Following more than 31 years of active duty, during which time he drew a Pentagon duty tour and served once again in Germany at the American Embassy, Bob retired in 1974 as a colonel, having logged 16,200 flying hours. He then moved back to Mobile, Alabama where he had previously spent five years flying C-74s at Brookley AFB and had amassed 3,500 hours in the giant cargo lifter. There, in 1975, he became director of aviation for the city's two airports, retiring a second time after fourteen years in that position. Despite Bob's modesty about his accomplishments in this position and his reluctance to talk about them, family members have reported that he lengthened the main runway and built an entire new terminal building. Secretary of Transportation Elizabeth Dole presided over the ceremony at which Bob's name was inscribed on the terminal's dedication plaque.

Today Bob and his wife Vi live in San Antonio's USAA towers, enjoy travel, play a lot of golf, and are regular attendants at BAVA annual reunions.

First Lieutenant Donald W. Measley, Pilot, Rhein-Main, Fassberg. Just about everyone who had anything to do with the airlift will remember the picture, broadcast worldwide, of a barefoot Berlin child presenting a bouquet of flowers to an American pilot at Tempelhof. The little girl, **Suzanne Joks**, is now Suzanne Riedi-Joks, lives in Lucerne, Switzerland, and has raised a beautiful family. The American pilot is Don Measley, whose hometown is Hammonton, New Jersey but who now lives in Santa Barbara, California. When the airlift commenced, Don was stationed at Elmendorf AFB, Alaska in the 54th Troop Carrier Squadron. "My squadron was one of the first troop carrier units ordered to Germany," Don remembers clearly. "We all packed in a hurry and quickly set out on the lengthy trip to Rhein-Main, where we started flying our airlift missions as soon as we arrived in early July." It was during one of his first trips to Tempelhof that Suzanne appeared to present her bouquet to Don.

Don and his fellow air crew members continued flying from their Rhein-Main base through September. "It wasn't any party," he points out. "The hours were long, the food was bad, and there were so many takeoffs and landings that it became tiresome." Still, it was all part of the job, and the allure of participating in an as yet undefined historical event was enough to make it worthwhile and interesting. "We were helping people to survive," he continues, "and everyone realized that much." Time would tell whether or not their efforts would be successful, but in midsummer 1948 no one was certain.

By early October Don had moved to Fassberg and the 29th Troop Carrier Squadron. This northern RAF station was bustling by that time with C-54 activity, and Don was in the middle of it, flying missions fast and furiously until by January 1, 1949 his tour of airlift duty came to an end, and he rotated to a new stateside assignment. By that time he had decided to pursue an air force career and ultimately served 21 years, retiring as a major. "Suzanne and I remain in touch, and it's good to see a friendship which began a half century ago continue even today," says Don with obvious pleasure.

Postscript: On May 12, 2001, Suzanne and Don met for the first time in a half century at the annual Tempelhof ceremonies marking the end of the Berlin blockade. Seeing one another again after so many years was thrilling for each of them. "He was a wonderful pilot," remembered Suzanne, "and he was a good father to me." The two were reunited by courtesy of the Allied Museum in Berlin. Despite the widespread publicity accorded to Don as a result of his meeting with Suzanne so many years ago, and again in 2001, he remains modest and self-effacing. He is truly a symbol of all those who, having taken part in the airlift, nevertheless felt that they had done nothing heroic—just ordinary people living in extraordinary times.

Ж

This portrayal commenced with brief biographies and eyewitness accounts offered in response to my circulated questionnaire centering on individual contributions to the airlift. In the assembly of these memoirs, certain personal characteristics became at once evident. First, the men and women of the ground support forces were for the most part very young; many of them enlisted immediately upon completing high school. Some did so even prior to completing high school. Those from the ground support grouping who returned the questionnaire ranged in age, as of June 26, 1948, from 17 to 31, with an average age of 20.4 years. Further, fewer than half of them, 43 per cent, chose to pursue a military career when their airlift duty was completed. A small number of men in this group also served occasionally on flying status, in order to perform periodic, specialized duties.

Second, the noncommissioned air crew members were next in the age group ranking, ranging from 18 to 35, with an average age of 24.2 years. Their ages too, as well as all in the questionnaire survey, are recorded as of June 26, 1948. As for carving out a military career, the pendulum swung the other way with this group. Almost 62 per cent opted to stay in after the airlift, all of them eventually achieving the rank of master sergeant, senior master sergeant, chief master sergeant, or officer status by the time of retirement. One enlisted navy pilot went on to a commission and ultimately the rank of commander. Third, commissioned air crew members comprised the oldest group, ranging in age from 20 to 32, with an average

age of 25.4 years. This group also had the greatest proportion, 67 per cent, opting for a career. Most of these careerists retired as majors, lieutenant colonels or colonels, with one, **Major Sterling P. Bettinger,** of Colorado Springs, Colorado, who was CALTF deputy chief, retiring as a brigadier general.

In this chapter's airlift biographies and memoirs, a sense of modesty and a feeling of merely having done one's duty are pervasive. As **Jim Spatafora** told us earlier in the chapter, "There were no heroes, just ordinary guys living in extraordinary times." Yet despite these noble and memorable sentiments, a mood of unease over media handling of airlift feats was reflected by some, to wit: air crews were glorified at the expense of the ground support forces. Some veterans wrote to me that despite their membership in the Berlin Airlift Veterans Association, they felt that they were not sufficiently identified with airlift operations to warrant their attendance at annual reunions. Others, among them some constabulary troopers, felt that the flyboys got all the credit. But these memoirs, in the end, clearly reflect the pride, professionalism, and a sense of accomplishment that won out over discontent and a feeling of being left out.

Americans who served on the Berlin airlift came from all walks of life and from all corners of the land. They left their homes in the inner cities, the affluent suburbs, and the rural farms to return to active duty, or like many already on active service, they hastily transferred from far-flung air bases in answer to the call from Germany. Together they joined proudly in the greatest humanitarian mission in modern history. Throughout the hurry up, makeshift procedures of summer 1948, the gradually maturing airlift operations of the autumn, the cold, formidable weather of the oncoming winter, and the efficient, streamlined deliveries of 1949, they carried out their responsibilities in a driven, professional manner. Theirs was a single mission: to stand firm in Berlin. That they succeeded is dramatically seen today in the fall of the Berlin Wall and the Iron Curtain, the collapse of the Soviet Union, a free, unified Berlin, a united Germany, and a democratic, prosperous Europe.

Figure 10. German laborers unloading a C-54 at Tempelhof, 1948. Courtesy Nicholas Rucci.

Figure 11. Circle C Cowboy, Cpl. Nicholas Rucci, Berlin, 1948. Courtesy Nicholas Rucci.

Figure 12. The 16th Constabulary guard mount, 1949, Roger Clift at the X. Courtesy Roger Clift.

Figure 13. The 16th Constabulary armored vehicles, Berlin, 1949. Courtesy Roger Clift.

Figure 14. Trauen civil laborers camp, Fassberg, 1948. Courtesy Rolf Kühne.

Figure 15. T/Sgt. Bill Michaels' C-54, No. 233, being loaded at Celle for yet another trip to Berlin. Courtesy Bill Michaels.

Figure 16. Kinzie Cole, Navy electronics technician, Rhein-Main, 1949. Courtesy Kinzie Cole.

Figure 17. Sgt. Sewart Farnham and Cpl. Bill Trackler, air policemen on airlift duty. Courtesy Bill Trackler.

Figure 18. Don Measley and Suzanne Riedi-Joks are reunited at the Allied Museum, Berlin, after 52 years, May 12, 2001. Courtesy Don Measley. Wall mural behind them shows Suzanne as a little girl presenting flowers to Don at Tempelhof 52 years ago.

Figure 19. Fred Murtishaw and his fellow line mechanics and technicians, Oberpfaffenhofen air depot, October 1948.

Rear row from left to right: Billy Melton, Paris, Texas; Charles Hollinbaugh, Indianapolis, Indiana; Alvin Schroder, Baton Rouge, Louisiana; John Fletcher, Warner, Oklahoma.

Front row, left to right: Fred Murtishaw (squatting), Portland, Oregon; Louis Anderson, Baton Rouge, Louisiana; Carlos Pizzolata, Denver, Colorado; George Collins, Woodbury, New Jersey; Harold Stroup, Willington, Oklahoma; Laurence Cripe (sitting), Dubuque, Iowa. Courtesy Fred Murtishaw.

Five

Airlift Personalities: British and Commonwealth Forces

Out of the night that covers me,
Black as the Pit from pole to pole,
I thank whatever gods may be
For my unconquerable soul.

William Ernest Henley, Invictus

BRITISH CONTRIBUTORS TO THE BERLIN airlift made up an impressive portion of the Combined Airlift Task Force, which was formed in October 1948 for overall coordination of the western allies' airlift effort. Other nations represented, in addition to England, were the United States, and the Commonwealth nations: Australia, Canada, New Zealand, and South Africa. Canada did not formally participate, but Canadians as individuals served with Royal Air Force units assigned to the airlift. France took part to the extent of flying a few ancient JU-52s during the earliest days of the airlift, and its air force crews also flew a B-17 to Berlin on a regular basis to stock the French garrison. The other three nations, Australia, New Zealand, and South Africa, dispatched air crews to the airlift effort but no aircraft.

Together, the air crews of these nations flew 542,236 of the 2,325,808 tons of vitally needed supplies delivered to Berlin, and they flew twelve different types of aircraft, compared to the Americans' five types, a factor that surely made the British task more complicated and difficult in terms of aircraft servicing, maintenance, flight coordination in the corridors, loading and unloading. The British also operated from more bases than did the Americans, if the seaplane base at Finkenwerder and the RAF operation from Fassberg early on, is considered. All this necessitated additional supply lines and administrative procedures.

Civilian contract carriers, too, formed a significant part of the British airlift effort; their crews flew ten different types of aircraft, including liquid fuel-carrying tankers. Another important factor about the British contribution is stressed by civilian **Radio Officer V.G. Sherwin**, whose home was in Newhaven, Sussex during the airlift. Sherwin, who flew 132 sorties in Yorks and Lancastrian tankers for Skyways, Ltd., states that "Britain was broke and still suffering the effects of World War II. Rationing of bread was introduced for the first time in order to supply Berlin with grain, but we still managed to contribute one third of the total effort."

As seen in the personal stories of Americans, the British and Commonwealth *chaps* in this chapter exude a healthy sense of modesty about their airlift duties. A strong feeling of simply having done one's job is exhibited overall. If there is any undercurrent of discontent noted, it is that the Yanks seemed to get more glory and credit than they, the Brits, did. Yet this unpleasant notation failed to replace the sturdy pride they all express in having been a part of that massive undertaking, the Berlin airlift. Individual eyewitness accounts commence with noncommissioned forces, most of them serving in ground support positions; followed by the commissioned ranks, most of them air crew members; then followed by those in the civilian contract carrier group. All are presented in the rank or job title held when they first entered upon airlift duty.

From the American point of view, geography played a significant role in British airlift morale, at least for air crews. The proximity of the United Kingdom to the continent permitted, and even necessitated, regular and frequent air travel between the two. Pilots, navigators, and signallers could easily reach home on a few days of off duty time. In fact, some squadrons set up their airlift flying schedules so that crews were on duty for, say, three weeks, as **Bob Davies** tells us later in this chapter, enjoy four days off, then back to the airlift for another three weeks. And with the abundance of air traffic between Germany and the UK, particularly regular courier flights from Bückeberg, it is quite probable that members of ground service forces also had opportunities to return home on short leave. Those who could not return home on leave often had an opportunity to visit British zone leave centers such as Bad Harzburg. Perhaps geography also played a role in how airlift personnel viewed their assignment to Germany. Many air crew members reported their airlift station as Waterbeach, Oakington, Abingdon, or other RAF station in the UK, all the while being on detached assignment at Wunstorf, Lübeck, or another German air base. Technically true, to be sure, but also a frame of mind?

Noncommissioned Forces

Most of the following personal stories are from noncoms who held aircraft-oriented jobs, such as: fitters, engineers, wireless operators, and instrument and radio mechanics. Others are told by loadmasters, construction engineers, and perimeter guards. Unfortunately, no supply sergeants, cooks, or finance clerks came forward. In this respect, eyewitness stories told in this segment perhaps do not represent a full cross section of the wide job spectrum extant throughout the ranks of Operation Plainfare. No matter. The stories told in the following pages are heartwarming.

Leading Aircraftsman Desmond Dawe, Fitter IIA Airframes, Wunstorf. Desmond Dawe wanted air crew duty, but the Berlin airlift got in his way. Stationed in early 1948 at Tangmere, Sussex as an airframe fitter on Gloster Meteor IVs, he applied for air crew training and was delighted when, in May, he learned that he had been selected. "I was in the process of toting the clearance chit around the station in preparation for departure," Desmond recalls, "when official word came from on high: 'You're on the airlift. Report forthwith to Transport Command, Abington.'" That was the end of his hopes for flying the wild blue yonder.

A native of Bristol, Desmond was still a young man when he entered the RAF Transport Command. He completed two years of training at the RAF School of Technical Training at Halton, Bucks, where he mastered the trade of airframe fitter but still yearned for a flying assignment. "As apprentices we were known as Trenchard's Brats, after the founder of the RAF aircraft apprentice scheme," he explains.

On the airlift, Desmond was stationed at Wunstorf from May 1948 through May 1949, working on major maintenance and inspections of Avro Yorks. He and his crew worked three shifts in rotation, the worst being the wee hours "digger" shift ("graveyard" shift to us Yanks). They performed daily preflight and fuselage inspections that required lifting floor panels under which lay grimy mounds of rancid flour and coal dust; landing gear retraction tests; hydraulic repairs; engine changes; fuel leak repairs, involving removal of hundreds of pop rivets; and a host of other maintenance tasks, all performed in the open except for major maintenance jobs carried out in hangars. Desmond and his fellow workers spent their long duty shifts exposed to the elements, even through the harsh winter.

"Another favorite recurring problem," recalls Desmond, "was the magnetisation of the tail strut assembly, which caused erroneous readings on the Distant Reading Compass installed in the rear fuselage." Since demagnetising equipment was not available, they usually had to replace the entire assembly, a nasty job, indeed.

Wunstorf had been a Luftwaffe fighter base, and as such, all facilities had been designed for fighter aircraft. Desmond experienced a rude awakening to this factor on the day they first towed a York into one of the large hangars for major maintenance. The heavy aircraft's main wheels promptly went through the thin concrete floor. More drudging repair work to be performed by more unsung airlift workers!

In 1959, following a successful RAF career from which he retired as a senior technician, Desmond and his wife left their homeland and took up residence in Levin, New Zealand. In thinking back on his time on the airlift, Desmond is reflective. "I consider it a great privilege and a memorable experience."

Sergeant John L. Bushell, Army Engineer, Fühlsbuttel. The airlift needed airfields and runways, and John Bushell was there to build them. A member of the army's Royal Engineers Corps, John was in charge of constructing the runways at Fühlsbuttel, near Hamburg. Skilled in civil engineering, he quickly became equally skilled in the fine art of laying pierced steel planking (PSP) for temporary runway surfaces. He also put in considerable time building concrete runways. John had an able work force made up of men from the German Civil Labor Organization They were all former Wehrmacht Pioneers, that is engineers, and their group was composed of former officers, noncommissioned officers, and ordinary soldiers. "They wore their old uniforms, minus badges of rank," reports John. "They still held to their command structure and were very well disciplined. Any conversations we had with them were purely orders and work instructions. It was all rather embarrassing, really, because they would jump to attention and salute when I approached them."

A native of Kenton, Middlesex, John was stationed at Fühlsbuttel from October 1948 until March 1949. Although primarily engaged in runway construction, he also carried out other general engineering tasks, such as blowing up structures left behind by retreating German forces in the final days of World War II. He enjoyed his own work very much, noting how long and hard the German laborers themselves toiled to help their fellow countrymen in Berlin. And what impressions from Operation Plainfare stand out in his memory? Quite a few, but just to name one, because he was prone to watch carefully the results of his own labors: the steel plank runway segments always formed a ripple wave in front of the wheels of landing aircraft. Had he and his German crew done their work well? Would the PSP sheer apart under the landing impact of the heavy aircraft? He was always apprehensive.

John chose not to make a career in the army and left the service at the end of his enlistment. Yet he continued in the same vein in private life as a civil engineer, spending many years planning and overseeing the construction of roads, bridges, drains, and buildings. Today John is a loyal British Berlin Airlift Association member but finds it a bit difficult, due to physical disabilities, to attend BBAA meetings. In looking back upon his memories of the airlift, he says that there were poseurs among both the Americans and British—those who unduly glorified the part they played. "But they were usually Americans," he concludes. In a more positive sense, however, John remembers the "close cooperation and extremely hard work of so many different nationalities."

Aircraftsman First Class George F. Morton, Teleprinter Operator, Bushy Park, London. No, they were not all stationed in Germany during the airlift time. British forces headquartered at Bushy Park in London were vital to Operation Plainfare's success, and George Morton was posted there in late September 1947, well before the airlift commenced, when his organization was staffed wholly by the RAF. American forces arrived at Bushy Park sometime later to round out the total British-American airlift effort. "The USAF chaps joined us just before the start of the airlift," he remembers. "We each had our own mess hall and billets, and the American teleprinter section was separate to our own, although we did share social gatherings. I remember an excellent American concert party visiting us on one occasion with a full orchestra."

George's Bushy Park duty, with eight-hour, albeit round-the-clock shifts, was a bit more on the normal side than the twelve-hour, seven-day grinds which both Brits and Yanks experienced at their German air bases. Yet the Bushy Park mission was an integral segment of the combined airlift operation. "I suppose that some of us had to be the backroom boys," responds George today. "I sincerely hope we were doing a worthwhile job, although it didn't seem like it at the time." Perhaps the serenity of Bushy Park lulled George and his colleagues into such a mood. He reports that it "was about the most tranquil posting anybody could ever wish for, with deer wandering around the camp, and all of us surrounded by nature." Constructed in 1942, the camp served during World War II as headquarters for the American 8th Air Force, and was known then as Camp Griffiss. Two years later General Eisenhower moved in with his staff, designating it as the Supreme Headquarters, Allied Expeditionary Forces (SHAEF), from which D-Day was planned and executed. George was there until July 1949 when he was demobbed.

In civilian life, George worked in the electrical industry, ultimately owning his own business, with a specialty in burglar alarm systems. As a BBAA member, this life-long native of Birmingham, like John Bushell, has difficulty traveling to association meetings because of physical problems. But when invited by the Royal Parks Commission to attend the May 14, 1999 unveiling of a plaque in his own Bushy Park to commemorate the fiftieth anniversary of the Berlin airlift, George was there, for on this occasion he was introduced to, and had his picture taken with, H.R.H. Prince Charles.

Signalman Ernest E. Gathercole, Army Keyboard Operator, Berlin. "Our transmitter site was located at the Olympic Stadium, enclosed in a barbed wire stockade," reports Ernest, who is from Preston, Lancashire. "The stockade interior was patrolled by an elderly German with his German shepherd dog. Our guard stood outside the stockade in a sentry box. He was issued only five rounds for his rifle; wasn't even allowed to have 'one up the spout.' What would happen if the Russians tried to take over the site? Should the sentry try to ring the bell to the guardhouse or fire his rifle in warning? We finally concluded that he should fire four shots, hoping the other guards would hear, and save the last bullet for himself!"

In June 1947, when he was eighteen years old, Ernest was called up for National Service. Following basic training he transferred to the Royal

Signals for trade training, where he qualified as an Operator Keyboard and Wireless. His first posting was to Hamburg, but soon after, he found himself riding bucket-seat style in a coal-laden Dakota to Berlin and his new airlift assignment with the Berlin Signals Squadron. It was interesting duty for the young man, and he enjoyed the cultural life that Berlin had to offer even at that time, taking in on one occasion a performance of *Carmen* at the *Komische Oper* in the city's Russian sector. Other duties may have been interesting but not so enjoyable. His unit's parade ground included an assault course "over which our C.O., Major Parker, used to delight in driving us every morning, no matter what the weather was like." Nonetheless, life was not all gloom and doom. Young Ernest worked diligently at his job of helping to maintain communications between the British military government in the city and in the west and took good advantage of his free time.

Ernest did not remain in the military service beyond his obligation time. In civilian life he fashioned a varied and interesting career, including service in the merchant navy as a radio officer, two years in the banking industry in Brazil, and several years in Australia. Yet his airlift time remains memorable. "As a National Serviceman, I am proud that I was able to put my training to good use," he concludes, "but I am dismayed that no official recognition of our service, including airlift service, has ever been made; no certificate, no medal, no thanks." He holds no detracting or negative airlift memories themselves, although he emphasizes that he and his colleagues were aware of what might happen if the Russians had been able to take over the entire city of Berlin.

Today Ernest is back in England, living in Hunstanton, Norfolk. In 1999 he attended the airlift fiftieth anniversary ceremonies in Berlin, but he reports that he is the only member of his original Berlin Signals Squadron who is a member of BBAA. Sadly, he has lost contact with all of the others.

PII James W. Peat, Pilot, Lübeck. Jim Peat won his wings as a noncommissioned pilot in March 1945 at No. 4 British Flying Training School in Mesa, Arizona. It was too late for the shooting war so, late in the year he joined the regular RAF for three years of active service and four years of reserve duty. This commitment took him to the Middle East for the full three years, followed by return in early 1949 to England and the choice to be based at either Oakington or Waterbeach. To make his decision, Jim asked the whereabouts of his dear friend **PII Ted Talbot**, with whom he had been in flying training. Learning that Ted was stationed at Oakington, he chose that station, happy in the knowledge that for once he had been given a choice in military postings.

Upon his arrival at Oakington, the airlift had been ongoing for six months, Jim's No. 10 Squadron was busily engaged at Lübeck, and he quickly found himself on the way to that northern Germany air base to take up duties as a Dakota pilot. "When I joined No. 10 Squadron, I found that air crews would fly the airlift for about ten days, then rotate back home for four days leave," he recalls with relish. This was enjoyable for

Jim, Ted, and other flying personnel, and as Jim points out, "it maintained the fiction that the squadron was still based in the UK, thus saving the RAF the expense of providing dependent quarters in Germany."

Given his late start on the airlift, Jim did not have much time to fly a significant number of missions to Gatow prior to his final flights in late July. "A round trip took about three hours," Jim points out. "We would have a meal and then do another trip, and that was a day's work for us." The next day he and his crew would start flying four hours later and gradually rotate around the clock until it was time to return to Oakington for four days off. "Generally, the Russians did not interfere with our flights, but once, while we were waiting for our aircraft to be unloaded, the airfield was buzzed by Russian fighters. There was also a flurry of antiaircraft fire in the corridor to the west, but it was only mild harassment, and we took off a few minutes later."

Jim might have been induced to remain in the RAF for a career, but he felt that the military environment was not friendly to enlisted men. "I loved the flying but realized I would be sent overseas again if I did re-enlist," he reports. "As an NCO, the pay was low for a single man but completely insufficient for a married man like me, and there was no certainty that I would always be fit for flying duties." Accordingly, he made the decision to move on with civilian life. He became a qualified accountant, then emigrated to Canada where he lives today in Don Mills, a Toronto suburb. Sadly, his wife Cynthia, who figured so importantly in his career decisions, passed away in August 1999, following a lengthy illness. And Jim, with physical limitations caused by arthritis, has been unable to attend any airlift reunions.

Sergeant Kenneth W. King, Army Loadmaster, Wunstorf. "As soldiers, we lived in poor conditions at Wunstorf and had to make the best of it," remembers Ken, a native of Ipswich in Suffolk. But he remembers, too, that given the pressures of the airlift, discipline was a bit relaxed. Now and then, he and his fellow barracks mates were lucky enough to get a long weekend at the British recreation center at Bad Harzburg.

At his Wunstorf post, Ken was in charge of German laborers who loaded the lorries. "My job at Wunstorf was to supervise the loading so that the correct food items were included in an aircraft load," explains Ken. His specific detail was to ensure that coal, flour, and other commodities stored in the supply hangars were loaded into the waiting lorries and then on the Yorks for air transport to Gatow. The RAF also maintained a loading operation at Wunstorf, as **Peter Izard** describes, but Ken was part of the Royal Army Service Corps (RASC); the two service branches nicely coordinated their efforts. "I was at Wunstorf on airlift duty from July 1948 until March 1949," he points out. "I then returned to my permanent unit in Hildesheim."

To Ken, his airlift time was memorable; the constant noise of trucks, aircraft, and other machines became part of the everyday routine, and everyone involved, he noticed, made a 100 per cent effort 24 hours a day. "It was a great humanitarian undertaking," he concludes today, and he was proud to have been a part of it. Yet with the prideful times came those occasions almost too sad to speak about. "Returning from the RAF cinema at around 10:00 p.m.," recalls Ken, "I witnessed an Avro York crash on takeoff with the loss of all five crew members. The plane was loaded with anthracite coal and burned all night."

Ken joined the army in 1944 and forged a fourteen-year career, retiring in 1958 as a staff sergeant. Following extra special training at Lanark, Scotland, in which only volunteers and regular soldiers with term commitments were accepted, he spent ten years with the 16th Independent Parachute Brigade, based at Hildesheim. His Operation Plainfare time was sandwiched in between. Part of his Lanark training had been in the art of air supply; hence, he was a natural for his airlift assignment. In his total years with the brigade, both before and after the airlift, he made approximately 100 parachute jumps.

Following his army career, Ken became a salesman with MARS, Ltd., the worldwide corporation that markets candy bars and confectionaries, including the well-known Mars bars. He retired from that second career in 1982.

Aircraftwoman Class I Joyce L. Peachey, Air Traffic Controller, Bad Eilsen. Yes, there were British women assigned to the Berlin airlift. They worked in many capacities—on the flight line, in hospitals, in headquarters units, and in special services, among others. A native of Brighton, Sussex, Joyce Peachey commenced her RAF training in 1947 at Uxbridge and Stanmore, specializing in air traffic control. Then, just prior to the airlift, she was posted to Bad Eilsen, at British Air Forces of Occupation (BAFO) headquarters, where she served through the end of June 1949. "I was in the control room and was one of the girls with the magnetic poles, plotting the routes of planes," writes Joyce about her service duties. "It was stressful work and tiring, but it was important to know the exact whereabouts of all aircraft, especially in the airlift corridors." She recalls that Bad Eilsen during World War II had been a "baby farm," where "flaxen-haired maidens had lived in splendor, provided they produced a child every year from the 'stud' of equally yellow-haired Teutons for Adolph Hitler's ideal Germany of the future. "Those babies must now be well past their mid fifties," she muses today.

Joyce and other RAF women were in the Women's Auxiliary Air Force (WAAF) which later became the Women's Royal Air Force (WRAF). At Bad Eilsen she met her future husband, **Jack Hargrave-Wright**, who was also assigned to airlift duty as a wireless operator. Both lovers and singers of classical music, they met in a local concert hall to the strains of the "Warsaw Concerto" and were married in 1950. While in Germany, Joyce continued with voice training under Friedrich Seufert, who had been a professor of music at the University of Frankfurt.

At one point during her airlift service, Joyce was dispatched with two other women on temporary duty to Lübeck. They flew in a Dakota that hedgehopped over the terrain, making them all violently air sick. "I lay on the floor and prayed for death," she recalls. Meanwhile, a request for accommodations at their destination had preceded them. Because her maiden name was Peachey, the Lübeck billeting people, thinking she was one of the other women's pet, reserved a dog kennel for her!

Following the airlift, Joyce had a splendid opportunity to attend teacher training, so she pursued graduate study in adult dyslexia, earned a PhD, and taught until retirement in 1989. Even now she continues to travel widely each year, lecturing at professional conferences and working in education. As for her military experience, she is very thoughtful. "I saw real life and struggles between nations and peoples, which I had never really understood, even during the actual 1939-1945 war itself. The Berlin Airlift Gratitude Foundation, which hosts our visits to Germany, has astounded me with its constant generosity in paying something back for that year, when we kept them going with coal, food, baby wear, etc. Yet three years before, we had been at war with each other."

Aircraftsman Second Class John B. Kite, Instrument Mechanic, Lübeck. "As a very lowly aircraftsman, having just passed out as an instrument mechanic from the No. 1 Instrument and Electrical Training School at RAF Melksham, I was told that my next posting, after a spell of leave, was to be to Transport Command," reports John Kite, who was only seventeen at the time. "During this leave a recall notice came ordering me to report immediately to RAF Oakington in Cambridgeshire." That meant only one thing to John: Operation Plainfare, because Oakington was supplying Dakotas and support personnel for the airlift. From Oakington, he very quickly found himself on the way to Lübeck to practice his trade desnagging instrument faults on the Dakotas.

"Lübeck was an ex-Luftwaffe night fighter base that had been operating Junkers JU-88s during the latter part of the war," John recalls. "The eastern boundary of the airfield was only two miles from the Soviet zone." Three fatal Plainfare crashes that occurred in the zone between November 1948 and March 1949 were unusually difficult to investigate due to the Soviets' generally uncooperative behavior.

But young John liked what he saw at Lübeck. "Accommodations for ground crews were sturdy brick buildings with large, double entrance doors to keep out the cold," according to his description. "Rooms contained only four beds with very efficient central heating. This was the epitome of luxury for RAF ground crews accustomed to Nissen-type huts containing thirty beds and two coke stoves! Herman Göring certainly knew how to look after his Luftwaffe." Nice, comfortable barracks were one thing, but working conditions were another. The Dakotas flying from Lübeck to Berlin hauled mostly coal, tobacco, and newsprint. This created real problems for the ground crews; even though the airplanes were cleaned and swept out after each mission, the coal and tobacco dust made them look like they had spent their work shift in a coal mine. When the dust caused them to sneeze, they all became enveloped in a huge black cloud.

John's airlift time ran from mid-October 1948 to mid-August 1949, and he remembers the winter of 1948 well. "When the east wind blows in from Siberia with the Ural mountains being the only natural barrier, you begin to find out what cold really is," he insists. "On one particular night of severe blizzards, all ground crews, even those off shift, were mobilised to sit in the Dakota cockpits and manually pump up the hydraulic pressure to ensure that the brakes were fully on," he recalls. "The vigorous pumping did help to keep us warm in the minus fifteen degree Celsius temperature, but it also prevented the Dakotas from being blown off their dispersal points."

After spending eight years in the RAF, during which time he attained the rank of corporal, John switched to civilian life at GEC Ltd., moving progressively from works foreman to planning engineer, and ultimately on to works manager. In 1993, always nurturing his keen interest in aviation, he and three colleagues opened the Museum of Berkshire Aviation in Woodley that is now recognized as the main authority on Berkshire aviation history worldwide.

Private Brian Cooper, Army Infantryman, Kladow. Nineteen-year-old Brian Cooper was apprehensive about being posted to the small, suburban Berlin village of Kladow, adjacent to Gatow airfield. His unit was the 1st Battalion of the famed Worcestershire Regiment, whose members were housed in Montgomery Barracks, once home to the SS. That his unit's location was only a hop, skip, and a jump from the Soviet zone border line was unnerving. "We were living right on the British sector and Russian zone border, young conscripts, still wet behind the ears and not realising that we were taking part in what was to be a monumental event of the Cold War," remembers Brian vividly. "We were kept very busy doing route marches, house-to-house infantry clearings," continues Brian, "drill, drill, and more drill, PT, range practice, camp guards, and on two occasions we provided guard duty at Sir Brian Robertson's' Berlin residence."

Brian's job during the cold winter of 1948-1949 was often night border patrol. Full length white sheepskin coats were available but not worn because they were infested with fleas. "I remember **Corporal Partridge** shouting our names, **'Woodcock, Wayne, Shredder, Pierce, Cooper,'** then the moans that followed, knowing that we were facing another cold, miserable night patrol, or guard duty at the Betelager petrol dump," recalls Brian, a native of Sheffield. Their mission on patrol was to stop the Russians from crossing over the border from their barracks and onto Gatow airfield where they would steal anything they could carry. The sergeant major, typical of his genre with a large, round, ruddy face and the traditional walrus moustache, had specific orders for his "lads" about to go on patrol: "Shoot the blighters, if you encounter them!"

"With these instructions," continues Brian, "we would patrol over the frozen, or sometimes wet, ground. One night, our patrol route took us past the Russian barracks on the other side of the road. They had a huge bonfire going, and as we crawled through the undergrowth we could see them as they all sat around singing and drinking. Many times we would rest up, then watch in wonderment at the glowing exhausts of aircraft, landing and taking off throughout our hours of patrol." At that time in their young lives, he and his colleagues were more interested in the creature comforts of off duty time than in the long, chilly hours of patrol; uppermost in their minds were the end of the patrol for the night, and the hot meal and cup of tea awaiting them. Now, a half century later, Brian, like all of us, thinks back upon that great enterprise with appreciation, saying, "Thank God for its success."

In later civilian life Brian worked in the construction industry, specializing in plastering and dry wall installation. In 1992 he was forced, for medical reasons, to retire, but he continues as a springboard diving instructor in Sheffield, an avocation he has enjoyed for 28 years.

Aircraftsman Edward W. Duck, Radar Operator, Wunstorf. In October 1947, Ted Duck was on a train in western Germany, heading for Berlin on four days leave from his radar unit at RAF Wahn, near Cologne. The train was halted at Helmstedt by the Russians, who alleged that its papers were not in order. "From the window we could see nothing," he reports. "With darkness outside, most of the blokes in the compartment dozed off and resigned themselves to the situation. Our train was delayed for nearly six hours before being permitted to move on to Berlin, where we arrived just before dawn the next morning." Ted's brief leave had been shortened considerably.

A native of Hull, Ted commenced his air corps training in 1943 as a cadet, earned a glider pilot certificate just before the war ended, then moved to the RAF in 1946 at age nineteen. In April 1948, Ted was abruptly posted to a master radar station situated close to the Russian border at a former Luftwaffe flying school at Wesendorf. "I settled in at Wesendorf," recalls Ted, "where I was extremely active as radar operator." His command of German was excellent; he had studied German for many years and now was fluent in the language, a factor which often came in handy. Speaking with an elderly German cleaning lady on the base one day, Ted learned from her that his unit would be moving to RAF Wunstorf in two weeks. Sure enough, it happened! The old World War II adage, "Loose lips sink ships" was very much alive!

Just as the German lady had predicted, Ted's unit was on site and operating in Wunstorf by the time the blockade was imposed. "The time at Wunstorf is impregnated indelibly on my brain," he notes. "I was active there from May 1948 until September, conducting radar surveillance of the air lanes into Gatow. My task was to keep a lookout for Soviet aircraft buzzing the air corridor from Wunstorf to Gatow and to ascertain their positions." And like all good noncoms, he doubled on occasion as a heavy goods truck driver. His commanding officer even pressed him into service as an interpreter. By late September, Ted had been posted again to RAF Uetersen as an education assistant; his active airlift radar involvement had come to an end.

Ted was not one to remain in the military service, although he did advance to the rank of sergeant. In a varied civilian career, he studied chemistry in London, then Cologne and Aachen, from which he received a doctoral degree in 1956. In his field, he directed research extensively and was a professor for 24 years. And having married a German girl, he has lived in Germany a total of 25 years. Today, he is back in England, living in Southampton, active in the BBAA despite a stroke in 1991, and reflecting on the massive effort to keep Berlin free so many years ago. "In addition to the airlift being a great humanitarian undertaking, it was a decisive factor in establishing the eventual democratic Germany in the west under Konrad Adenauer," concludes this interesting airlift veteran.

Leading Aircraftsman Terence O'Neil Crowley, Engine Fitter, Hamburg (RAF Uetersen). Terence Crowley was explaining his job to a visiting American airman. "Yes, I am the cylinder man," he said, responding to the pointed question.

"Well, in our service," explained the young American, "we have mechanics who specialize in carburetors, magnetos, propellers, and so on."

Terence was quick on the comeback. "I am afraid you are looking at all of them," he smiled. "I also fit new engines, run them on test, refuel, and generally ensure the aircraft is safe to fly in relation to its power plants."

The American was amazed. "No kidding? Then you must have a high NCO ranking."

"Afraid not," continued Terence. "I am known as a leading aircraftsman."

"Let me tell you, sir. In the U.S. Air Force, you would be a top sergeant with all that know-how." The airman left, shaking his head in mock disbelief.

RAF Uetersen was not a basic Plainfare departure air base, but it was an important cog in the airlift machinery, providing, with its fleet of light aircraft, vital liaison and communication between scattered front line air bases. It was also a welcome haven for airlift planes diverted from their home bases because of weather. Many VIPs, such as Field Marshal Bernard Montgomery and Air Marshal Arthur Tedder, passed through Uetersen. On such occasions Terence and his fellow mechanics followed a fixed routine. They worked in their standard coveralls—dirt, grease, and all—for repairs and servicing, but as soon as the VIP-carrying aircraft arrived, they quickly changed into spanking clean, white overalls and smartly hurried to fix wheel chocks, open cabin doors for the dignitaries and crew, and otherwise make themselves a neatly attired, visible presence. Then back to the dirty coveralls once more as the VIPs departed.

To prepare for his work as an engine fitter, Terence, a native of Brighton, Sussex, underwent an extensive period of training in RAF technical schools. Then, in July 1948 he was posted to Uetersen, remaining there through May 1950. From time to time, he flew to Berlin as crew on the base's seven-seater, twin-engine Anson used to deliver newspapers to the blockaded city. Such flights raised a bit of havoc with Vittles and Plainfare block times, however, because the Anson lumbered along the corridor at no more than 100 mph.

Terence served ten years in the RAF, attaining the rank of sergeant aircraft engine fitter, then moved to civilian life as an aircraft technical author, public relations executive, and technical publications manager. Now living in Coggeshall, Essex, he writes poetry, technical articles, and short stories. One of his poems, on the subject of the airlift, was published in the BBAA *Newsletter* just prior to the 1999 fiftieth anniversary reunion in Berlin. He has also published a small, delightful book of poems entitled *Meandering*, sales of which have raised over £300 for the RAF Association and the RAF Benevolent Fund.

Corporal Peter Izard, Loadmaster, Wunstorf. "I joined No. 51 Squadron at RAF Waterbeach in 1947 and flew with them as an air quartermaster on the India-Singapore route throughout that year and into 1948," reminisces Peter. "We then moved to RAF Abingdon and settled down to life on the new station." But Peter and his colleagues did not remain settled for long. On July 1, 1948, orders came through alerting many at his base for movement to Wunstorf and duty on the airlift. The first Avro York to depart was off the ground a mere 45 minutes later. Peter was on board.

The inevitable confusion existent at any military base in the early stages of a new operation was soon eased by the arrival of **Major Ken Crisp-Jones** of the Royal Army Service Corps. As Peter reports, "He brought with him all the expertise needed to put the ground side of the operations on a professional footing." Still, not everything moved smoothly; little gaffes persisted from time to time. Once in a while an aircraft was overloaded, and on one evening some bumblers put a York load into a Dakota. That's roughly a nine-ton load stashed into an aircraft that can lift only three. "Needless to say, the Dakota did not get airborne," Peter recalls, "except for the time it took to clear the train chugging across the far end of the runway. Fortunately, the terrain was flat on the other side of the tracks, and the only mishap was that the farmer out there harvested his turnips a bit earlier than he intended!"

Peter and his crew literally learned the tricks of the loading trade as they went along. Assigned to loading duties on not only RAF aircraft but also some of the civilian contract carriers based at Wunstorf, they became fascinated at one point with the Consolidated Liberators used by Scottish Airways, since they were the first tricycle landing gear aircraft on which they would work. Loading them presented a problem. "Just stack the flour sacks from front to rear until she drops back on her tail," explained the airline's flight engineer. Sure enough, when the captain started engines for the Berlin run, the Liberator thrust forward on its nose wheel and leveled itself.

On another mission to Gatow, this time in a Handley Page Halton, they were accosted in the corridor by a Russian Yak fighter whose pilot buzzed them from several angles. After a few passes he came so close that the captain rolled the Halton onto its starboard wingtip until the wings were actually vertical. At this point the captain cried, "What the hell," and continued on over into a slow barrel roll. "As we became inverted," explains Peter, "my jump seat came out of its clip, my head hit the canopy, and cigarette packets and candy papers came out of the floor like confetti." This four-engined aerobatic maneuver was one for the record books, except that it almost certainly was never recorded.

After Peter left active RAF duty, he joined the Royal Air Force Volunteer Reserve, similar to the American Air National guard, was later commissioned as a pilot officer, and served 39 years, retiring as a squadron leader at age 61. He is presently active in the BBAA as supplies officer and also served as supplies officer in the RAFVR (Retired).

Corporal Robert G. George, Draftsman and Surveyor, Gatow. Bob George arrived at Gatow in August 1947, well before imposition of the blockade. Assigned to the airfield design and construction unit, his job included building a new runway, taxi tracks, and hardstands. By the summer of 1948, with the airlift building up forces, it became urgent to finish the construction, as aircraft were taxiing and unloading on grass. "We knew that the operation would bog down in the October mud and rain if we didn't complete our work," explains Bob. His unit was small: a squadron leader, a flight lieutenant, pilot officers, several RAF technical staff, of which Bob was one, and some German draftsmen. "We also had an excellent German engineer maintaining liaison between the office and the work force."

Bob had to survey on and near the runway without interrupting aircraft landing and taking off. "It was sometimes necessary to locate the theodolite, or transit instrument, at the end of the runway on the centreline," he continues. "We lay flat on the ground with the instrument inches from the surface. On one occasion, absorbed in my calculations, I looked up quickly and saw a plane only yards away on final approach. I could see the look of horror on the pilot's face as I dove for safety to the ground with only seconds to spare."

At Gatow, the original concrete runway, only about six inches thick with no reinforcement, had been designed for infrequent flights by British European Airways. Inevitably, with the onset of the airlift, it commenced to break down under consistent, heavy Plainfare usage. One might say Vittles usage as well, for a giant C-74 Globemaster landing at the British air base made virtual rubble of the taxiway, too narrow for the heavy aircraft's wide landing gear.

An accomplished piano player, Bob soon met at Gatow a saxophone player and a drummer, so during their off duty time they began to do gigs in such places as the sergeants mess, officers mess, and Malcolm Club, all with their commanding officer's blessing. The threesome gradually grew into a reputable eight-piece dance band, and their fame spread around the British sector occupation community. Saturday night at the NAAFI club on Reichskanzler Platz was their favorite gig; there on one occasion Bob accompanied Bonar Coleano, the American film star, on piano.

But an RAF career was not for Bob, a native of Bristol, Avon. He left the service in August 1949, then pursued his love of architecture and design at the Royal West of England school of architecture in Bristol for four years, receiving his license in 1955. "After working in a variety of private and commercial architects' offices, I spent the bulk of my career in the architect department of the South West Regional Health Authority," Bob continues. "There I designed and supervised construction of district general hospitals." Retired since 1989, Bob now lives in Portishead, about ten miles from Bristol.

Aircraftsman First Class W. L. Ball, Engine Fitter, Wunstorf, Lübeck. "We were told we were going for only a short while," says Bill Ball, "so we took only a small kit, enough for a few days. That few days turned out to be a whole year." He and his RAF colleagues were given inoculations for yellow fever and other diseases endemic to the Far East. They were issued tropical kits in further preparation for assignment to the other side of the world, only to end up at Wunstorf. There he was assigned the task of servicing Dakotas, that is, giving the engines ground checks and generally getting them ready for flights to Berlin. Upon their return, Bill had to follow through on any faults noticed by the pilot and correct them for the return flight.

Bill entered military service in early 1947, not yet eighteen, and trained at RAF Wilslow in Cheshire. Following further technical training at RAF Cosford, he was posted to No. 77 Squadron at Waterbeach. When the airlift began, he was among those in Transport Command who very quickly found themselves at Wunstorf, where the Dakotas were temporarily concentrated. As organization of the airlift proceeded, however, Bill and his unit were moved to various bases, including Fassberg and Lübeck. "Living conditions at Wunstorf were not too bad," he remembers. "Since we were one of the first there, our squadron had the pick of what there was. But the other stations, as I remember, were cramped, to say the least."

Bill may have liked the living conditions, but shift work was another matter; it was nonstop, around the clock. Night work was the worst; many checks had to be made by torch light, and fuel had to be checked with dip sticks. In the dark and cold of night, it was difficult to get a true reading, and doing a preflight check under such conditions was challenging, indeed. His airlift duties continued through June 1949, always under the most arduous circumstances. Thereafter he enjoyed a series of post-airlift assignments working on Dakotas and Vampire jets, finishing twelve years of service as a corporal and personal fitter to Air Chief Marshal Sir John Baker.

Returning to civilian life, Bill studied building construction and mathematics at Lime Grove Arts and Crafts College in London, then after several years of owning and managing two shops, he worked with a building company until retirement. Throughout life Bill has used poetry as a means of expression, and he has written several touching poems about sacrifices made during the airlift, some of them published in the BBAA *Newsletter* and BAVA's *The Legacy*.

Master Signaller Robert A. Hide, Fassberg, Lübeck. One early summer morning in 1948 Bob Hide was piloting his RAF Dakota from the right seat, on a course set for Frohnau beacon in Berlin's northern French sector. Pilots approaching through the northwest corridor typically reported their position over Frohnau since it marked the first turning point in their letdown and landing pattern to Gatow. Bob's skipper, in the left seat, had been reading a book but then dozed off. Having logged 400 hours in the Dakota, Bob decided to take it on in to a landing, rather than awaken the pilot. Making the mandatory position report over Frohnau ("over the fräulein," in airlift jargon), he received clearance to proceed in the pattern, turn onto final approach, and to land. "With undercarriage lowered, flaps extended, and the runway dead ahead," explains Bob, "I suddenly decided I had gone as far as I dared and gave the pilot a dig in the ribs. He awoke with a start; I advised him that I had done my bit, and it was time for him to complete the trip."

"You have come this far, why not take it on in?" responded his skipper. "I like living," was Bob's deadpan answer.

Bob received his early training at RAF Cardington, then Blackpool for basic training or square bashing, and on to RAF Yatesbury for radio school. His first Plainfare station was Fassberg where he became the radio operator, or signaller, on a three-man Dakota crew. He carried out second pilot duties and handled all radio communications during flights. When the Americans moved into Fassberg with their C-54s, Bob's unit moved on to Lübeck, where all RAF Dakotas were being concentrated, and its members continued their airlift duties. From August 1 through November 13, 1948 Bob flew eighty missions, return trips, in British terms, before being posted to plush duty with a VIP flight unit. In this new assignment, he transported high-ranking airlift officials around much of Europe, visiting numerous American and British airlift bases.

In March 1944, Bob was on a bombing mission to Berlin when his aircraft was shot down over northwest Germany. He and the rear gunner were the only survivors. Badly burned on his hands and face, he and the gunner were captured by a farmer, then taken to the nearest village where they were treated with unbelievable compassion, sympathy, and first aid. "I could only conclude that being in a remote part of the country, they had no direct experience with the horrors of war, and therefore treated us humanely," explains Bob. During the airlift, this experience kept coming back to Bob and helped to mold his general feeling about the German populace. "I felt that I should at least try to reciprocate the compassion and sympathy that had been afforded me in my hour of need."

In 1955, after retirement from the military, Bob emigrated to Canada, first to Ontario where he worked another 32 years at Canadian Westinghouse as a senior electrician, then to British Columbia to be closer to his only son. But his airlift memories remain strong. "I remember the determination of all ground and air crews to complete what some thought was the impossible, and I remember, too, the willingness of the West Berliners to help us succeed."

Aircraftsman First Class David T. Hines, Radar Operator, Tremsbüttel. Where, oh where is Tremsbüttel, you might ask? David Hines perhaps asked himself the same question when he learned that he would be posted there during the airlift. "Tremsbüttel was an outstation halfway between Hamburg and Lübeck," David explains. "I had to set up and operate a radio/radar beacon there. My first task was to supervise the construction of the beacon site and decide on the positioning of buildings." When this was done, he installed a T1154 aircraft transmitter and a Eureka beacon transponder. David and one or two other persons operated the site, eventually developing it into a 24-hour activity.

David commenced his military service in February 1947 with training at the radio schools at RAF Yatesbury and RAF Cranwell. In early September 1948 he was posted to the Tremsbüttel site, remaining there until March 1949. It was very much a lonely and independent life, with no air base environment or camaraderie whatsoever. Given his geographical isolation from Lübeck, he was a part of the airlift yet did not feel as if he belonged to it. He and his fellow workers were billeted in transient barracks in Hamburg; and according to David, they were "appalling, being little more than the least war-damaged buildings in the city." Off duty time was equally as dismal. "We were miles from any other British military establishment," laments David. "We made our own entertainment or walked to nearby Bargteheide for shops and cinema."

A native of Harrow, David remained in military service for only two-and-a half years, serving also with an air/sea rescue unit at St. Eval. About six months after leaving the RAF, his health worsened, with the result that he was in and out of hospitals for the next five years. This state of affairs hampered his transition to civilian life, and he feels that the poor living accommodations in the Hamburg area had a lot to do with it. Nonetheless, he succeeded in building a successful career in the electronics industry, specializing in instrumentation. Happily, this new life lasted for many years past his airlift and RAF time.

Now living in Eaton, near Cambridge, David is busy supervising new electrical installations in his home as it undergoes extensive remodeling. One very important factor of his airlift time continues to bother David, however. "The strange thing about my radio beacon is that although I am a member of the BBAA, I have not met up with anybody who has ever heard of it." If nobody ever heard of it, then did anybody ever make use of it? He really should not be left with these doubts; hopefully, someone will come forward and confirm for David that his airlift contribution was not in vain.

Aircraftsman First Class Ronald E. Travell, Aircraft Electrician, Wunstorf, Lübeck. "I went right through the airlift, flying from RAF Waterbeach on June 26, 1948 to Wunstorf, where we had to organize the start of the operation," explains Ron Travell, an airlift veteran right from the first day. When things were running well at Wunstorf, Ron and others moved to Fassberg, where they did the same thing, then in the same fashion at Celle and finally, Lübeck. "If an aircraft got into trouble in

Berlin, I had to fly in with parts, fix it and come back, sometimes with a plane load of children, one of whom I met fifty years later during the anniversary celebrations." He was assigned on the airlift through the end of the blockade in May 1949, following which he returned to civilian life after over three years of service. "I could have gone for further promotion," says Ron, "but the airlift meant my job was the one the air force needed most for that period, and as I couldn't change to pilot status, that was what I settled for until I was demobbed."

Ron grew up on the streets of London, and as a young boy he watched German bombers coming in formation to drop their lethal loads on the rail yards near his house. "I lost school pals in the bombings," recalls this talented man who found it strange to be helping Berlin remain free a few short years after not only the airborne bombs but also the V1s and V2s exploded in his neighborhood. Later in the World War II period, he enlisted in the air cadets and flew in many of the famous aircraft types of that time. On the airlift, he was a specialist in electrical installations and repairs. He had to know other systems as well, and when flying on air tests to check out fuel lines, hydraulic systems, and engines, he usually got a chance to pilot the Dakota, or whatever aircraft he was flying in, but only on an unofficial basis.

Upon return to civilian life, Ron worked several years in telephone electronics, then moved to Canada in 1956 at the urging of a friend who had seen the wide world and implored him to "Go west, young man." There he moved into aviation electronics, joined the A.V. Roe corporation to work on the Avro Arrow project, and always the flying enthusiast, owned his own Auster airplane for many years. Now, having recently become a member of the *Spirit of Freedom* C-54 crew, he is enthusiastic about this fresh, new segment of his life and looks forward to many missions spreading the word of the Berlin airlift and the Berlin Airlift Historical Foundation, sponsor of the *Spirit*.

Master Pilot Walter "Dickie" Dougan, Fassberg, Lübeck. Dickie Dougan has spent a considerable portion of his life in the air—about 20,000 hours worth. Entering the RAF as an apprentice in 1934 at No.1 School of Technical Training at RAF Halton, he moved through his early training and graduated a year later. "My first posting was to 83B Squadron," he remembers. "I was friendly with the pilots, and I got a lot of dual time on Tigers and Hawker Harts." When World War II commenced, Dickie volunteered for pilot training, completed the course, and flew Vickers Wellington and Liberator bombers in North Africa. At war's end, he transferred to Transport Command and No. 53 Squadron where he flew Dakotas on scheduled runs in Europe and the Middle East.

At the start of the airlift, Dickie's squadron moved to Fassberg, then to Lübeck, where the Dakotas eventually were concentrated. "During the lift I flew Dakota KN566," he points out, "and 48 years later I happened to fly this aircraft again at Inverness. It still had a hole in the cockpit lining where I kept my pencil a half century ago!" On another airlift mission from

Gatow to Lübeck, Dickie had a passenger on board who was under close medical supervision and was manifested as an "imbecile."

"I was briefed to warn Lübeck that he was to be met by a medical officer, and Lübeck's reply to my transmission was '566, what is the name of your imbecile?' Quick as a flash, my pal flying two aircraft behind me shouted over his radio, 'Master Pilot Dougan!' "

Later in his lengthy flying career, Dickie was loaned to the German Luftwaffe at Landsberg am Lech in Bavaria, where he served as a flying instructor for five years. After retiring from the RAF in the rank of flight lieutenant, he secured a civilian pilot's license and continued to train instructors on a variety of aircraft, working at such widely separated locations as the United Kingdom, Africa, and the Middle East. Dickie now lives in Topsham, Devon, but his real home continues to be in the air. At age 79, he lost his license on medical grounds but now, five years later at this writing, he continues to teach aerobatics to licensed pilots.

Sergeant John Overington, Army Line Mechanic, Bückeburg. John Overington always felt that mandatory military service had its good points. "I applauded the idea of some form of National Service," he states. "Young men, removed from the environment they were raised in, have the opportunity to learn self-reliance, discipline, and to find direction in their lives. Going away boys and coming back men has something to commend it." Such a mood did not, however, impel John to seek a military career. Called to National Service himself in May 1948, he graduated from line mechanic training in October but was at the time anxious to transfer to the paratroops. This would have necessitated a two-year commitment, which he was not about to make.

"Instead, I was posted to the 11th Air Formation Signals Regiment in Bückeburg," recalls John, a native of Hersham, Surrey. "Our mission was to service the land communication network of the British Air Force of Occupation, which had its headquarters in a spa hotel in Bad Eilsen. With the airlift in full swing, this place was a hive of activity."

John's duties on the Royal Signals team took him to Celle, Fassberg, Gutersloh, Wahn, Wunstorf, and several other posts throughout the British occupation zone, working on and maintaining the communications network that was so vital to smooth airlift operations. Once, just once, he secured a completely unauthorized trip to Berlin on a supply Dakota. In awe and wonderment at the bustle of airlift-related activity in the blockaded city, he suddenly appreciated how important his own duties were.

"Most of the communications network stations were manned by Germans and supervised by Royal Signals personnel," John points out. "Many had worked for the German post office, were very knowledgeable and could speak good English. None of them were ever Nazis, to hear them tell it, and although I could not forgive them for the hurt they had caused the world, individually they could be nice people. But collectively, Nazis or not, they had been a bunch of real bastards!"

Although John and his colleagues worked long and diligently in their maintenance duties, service in Germany also had its pleasant side. "I played cricket, football, and hockey for the regiment and ran on the track team," he remembers with obvious pleasure. John was also selected, despite his army status, to play football for the all-Germany RAF team.

In February 1950, John was demobbed, moved to Canada a few years later to a job with Bell Telephone of Canada, then moved to the United States for a career with IBM. Today, he lives in Doylestown, Pennsylvania, has become an American citizen, and is a proud member of the Philadelphia branch of the Royal British Legion. He also retains his membership in BBAA. "In retrospect, I believe my service meant something," concludes John. "It was never tiresome or tedious, and I believe my role was a meaningful contribution to the success of the airlift."

Sergeant Victor J. Taylor, Flight Line Supervisor, Lübeck. "The variety of goods flown into Gatow from Lübeck was simply amazing," Vic Taylor remembers. "Loads of toilet paper, metal lavatory buckets, gold bullion, newsprint, flour, coal, of course, and even a goat mascot for the South Wales Borderers Regiment." As flight line supervisor at the Lübeck RAF station, Vic got a good look everyday at goods being loaded on Dakotas. And when they returned from Gatow, he almost always saw Berlin children and adults unloading after a usually terrifying (to them) trip.

But Vic's primary duty at Lübeck, although a bit at odds with his basic professional skills as an engine fitter, was actually a move up the ladder of responsibility. Based at Oakington in the days immediately prior to the airlift, he was senior NCO, an Engine Fitter I, in charge of the top ground crew responsible for keeping the Dakotas in running order. His crew was involved daily in the rebuilding of Pratt and Whitney engines for the four squadrons of Dakotas based there. Then came the airlift, the move to Lübeck, and his assignment as flight line supervisor.

"Before the airlift, I had an experience that I can't shake," continues Vic. "In 1947, I was selected by Transport Command to crew with No. 617 Squadron [the renowned World War II dambusters] on a three-month good will tour of the United States. I was ground crew chief on Avro York MW 288. A year later the same aircraft crashed on the first fatal accident of the airlift, with the death of all five crew members."

Vic completed twelve years of regular military service in 1950 and retired in the rank of sergeant. He then moved into civilian work in mechanical engineering, specifically in scientific instrument manufacturing, and retired in 1984, rounding out two successful careers. Now living in Girton, Cambridge, Vic, as a BBAA member, was interviewed in 1997 at the American embassy in London and appeared on the USAF video of the airlift.

What was most memorable to this RAF veteran about the airlift? "The professionalism of the entire operation," Vic emphasizes, "and the hard work by ground crew members who maintained their aircraft in serviceable condition, so that they could meet their flight schedules. Not enough of this devotion to duty has been recognized."

Commissioned Forces

Flight Lieutenant Graeme Bushell, who flew as a York pilot with No. 242 Squadron at Wunstorf, advises that Transport Command established several official categories of pilot skill and the legal load that a pilot was authorized to carry: 1) freight only, 2) passengers, and 3) VIPs, in that ascending order. If, for example, a pilot certified for freight only carried his load into Berlin but faced a load of German children to be flown back to the west, he could not take them. On the other hand, a VIP certified pilot was authorized to carry anything from a bag of coal to Field Marshal Bernard Montgomery. Such categorizations were determined by training, hours flown, and overall experience.

USAF pilot certifications were also of several rankings: pilot, senior pilot, and command pilot, based on number of hours flown and years of active service. Obviously, no freshly minted, young American pilot would be instantly eligible to fly the air force chief of staff around. However, the distinctions between flying skills and assignments during the airlift seemed to be less subtle for USAF pilots. They classified freight and passengers the same.

An airlift tale is told by **Lieutenant Duncan Ralston**, a South African Air Force pilot-navigator, who retired as a major general, and was one of 81 SAAF air crew members who flew with No. 42 Group. He reports that in a night thunderstorm and low ceilings at Gatow, GCA lost contact with **Lieutenant Tom Condon** on final approach, and he was advised to pull up and go around. As Tom maneuvered his Dakota around the pattern for another landing attempt, his crew jettisoned their 100-pound coal sacks so as to maintain altitude. One of the sacks crashed through the roof of General Sir Brian Robertson's Berlin house. In Duncan's words, "This was believed to be the only direct delivery of coal to a private home during the whole airlift!" On a more serious note, Lieutenant Condon was awarded the Air Force Cross for his airmanship in bringing the aircraft around the pattern to a safe landing. The following are selected personal experience stories as described by British and Commonwealth commissioned air crew members.

Flight Lieutenant B. D. Davies, Pilot, Wunstorf. Bob Davies is one-fourth German by birth. During World War II, as he was flying bombing missions against Germany, his cousin Erwin Bückle served with a Luftwaffe flak battery on Jersey in the Channel Islands. He was later transferred to the Russian front and lost a leg in heavy combat. Bob's two female cousins, Ilse and Marga Kaiser, spent the war years in the Sudetenland, only to be apprehended at the war's end by Czech partisans and shot. Marga died from her wounds while Ilse survived and lives today in Munich. It is understandable, then, why Bob had a variety of feelings about flying first in the war against Germany, then flying to feed Berlin a few years later.

"I joined the airlift in August 1948 as a member of No. 40 Squadron after it had left RAF Abingdon for Wunstorf," recalls Bob, a native of Gravesend, Kent. The squadron was equipped with four-engined Avro Yorks that carried about nine tons. "Our York crews worked on a fixed schedule," he continues. "It meant flying thirty round trips into Berlin in 21 days before returning to the UK for about four days, and then back to Wunstorf for another three week stint." While off duty during the winter flying weeks, there wasn't much for the air crews to do except sleep or spend time at the bar. Such boredom often led to an excessive amount of drinking by many pilots, but the summer months offered more recreational opportunities, such as sailing on the nearby *Steinhuder Meer*, having dinner at the clubhouse, or simply enjoying quiet walks in the lush surrounding woodlands.

During his time at Wunstorf, Bob had two experiences that have remained firm in his memory to this day. First, shortly after midnight on September 19, 1948 as he was making an approach to landing at the end of a return trip from Gatow, Bob was unnerved as he witnessed the fatal York crash of MW 288, cited in this chapter by Vic Taylor, and also described in chapter eight. It was the only fatal airlift accident at Wunstorf, and sadly, all five crew members were killed. Second, "As we climbed in on several return flights from Gatow to Wunstorf, instead of coal, on the floor behind the flight deck sat civilians—old men, women, sometimes children, being flown out to western Germany. Our only contact with them was when our eyes met as we walked past them to the front of the aircraft. After the noisy, bumpy one-hour flight with us, they left, and to all intents disappeared to, we hoped, better places."

Bob's rich, lengthy military career, almost all of which was spent on flying status all over the world, would fill volumes. Suffice it to say that he flew about everything in the RAF inventory, carried everything from freight to VIPs, was court-martialed in early 1948, but only reprimanded, for allowing his York to collide in midair with another York over Karachi, Pakistan, and retired in 1963 at age 43 as a squadron leader after 24 years of service.

Flying Officer Frank Stillwell, Navigator, Wunstorf, Fassberg, Lübeck. In late April 1948, Frank Stillwell's No. 30 Squadron, equipped with Dakotas, was ordered from its permanent station at Oakington, to Schleswigland for two months of transport support field training. Its members had barely returned to their home base when, only four days later, they were sent back to Germany, this time to Wunstorf, for duty on the three-day-old Berlin airlift. It was late June, and the first hurried allied responses to the Soviet blockade of Berlin were being implemented. Six Dakota squadrons suddenly converged on Wunstorf, followed not long thereafter by York units, causing the inevitable crunch, which Frank describes. "We in No. 30 together with No. 46 flew to Wunstorf on 29 June. The other four Dakota squadrons had arrived before us, and the accommodations were full, with rooms built for one officer now having four occupants. In addition, beds were put in the lofts of the blocks, with a rudimentary system of lighting." The operations staff organized quickly, however, and Frank and his crew flew their first sortie to Gatow the very next day. His pilot on that first mission was **Flight Lieutenant James F. Manning**, and his wireless operator was **Signaller 1 Leslie Barlow**. The three flew as a crew throughout most of their Dakota missions.

In July, with the flight missions settling down to an average of two per day, Dakota squadrons were moved to Fassberg, to relieve the pressure caused by too many aircraft at Wunstorf. Frank's crew arrived there on July 28. "Throughout August the USAF C-54s started arriving at Fassberg," explains Frank about the airlift task force command decision to move American squadrons to British air bases, "and during September the Dakotas were gradually moved to Lübeck. Our crew transferred on 18 September." There the Dakota squadrons remained until the airlift's end in late September of the following year.

In writing about his duties as navigator throughout his lengthy airlift duty tour, Frank nicely describes a typical mission and the use of his precision navigational equipment. After takeoff, and once the aircraft has reached flying elevation and turned on a course for Berlin, his work begins in earnest. "I now check progress with fixes from my Gee receiver and give the pilot a new heading to steer. Then I use my Dalton computer to check ground speed and ETA at the Frohnau beacon. About 70 miles from Frohnau the airborne Rebecca equipment will pick up the Eureka beacon at Frohnau, which will give an instant range indication." On each of his 265 flights, or sorties, Frank kept meticulous records of the loads he was carrying, ranging from flour to coal, to tinned meat, to dried carrots, and powdered soap.

Following the airlift, Frank completed a successful RAF career, retired as a squadron leader, and today enjoys life at home in Marlow, Bucks. Having served long and faithfully as BBAA secretary, he became chairman upon the death of Alan Smith. In thinking back to the airlift and its place in cold war history, he is reflective. "It was the greatest ever humanitarian undertaking, providing the essential supplies to 2.2 million Berlin inhabitants. If we had failed, the Russians would have taken over Berlin completely, with the spread of communism westward."

Lieutenant Steve Stevens, DFC, Pilot, Lübeck. Steve Stevens traveled a lengthy distance to fly on the Berlin airlift. "I was serving with the South African Air Force in Zululand, spraying three game reserves against the tsetse fly in ancient, twin-engined Avro Ansons, when I was ordered to report to Zwartkops, near Pretoria, for overseas posting," writes Steve. There, he learned that the movement would be to England, then Germany, to take part in the Berlin airlift. He and a small group of other pilots, navigators, and signallers eventually arrived at Bassingbourne in Cambridgeshire where they underwent refresher training in Dakotas, although most all had previous Dakota experience.

From England they traveled to Lübeck and No. 24 Commonwealth Squadron to commence their airlift missions. Steve got a rude awakening when he learned that he would have no second pilot in the Dakota. This was his first experience flying as a crew of pilot, navigator, and signaller, but he warmed to the idea. His signaller showed that he could ably handle right seat duties, including raising and lowering the undercarriage, as well as any copilot.

On one very wet night mission to Berlin, Steve had an experience that quite a few others reported during the long airlift months. His Dakota felt extremely sluggish on takeoff, causing him to wonder if it had been overloaded. "Perhaps we had been wrongly loaded with a York, rather than a Dakota, load," reminisces Steve. "I used full power, eventually made it to 5,500 feet, our cruising altitude, and fortunately landed safely at Gatow." On the ground, he left instructions for the number of bags to be counted, so that he could clear up his doubts. Upon returning from his cup of coffee, however, the aircraft was empty and the unloading crew had departed. Steve suspected that the unloading crew disappeared to cover up for their fellow loaders at Lübeck, who might be fired if the truth came out; he never did get to the bottom of the problem.

Steve's second memorable airlift experience is vividly remembered. On a midnight preflight check in the dark and in steady rain, he hastily skimped on the details. After takeoff, he discovered that his airspeed indicator showed zero. "I had forgotten to remove the cloth cover from the pitot tube, despite the long red warning piece of material attached to it that only a fool could miss," he recalls, as if still embarrassed about it after so many years. He opted to continue on to Gatow, using his knowledge of exact power settings to maintain speed and altitude. "Why didn't you burn it off with pitot heat?" asked one of his colleagues after his return to Lübeck. "*Ja* man, why didn't I think of that!"

With the airlift at an end in October 1949, Steve flew back home, resigned his permanent SAAF commission, and became a missionary pilot in central Africa, flying an old DeHaviland Rapide. In this capacity he became Africa's first "mercy flight" pilot, based with his wife and family on a remote mission station near the equator in South Sudan, one of the most isolated spots in the world. Today he and his wife Kay, having left their lifelong South African home, are enjoying retirement in Worthing, West Sussex.

Flight Lieutenant E. F. "Ted" Edwards, Pilot, Wunstorf. Ted Edwards has been around the block, aeronautically speaking. A native New Zealander, he spent his military career in both the Royal New Zealand and Royal Air Forces, flew more than a dozen different types of aircraft in his flying years, possessed the coveted green instrument rating certificate, and was posted to just about every air force station in the British empire. Along the way, he flew 222 Plainfare trips on the airlift from July 1948 through August 1949. "I went into the air force in 1940, did my initial training at Wellington, which consisted of square-bashing, route marches, and more exams," he recollects. "After that it was elementary flying training at Auckland, then senior flying school at Saskatoon in Saskatchewan, Canada. I got my wings in October 1941."

By 1947, following many interesting worldwide assignments, Ted had transferred to the RAF, had checked out in the Avro York, and had been posted to No. 511 Squadron at Lyneham, Wiltshire. Then came the blockade. No. 511 Squadron moved to Wunstorf, and the fun began. "We were on duty eight hours a day, doing two flights daily into Berlin for 21 days on end," he remembers. "Then back to England for a much needed rest of seven days. This just went on indefinitely; the only times we didn't fly were due to aircraft unserviceability or sickness."

On a typical Plainfare mission, Ted's navigator was **Flight Sergeant Eade**, the signaller was **Paddy Lewis**, and **Mike Malone**, a big, burly Irishman with a heart of gold was the flight engineer. "I always have difficulty in scrambling up on to the floor of the York because it is just a little bit too big," he explains. "On the second attempt big Mike gives me a nudge under the seat with a grin, which sends me sprawling gracelessly on hands and knees." Once the flight is under way, in darkness or in weather, "the thin shield of survival is those banks of instruments, our training, and our complete confidence in each other's skill and competence. This is truly precision flying, and it is carried out by every airlift pilot to the best of his ability. Few fail to take pride in this achievement, and there is no room for those who cannot do it."

On the lighter side, Ted points out that at cruising altitude on a return trip, the crew was fond of turning on George, the automatic pilot, and retreating to the main cabin for a round of cards, much to the anxiety of the already nervous German passengers. After forty minutes, the crew calmly returned to their posts, preparatory to descent and landing at Wunstorf. Ted's favorite remembrances are of his close, dear friend, **Frosty Winterbottom**, a soldier of fortune of sorts who had a colorful, worldwide career as a pilot. Frosty was to the Brits what **Sergeant Jake Schuffert** was to the Americans, a superb cartoonist who poked fun at airlift life with his sizzling, irreverent drawings.

Ted ultimately returned in 1951 to New Zealand to settle down, but he clearly savors the day in December 1949 when he was one of those presented to H.R.H. King George VI and the Royal Family at Buckingham Palace on the occasion of recognizing those who had taken part in the airlift.

Civilian Contract Flyers

One of England's civilian contract airlift flyers, **Captain Stan Sickelmore of Airflight, Ltd.**, wrote in July 2000, "I was talking to a colleague recently, who had been to the U.S. and talked to a number of people about the Berlin airlift. He was surprised at how little so many of these persons knew of the part the RAF had played in this great operation. I found a similar situation here in our country. Most people knew of the efforts made by the American air force and the RAF, but they didn't realise that civil aviation companies also made a big contribution." In fact, the need to bolster the RAF's supply efforts to Berlin brought numerous civilian carriers to the rescue, lured by the profits to be made from contract flying. Stan's company, flying Avro Tudors, was one of them. He joined Airflight in October 1948 as copilot to **Captain Clem Utting,** who on the night of December 8 was run down by a lorry at Gatow and killed. Utting's radio officer on that flight, **John Kilburn**, conjectures that the truck driver could have been a disgruntled German who perceived Utting to resemble **Captain Donald Bennett** of World War II Pathfinder fame, and in mistaken identity, sought revenge for "Bennett's not inconsiderable participation in the bombing of Germany." John cautions that this is theory only, yet plausible. As for Stan, he was very soon promoted to captain and made 226 trips to Berlin, hauling bulk diesel fuel.

Civilian contract flyers also laid claim to having the youngest. He is **Derek W. Hermiston-Hooper**, a captain with Bond Air Services, who flew 175 airlift sorties in Halifax aircraft, and who now lives on the Isle of Wight. Derek was all of seventeen when he commenced his airlift duties.

Throughout the months of the airlift, a total of 25 civilian carriers worked the airlift corridors at one time or another. They ranged in size from Air Transport and Horton Airways with one Dakota each, to Lancashire Aircraft Corporation with thirteen Haltons. Altogether, they flew 21,921 sorties and delivered 146,980 tons of food, coal, machinery, and liquid fuel. Their air crews also paid a high price; 21 were killed in air and ground accidents. The following are personal, eyewitness stories as told by airlift civil contract flyers.

Bert G. Cramp, Radio Engineer, Wunstorf and Schleswigland. A reading of Bert Cramp's memoirs persuades one that he was a happy-go-lucky, good time flyboy, in the tradition of flyboys everywhere. A generous portion of his reminiscences about airlift civilian service is devoted to off duty social activities in the downtown night clubs and pubs of Wunstorf and Schleswigland, where tipsy off duty flyers, both military and civilian, romanced the local women and on several occasions urinated in unison into the centerpiece fish tank at a particular establishment in Schleswigland known as the *Schlei Halle.*

Yet Bert got serious when duty called—again in the tradition of flyboys everywhere. A veteran of the Royal Navy during World War II, young Bert was then still in his teens, training as a pilot in Canada. The war's end brought an end to flying as well. "So I became an air radio mechanic in the Fleet Air Arm," he recalls with intensity. "After my release from the navy in 1947, I joined Lancashire Aircraft Corporation as a radio engineer. Then I left and emigrated to Newburyport, Massachusetts and became engaged to a girl I had met there during the war." Their engagement didn't work out, so Bert returned to England, rejoined Lancashire, and quickly found himself in Germany on the airlift.

Arriving at his first station assignment, Wunstorf, in late October 1948, Bert joined a crew of engineers maintaining radio equipment on the company's Halifaxes. "During the night shift the waves of aircraft were maintained by a three-man crew: an engine fitter, an airframe rigger, and a radio engineer—me," explains Bert. "It was an unwritten rule that if returning aircraft had no snags requiring the attention of a particular tradesman, that man would then help out with anything else, usually refueling and reoiling." Work shifts were twelve hours long, often in brutally cold temperatures and winds so strong that aircraft were blown completely backwards against their brakes. Crews worked seven days a week for five weeks, then received five days off to return to the U.K. or otherwise enjoy free time, after which the seven-day work cycle began anew.

In December 1948, Lancashire Aircraft commenced liquid fuel-carrying operations, for which it became noted. The early flights, however, exposed problems that had to be corrected. The fuel tanks, for example, had no baffles installed to prevent sloshing in flight, with the result that the slightest turbulence caused the tankers to careen all over the sky. Lancashire continued its fuel-carrying program as it moved from Wunstorf to Schleswigland, where Bert found better working conditions: good line shops, comfortable rest huts, and a great air crew buffet on the field. He enjoyed his airlift months and along with his ground crew duties made several flights to Berlin, often on orders to scrounge certain pieces of needed radio or engine parts from the wrecked aircraft dump. On one flight, a crew member suddenly shouted that the Russians were at it again. "Everybody on board looked out, and we saw a Yak fighter making passes at the several aircraft in front of us." He continued to buzz the line of inbound aircraft until he suddenly broke off and landed at his base directly below the line.

With the end of his airlift assignment in February 1949, Bert joined the RAF in order to fly again as a pilot. He served in Egypt and Aden, then became a staff pilot at the Air Navigation School, remaining on active duty until 1956. Still in love with flying, he moved to the airlines and ultimately became chief training captain for British Midland Airways. There was just one thing that would keep this flyboy out of the air, and ultimately it happened; he lost his license on medical grounds. But he has pleasant memories. Bert is now retired and lives in Crawley, West Sussex.

Ken Nichol, Flight Engineer, Wunstorf, Hamburg. Ken Nichol is another RAF veteran of World War II who in 1948 found himself on the airlift. He had served in the Middle East and Italy, flying on B-24s from the latter. Postwar life took him into the world of civilian flying—Scottish Airlines in Prestwick, Hellenic Airlines in Athens, Alpha Airlines in South Africa, and Eagle Aviation, based in the U.K. One of the smaller civilian contractors on the airlift, Eagle had hauled mostly freight at home, since the British Overseas Airways Corporation (BOAC) held at that time a virtual lock on the passenger business, according to Ken. On the airlift, the company had four Haltons, one of them painted bright red!

"My first flight was from Wunstorf into Gatow on 12 September 1948," recalls Ken. "And my last flight took place on 15 August 1949, going from Hamburg to Tegel." This was also the last civilian flight of the airlift with his pilot, Captain Villas, at the controls. He remembers it vividly. "We landed at 23:49 hours and took off again seventeen minutes later at 00:06 hours. It was my 258th trip into Berlin."

At Wunstorf the crews' only sleeping accommodations were in cramped attic space above the officers mess, so Ken and his colleagues were pleased when Eagle was moved to Hamburg. There they were billeted in a downtown hotel with all its amenities. This change made life a bit easier, but they still worked a twelve-hour shift that included loading, unloading, and three round trips of flying time. "It was just another job," Ken insists. But he does recall such events as his bright red Halton being "inspected by the other side, flying off a wing tip, snapping a picture, giving a wave, and peeling away."

"As civil carriers, our aircraft did not have access to the navigation aids used by the RAF," Ken points out rather remorsefully. "Even the VHF crystals for communication were borrowed. The ground controlled approach [eventually installed at all three Berlin airfields], however, was very useful in dirty weather."

Two days after the last civilian flight, the Eagle people returned to the U.K., and most of them started looking for other jobs. Ken found his in the design office of Fairey Aviation, Ltd., well known for its manufacture of carrier-borne aircraft. But down the road, carriers were not in the Royal Navy's thinking, and he once more went job hunting, winding up in the computer industry where he fashioned an interesting and comfortable career until retirement. Living today in Sandhurst, Berks, Ken retains his lifelong love affair with aviation and follows developments in light aircraft as well as events transpiring at nearby Farnsborough, the "home of British aviation."

David Lawrence, Flight Engineer, Fühlsbuttel. On the airlift, David Lawrence was based at Fühlsbuttel, flying Haltons and Halifax CVIIIs with Bond Air Services, one of the larger civilian airlift contractors. "But we were billeted in downtown Hamburg in the Hotel Baslerhof," he recalls today. "The food was pretty awful, but by that time we'd been through wartime rationing since 1939, so we didn't expect too much." The air crew duty shifts ran close to twelve hours, about sixty per cent of which were spent in the air. "Night or day, we generally got in three trips," continues this native of Watford, Hertfordshire. "The rest of the time was taken up with loading, unloading, refueling, and mealtime. We much appreciated the PX wagon on the ramp at both Tegel and Gatow. They had quite good coffee, and I was introduced to the American ham salad sandwich, often better than anything we had for breakfast."

Trained in the RAF, David flew during World War II with Bomber Command from May 1943 through May 1947. Being a flight engineer was a rather busy job in the British crew setup, because he was also the copilot, handled flaps, landing gear, throttle settings, and all engine functions. He was responsible, too, for fuel, hydraulic, pneumatic, and electrical systems. "On the airlift, it was the same. We usually flew with a crew of three: pilot, flight engineer, and radio operator. In rare instances, a specialist navigator, was available."

As his airlift sorties, which commenced on August 31, 1948 and lasted through the following August 15, continued, David remained keenly aware of the kinds of loads his aircraft carried. "We were still under food rationing in Britain at that time, and the butter and margarine we took to Berlin was all produced back there. I hope those folks in Berlin realized how deeply we were cutting into our own rations. We had candy rationing in the U.K. until 1950, which is the reason we couldn't join the USAF guys in dropping it to the kids. We didn't have any to drop."

David's 215 airlift sorties, despite the long duty hours, were, in his view, more or less routine, except for a GCA approach to Gatow late in September 1949, just days before it all came to an official end. The weather was wretched. "It got a bit sweaty if you got down to 200 feet and still couldn't see anything," he recalls as if it were yesterday. "We were, the GCA man said, lined up nicely, a half mile from the runway threshhold. Right about then we broke into the clear and were flying straight between the factory chimneys at Spandau!" Needless to say, they executed a missed approach and headed for home.

After the airlift, David worked at home in civil aviation, moved in 1954 to Canada, and then to the United States a year later, where he established a career as an advertising copywriter in Detroit and San Francisco. From this he moved into publishing automotive magazines until retirement. Living today in Florida with his American-born wife, he has joined BAVA but retains British citizenship. Looking back on his airlift service, David proudly proclaims it as "the best year of my life."

Ж

As with the preceding chapter, this presents brief biographies and eyewitness stories of British and Commonwealth forces members who completed the same questionnaire as did the Americans. In like fashion, the characteristics of age and career service are noteworthy. Those noncommissioned officers serving in ground support posts ranged in age, as of June 26, 1948, from 17 to 28, with an average age of 20.5 years. Unlike their American colleagues, however, only a very small proportion of them, 23.7 per cent, chose to follow a military career beyond airlift service to retirement Air crew members are included in this grouping because the number serving on flight status, unlike the larger American group of flight engineers, was quite small. Aircraft such as the Dakota carried no flight engineer, while most noncommissioned air crew members were enlisted pilots or signallers. Some mechanics, whose primary duty was the maintenance of aircraft, made occasional Plainfare flights. As in chapter four, those whose experiences are portrayed in this chapter are presented in the rank they held when first entering upon airlift service.

Most commissioned officers cited in this chapter were air crew members. Those in this category were older than their colleagues in the ground forces, as were their American counterparts. With an age group ranging from 18 to 33, they had an average age of 25.0 years, about on a par with the Americans' average of 25.4 years. These ages, too, are recorded as of June 26, 1948. With respect to remaining in the military service for a career, the British far surpassed the Americans; 80.64 per cent opted to fashion a military career, with most of the respondents retiring as a squadron or group leader. Two, however, finished their careers a step or two up, one as an air marshal, and one as a major general.

Finally, civilian contract flyers from many different carriers made an impressive contribution to overall airlift deliveries. Of those responding to the questionnaire, their ages ranged from 17 to 28 with an average of 23.5 years. And most of them, if they were old enough, had seen World War II service in the RAF; a few others flew in the RAF following their civilian airlift time. Most of this group, however, rather than pursuing or resuming a military career, continued in civil aviation and flew many years thereafter with major British airlines.

At the onset of the Berlin blockade, British forces rallied at once to forge a strong, committed airlift participation, backed vigorously by their political leaders. In a matter of months they were joined by flying crews from Australia, New Zealand, and South Africa, as well as by individual Canadians serving with the RAF. Still coping with food shortages at home, and mindful of the bombings of their homeland by the Germans a mere three years previously, the British, nonetheless, responded valiantly and selflessly to sustain the people of West Berlin through the long months of the blockade. Anxious to be a strong partner in the airlift operations, they called upon numerous civilian carriers to augment the RAF in hauling supplies to the besieged city. Their mission, as it was with the Americans, was to stand firm in Berlin, and they did so, extremely proud and thankful to have a role in that massive humanitarian enterprise that was the Berlin airlift.

Figure 20. RAF Master Signaller Bob Hide (left and friend. Courtesy Robert Hide.

Figure 21. Derek Hermiston-Hooper, 70 years old, March 2000. Youngest British airman on the airlift. Courtesy Derek Hermiston-Hooper.

Figure 22. George Morton, airlift teleprinter at Bushy Park, London, being introduced to H.R.H. Prince Charles, May 14, 1999. Frank Stillwell, BBAA secretary, on his right; the late Alan Smith, BBAA chairman, on his left. Courtesy George Morton.

Six

Berlin and the Berliners

Cold. Fifteen degrees below zero centigrade outside my window. Half the population freezing in their homes and offices and workshops because there's no coal.

William L. Shirer, Berlin Diary, January 11, 1940

IN HER 1981 BOOK, *Das War Berlin*, Susanne Everett, English-born daughter of a British father and a German mother, wrote colorfully of the euphoric years between 1918 and 1945 when her beloved Berlin strove to become a world class city. Humbled by Germany's defeat in World War I and torn asunder by political strife during the 1920s as veteran communists and embryo national socialists battled for supremacy, Berlin struggled through a decade or more of virtual self-denial as many of its citizens, and Germans everywhere, raced to compensate for the realities of national defeat, massive physical destruction, widespread unemployment, poverty, and loss of much of its young male population. Staggered by the harsh terms imposed on their nation by the Treaty of Versailles, and disillusioned by the inability of the Weimar Republic to combat rampant unemployment and inflation, Germans turned inward in self-pity and isolation; by the end of the decade they were ready to embrace a most severe form of nationalism by submitting to the national socialists.

In the capital city, a wave of escapism swept through much of Berlin's upper-class population as those who could afford it sought to forget the past by living only for the present. On the city's most prominent avenue, the renowned *Kurfürstendamm*, its popular cafes and cabarets knew no closing hour. Attendance at its numerous theaters reached record proportions, and in the "Golden Twenties," the arts flourished as never before.

cWriters, musicians, artists, actors, and actresses—all came to Berlin and prominence in that time. In the accompanying culture of loose living, drugs, and prostitution, Berlin became known to many as Babylon on the Spree. Although Germany ultimately succumbed to Hitler and his national socialists, Berlin survived the decade of the twenties and carved out its own distinct life style, despite the fact that the Nazis made it their *Haupstadt,* resplendent with government and military headquarters buildings as well as massive architectural construction plans for the "thousand year Reich."

Berlin, true to its tradition, remained a major center of resistance and indifference to the Nazi movement. Reporting on the German invasion of Holland, Belgium, and Luxemburg in May 1940, American correspondent in Berlin, William L. Shirer, wrote in his May 10 dispatch to New York, "The people in Berlin, I must say, have taken the news of the battle, which Hitler says is going to decide the future of their nation for the next thousand years, with their usual calm. None of them gathered before the Chancellery as usually happens when big events occur. Few bothered to buy the noon papers which carried the news." Many years later, Frank Donovan, in his 1968 book on the blockade and airlift, wrote, "Berliners were a rather special breed of Germans, somewhat cynical, sophisticated, and apt to regard politics and politicians with a jaundiced eye. Hitler's national socialism had much less support in Berlin than in any other part of Germany; Berliners had voted against Hitler so long as free elections were allowed in Germany."

Historic Berlin

Early in the thirteenth century, Berlin was a tiny, rural trading community situated on the banks of the Spree River; on the southern, or opposite, side was the town of Cölln. The two villages lay almost in the center of the Mark Brandenburg, a wild, remote, northern border region of the Holy Roman Empire. By constructing a *Mühlendamm*, a milldam, between them, the two towns joined physically, largely for purposes of trade and a sense of community. Later, each village dredged out a protective moat between itself and its riverbank; hence, the citizens of the two towns found themselves situated on a man-made island. Today, this is the Museum Island, in the center of modern Berlin, home of the renowned Pergamon and Bode Museums, as well as the National Gallery.

By 1359 the two towns had linked with numerous other cities of Europe in the Hanseatic League, thus nurturing their desire for greater trade and prosperity. By late in the fifteenth century, the city was enjoying celebrity status as the seat of the Brandenburg electors, but during this time the need for mutual security and defense prompted the two communities to formalize their unity, and so they merged administratively, taking the name of Berlin, although it was not until 1709 that they were officially merged by the first king of Prussia, Friedrich I, who ruled from 1701 to

1713. The name, Berlin, rather than Germanic, is probably of Slavic origin, linked with the swampy, marshy nature of the surrounding region.

By the time of Friedrich's death in 1713, the newly established city had a population of approximately 60,000. In the late eighteenth century, Berlin increased steadily in population as the Prussian capital under the kings of Hohenzollern, and by 1786, when the ruler Friedrich II (Frederick the Great) died, the city had grown to a population of about 150,000.

Das Brandenburger Tor, the noted Brandenburg Gate situated at the head of what is now the broad avenue *Unter den Linden*, is perhaps the most prominent symbol of Berlin today. Constructed during the regime of Friedrich Wilhelm II and finished in 1791 by the noted architect Karl Langhans, its grandeur is enhanced by sculptor Gottfried Schadow's majestic Victory Quadriga, the four-horse chariot memorializing Friedrich's battle victories, mounted atop the gate itself. Seven years later, Napoleon, flush with victory against the Prussians, ordered the Quadriga moved to Paris. By 1814, however, the Prussians had decisively defeated the French in a climactic battle of the Napoleonic wars and painstakingly transported the Quadriga back to Berlin "on six great wagons each drawn by 32 horses," where it was carefully restored to its place atop the Brandenburg gate. Destroyed in World War II, the Quadriga was replaced by a copy presented to the East Berlin city council by the West Berlin Senate as a gesture of friendship.

When Otto von Bismark, the Iron Chancellor, came to power in 1871 to found the second Reich, Berlin was designated as capital of a united German empire, at which time its population had grown to 871,000. By the turn of the century, it was one of the great cities of the world, with its population now 2.7 million. In response to its early twentieth century growth, Berlin's numerous surrounding communities were annexed in 1920 to the city proper, creating a metropolitan Berlin that provided a greater ease of administration, service delivery, economic unity, and political integrity. The merger brought the population of Greater Berlin to 3.85 million.

Airlift veterans remember that the Berlin of 1948, a mere three years after the devastation wrought by war, was not a very pretty sight to behold. Allied bombing between 1943 and 1945 destroyed almost one-third of the city's 1.5 million buildings, and the remnants of this destruction continued to scar the landscape for several years thereafter. Traffic flow during the year of the blockade was still diverted around avenues and alleys choked with the rubble of war. The people of Berlin continued to move about on foot, with bicycles, or by means of the partially restored bus and S-Bahn systems. There were very few private motor vehicles, and many of those that did operate on the city's streets were equipped with a strange looking, rear-mounted firebox mechanism that burned wood and belched a black, filthy smoke, causing the machine in some mysterious fashion to propel itself forward.

Geographically speaking, Berlin is vast. "[It] is bigger than all of Chicago," wrote Walter Henry Nelson, "five times as big as the District of Columbia, fifteen times the size of Bermuda, and just about as large as all five boroughs of New York City put together." Sheer size has given Berliners considerable mobility; this was true even during the year of the blockade. And despite the stark impositions of the blockade, those in the western sectors were able to view their plight with a grain of salt, which many attributed to the ample reservoir of forests, open space, beaches, water courses, and rural land. Water areas aside, open space itself covers well more than one-third of the city's approximately 889 square kilometers. In some of the city's outer reaches, where a few small farms remain today, people still speak of "going to Berlin" on market day.

The citizens of the entire city, east and west, have always enjoyed broad access to greenery and a general sense of openness and freedom not readily available in other large cities of the world. The *Havelsee, Tegelersee, Wannsee, Großer Müggelsee*, and other delightful bodies of water provide relaxation, swimming, sailing, and boating for the city's population. On the beaches topless sunbathers may often be observed. The famous *Grünewald*, green forest, in the city's western districts; the parklands of the *Tiergarten*; the Zoo, which was heavily damaged by allied bombs; and the city's numerous playing fields, have provided Berliners with a tension-easing environment, within which those in the western sectors have felt confident they could survive any crisis—the blockade included—that might confront them.

It is sometimes noted in casual discussions about Berlin that the city, because of its numerous parklands, possesses over 200,000 trees, but that there are also approximately 100,000 dogs running around. Two trees for each dog, so goes the conventional wisdom. During the blockade, however, thousands of trees were sacrificed for firewood in fervent attempts by citizens to secure fuel for heating and cooking. Berliners take great pride, too, in their noted *Berliner Luft*, that wonderful, exhilarating, stimulating air that wafts gently throughout the city and reputedly contributes to the distinct Berlin personality and possibly, well-being.

In addition to enjoying a favorable environment, Berliners are notorious for possessing a certain psyche, evident in some of the personal stories to follow. "Once a Berliner, always a Berliner," is a phrase that seems to sum up this mood. Another affectionate thought, popularized years ago in song by Marlene Dietrich, *Ich hab' noch einen Koffer in Berlin*, further reflects the native Berliner's romantic attachment to this remarkable metropolis. "I still keep a suitcase [sentimental baggage] in Berlin," rings true year after year.

Yet another quality characteristic of Berliners is irreverence. They simply have a way of poking fun at people, events and, if need be, themselves. Everything is fair game; nothing is sacred. In the 1920s and early 1930s, when Hitler and his national socialists were coming to power, Berlin's nightclubs and cafes were packed nightly as musicians and comedians, often at great personal risk, ridiculed and poked fun at "Uncle

Adolph," his Brownshirts, and the Nazi party in general. Following dedication of the *Luftbrückendenkmal*, the airlift memorial, in 1951, Berliners took note of its three arches curving skyward to denote the three air corridors to and from the city, and promptly dubbed it *Die Hunger Harke*, the hunger rake, since it resembled a farmer's handheld haying tool. In the 1960s, after the Berlin Wall had gone up and the East German government had constructed the showcase 362-meter TV tower high over *Alexanderplatz*, it was noticed that the sun's rays formed a perfect cross on the face of the tower's glass-walled revolving restaurant. Berliners, irreverent as always, immediately named the cross "The Pope's Revenge." When the Congress Hall, a gift from the United States of debatable architectural design, was constructed in the form of a huge shell, the citizens jokingly referred to it as the "pregnant oyster." Berliners today still cast a jaundiced eye at the architectural style of numerous contemporary and some proposed buildings, and for some they reserve the caustic comment, "This looks like something that Albert Speer [Hitler's architect] might have designed."

Capital city of the second Reich from 1871 to 1918, of the ill-fated Weimar Republic from 1919 to 1932, of the third Reich from 1933 to 1945, and of the German Democratic Republic from 1949 to 1989, Berlin is once again, since 1990, capital of a reunited German nation, the Federal Republic of Germany. Berliners and all Germans enjoy today a unity and a time of peace not too often experienced in their lengthy history. Through the decades, yes, through the centuries, whatever happens in Berlin or to the Berliners—war, destruction, invasion, occupation, blockade, partition by the Wall, peace now and then—its people always seem to shrug it off and then go on about the task of rebuilding, replacing, modernizing, always looking ahead to some distant time when the city might, just might, stand still for a moment. To the Berliners, and most likely to the rest of the world, *Berlin bleibt doch Berlin*.

The Berliners of 1948-1949

Another characteristic of the Berliners is that they are tough. As the barriers were brought down across highways, railroads, and water courses in June 1948, making it plain that a blockade was in full force, the people of Berlin's western sectors, as the implications set in, reacted in bewilderment and fright, uncertain of what the future held. Would the Soviets overrun the city? Would the western allies stand firm and resist? Would there be enough food and fuel for the 2.24 million citizens of the western sectors? These and similar questions were swiftly answered as the British and American military and political leaders came to the fateful decision to attempt to provision the blockaded city by air. It was the toughness and resolve of the West Berliners, however, as Ernst Reuter assured General Clay would be the case, that in the end proved to be decisive. They stood tough and hung in through the long winter months of 1948-1949, enduring the cold, hunger, and privations, until on May 12, 1949 at one minute past midnight, the blockade was broken and they were once again in command of their own destiny.

When the improvised airlift commenced operations, one advantageous by-product of the massive endeavor was the need to hire thousands of Berliners, desperate for work, in a variety of support jobs. Responding eagerly to the call for help, they found quick employment, men and women both, as unloaders, truck drivers, security guards, mechanics, runway builders and repairers, and common laborers. Securing an airlift-related job was a fortunate turn of events for those so employed, for it meant decent pay and more important, a daily hot meal.

Because of the Berliners' love for their city and their dogged persistence to help save it, the airlift in the end succeeded. Without their noble, determined copartnership with the western allies, urged on daily by Reuter and deputy mayor Louise Schroeder, it is problematical if the Soviets could have been stopped. In the following pages are the personal, eyewitness stories of a tiny fraction of those who labored long and lovingly to secure and maintain their city's freedom. Included among these are stories told by Berliners who were children during the year of the blockade. These stories were assembled largely from personal interviews and returned questionnaires, and in almost all instances with telephone, e-mail, or mail follow-up.

Some seeming discrepancies tend to arise from witness to witness, for example, Did Berliners receive one bucket of coal weekly or only one bucket for the entire winter? But all these events occurred a half century ago; memories have become fogged, and obviously, not everyone's experiences were the same. As Inge Stanneck Gross, whose story as a little girl in blockaded Berlin follows in this chapter, observed, "There seems to be a great coping mechanism installed in human beings, which tends to make them forget the bad and remember the good." Quite likely it is, then, that Inge has the answer to why people had trouble recollecting their experiences and why some even declined to do so. These stories that do follow, in addition to those told by Dietmar Kurnoth and Herta Tiede in chapter three, are those of a proud and determined people who refused to give up amidst an atmosphere of fright, constant uncertainty, cold, hunger, and deprivation. These are the stories of struggling Berliners during the blockade. In their minds, they were not heroes; they were simply ordinary people living in extraordinary times, doing what they had to do. In every sense they were heroes, unheralded heroes, but heroes nonetheless. They loved their city and were determined by any means to preserve it from the Soviet grasp.

Werner Demitrowitz, Spandau. In 1945, when the Soviet armies entered Berlin and crushed what scant German resistance remained, Werner Demitrowitz was a frightened, confused seventeen-year-old. Life looked completely hopeless for him and his family. "I had no real concept of what a normal life was like," he told me 55 years later. Yet as the allies took over their designated occupation sectors of the city, the young man rejoiced that his family's residence would lie in the British sector, even though the Soviet zone border was only a few blocks distant. With reestablishment of the city government and a program of rebuilding the devastated metropolis in force, a semblance of normalcy soon settled in. For the first time, Werner felt a new hope for the future.

"Then came the 24th of June 1948 when the Soviets closed the borders! We were devastated and shocked!" Werner continues. "What was to become of us? Will the western allies leave and turn West Berlin over to the Russians? I cannot put into words the feelings and anxieties that overwhelmed us."

In 1947, prior to the blockade, young Werner worked at Gatow as a laborer, wielding a shovel to construct the airfield runways. At the onset of the airlift less than a year later, he was building teleprinters as a specialty mechanic at the large Siemens plant in West Berlin. But he also was given an opportunity, under released time, to divide his energies and work unloading the American and British aircraft as they arrived at the Gatow air base. He and his fellow unloaders toiled on long duty shifts, happy to be part of the massive airlift effort to supply the encircled city. "The airlift was an adventure for the children," notes this modest, talented man. "They would get behind the propeller blasts and hold something to blow in the air." Werner, of course, considered himself too mature for such amusements.

Skilled in model building since childhood, Werner was tapped by the Hitler Youth to construct models of enemy bombers for classes in aircraft recognition. Then, during the war, he served as a specialized mechanic in a Spandau aviation instrument factory. Today, in his retirement, he has carefully crafted beautiful models of each allied aircraft that brought lifesaving supplies to the blockaded city many years ago. He has also constructed models of the three Berlin air bases as they appeared during the airlift time. And when the *Spirit of Freedom* visited Berlin in 1998, Werner and his family met its crew at Tempelhof and presented each member with a relief plaque of an airlift C-47 and C-54. His models, each of which required many hours of loving, skillful toil, stand proudly on display in such locations as the Allied Museum, City Hall, the Gatow airlift museum, and the Airlift Gratitude Foundation offices.

Today Werner lives with his wife, Erika, in their pleasant Spandau home situated only a few blocks from his childhood residence. His cousin, Maryann Kozelka, an American from Connecticut now living in Berlin, visits often, as does another American resident of the city, Frank Reynolds of Massachusetts, a civilian official with the Air Force Communications Agency. Werner remains eternally grateful for the freedom preserved by the airlift. "You flew in food and the basic necessities of life," he remembers, "but more important was your gift of freedom, hope, trust, and faith, the knowledge that you cared for the people of West Berlin."

Michael Foppe-Vorpahl, Wedding. As a small boy, Michael Foppe-Vorpahl was fond of playing ball in the streets with his friends. Trying to have fun in the midst of the rubble, however, was a challenge, but they made the most of it. Like children everywhere, Michael and his friends remained undaunted in circumstances that tried their parents' courage and determination. In postwar Berlin, even prior to the blockade, the standard of living was extremely poor as people struggled to keep food on the table and a roof over their heads. Then came the blockade, with its terribly severe restrictions on Berliners. But Michael revelled in the new found children's game of playing "airlift" in the streets with crudely fashioned model airplanes.

The Foppe-Vorpahl family endured the year of the blockade with its deprivations, then set about on a return to normal living. Michael finished his schooling, and having decided on a career in law enforcement, moved toward his goal. Down the road, he ultimately realized his dream of establishing his own private detective agency, setting up within it a special institute for white-collar crime. During this time he married his long-time sweetheart, Monika, and in due course they had a son, Fabian.

In September 1989, as airlift veterans arrived in Berlin to celebrate the fortieth anniversary of the end of the fifteen-month-long airlift, many Berlin residents were asked to host returning Americans and Britons for an evening in their homes. Michael and Monika quickly volunteered to do so and soon found themselves swept up in the excitement of drawing lots to match hosts and guests. My wife and I were pleased to be paired with the Foppe-Vorpahls, who picked us up in their Mercedes and whisked us to their comfortable apartment in Wedding, where we exchanged small gifts and spent a very pleasant evening, with dinner, wine, and good conversation. Fabian, then about ten years old, and Monika's mother, who lives with them, were also present. Since most of the Berlin hosts were of the age to have lived through the blockade as adults, my curiosity moved me to ask Michael, only in his forties, why he wanted to take part in this particular reunion program. "During the blockade, as you know," explained Michael, "I was a small boy. During that winter I contracted pneumonia. The medicines which saved my life were flown in by an airlift crew, and although I'll never know precisely which crew it was, this is my small way of saying 'thank you.' " At the end of that memorable evening the six of us said a tearful goodbye.

Horst Molkenbuhr, Wilmersdorf. Horst Molkenbuhr resides today in a pleasant, comfortable home in Wilmersdorf, not too far distant from where he lived as a teenager during the blockade. As my son Jonathan and I arrived for a stimulating evening of dinner and good conversation, our host invited us to his expansive wine cellar, from which he selected several vintages to accompany Frau Molkenbuhr's outstanding dinner menu.

Horst's family background is interesting and extensive. His great-grandfather founded the Socialist Party in Berlin; his father was also active before the war in socialist politics and was a party colleague with Willy Brandt, who later in 1957 was elected mayor of West Berlin and in 1969 became chancellor of the Federal Republic. His elders' involvement in public affairs came to an end, however, when Hitler came to power, for the Molkenbuhrs were Jewish. During World War II, young Horst, only nine years old, was sent from one Jewish youth camp to another, where he had schooling and played sports, yet still was confined to camp. He was permitted, however, to go home for short periods on occasion. No one explained to him why he was sent to camp; he thought his parents didn't love him.

After the war, the young man returned home and resumed his education in the regular Berlin schools. He joined the German Jewish Activities (GJA), a sports club for Jewish youth sponsored by the Americans. Its young members played table tennis, basketball, and other sports; they also formed several very good musical bands. As a sixteen-year old school boy at the start of the so-called Little Airlift in April 1948, Horst and his GJA clubmates were offered a chance to help unload airplanes at Tempelhof. They accepted eagerly and enjoyed the diversion, even though they were not paid, except for one meal a day. This action, however, which got them out of school every third day, lasted only a month. Later, when the big airlift commenced, the boys were called to be unloaders again. Even young Horst and his friends could see at that early time that there was little organization to the embryo airlift. As they went about their unloading duties, they observed pilots sleeping under the wings of their airplanes, leisurely awaiting the time to head back to their bases. Soon, however, in the same fashion that airlift procedures became modernized and more efficient with the passage of time, so did unloading procedures. By the time that the airlift was four months old, the boys were no longer needed. The airlift now wanted twelve-man teams of grown men, men who were not only physically stronger than the boys, but who also badly needed employment.

In the postblockade years, "it was difficult to develop a profession or even to find a job," explains Horst. "I worked long and hard in the women's clothing industry for six years, then, through a stroke of good fortune, became the director of a candy factory, but the job didn't pay very well." Following that, he was with the giant AEG conglomerate for ten years in a variety of construction activities. In the 1970s he moved into the insurance business, rose quickly through the ranks, and retired comfortably at age 65. "Like all retired people," says Horst, "I have little free time. But I still make time for tennis and skiing."

Gisela Irene Marianne Scholtz, Friedenau. For Gisela, her early childhood years were replete with difficult times. Only twelve years old at the end of World War II, she emphasizes that life was full of hardships long before the blockade was imposed. "We were on food rations since the 1940s," she recalls, "and things got really bad after the war. My mom, my one-year-old sister, and I lived as refugees in Kieselwitz, a small village east of Berlin and close to Frankfurt on Oder." As the Russian armies closed in on Berlin early in 1945, Gisela fled west with her mother and sister, hoping to reach the American lines and relative safety. For most of the distance, they had to walk, all the time looking over their shoulders in fear of the advancing Soviet troops. "It was all for nothing when the

Americans pulled back to west of the Elbe," she continues, "and we got stuck in the Russian zone."

Later in the year, they learned that her father, an army draftee last heard from in Italy, had been taken prisoner by the Americans in January, was released in July, and was in Braunschweig working as a janitor. The three secured permission to leave the Russian zone, but they could not take their little dachshund through the clearing camp. "Rather than turn him loose," explains Gisela, "my Mom asked one of the Russian soldiers to shoot him, but even Russians have soft hearts and not one of them would do it." Fortunately, they found a forest worker who took the dog. The family then made their way west in an open cattle car, reunited with her father, then took up residence in Braunschweig. Gisela returned to school, having missed a year due to the war.

"We should have stayed there in Braunschweig," ruminates Gisela, "but once a Berliner, always a Berliner." A few months later, in the spring of 1946, the family returned to their Berlin apartment in Steglitz, which had been partially destroyed in the war. Her father secured work as a city garbage collector, a fortunate turn of events because he was able to salvage leftover food from friends at the American army barracks who saved it for him in separate containers. Then came the blockade and the harsh conditions it imposed on all Berliners, Gisela and her family included. By then, there was a new baby girl in the family, and her baby carriage proved important to them as they foraged in the fields of the Russian zone for vegetables; the carriage had a false bottom that permitted them to smuggle potatoes back home right under the watchful eyes of Russian guards. Late in 1948 the family moved to Lichterfelde-West, always seeking to improve their quality of life.

"I remember the planes of the airlift," says Gisela. "If we had 25 pfennigs for the S-Bahn, my girl friend and I would ride out to Tempelhof and watch the airplanes coming and going. We had heard about the candy drops but were never lucky enough to be there at the right time." Gisela was fortunate in another way, however, for her father obtained a better job at a city children's home. A nice apartment with central heat and hot water came with it, making life much more pleasant for them.

Two years after the airlift, in 1951, Gisela met an American soldier stationed in Berlin. After much red tape, they were married the following year, and her name became **Irene Stevenson**. She and her husband then moved to the United States where they bought a farm in Burnettsville, Indiana and raised five children. Irene looks back with pride on her storybook life, despite its ups and downs. "Although we had many hardships in Berlin," she reminisces, "we always found ways to have fun during this austere time. We did all the normal things teenagers do—dances, swimming, movies, even an opera club in school. We survived." Today, believe it or not, she is a proud member of the Berlin Airlift Veterans Association. Her cousin, Alexander Gunkel, also tells his story in this chapter.

Karl Pohmer, Neukölln. In World War II Karl Pohmer was in the German submarine service, assigned to U-boat 161. Excited, as were all young submarine recruits, at the prospect of crewing on an *Unterseeboot*, he marveled at the sonar, radar, and other high-technology systems installed in his submarine. But his passions cooled down after the first several encounters with the enemy. "It was a dangerous life," recalls Karl grimly as he sipped a beer in my Berlin hotel room. "Many of my *kamaraden* did not survive. I was one of the lucky ones." By 1943 his unit was stationed at a submarine base in Norway, where the crew lived on King Haakon's yacht, the *Stella Polaris*, when they were in port. During our afternoon conversation he spoke half English, half German, and half body language as he recalled his wartime and blockade experiences.

The war's end found Karl in Copenhagen, from whence he moved on to Norway as a civilian until 1947, working on ships. Returning to Berlin shortly thereafter, he found his beloved city still in rubble and factories virtually nonexistent. He was unable to find any work in the ravaged city until the following year when the airlift provided him with employment at Tempelhof as an unloader. At Tempelhof, he worked steadily for an entire year, with the exception of a convalescent period following an injury on the job. A staff sergeant attached to the American hospital examined Karl and made the decision that he should not work for four weeks. While working, the hot meal that each unloader received on shift was a big plus; it was a real incentive to their performance. Yet he and his fellow unloaders were very proud of their work, at any rate, in service of their besieged city, and they strove constantly for maximum efficiency.

Karl's work schedule ran from 0600 to 1400 hours; then it rotated after a few weeks from 1400 to 2200 hours; and again it moved from 2200 to 0600 hours. "There were twelve men on my unloading team, including a disagreeable former SS man," Karl reminisces, "and our best unloading time was a record three minutes and two seconds! I know of no other team that ever beat that time. We were all very proud that day." Because he had learned English in school, he enjoyed speaking with the pilots and flight engineers as they awaited their aircraft unloading, always asking them where in the states they came from.

Now retired from a satisfying career as a customs official, but still living in the same Neukölln district house, 100 meters from the former Russian sector, where he was born in 1924 and in which he grew up, Karl enjoys coffee and pastries almost every day with his daughter, who lives next door. One son also lives in Berlin while a second makes his home in Bavaria. Thinking back on the airlift time, he remembers such events as a U.S. Air Force flying boxcar delivering an ambulance in early 1949 to Tempelhof, as his team was busily unloading a C-54. He and his family endured the deprivations wrought by the blockade—only four hours of electricity a day, washing and cooking late at night, and learning to do without—which are now just memories. But his proudest memory is of 1999 and the fiftieth anniversary Berlin celebrations when he and other civilian laborers who did the dirty work of the airlift were honored guests at the May 12 official anniversary functions.

Eva Beeskow, Steglitz. Another lifelong *Berlinerin* is Eva Beeskow, who early in the occupation took a job with the U.S. Army as an ordnance supply specialist. With this job, she was able to support herself and her widowed mother, with whom she lived in Steglitz. Her father died when Eva was only five years old. Happy in her work, and surrounded by friendly and helpful co-workers, she served in her position from January 1946 until retirement on March 31, 1989, a total of 43 years. Through her work, she benefited from numerous amenities, including access to the regular American daily diet, a huge plus factor in those days when food was scarce, even prior to the blockade.

During the blockade, an incident occurred that, because of her fluency in English, led to her being called as an interpreter at a court-martial proceeding. "While unloading the planes," Eva explains, "an American GI stole sacks of sugar, took them to his German girl friend, and she and her family sold the sugar on the black market, making a lot of money for the GI." The soldier was eventually caught and brought before the court, together with his girl friend and her family as witnesses. He was found guilty but according to Eva, he got off lightly with a demotion in rank, a fine, and an assignment to clean up the compound for a few months. She tells this story to emphasize that although such crimes occurred during the airlift, only a small number were covered by the press.

In school Eva studied "Oxford" English for six years, and as a result, she had a bit of difficulty getting started on her job, surrounded by Americans who spoke a different sounding version of English. For a lengthy period of time it was hard for her to understand "American" English. With constant daily exposure, however, to English as spoken by Yanks, she soon made the transition. Before long, she was accused of having a southern drawl!

In September 1999, Eva unexpectedly encountered the airlift veterans at their annual reunion, this time in St. Louis, where she maintains an apartment and visits two or three times a year. What a fortunate turn of events for her! "It was such a joy and coincidence that I was able to meet all of you in St. Louis," Eva writes. "It was a chance to finally say 'Thanks' for all you did for West Berlin. Thank you again for your help, for an outstanding and also dangerous job. We Berliners will never forget that!" Now, after a virtual lifetime of working for the Americans, she feels fully Americanized and spends an increasing amount of time in St. Louis. "I still love Berlin," insists this amazing lady, "but my heart is more and more American."

Louis von Egloff, Tempelhof. Literature of the blockade often mentions that Berliners from all walks of life worked side by side to help unload airplanes, build and repair runways, drive trucks, and perform the many other tasks required to keep the airlift going. Former doctors, teachers, other professionals, and blue collar workers of many backgrounds answered the call to preserve their city, even some whose family name marks them as of the nobility at some time in the distant past. Louis von Egloff is one. He traces his ancestry as far back as 745 A.D. and the tiny village of Egloffstein in the Jura mountains just north of Nurnberg. The family was Prussian and in later years all from Berlin. "My great grandfather," says Louis, "took Marshall Ney, Napoleon's top general, prisoner in 1813 in the Battle of Dennewitz. But my grandfather was the last one in the family to have any money," he notes with a smile.

During the war Louis moved with his parents to eastern Germany near Chemnitz, to escape the allied bombing. When Dresden was bombed by the allies, he was sent to Bratislava in the former Czechoslovakia where he attended school for almost a year. Then, at war's end, he and his mother made their way back, hoping to return to Chemnitz. When they learned that the city would be in the Russian occupation zone, they decided to push on to Berlin, to which his father had returned earlier. But with no trains or buses, they had to walk almost the entire distance, pushing a little handcart over bombed out bridges and roads until they reached their destination. In Berlin, young Louis, desperately needing work, was lucky enough to find a job clearing rubble from bombed out buildings.

When the blockade commenced on June 24, 1948, Louis was barely nineteen. He had been too young to serve in World War II, but he clearly remembers the devastation and destruction that reduced Berlin and other cities to rubble. He was fortunate enough to secure a job at Tempelhof air base laying pierced steel planking (PSP) on the runway. "Then I graduated to rock crusher operator, crushing cobblestones from Berlin's streets for the building of the runway extension," he recalls. The work was very hard; the work shift was normally eight hours, seven days a week, but often he and his fellow workers labored twelve or more hours a day. "I don't remember how much money I made, but it was the most I had ever earned, and the hot meal every day was the best part of the job."

Louis also remembers working on runway repairs, a task requiring the laborers to be fleet of foot. As the giant airplanes neared touchdown on their final approach, the workers filling in runway dips and holes had to scurry out of the way, then hurry back to their task between landings. On one occasion after they had filled in runway portions with fresh cement, a Skymaster bogged down in the newly poured mixture and had to be painstakingly extracted from its embarrassing dilemma. Feeling lucky to have a job, Louis liked his work and enjoyed good relations with his American army supervisors during the seven months he was at Tempelhof. They were so good, in fact, that one GI friend even taught him, to his great delight, to drive a truck and a caterpillar tractor, something that didn't happen to too many civil laborers.

In 1955 Louis emigrated to the United States, settled in California, worked 22 years as a radio and television mechanic at Sears, and later worked in sales. "I have never been back to Germany," he says a bit wistfully. And although he is a BAVA member, regretfully he has not been able to attend any of the recent annual reunions.

Rainer Baronsky, Wilmersdorf. Rainer was driving his 1942 American jeep to the end of the Tempelhof runway. It was the same jeep in which General Clay rode during his years in Berlin as commander of U.S. forces in Germany, and Rainer had acquired it in 1970. Riding in the jeep with him were Sylvia Rakow, his longtime lady friend, and Gerry Munn, from Bradenton, Florida, whose personal story is seen in chapter four. "See, Rainer," says Gerry, a member of the *Spirit of Freedom* crew visiting Tempelhof in June 1998 for the fiftieth anniversary observances of the airlift's beginning, "this is Runway 28, where I came down with the plane, every time." Gerry, of course, was referring to the distant past, fifty years earlier, when he was an airlift pilot flying the Rhein-Main to Berlin run.

In 1945, late in the war, Rainer, his parents, his brother, and his grandmother fled Berlin and made their way to Hamburg to stay with his other grandparents. It took them six weeks of walking through thick woods, part of the time with all of them riding an old motorcycle with a handwagon hooked to it. At the end of the year, his father hopped a coal train back to Berlin to check on their apartment, and finding it in good order, sent for the family to come back. Once a Berliner, always a Berliner.

When the blockade was imposed, Rainer was an eleven-year-old boy, playing with his friends after school in the streets choked with rubble and devoid of traffic. "We were always hungry, always cold," remembers this personable Berliner, 62 years old when we talked in March 2000. "The schools were open from 8:00 a.m. until 2:00 p.m.; after that there was no more heat. We had to rustle our potatoes and vegetables from the Soviet zone and bring them home in a wheelbarrow."

One day, as he and his brother were listening to the noise of many airplane engines and watching the heavens filled with Skymasters, they hurried to the nearest S-Bahn station, sneaked past the gate controller as they had no money, and rode to Tempelhof. Together with other children and adults, they climbed the small mountain of rubble close to the end of the runway. Suddenly, tiny parachutes filled the air; all the children screamed and ran toward them as they reached the ground, not knowing immediately what was dangling from them as they fell. "One parachute got snagged in a tree, so we took a long stick and jarred it loose," remembers Rainer as if it were yesterday. "My little brother and I opened up the package dangling from the bottom of the chute and found candy! What was candy? We would later find out about its sweet chocolate taste—Hershey bars, Butterfingers—it all looked so good." But they took it home where their father that night explained that it was sweets from the Americans. They then proceeded to divide the chocolate bars into five pieces, and they chewed the gum that also came in the package. The next day they dipped the gum wad in the sugar bowl and started all over again.

On Sundays Rainer always ran to his grandmother's (Oma's) apartment, about fifteen minutes away, to fetch her newspaper that she had read, and take it home for his parents to read. On one particular Sunday, he came upon two American GIs fast asleep outside Oma's door. Rainer was alarmed; Oma lived on the fifth floor. What were they doing up there?

An hour later they woke up, knocked on the door, Oma let them in, and one of them commenced to play Glenn Miller's "In the Mood" on her piano. Having brought some Maxwell House coffee with them, they asked Oma to brew a pot. Other friends in the apartment house, plus more GIs who happened to be MPs, joined in with bourbon whiskey and cigarettes, and Rainer suddenly was a little boy participating in a grown-up party that he has never forgotten.

Ursula Alker, Staaken. In 1948 Ursula was a 25-year-old, living in her elderly parents' home and acting, since the end of the war, as the family breadwinner. The house was situated smack on the border between the British sector and the Russian zone, so much so that she always exited and returned to the house door that faced towards the British side, since the Russians patrolled the area on the other side.

When the blockade began, Ursula had been unloading cargo from ships with a wheelbarrow and loading it onto conveyor belts. It was tough work, but it got her a class 2 food card and later a job at Gatow airfield, helping to unload and control the cargo that the huge Yorks airlifted from Wunstorf. "We worked in three shifts, seven days a week," she reminisces. "Nobody ever dared get sick. For the early shift, I left home in Staaken, in northwest Berlin, at 7:00 a.m. and traveled in an old Haru bus to Klosterstrasse. From there we were picked up by a British military truck and driven to Gatow."

At Gatow, Ursula's foreman assigned the women to Hall 6 where they all handled cargo but were actually responsible only for controlling it through an accurate count. "Nobody ever had enough to eat during the blockade, so it was important to make sure that nothing disappeared," she continues. "Often whole parcels of chocolate were ransacked." Sugar, chocolate, dried carrots, and the ubiquitous potato powder (pom), and other food products were all flown to Gatow and then distributed throughout the many city districts by means of a well-organized system. Compared to many other Berliners, Ursula feels that she and her fellow workers did quite well in terms of having enough to eat. At noon on the job, the British served the workers a gruel of corned beef, some dried potatoes, and margarine. What was left over she wrapped in her work coat and took home to her father and sister.

In the autumn of 1948, after Ursula had been working for several months at Gatow, the one-millionth ton of food supplies arrived at the airfield. Amid much fanfare, the York bringing it in came to a stop on the tarmac with flags flying and zeros denoting "one million" flapping in the wind. So many reporters monopolized the scene that no one else could get near the aircraft. Ursula was supposed to provide an accurate count for the one millionth ton, but she maintained that it was simply impossible to do so. As a result, she wrote in her report, "Millionth ton—not possible to count."

Alexander Gunkel, Friedenau. During the blockade Alexander was a seventh grader in the Rheingau high school, in which the junior high and high schools were traditionally combined. "I don't recall specifically looking for airlift planes," he says today. "One reason was that during the daytime I was in school and thereafter did my homework and performed what odd tasks had to be done." Such tasks included gathering fallen twigs and branches after a storm, with which to start a quick, hot fire in the kitchen stove. Firewood was very scarce and hard to obtain. "One day we took a flat handcart by streetcar to Dahlem where we owned some property," Alexander remembers. "There we cut down a fir tree, cut it into one meter lengths, loaded them on the cart, and returned by streetcar to Friedenau." He recalls, too, that older men sometimes dug out tree stumps and hauled them home, so serious was the fuel shortage. "In a search for firewood, my Uncle Hans and my aunt tore down a wooden slat fence one night," he continues. "She kept a watch for the police, and if they approached, the couple embraced and pretended to be lovers." They then toted the slats safely home in a gunny sack. Each family received about one bucket of coal per week, a ration that didn't go very far. People were cold most of the time, so they dressed in extra clothing, and at night the feather beds kept them warm.

The situation over food was as grim as it was over firewood. "My family, which consisted of my widowed mother, my grandmother, three boys, and a girl, was allotted one stick of margarine a week," Alexander points out as if it were yesterday. "My grandmother sliced it so thin, you couldn't see it when spread on a slice of dark bread."

Alexander's fortunes changed considerably after the airlift, and events thereafter altered his life in a way he never could have imagined as a small boy during the blockade. In 1950 his mother married an American air force sergeant; the entire family then moved to Prosser, Washington, and Alexander commenced a formal education regimen that resulted eventually in bachelor and master degrees at Washington State College. There, through ROTC, he also earned a commission in the army medical service corps, served the obligatory two years of active duty, and then moved to reserve activity until retirement in 1987 as a lieutenant colonel, a storybook accomplishment for a young boy from Berlin! In the late 1970s, he was awarded a doctoral degree in cultural anthropology from Southern Illinois University, but due to a glut of PhDs and a dearth of teaching positions, Alexander moved into the health field, ultimately accepting a position with the Veterans Administration in Kansas City as a surgical instrument technician.

Alexander's marriage to Rozanna Kaaz in 1979 ended in a 1995 divorce, but the couple had two daughters who remain very much a part of his life. Now, as he looks back upon a varied, interesting dual career in both the military and civilian worlds, he contemplates retirement and whatever comes beyond it. "Thus, in a sense, we have come full circle," says Alexander of his rich experiences. "During the airlift, the U.S. Air Force helped us Berliners, and now I, the former Berliner, help U.S. veterans, including of course, even airlift veterans, at the Kansas City Veterans Hospital." Needless to say, in view of his many, varied lifelong experiences, Alexander maintains membership in BAVA.

Ilse Moschberger, Prenzlauerberg. At the end of the war, Ilse Moschberger was living in Meissen, near Dresden, with her widowed mother. She remembers nothing about Bremerhaven, where she was born, since her parents moved from that northern port city to Lörrach near the Swiss border, when she was only six months old. As a customs official, her father had to move frequently; the family lived, after Lörrach, in Mannheim, then Heidelberg. There she spent her school years, and tragically, there her father died in an accident. After that it was a move to Rostock on the North Sea, to her mother's hometown. Then on to Meissen and life under the Russian occupation. In Meissen her mother bought a small business that she eventually sold to an East Berlin family who exchanged their Prenzlauerberg apartment in payment. So Ilse and her mother moved to Berlin and into the apartment, while Ilse first attended interpreter college, then later secured an office job with the British Control Commission for Germany (CCG) as a bilingual shorthand typist.

In those preblockade years, it was still possible to travel freely and without fear throughout the city; Ilse experienced little trouble living in the Russian sector while working in the British sector. She enjoyed her work, which continued through the blockade years of 1948-1949. She points out "that in the constricted environment of the blockade, with food rationing and barely any daily necessities in the shops, people looked like skeletons; many of them became ill. There were plenty of Russian guards about, but in such a big city they had to spread themselves out, whereas in a small town like Meissen they were everywhere." Still, life slowly improved for her and her mother.

While honing her language and secretarial skills on the job, Ilse kept up a correspondence with long-standing friends in the International Friendship League in London, who ultimately invited her to visit. She used their letter of invitation and a strong supporting letter from her superiors at the CCG to secure permission to leave Berlin on a Plainfare aircraft. The paperwork was slow-moving and painstaking, but she ultimately received approval. "I was flown from Gatow Flugplatz on 10 May 1949 to Lübeck-Blankensee," says Ilse, whose name through translation and marriage is now **Barbara Fairall**. "I had left behind my widowed mother in East Berlin." Although the blockade was lifted two days later, Ilse had spent weeks completing formalities to secure temporary travel papers valid through September 1950. Her plans had been set in motion, not to be lightly halted. "We flew in one of the small cargo aircraft, coal dust still being brushed off the seats that were to be used by passengers." From Lübeck she traveled to Bremen, then to the Hook of Holland where she boarded a boat for Harwich and a six-month stay in England.

Instead of returning to Berlin, where she had lived for only two years before and during the blockade, she found work with the British Disposals Group in Hamburg and remained there for a year and a half until she returned to England permanently. Shortly before the notorious Berlin Wall was constructed in 1961, Barbara succeeded in extricating her mother from East Berlin and moving her to England.

Today, happy with life in England, Barbara is retired from her own cosmetic import business that she built up and directed for many years. One evening a few years ago, she was watching a television program that suddenly evoked faded memories. "It was not until I saw the TV documentary *Secret History, The Berlin Airlift*, that I realized I had taken part in an historic event," she recalls. Viewing it prompted her to contact Geoffrey Smith, editor of the British Berlin Airlift Association's *Newsletter*. She is now a proud member of BBAA.

Inge Stanneck, Steglitz. Inge and I met in September 1999 at BAVA's St. Louis reunion. Now Inge Gross, she has lived in the United States since 1954 and as an active BAVA member attends each annual reunion with her husband, Mal. Her story of life as a little thirteen-year-old girl in blockaded Berlin, which she has written in memoir form, is heart-stirring. "We were all swept away by the spirit of the airlift," explains Inge. "To hear the plane's engines above us, continuously, day and night, was very reassuring. But how can it last? How long can they keep supplies coming at this impossible rate?" Such questions were on every Berliner's mind.

During the blockade months, gas for cooking was rationed to households, and severe measures were taken when several families had to use one kitchen, a common practice. "We read the gas meter at the start and finish, each time anyone used the stove," Inge recalls. "If three parties were cooking and one finished, the gas meter was read and the usage divided by three. After the next party finished, the meter was read again and the usage divided by two. It *had* to be exact." Everything was rationed; gas, electricity, food, coal, everything. Streetcars and subways stopped by 6:00 p.m., and when electricity came on at night at no specific time, "we got up and frantically worked on ironing, mending and darning socks, unfinished homework, and most importantly, cooking the next day's meal." Inside temperatures were only a bit above freezing, and people often stayed warm by remaining in bed.

Schools in Berlin remained open during the blockade months, and Inge attended every day, riding the street car, although school attendance was not mandatory. But as winter wore on that year, constant hunger and cold took its toll. "We had trouble concentrating and our reactions were slow," she points out. "The simplest math problems seemed like advanced calculus. We had trouble staying awake." Inge moved on to business school, with the city still blockaded, and was riding the streetcar to school one morning when it suddenly came to a halt, due to an electricity stoppage. She and her girl friend jumped off and ran the remaining distance to school, but they were still six-and-a-half minutes late. Result? Tardiness recorded on their report cards!

Inge, her mother, and little brother Peter lived with the Klemm family, escapees from the Russian revolution in 1919. Altogether, there were ten persons in the Klemm's apartment, but humor, music, games, and even Russian language practice were in good supply, permitting them all to make the best of the dark blockade days.

In late autumn 1948, Inge's brother Peter was one of two lucky children from his school sent to western Germany, where large mansions and old castles were being renovated to house children from Berlin. There they had enough food to eat, warm clothing, and a better life than they had in the blockaded city. Peter departed from Gatow the day after Christmas on an RAF airlift plane. He was excited, yet the prospect of sending her child off into total uncertainty was agonizing for his mother, and Inge, too. In the end, his mother concluded that the risk had sufficient benefits, which clearly turned out to be the case. Peter and his friends returned by train to Berlin the following August, full of excitement and unforgettable memories of their time in the village of Walkemühle, which they had named "Little Berlin."

Werner Erdmann, Wedding. Son Jonathan and I were warmly welcomed by Werner Erdmann and his wife, Wera, for a pleasant mid-morning coffee session and chat in their comfortable Reinickendorf home, situated just north of the former German army artillery range where, as a twenty-year-old, Werner, a lifelong resident of Berlin, was one of its 17,000 citizens who constructed the Tegel air field in record time. "It was hard work," recalls Werner, "but the pay was pretty good for the times, and we got a hot meal every day." In 1948, his home was in Wedding, from which he went to work daily on construction of the Tegel runway. The workers, who came from all walks of life—teachers, doctors, academics, housewives, and businessmen, among others—labored around the clock in the late summer and early autumn of 1948, and using mostly hand tools, they completed that badly needed third air field before the year was out.

During World War II, Werner served briefly in the German army. "I was a simple soldier," he explains, "only seventeen years old at the war's end." How he got in the army at such a young age is a story itself. When Werner was only four, his father divorced his mother and married another woman, who was mean and didn't like the boy. Discovering that his birth mother was of Jewish ancestry, she threatened to denounce young Werner to the Nazi authorities, but luckily he received a friendly tip that the best thing for him to do was to volunteer for military service. In January 1945, he reported for panzer training only to discover that it had been cancelled; it was the infantry for him. By March he was on the eastern front near Stettin, with his unit ordered to halt the Russian march on Berlin. Nothing doing! Instead, his company commander marched his unit westward to Schwerin where it surrendered to the Americans.

Returning to Berlin and civilian life at the war's end, Werner became one of thousands who had a hard time finding work, until the blockade was imposed. After the work at Tegel had come to an end late in 1948, he found employment at Tempelhof airfield as an unloader for the arriving C-54s. The loads always seemed to be coal and nothing else. "We worked three shifts," explains Werner. "Three days' work, the next day free, then three days' work again, rotating around the clock from the morning shift, then to the late afternoon shift, and on to the late night shift." This twelve-hour work schedule was quite different from the usual airlift regimen of seven-day weeks, but nonetheless, it was a successful work routine for his unloading team. The hot meal was eagerly awaited on this job, too, and his team developed a great spirit among themselves by striving for maximum speed and efficiency. Average unloading time was six to seven minutes, with five minutes the fastest for his team. "We saw it as a great sport," smiles Werner, "a friendly sort of competition to keep our skills sharp." There was an ancillary motive as well for the unloading crews. With crew unloading times officially recorded, the best crew was singled out at the end of each month and awarded cigarettes and chocolate by the American commander at Tempelhof. Such prizes were, of course, a great incentive for the unloading crews to do their very best, yet each worker felt a distinct pride in simply doing it for his city and fellow Berliners.

Werner continued on his unloading team until the very end of the blockade, following which he returned to his early trade as a tool maker with various firms. In 1967 he took his skills to the Berlin BMW motorcycle plant and worked there until retirement in 1988.

Wera Erdmann, Wedding. Werner's wife, Wera, also lived in Berlin during the blockade, although the two were not married until 1951. Originally from Munich, she moved with her family to Berlin in 1941 as a young girl. "We were constantly in fear of the Russians during the blockade," she remembers. "We often went into the Russian zone to get potatoes to trade for other food items. But we always had to be careful on the return trip to West Berlin to stay clear of the Russian soldiers." Fear that the Russians might take over all of Berlin was constantly on everyone's mind and was highly distressing during the entire time of the blockade. But there were pleasant moments as well. "My boy friend at the time occasionally surprised us with a bar of chocolate, and we shared it with my little sisters. What joy!"

In 1949, as the blockade came to an end, all of the German civil workers were invited to a farewell dance. "I had no decent dress, I had no shoes, I was very unhappy about it all," she remembers. But it all went off very well in the end. Today, she and her husband look back upon those dark days and rejoice that after so much deprivation and hardship it all turned out so well. And it still is turning out well for the couple; in 2001 they happily celebrated their golden wedding anniversary.

Christian Seifert, Pankow. In September 2000, Christian spoke to the assembled airlift veterans at their annual reunion, this time in Seattle. As he addressed the BAVA members in the German-American club, Christian recalled almost tearfully the early days of the blockade when not many Berliners felt that the western allies would come to their rescue after the Russians cut off transit to and from the besieged city. "When the Soviets started the blockade," he points out, "a terrible sigh of torment went through the 2.24 million Berliners living in the three western sectors. Everybody believed the British and Americans would give up Berlin and succumb to the Soviets. For many people suicide seemed the only way out."

Christian clearly remembers the endless debates in which his parents and friends engaged, so negative in tone. No one had hope. A distinct cynicism about the Americans and British colored their discussions, clearly indicating that the embryo blockade and airlift were a day-by-day experiment, with no one knowing if they would last a week, a month, or a year. Pessimism, despair, a feeling of hopelessness; then, as the airlift grew in its ability to deliver food and coal, a small change in mood, improving ever so slightly with increased daily tonnage figures. Christian looks back upon his fellow Berliners' fluctuating attitude then and firmly avows today, "The fact is, the allies did help! And how they helped! Fast and decisive!"

Christian was born in Berlin in 1943. As a young lad, he grew up among the ruins and the rubble of the devastated postwar city, with images of soldiers returning from POW camps in their dirty, torn uniforms, some with amputated limbs, and most of them with gray, bearded faces exuding hopelessness and despair. "Life was sad, empty, without color," he continues, "ruins spreading as far as the eye could see. Food was sparse to barely existent, and a lead-like silence cast a gloomy spell over the city. We kids collected dandelions for our rabbits and coal from the railroad cars that ran behind the house." Christian felt that the country had fallen under the spell of a horrifying past, from which its people could not imagine how to extricate themselves. Yet Berliners in the end survived the immediate postwar years and the blockade as well, showing the world that they could be tough under extreme adversity.

With the blockade at an end, the people of the western sectors, within a year or two, commenced to turn things around. The currency was stabilized, and Berlin began to exhibit once more its bustling, colorful, large-city characteristics. Its citizens returned to their traditional positive, can-do spirit. But they remembered the airlift with thanks, especially General Clay whose name even today rings warmly in Berlin, while elsewhere he is all but forgotten.

In 1996, after years of visiting on business, Christian moved to the United States and became a permanent resident. He now works with other Berliners who have migrated to America, to help keep alive the memory of those uncertain days many years ago when the western allies came to the help of a desperate people.

Werner Dargatz, Reinickendorf. When the blockade was imposed in June 1948, Werner was a young boy of nineteen. To that time he had always been a Berliner, and today he remains a lifelong Berliner, living with his wife, Suzanne, in their pleasant home in the city's northern Reinickendorf district. The couple warmly welcomed son Jonathan and me on the day of our visit, and we were treated to a genuine old-fashioned German dinner of sauerbraten, red cabbage, boiled potatoes—the works, washed down with potent schnaps.

During World War II, Werner was a very young conscript, only sixteen. He underwent his formal infantry training at Wittstock and in the last days of the war was assigned to an anti-aircraft battery in the defense of Berlin. "Many of my comrades fell in this battle," he recalls. "My flak battery was regrouped and we ended up in house-to-house fighting. On April 30, 1945 I was captured and sent to a Russian prisoner of war camp." Six months later, because of his youth and illness contracted in captivity, Werner was released and sent home. He weighed only 88 pounds.

Back in civilian life, hoping to return to his old firm, he found that it no longer existed. Despondent, he experienced great difficulty finding a job anywhere and so enlisted in the *Reichsarbeitsdienst*, a German youth organization similar to the American Civilian Conservation Corps (CCC) of the 1930s, whereby young men were assigned to public works projects. "Later, however, I found a job at Gatow military base unloading trucks that had brought in supplies," explains Werner about those early postwar years when there was much unemployment, confusion, and despair. When the blockade was imposed, he had been working at Gatow for some time, so he and his fellow workers were simply switched to airlift duties unloading incoming British airplanes. Now assigned to a regular unloading crew, Werner commenced working a new, lengthy twelve-hour shift. Life had some meaning once more. It was hard work, and it was difficult, but not every nineteen-year-old had a chance to help his beloved city in this manner. Werner considered himself very lucky.

In the early weeks of the airlift, Werner and his crew were busy unloading RAF Dakotas arriving at Gatow. By August, the western air base at Fassberg had been taken over by the Americans who commenced regular flights to Gatow with C–54s. Young Werner and his crew quickly learned the new procedures necessary to unload the larger Skymasters.

With the airlift at an end, young Werner was once more hunting for a job. But through a stroke of good fortune he secured a training position with the firm that is now Otis elevator. "Following my training," continues Werner, "I worked as a mechanic at Otis until 1980, at which time, due to my lengthy illness from the prisoner of war camp, I applied for retirement." Today Werner and his wife Suzanne enjoy their home, their garden, and the knowledge that their lifelong city of Berlin is united once more.

Ж

The eyewitness stories told above seek to portray different personal experiences of Berliners caught in the blockade of 1948-1949. Yet the surface has barely been scratched, for it was not possible to locate blockade veterans who represented every conceivable individual situation that then prevailed. When the barriers came down in June 1948, some Berliners were little school children, some were teenagers, and some were adults; others were battle-hardened veterans of World War II. Some were not even Berliners; they were simply trapped in the capital city on a business trip or vacation from the west when the blockade was imposed, and they became marooned there for the duration, or until they could be evacuated by air. Whatever their personal circumstances might have been, those who knew Berlin long enough to call it home displayed unbelievable courage and determination through the long months of the blockade. Their common bond was a love for their city and a will to stand tough against the harsh cruelty they were forced to suffer. They were the unheralded.

Berliners at Heart: West Germans and the Airlift

Countless numbers of Germans living in the western zones of occupation also became airlift veterans by virtue of their employment at western air bases and other military installations. They worked as aviation mechanics, truck drivers, mess hall assistants, hospital orderlies, maids, aircraft loaders, finance and office assistants, and in numerous other capacities.

One such West German was **Dorothea Meier**, a chambermaid in the Fassberg air base barracks. A resident of the tiny nearby village of Unterlüß, Dorothea commenced work at the giant air base soon after the British took it over following the war's end. When the airlift commenced, she was well-experienced in her job and had come to know many British airmen stationed there. Then, in August 1948, Americans began to move in as the C-54s transferred from Wiesbaden and Rhein-Main, and she had dozens of new faces and names to learn. Always cheerful, always jolly, Dorothea went about her work with the certain knowledge that unimportant as the job of a chambermaid might seem to others, she was making her own contribution to the larger effort that the airlift represented. She swept and mopped floors, washed windows, made beds, did personal laundry, and performed dozens of additional tasks to help make life a little better for the airmen stationed there. Her friendliness and willingness to help others quickly became known among the Americans as it had been with the British.

When airlift veterans returned to Fassberg in 1989 for the fortieth anniversary reunion events, Dorothea was there to greet them. By then, she was **Dorothea Kühne**, having married **Karl Kühne**, a fellow air base worker. The couple had two sons, one of whom, Rolf, took up the family tradition, secured an air base job with the RAF, and continues to work there today, a civilian employee of the German air force. Dorothea enthusiastically greeted the returning veterans whom she remembered from so long ago, reminisced with them and their wives about old times, and mixed easily with all those whom she had long considered her "extended family."

By 1999 and the fiftieth anniversary reunion, sadly, both Dorothea and husband Karl had passed on. Son Rolf, however, who now owns and continues to live in his parents' former house in Unterlüß, was in attendance and warmly greeted those whom he remembered from 1989. As all airlift veterans, British, Commonwealth, and American, know, there were many "Dorotheas" at each of their bases, going about their jobs, seeking to make living conditions more comfortable for the soldiers and airmen, and spreading cheer in an otherwise often cheerless environment.

Another such "Dorothea"—her name was **Olga**—did laundry for several airmen at Rhein-Main. One of them who wishes to remain anonymous tells the story. "Olga would do five days laundry for two packs of cigarettes. One day, she asked for chocolate instead of cigarettes, and when I advised her that chocolate was not bringing much on the market, she explained that she did not want it for sale—it was for her child. Suddenly, I realized that a very small, hollow-eyed child was hanging on to her skirt. He was five years old and had never even tasted chocolate. His father had gone to the eastern front in 1944, and Olga never again heard from him. I don't know if Olga was telling the truth. Who cares? The look on that child's face was no fake. I went to my locker and returned with a box of Hershey bars. 'Olga,' I said, 'the boy will be sick as a horse, but he gets to eat all 24 bars.' Upon bringing my laundry the next time, she reported that the boy was somewhat ill but very happy."

On September 1, 1949, as Navy VR-6 Squadron made ready to depart on its return trip to Hawaii, the many women who had mopped floors, made beds, and laundered uniforms in the Betts housing area at Rhein-Main gathered at the gate, most of them in tears, but all of them waving goodbye. As one of the departing navy pilots said, "We left a lot of good friends there." Those "friends" did not come from Berlin, and they didn't suffer the severe privations that Berliners endured during 1948 and 1949, but through the long months of the blockade they were Berliners at heart. Heroines? There were no heroines, just ordinary gals living in extraordinary times. But they did their noble part in helping Berliners to survive.

Figure 23. Werner Dargatz, left, during an interview with Ed Gere at Werner's home in Reinickendorf, Berlin, March 2000. Author's photo.

Figure 24. Dietmar Kurnoth, eleven years old during the blockade. Today a successful insurance executive in Berlin. Author's photo.

Figure 25. Werner and Wera Erdmann, Berlin, 1973. Courtesy Werner Erdmann.

Figure 26. Werner Demitrowitz, seventeen years old as an airlift unloader, in his Berlin home, March 2000. Author's photo.

Figure 27. Horst Molkenbuhr, teenage airlift unloader, in his Wilmersdorf, Berlin, home, March 2000. Author's photo.

Figure 28. Jon Gere and Rainer Baronsky, Berlin, March 2000. Rainer was eleven during the blockade. Author's photo.

Figure 29. Herta Tiede, a *Berlinerin* who was a secretary at Fassberg RAF station during the airlift. She returned to Berlin and lives there today. Courtesy Herta Tiede.

Seven

Full Measure of Devotion: Commonwealth and German Casualties

For though from out our bourne of time and place
The flood may bear me far,
I hope to see my Pilot face to face
When I have crossed the bar.

Alfred, Lord Tennyson, Crossing the Bar

ON MONDAY, MAY 10, 1999, at the former RAF Gatow, Berlin, representatives of the British Berlin Airlift Association laid a wreath at the memorial stone in remembrance of the 38 Britons and one Australian who lost their lives in Operation Plainfare accidents. On November 11, 1999, members of the Berlin Airlift Veterans Association were present at Dover AFB, Delaware, to dedicate the Berlin airlift memorial plaque and to lay a memorial wreath on the site. The memorial pays homage to the 32 Americans who died in Operation Vittles accidents. These scenes have been, and will continue to be repeated in testimony to the courage and bravery of those men who died in the first, tension-filled, major confrontation of the cold war.

British and Commonwealth Casualties

I am very much indebted to **Squadron Leader Frank Stillwell**, BBAA chairman, for the association's book of remembrance in which British and Commonwealth casualties are cited, and also for information on several individuals whose biographies are seen in this chapter. Frank was engaged in a valiant effort to secure personal information on those who were killed whilst (now he even has me saying it) serving in Operation Plainfare, and this chapter is much better for his contributions. For others who lost their lives, it was possible to secure fragmentary biographical notes on only a few. A bit of additional detail on British and Commonwealth accidents became available from eyewitnesses and published sources.

RAF and civilian contract crew members suffered eleven fatal airlift accidents between September 19, 1948 and July 16, 1949, six of which were civilian. Altogether, 21 of the 39 fatalities were civilian. The names of those who lost their lives are listed below, followed by brief circumstances of each accident:

Engineer Officer John Anderson	April 30, 1949
Navigation Officer Alan John Burton	November 22, 1948
Navigation Officer Edward Ernest Carroll	April 30, 1949
Navigation Officer Michael Edwin Casey	November 22, 1948
Captain William Cusack	November 22, 1948
Flying Officer Ian Ronald Donaldson	July 16, 1949
Sergeant Frank Dowling	November 17, 1948
Signaller II Alexander Dunsire	July 16, 1949
Radio Officer Peter James Edwards	March 15, 1949
Captain Robert John Freight	March 21, 1949
Engineer II Roy Reginald Gibbs	July 16, 1949
Navigator II Lawrence Edward Hope Gilbert	September 19, 1948
Captain Cecil Golding	March 15, 1949
Ground Engineer Patrick James Griffin	January 15, 1949
Signaller I John Ernest Grout	January 24, 1949
Captain Reginald Merrick Watson Heath, DFC	November 22, 1949
Flight Lieutenant Geoffrey Kell	September 19, 1948
Captain William Richard Donald Lewis	April 30, 1949
Signaller III Philip Arthur Louch	November 17, 1948
First Officer Henry Thomas Newman	March 15, 1949
Ground Engineer Edward O'Neil	January 15, 1949
Navigator I William George Page	July 16, 1949
Engineer Officer Henry Patterson	March 21, 1949
Master Signaller Alan Penny, AFC	March 22, 1949
Flight Lieutenant Mel Joseph Quinn, RAAF	March 22, 1949
Flying Officer Kenneth Arthur Reeves	March 22, 1949
Radio Officer Dornford Winstan Robertson	November 22, 1949

Flight Engineer Kenneth Arthur Seaborne, DFM	November 22, 1949
Navigation Officer James Patrick Lewin Sharp, DFC	March 21, 1949
Ground Engineer Theodor Supernat	January 15, 1949
Captain Cyril Taylor, DFC, AFM	November 22, 1948
Flight Lieutenant Hugh Wallace Thompson, MC, DFC	September 19, 1948
Sergeant Joseph Toal	July 16, 1949
Signaller II Sidney Mark Lewis Towersey	September 19, 1948
Pilot I Francis Ivor Trezona	November 17, 1948
Captain Clement Wilbur Utting	December 8, 1948
Engineer II Ernest William Watson	September 19, 1948
Flight Lieutenant John Graham Wilkins	November 17, 1948
Radio Officer Kenneth George Wood	April 30, 1949

September 19, 1948. On this date an RAF York bound from Wunstorf to Gatow crashed following a night takeoff. The cause was engine failure, and the entire crew of five was killed. This crash was witnessed by **Kenneth King**, Royal Army Service Corps, whose personal story is told in chapter five. The airmen killed were:

Flight Lieutenant Hugh W. Thomson, MC, DFC

Flight Lieutenant Geoffrey Kell

Navigator II Lawrence E. H. Gilbert

Signaller II Sidney M. L. Towersey

Engineer II Ernest W.Watson

Hugh Wallace Thompson was born in India in 1917, where his father served in the army. The family moved to England when Hugh was six, and he moved through his school years, passing his School Certificate at age seventeen. He later joined the territorial army in the Royal Artillery.

In September 1939, following the German attack on Poland, Hugh was called to active service and sent to Brussels. The following May his regiment was caught in the Dunkirk evacuation, but the ship that rescued his unit was sunk, and Hugh reached England in nothing but his trousers. In 1941 he transferred to the RAF, received pilot training in Canada, and flew with Bomber Command on many aerial raids over Germany and the occupied countries. On one such raid in June 1944, his aircraft was damaged and crashed in Belgium. Hugh was the only survivor. He was rescued by farmers who moved him from one farm to another until he could be turned over to resistance forces. In Lille he fought with the Maquis, a French underground resistance group, helping to blow bridges and trains until picked up by British troops and returned to England. For his deeds with the Maquis, Hugh was awarded the Military Cross.

When the airlift was mounted in 1948, Hugh was assigned to route flying with Transport Command. He was quickly transferred to RAF Wunstorf to join others flying Yorks between that base and Berlin.

Missions to Berlin continued on a steady basis for Hugh and his crew members until that fateful night takeoff from Wunstorf.

November 17, 1948. An RAF Dakota on a night landing approach to Lübeck caught fire after hitting trees and crashed in the Russian zone. Killed immediately were:

> Pilot I Francis I. Trezona
>
> Flight Lieutenant John G. Wilkins
>
> Signaller III Philip A. Louch
>
> Sergeant Frank Dowling

John Graham Wilkins, born in Coleford, Gloucestershire in February 1922, was an army "brat," his father being a retired regimental sergeant major in the Royal Gloucesters who spent the greater part of his military career in India. In 1938, young John joined the RAF and continued his service through World War II. During part of that time he was attached to a Canadian squadron, flying as a navigator on Mosquito bombers. During this assignment he met Marjorie Broadbent, and on June 27, 1942 they were married. John's pilot, Ken Moore, a Toronto native, married a girl named Millie, so the twin engines on their Mosquito were dubbed Marjorie and Millie!

After the war, John remained in the RAF as a regular officer and by 1948 was posted to Lübeck and airlift duty with a Dakota squadron. In the fatal crash on the night of November 17, 1948, John, severely injured, was taken to Schönberg hospital in the Russian zone where he was attended by Professor Lehman, a German surgeon. His wife Marjorie, Flight Lieutenant L. F. Levy, an RAF medical officer, and Jeanne Burns, a WAAF nursing orderly, were uncharacteristically permitted to visit him in the hospital and to remain until he died on November 25, eight days following the accident. RAF authorities later sent a letter to Lieut. General Lukyanchenko, Soviet chief of staff, in thanks for John's humane treatment. On December 18, 1948, John was buried with full military honors in Ohlsdorf Cemetery, Hamburg.

Philip Arthur Louch was a happy school boy who loved singing, dancing, and music in general but was not very much interested in his studies. Born in Leicester in May 1926, he was the only boy in a family of three children. Leaving school at age fourteen, Philip worked in a grocery store, then joined the air cadets as war came on. Before his eighteenth birthday, he enlisted in the RAF, saw service in Anglesea and Northern Ireland, then moved on to air crew training at St. Helens. He graduated as a Signaller III.

After the war, Philip chose to remain on military service and entered the Dakota Operational Conversion Unit Course at North Luffenham. From this base he was posted on October 22, 1948 to No. 30 Squadron at Lübeck for Operation Plainfare duty. Only three-and-a-half weeks later he died in the November 17 crash sixteen kilometers inside the Russian zone of occupation.

Frank Dowling was born in Nantyglo, Monmouthshire on September 7, 1925. He lost his mother while still a young boy and grew up with his brother, George, both of whom enjoyed riding and sailing. In 1942, at the very young age of seventeen, he enlisted in the RAF and pursued flight engineer training. Upon completion of his training, he was posted to southeast Asia where he crewed on Lancasters and advanced to the rank of flight sergeant.

After World War II, Frank found civilian life rather dull, so he re-enlisted. An ear injury, however, ruled out further flight duty; he had to train as a fitter and literally start over again as a corporal. At RAF Chigwell, he met Sergeant Hazel Bishop, a special duties clerk on the airbase. The two fell in love, and in due course they were married, but Frank had to move on to Heathrow, anticipating further training and duty as an air traffic controller, while Hazel returned to civilian life. By this time, the airlift was calling many RAF specialists to service in Germany, and Frank's engineering skills were needed at RAF Gatow in Berlin.

On the fateful night of November 17, 1948, Frank was an eager passenger, catching a ride on the Lübeck-bound Dakota, anxious to head home on leave to his pregnant wife. He was killed instantly in the crash.

November 22, 1948. On this date a Lancaster aircraft from Flight Refueling, Ltd., crashed into a hillside in Thruxton, England, carrying a crew of four and a supernumerary crew of four heading for home leave. The Lancaster was bound for Tarrant Rushton, Dorset. A local resident, F. Green, and his wife, from nearby Chute, upon hearing the crash sought to render aid, but a persistent, heavy fog impeded their search. It took them an hour to locate the burning aircraft. **Radio Officer Vincent Stanley** was the only person to survive the crash. The other seven airmen aboard, listed below, lost their lives.

Captain Cyril Taylor

Captain Reginald M. W. Heath

Navigation Officer Michael E. Casey

Captain William Cusack

Navigation Officer Alan J. Burton

Radio Officer Dornford W. Robertson

Flight Engineer Kenneth A. Seaborne

Cyril Taylor, a native of West Bridgeford, Nottinghamshire, was born on December 14, 1913. He was 25 years of age when, in February 1939, he enlisted in the RAF and proceeded through several training schools and graduated with a pilot designation in May 1940, in the rank of sergeant. In World War II, he advanced through further operational training and flew the Takoradi route across Central Africa in 1940 and 1941 to ferry supplies to Egypt in support of the North African campaign. In June 1945, Cyril was awarded the Air Force Medal by King George VI at Buckingham Palace. During the Berlin airlift, he flew as a civilian.

The sole survivor of the crash, Radio Officer Vincent Stanley, was thrown clear, but with his clothes on fire he was very much in danger of perishing. A farmer wrapped him in a blanket, and he was transferred to a local hospital in serious condition.

On May 12, 1959, at Tempelhof ceremonies marking the tenth anniversary of the lifting of the blockade, **Captain Taylor's** daughter, Ms Lynn Taylor, was selected to represent all of the daughters of airmen who had lost their lives in airlift operations.

December 8, 1948. Captain Clement W. Utting, a senior pilot of Airflight, Ltd., was killed at Gatow airfield when he was struck by a lorry as he walked toward his Tudor aircraft. He died later in Spandau hospital. His tragic accident was widely reported in the press at the time, and later in much of airlift literature. Over time, there was considerable speculation that he was deliberately run down by an unknown German driver who believed Utting to be Air Vice Marshal Donald Bennett of Bomber Command's famous Pathfinder force in World War II, and who was seeking revenge for the heavy damage inflicted on German targets by his forces. The lorry driver sped away in the dark on that evening and was never apprehended.

January 15, 1949. Three civilian ground engineers from the Lancashire Aircraft Corporation and a German truck driver were killed at Schleswigland on January 15 when their vehicle was struck by the propeller of an RAF Hastings that was proceeding on the taxiway. **John Dury** from No. 297 Squadron was a witness to this accident. The victims were:

> Ground Engineer Theodore Supernat
>
> Ground Engineer Patrick J. Griffin
>
> Ground Engineer Edward O'Neil

Theodore Supernat was born Teodor Supernat in December 1914 at Radom, Poland. As a relatively young man, he joined the Polish air force in 1937. Two years later, he left Poland and moved through Hungary to Greece, where he joined Polish resistance forces. Some indeterminate time later, he joined the RAF and during this military period was a corporal in No. 308 Squadron at Bovingdon, serving as an aircraft electrician. Ted was struck by the Hastings propeller and died 24 hours later. Notes from the December 2001 issue of the BBAA *Newsletter* indicate that he had also been posted to France, Belgium, Holland, and Germany with the British Air Forces of Occupation. He later was associated with Airtech, Ltd., in Bovingdon and was employed by Lancashire Aircraft Association during the airlift.

During the war, Ted's father, three sisters, and four brothers suffered terribly and were put to death in concentration camps, but a younger brother was interned in Norway and survived. For his war service, Ted was awarded the French Cross Combatants Volontaires, the Medal LOTNICCZY of the Polish Air Force, the UK, France, and Germany Star, and the UK Defence Medal. He is buried in the Catholic cemetery in North London.

January 24, 1949. On this date an RAF Dakota crashed in the Russian zone while making a night landing approach to Lübeck in poor weather. The pilot and navigator were injured, but **Signaller I John E. Grout** and seven German passengers were killed. This accident is remembered, in terms of lives lost, as one of the worst in the history of the airlift. The accident and the explosion that followed were witnessed by **Warrant Officer Douglas Raw**, another Dakota signaller stationed at Lübeck. John was buried in the Ohlsdorfer cemetery in Hamburg.

March 15, 1949. A Skyways, Ltd., York aircraft stalled and crashed on final approach to RAF Gatow, resulting in the death of all three crew members, who were:

> Captain Cecil Golding
>
> First Officer Henry T. Newman
>
> Radio Officer Peter J. Edwards

March 21, 1949. A Halton aircraft of the Lancashire Aircraft Corporation struck the ground while on a landing approach to Schleswigland in marginal weather and visibility. **Radio Officer James Hamilton** survived his injuries, but the other three crew members, named below, lost their lives.

> Captain Robert J. Freight
>
> Navigation Officer James P.L. Sharp, DFC
>
> Engineer Officer Henry Patterson

March 22, 1949. Still another Russian zone crash occurred near Lübeck on this date as an RAF Dakota made a landing approach in poor weather with a loss of all lives. The crew, whose names appear below, were:

> Flight Lieutenant Mel J. Quinn, RAAF
>
> Flying Officer Kenneth A. Reeves, a South African serving with the RAF
>
> Master Signaller Alan Penny, AFC, who died later from his injuries

Flight Lieutenant Mel Joseph Quinn was a native Australian, born in West Maitland, South Australia, in 1922. Following schooling at Muswellbrook, New South Wales, young Mel enlisted in 1941 as a pilot trainee with the rank of aircraftsman, and eleven months later was commissioned a pilot officer in the Royal Australian Air Force (RAAF), only three days past his twentieth birthday. By December he was promoted to flying officer and served during World War II in the United Kingdom, India, and the Burma campaign, with promotion to flight lieutenant in June 1944. Before demobilisation in late 1945, many decorations came Mel's way, including the Burma Star, War Medal, and the Defence Medal. He spent less than a year in civilian life, however, before being reappointed to his commission, followed by Dakota crew training and service in Indonesia.

In 1947 Mel married Margaret Squelch, an English woman, in Sydney, and a son, Mel Galvin, was born in September 1949, six months after his father's death. Later in 1947, Mel was posted to refresher training with No. 24 Squadron at RAF Bassingbourne in the United Kingdom, followed by further navigation and transport training at RAF bases in England. Then, on September 15, 1948, Mel, as part of a ten-crew RAAF contingent, transferred to No. 46 Squadron at RAF Lübeck for airlift duty, until sadly, on March 22, 1949, the Dakota he was piloting crashed in poor weather while approaching Lübeck. He was the only Australian casualty of the Berlin airlift.

Flying Officer Kenneth Reeves was a South African, born in Johannesburg in 1920. The eldest of four children, Ken was an excellent student in his school years and also was a keen sportsman, especially in rugby, his favorite sport. Good pupil that he was, he nonetheless left school at age fifteen to become an apprentice mechanic, and by the time war broke out in Europe in 1939 he had completed his training. In 1940 he joined the South African Air Force (SAAF) and entered navigator training in East London, South Africa, where he met Joan Triggs, who was evacuated with her military family from Egypt to South Africa as German Field Marshal Erwin Rommel advanced toward Cairo in his desert offensive.

Following the Battle of El Alamein in 1942, Joan returned to Egypt while Ken, by then a lieutenant in the SAAF, flew bombing missions over German-occupied Europe. On a rare leave in December 1944, the two were married in Cairo, then returned to Johannesburg at war's end to take up a new life in the business world. In much the same fashion as Mel Quinn, however, Ken was anxious to remain in flying. In May 1947, he was offered a commission in the RAF and quickly found himself in England on air crew duty. Assigned by December 1948 to No. 24 Commonwealth Squadron in Bassingbourne, Ken was requested the following March to transfer to Germany for the Berlin airlift. Reluctant to go because his wife was pregnant with their second child, he was assured it would be for only a short time.

Ken had only a few short weeks of airlift service. Then came March 22 and the fatal Dakota crash at Lübeck. He left his wife, a two-year-old son, Michael John, and a soon-to-be born daughter, Pamela, whom he never knew.

April 30, 1949. On this date, a World Air Freight Halton crashed fourteen kilometers west of Oranienburg in the Russian zone while returning to Fuhlsbüttel from Tegel. All four crew members, listed here, were killed.

Captain William R. D. Lewis

Navigation Officer Edward E. Carroll

Engineer Officer John Anderson

Radio Officer Kenneth G. Wood

July 16, 1949. An RAF Hastings crashed on an early morning takeoff from Tegel, following engine failure. All five crew members, as follows, were killed in the last British fatal crash of the airlift.

Flying Officer Ian R. Donaldson

Sergeant Joseph Toal, Glider Pilot Regiment

Navigator I William G. Page

Signaller II Alexander Dunsire

Engineer II Roy R. Gibbs

Roy Reginald Gibbs was born in November 1925 at Portsmouth, Hampshire. The third of four brothers, he also had four sisters—a large family, indeed. One of his brothers, John, reported that Roy was "a born mechanical engineer." At an early age, he could take apart any type of machinery and put it back together. Clocks were his favorite. After passing the examination for grammar school, he soon left to apprentice as a mechanic with a Plymouth coach manufacturing company. By this time, however, the war was on, so upon reaching age he enlisted in the RAF, went through engineer training, and flew with an Australian crew as flight engineer on Bomber Command's Halifaxes. Roy was fond of bringing his entire crew home with him on leave!

Temporarily grounded due to ear problems, Roy was sent to Liverpool "Liver Buildings" where he met the woman he would marry. During his duty times in Huntingdon and St. Mawgan, they enjoyed a marvelous year and a half together and looked forward to a bright future. In early 1949, he volunteered for airlift service and following OCU training at Dishforth he was posted to No. 47 Squadron at Schleswigland, crewing on Handley Page Hastings. On June 9, 1949, his daughter Elaine was born in Liverpool, and Roy was fortunate to secure a trip home to see her at the end of the month. Two weeks later came the fatal takeoff crash at Tegel. But he saw his baby daughter before he died.

Ж

In the eleven fatal British and Commonwealth airlift-related accidents, fourteen RAF officers, four RAF enlisted men, and 21 civilians lost their lives. Aircraft involved were three Dakotas, two Hastings, two Yorks, two Haltons, and one Lancaster. Six accidents occurred at night; four took place in poor weather; and some of those four happened at night as well. Two of the eleven accidents took place on the ground. In Berlin, two accidents occurred at Gatow, and one at Tegel. At the air bases and elsewhere, three crashes took place at Lübeck, two at Schleswigland, one at Wunstorf, one over England, and one in the corridor. It is difficult to perceive any distinct causal patterns from such statistics, except possibly those of night and marginal weather.

German Casualties

Ich hatte einen Kamerad
German hymn, traditionally sung at military funerals

Germans killed in airlift accidents were all civilians, but they crashed in military aircraft or lost their lives in an otherwise military environment. Hence, the hymn, *Ich hatte einen Kamerad* (I had a pal), seems appropriate. Seven Germans were aboard an RAF Dakota that crashed on January 24, 1949. On March 11, 1949, a Berlin policeman tragically walked into the whirling propeller of an RAF York at Gatow and was instantly killed. Two German truck drivers were killed in separate accidents at Rhein-Main and Schleswigland. Families of those Americans, Britons, one Australian, and Germans killed in airlift related accidents were guests of the city of Berlin at the May 12, 1959 tenth anniversary ceremonies marking the end of the blockade.

It has always been an anomaly of airlift record keeping that so little is known about the indeterminate number of Germans who were killed in airlift-related accidents. Some lost their lives as aircraft passengers flying from Berlin to the west; others were truck drivers, transport workers, and policemen, yet complete, accurate records of these casualties seem not to exist. Daniel Harrington's careful compilation, summarized below, and Wolfgang Huschke's detail are the best sources for the German casualties.

January 15, 1949. In the same truck collision in which three British ground engineers were killed at Schleswigland, the truck driver, **Richard K. O. Neumann,** from Busdorf, also lost his life.

January 24, 1949. When an RAF Dakota crashed at night inside the Russian zone as it approached Lübeck for landing, seven German passengers were killed as was Signaller I John E. Grout. The Germans, who were buried in Lübeck, were:

> Frau Ursula Gashoff, Bielefeld
> Frau Gudrun Giesdler, Bonn
> Emanuel Kelch, Berlin
> Frau Irmgard Kelch, Berlin
> Johann Lercher
> Frau Gerti Zimmerman, Berlin
> Fraulein Silvia Zimmerman, Berlin

March 11, 1949. Kurt Zülsdorf, a German policeman from Berlin-Spandau, walked into a spinning York propeller in the dark of night at Gatow.

April 1949. An unknown truck driver was killed when he drove his gasoline truck into the propeller of a parked aircraft at Rhein-Main.

Additionally, four other Germans, all transport workers, were killed in various airlift-related accidents in Berlin. Their names are known, yet the dates and exact locations of the accidents are not. They were:

Willi Dühring, transport worker, Berlin-Kreuzberg

Hans Fiedler, transport worker, Berlin-Moabit

Kurt Schlinsog, transport worker, Berlin-Lübars

Herman Schwarz, transport worker, Berlin-Kreuzberg

At the May 12, 1959 Tempelhof ceremonies marking the tenth anniversary of the end of the blockade, families of those who lost their lives in airlift accidents were guests of the Berlin city government. On that occasion, **Herr Wilhelm Schwarz**, father of **Herman Schwarz**, was selected to represent all those German civilians who lost their lives.

Ж

"If I should die, think only this of me;" wrote the poet Rupert Brooke in his classic, 'The Soldier', "that there's some corner of a foreign field that is forever England." The courageous Englishmen and one Australian who lost their lives in Plainfare operations would no doubt agree with Brooke, who died in World War I of blood poisoning. Only 28 at the time, he was not much older than those who died trying to save Berlin from a slow death.

Those Berlin workers killed in ground accidents and Berliners who lost their lives while being airlifted to the west remain firm in the memories of all their compatriots who endured the privations of the blockade. Their losses will forever be remembered in the annals of the cold war. They, too, were the unheralded.

Figure 30. Lindsey Air Station photo of Americans killed on the airlift. Courtesy Ronald M. A. Hirst.

Figure 31. John and Patricia Hanlon standing before memorial to Lt. Royce Stephens, erected by citizens of Heroldishausen, Germany at the site of Stephen's fatal crash. John was flight engineer of the doomed C–54 that crashed almost exactly fifty years earlier, on March 4, 1949. Courtesy John Hanlon.

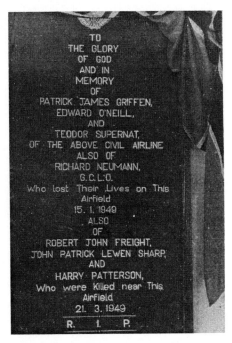

Figure 32. Memorial to British flyers who died in crashes in Schleswigland. Courtesy Frank Stillwell.

Figure 33. Ground Engineer Theodore Supernat, killed January 15, 1949 at Schleswigland. Courtesy Frank Stillwell.

Figure 34. Flying Officer Kenneth Arthur Reeves, South African serving with the RAF. Killed March 22, 1949. Shown in South African Air Force uniform. Courtesy Frank Stillwell.

Eight

Full Measure of Devotion: American Casualties

I would be true, for there are those who trust me;
I would be pure, for there are those who care;
I would be strong, for there is much to suffer;
I would be brave, for there is much to dare.

Howard Arnold Walter, My Creed

FOR DETAILED BIOGRAPHICAL information on each American who died in an airlift-related accident, I am immeasurably indebted to Ronald M. A. "Scotty" Hirst, of Wiesbaden, Germany. A much decorated American combat veteran of World War II who took part in the D-Day landings in France, "Scotty" has devoted a considerable part of his life to collecting and assembling the personal, individual information that appears in this chapter. Over the years, he has painstakingly searched military records, local newspapers, schools, libraries, and family sources in his quest for full, accurate information on those who died. At his own expense, he has contacted families and next of kin in an ongoing effort to insure that those who lost their lives in 1948 and 1949 will not be forgotten. On the occasion of airlift veteran reunions in Germany, Scotty has been a constant behind-the-scenes activist. For the tenth anniversary reunion in May 1959, at which family members of those who lost their lives were guests of the Berlin city government, he quietly assisted with arrangements. And prior to the fiftieth anniversary reunion in May 1999, he made sure that surviving family members were extended invitations to attend the Berlin ceremonies, and that they were suitably housed and hosted during their visit.

Aggregate information on American casualties, which Scotty published privately, now has been turned over to the Hoover Institution on War, Revolution and Peace at Stanford University where it will be, in his words, "on permanent display for eternity for students, scholars, and persons of interest on an achievement which ensured the permanency of Germany and the ultimate demise of the Soviet Union. There is no doubt in the mind of the world," he continues, "that had the Berlin airlift not succeeded, we would live today in a much different world, had we all survived the consequences of its failure."

In addition to donating his airlift papers to Stanford, Scotty has very generously made them available to me for the writing of this chapter, and I am deeply grateful to him for doing so. It seemed to me that having devoted so much time, energy, and effort to his work on the casualties, Scotty should be named co-author of this chapter, but he modestly declined. The least that I can do, then, is to acknowledge with deep thanks his vital role in the process. Additional personal and biographical details on American dead have been obtained from direct contact with family members, newspaper sources, and BAVA members.

American Casualties

Thirty-two Americans lost their lives in airlift-related accidents between July 8, 1948 and July 12, 1949: 28 air force, one navy, two army, and one army civilian. Of this number, 21 were officers, ten were enlisted men, and one was a civilian. For many years the official tally remained at 31. In 1998, however, air force historian Roger Miller learned of Corporal George S. Burn's death in October 1948. Roger's historian colleague at Ramstein air base, Germany, Daniel Harrington, concurred in Miller's findings. On this account, the amended list appears below.

The 32 Americans were killed in thirteen accidents. One was a mid-air collision between two C-47s, while two accidents occurred on the ground. Aircraft involved were four C-47s, eight C-54s, and one R5D, the navy version of the C-54. More importantly, for each American who died, a street was later named in his honor at Lindsey air station in Wiesbaden. When the widows and other next of kin of those who died were present as guests of the Berlin city government for the May 12, 1959 tenth anniversary ceremonies, each guest was hosted by and stayed in the home of a Berlin family. The names of those killed are listed below, followed by circumstances of each accident and a biographical sketch of each person.

First Lieutenant Ralph H. Boyd	January 12, 1949
Corporal George S. Burns	October 29, 1948
AMM3/c Harry R. Crites, Jr.	December 11, 1948
Captain Joel M. DeVolentine	August 24, 1948

Major Edwin C. Diltz	August 24, 1948
First Lieutenant Eugene Erickson	October 18, 1948
Karl V. Hagen	July 8, 1948
First Lieutenant Willis F. Hargis	December 5, 1948
Technical Sergeant Herbert F. Heinig	July 12, 1949
Captain William R. Howard	August 24, 1948
First Lieutenant Charles H. King	July 25, 1948
First Lieutenant Craig B. Ladd	January 12, 1949
Second Lieutenant Donald J. Leemon	July 12, 1949
First Lieutenant William T. Lucas	August 24, 1948
First Lieutenant Robert C. von Luehrte	July 12, 1949
Private First Class Johnnie T. Orms	October 2, 1948
Captain Billy E. Phelps	December 5, 1948
Technical Sergeant Charles L. Putnam	January 12, 1949
Captain William A. Rathgeber	January 7, 1949
First Lieutenant George B. Smith	July 8, 1948
First Lieutenant Royce C. Stephens	March 4, 1949
Private First Class Donald E. Stone	January 7, 1949
First Lieutenant Robert W. Stuber	July 25, 1948
Corporal Norbert H. Theis	January 7, 1949
Captain James A. Vaughan	October 18, 1948
Sergeant Bernard J. Watkins	January 7, 1949
First Lieutenant Robert P. Weaver	January 18, 1949
Technical Sergeant Lloyd C. Wells	December 5, 1948
First Lieutenant Lowell A. Wheaton, Jr.	January 7, 1949
First Lieutenant Leland W. Williams	July 8, 1948
Sergeant Richard Winter	October 18, 1948
First Lieutenant Richard M. Wurgel	January 7, 1949

July 8, 1948. The very first Operation Vittles fatal accident occurred barely two weeks after the airlift's beginning. Killed in the crash were:

First Lieutenant Leland V. Williams

First Lieutenant George B. Smith

Karl V. Hagen

The C-47 that Williams piloted was cleared from Wiesbaden to Tempelhof on the night of July 8, loaded with a three-ton cargo of powdered milk. Poor weather prevailed, with a low ceiling and light rain. Seven minutes after takeoff, at 10:35 p.m., the aircraft crashed near Königstein, situated about sixteen kilometers to the northeast. The aircraft was totally destroyed, but the specific cause of the crash was never firmly determined.

Leland Vee Williams was born March 6, 1920 in Tuscola, Texas, the only son of Rosa P. Flippo and John O. Williams. When the boy was four, the family, with his sister Lanelle, moved to Abilene. He graduated from high school there in 1939, enlisted as an aviation cadet on the day after

Pearl Harbor, and was awarded pilot wings and a commission on July 29, 1943 at Altus, Oklahoma. In World War II, due to his excellence in training, he was retained at Fort Worth army air field as a B-24 instructor pilot.

In 1946 Leland was assigned to Ansbach air depot in Germany, then to Erding air depot as commander of the 7236th Motor Vehicle Squadron. Sometime later his wife joined him from the states, and they settled into occupation duty in Bavaria. Then came the blockade of Berlin, the onset of the airlift, and a temporary duty move to Wiesbaden. In his military flying career, Leland had amassed over 2,200 hours in the air, and when assigned to the airlift he had recently been recertified for instrument flying.

After his death, Leland was brought home and buried in the same plot with his parents at the Elmwood Memorial Park in Abilene. His widow later remarried and raised three sons. In June 1951, the American dependent housing area at Erding air depot was named Williamsville in his memory. Although it is today a German Luftwaffe base, the name has been retained in a small garden plot facing the entrance to the housing area, where a stone memorial stands in remembrance of Leland Williams. A bronze tablet attached to the stone reads:

> Though death came in time of peace, his name must be
> added to the honor roll of those courageous Americans who
> have valiantly fought and died on the battlefields to pre-
> serve freedom and the principles of democracy.

George Bates Smith was born in Los Angeles on December 26, 1918, the son of Mildred Jackson and Frank Smith. Unfortunately, nothing is known about his early life or his aviation cadet training. At the time of the crash he was assigned to the 7234th Food Service Squadron at Wiesbaden, and like Leland Williams, he was taken from his desk and pressed into pilot duties at the onset of the airlift. George was well-qualified as a pilot with over 2,000 hours of flying time. On the night of the ill-fated flight, he was flying as copilot with Lieutenant Williams. He was listed by the air force as being from Tuscaloosa, Alabama, but shortly thereafter the veterans administration advised that he was from Los Angeles. He left his widow, Harriet, and two children.

Karl Victor Hagen. In October 1935, Louis and Victoria Hagen fled Berlin, Germany and emigrated to the United States, taking with them their son, Karl Victor, who was born in Berlin on October 4, 1912. Karl's widow, Yvonne, told the story of his early life. "Karl Victor Hagen was the oldest son of Louis Hagen, a banker, who was the son of Karl Hagen, also a banker and founder of the *Bayerische Motor Werke* (BMW) before World War I. Although brought up as a Lutheran, his family was of Jewish origin, a fact Hitler unearthed when he moved to take over the BMW factory. I married Karl in 1940 while I was still in school at the Art Students' League."

Karl's formal education ended in 1932 when he left the University of Berlin and took a bank clerk job in Strasbourg, France. From there he moved to England temporarily until emigrating with his parents to America. During World War II, because of his language skills, he was recruited by the OSS. Back in Germany in 1945 with the Office of Military Government in Berlin, Karl warmed to his duties as a civilian member of the occupation force. By 1947 he was named the United States representative to a four-power group working on currency reform and spent increasing amounts of time in Frankfurt coordinating mint activities. On the night of July 8, 1948, having completed his work in Frankfurt for the time being, Karl was impatient to return to Berlin. At Rhein-Main airport in Frankfurt, traffic was clogged with awaiting passengers, so he arranged ground transportation to Wiesbaden and caught a ride with Lieutenants Williams and Smith, only to have his life cut short at age 35.

July 25, 1948. The airlift was officially less than a month old when its second fatal crash occurred. On its final approach to a landing at Tempelhof at approximately 1:00 a.m. on July 25, a C-47 plowed into a street in front of an apartment house in the Friedenau district. First Lieutenant Charles H. King and First Lieutenant Robert W. Stuber, the pilot and copilot, respectively, were killed instantly in the fiery crash. The accident, which happened close to the center of downtown Berlin and only a few city blocks distant from touchdown, resulted in an immediate outpouring of sympathy from Berliners, best expressed by a nameless person who placed a simple plaque on the crash site, reading: "Two American flyers became victims of the Berlin blockade here. You gave your lives for us! The Berliners of the west sectors will never forget you! We stand deeply moved on this spot that has been dedicated by your death. Once we were enemies, and yet you gave your lives for us. We are now doubly obligated to you." Coincidentally, General Clay and Chip Bohlen had arrived at Tempelhof only minutes prior to the crash, after a long, tiring flight from Washington.

Charles Howard King, the son of Judge Harold W. King and Lyla Buss, was born on June 18, 1922 in Aberdeen, South Dakota, the closest hospital to his family's home in tiny Britton. Charles later graduated from high school in Britton. After two years at the University of South Dakota at Vermillion, he entered West Point Military Academy, graduating in a wartime-accelerated class on June 5, 1945 with both a commission as second lieutenant and pilot wings.

Early in 1946 Charles was assigned to headquarters USAFE, with duty as a personnel staff officer at Lindsey air station in Wiesbaden. There he met Natalie O'Keefe, a civilian nurse in the military hospital. They married in the 317th Base Hospital chapel on July 19, 1947, and a son, William, was born the following May. His widow later described the early airlift conditions: "In the early days of the airlift...all available planes and pilots were utilized. Chuck was delighted to have a part in that dramatic and humanitarian enterprise. He flew regularly and served long hours." On the news of his death, she continued: "News spreads fast and all of our friends rallied—also, friends I didn't know I had. I received condolences and prayers from the German people, including those in the apartments! I cherish a beautiful silver bracelet, no doubt her most prized possession, sent to me by one of those wonderful women."

Eleven years later, Natalie, son William, and Charles' mother returned to Berlin for the 1959 tenth anniversary ceremonies at the airlift memorial in Tempelhof. Natalie reported on her trip: "We airlift families returned to West Berlin as guests of those wonderful people. The kindness, the sharing, is almost indescribable. For a little ten-year-old boy it was very special. My son had never known his father; he only heard us tell him how fine he was. Here he was able to see an entire city as well as three other governments pay honor and call him a hero. Little guys need that."

Natalie later married again, to a World War II infantry officer who was wounded in the Battle of the Bulge. He gave her a stepdaughter, and now she has three fine grandchildren. "If I were a philosopher," she concluded, "I might give some deep thought to the twists and turns that life brings us and even to some of the 'might have beens.' We have survived and made a good life. It is better to forget some of the gaps."

Robert Wallace Stuber. In February 1945, Robert Stuber, copilot of a B-17, was reported missing in action over Germany. But in the end, he survived the war and went on to postwar duty in the now defeated and occupied country. Early in 1948, he was assigned to headquarters USAFE and served in the same military personnel unit with Charles King. It was well-known around his office that he preferred flying.

Robert was born on August 28, 1920 in St. Joseph, Missouri. At Central High he starred in football, basketball, and track, thus carrying on the noted athletic tradition of his family. After graduation in 1939, the young athlete attended the University of Missouri for a year, then moved on to California and a position with Douglas Aircraft. Later, in March 1943, he enlisted in the aviation cadet program, moved steadily through his training phases, and was commissioned at Marfa, Texas the following year.

Bob's wife, Maxine, of Santa Monica, California, and their eighteen-month-old son, Robert, Jr., accompanied him to Germany in 1948, and at the time of the crash they were living in a Wiesbaden hotel while awaiting a permanent quarters assignment. On August 7, 1948, the *Los Angeles Times* reported that Berlin citizens sent bouquets of flowers to the widows of both Lieutenant King and Lieutenant Stuber on an Operation Vittles aircraft. Many notes of sympathy accompanied the flowers, including one which poignantly read, "In bringing us life, you gave yours."

Bob's widow remarried but returned to Berlin in 1959 with twelve-year-old Robert, Jr. to attend the tenth anniversary ceremonies.

August 24, 1948. One month after the crash that took the lives of Lieutenants King and Stuber, two C-47s collided in mid-air only a few kilometers from Rhein-Main airfield in Frankfurt. In the early morning of August 24, 1948, Captain Joel M. DeVolentine and his copilot First Lieutenant William T. Lucas departed Wiesbaden for Tempelhof, their C-47 loaded with foodstuffs for blockaded Berlin. Upon arrival, the aircraft was unloaded, and the two pilots departed at 6:18 a.m. for the return flight. A second C-47, piloted by Major Edwin C. Diltz with Captain William R. Howard as copilot, had departed Tempelhof 27 minutes earlier. Inexplicably, the two aircraft collided at 8:30 a.m. over the village of Ravolzhausen, just a short distance from their destination, when one of the C-47s rammed the other and severed its tail structure. It is unknown if weather was a factor, although circumstances of almost any midair collision strongly suggest either limited or zero visibility. Of the eleven aerial crashes of Operation Vittles, this was the only one in which two aircraft were involved, and in terms of fatalities it was the second most costly accident.

Joel Monroe DeVolentine was the son of Minnie and Frank DeVolentine of Lawrenceville, Georgia. He was born there on February 1, 1917, but his father's business as a contractor forced the family to move often, and as a result, young Joel graduated from high school not in Lawrenceville but from Miami, Florida in 1936. He went on to college at Duke University, played end on the Blue Devil's football team, joined the Young Republicans, graduated, and became vice-president of an insurance firm prior to entering military service. In January 1942, Joel graduated from aviation cadet school at Kelly Field, Texas, earning a commission and pilot wings. During World War II he served as a B-29 instructor pilot at Randolph Field, Texas, and by the time he reported for airlift duty he had amassed 2,500 hours of flying time. In May, three months before the accident, he passed an instrument check and had 65 hours as a C-47 first pilot. Assigned as a special services officer at headquarters USAFE, Joel was another of many pilots stationed in Germany who were rushed into duty to meet the need for air crews in those early weeks of the airlift. His wife and two children were living with him in Wiesbaden at the time of the accident. Joel's mother attended the 1959 ceremonies in Berlin and was very much impressed by the generosity and kindness not only of her German hosts but of all Berliners who remembered the airlift.

William T. Lucas, Jr. was known to his childhood friends as "Ham" and on some occasions as "Hambone." Born in Wilson, North Carolina on June 3, 1922, he was the son of Sallie and William T. Lucas, Sr. At the Charles L. Coon High School, he owned a Model A Ford and played baseball and football. He left high school without graduating, entered the service in February 1943, and although details about his military training are skimpy, it is known that later in the year he was awarded pilot wings and a commission at aviation cadet graduation exercises. By the time that he entered on airlift duty, he had been promoted to first lieutenant. Following the tragic accident, "Ham" was borne home and buried with full military honors in the family cemetery plot in Wilson. Eleven years later his mother and sister attended the May 12, 1959 tenth anniversary ceremonies at the airlift memorial in Tempelhof, to and from which "Ham" had flown so many times. They were presented with a porcelain copy of the Berlin Freedom Bell, one of which was presented to each family of an airlift casualty.

Edwin Cary Diltz was the son of a Methodist minister, Rev. Charles B. Diltz. His mother was Elizabeth Buna. "Jack," as he was known in college, was born October 14, 1916 in Hamilton, Texas. The family moved around Texas frequently during Jack's childhood and teen years, and in 1929 he graduated from Killeen Elementary School, followed by graduation from San Marcos High School in 1934. After three-and-a-half years of college, he became a railroad telegrapher, remaining in this job until late 1940 when he entered the aviation cadet program in Ontario, California. Eight months later he was commissioned and awarded pilot wings at Barksdale Field, Louisiana.

Jack did not see combat in World War II. Instead, he fought "the battle of Carlsbad," as he called it, referring to his assignment to Carlsbad air base in New Mexico where he spent three years. Then followed a series of assignments around the country during which he flew the new B-29 long-range bomber. In 1946 all that changed. He was transferred to occupation duty in Germany, first to Erlangen, then to Oberpfaffenhofen. His wife, Doris, was one of the first American dependents to arrive—in May 1946. She wrote after his death, "I do believe for once in his short lifetime he felt really being part of a very great move, and his last letters [he had sent his wife home in April 1948 during the Russian's "Little Blockade"] reflected how proud he was to have Captain Howard as his copilot."

Doris Diltz flew to Berlin in May 1959 to attend the memorial ceremonies and while there visited her brother-in-law, General Theo Diltz, whose unofficial investigations found that the accident was caused by human error: control tower communications.

William Riley Howard was born on July 18, 1920 in Una, Mississippi. He was the eldest of four sons who were raised on a plantation in the delta. His grammar and high school educations were taken in Gunnison, and he later attended Mississippi State College in Starksville, leaving in October 1941, in the final quarter of his senior year to join the aviation cadet program. By May 1942 he had completed all of his flight training and won his commission and pilot wings at Moody Field, Georgia. Following a short assignment as an instructor pilot at Moody and Fort Worth, Bill transitioned to the new B-29 Superfortress, then moved with his crew to Chakulia, India. From this base, he and his crew flew many combat missions, returning to the states in March 1945.

In recognition of his combat achievements, he was awarded the Distinguished Flying Cross and the Air Medal with two oak leaf clusters. Bill married his fiancée, Eleanor Morgan, while on home leave, then later traveled to his new post at Erlangen, Germany, with subsequent assignment to Oberpfaffenhofen as assistant operations officer with duties, among others, as chief of instrument training. Eleanor joined him in September 1946, and a son, William, Jr., was born in Munich on December 1, 1947. Drafted for airlift duty, as were so many pilots stationed in Germany in the summer of 1948, Bill was assigned to Wiesbaden with the 60th Troop Carrier Group. By this time in his career, he had accumulated over 3,000 hours in the cockpit, and his commanding officer at Obie called him one of the three best pilots in the European theater. He made his first airlift flight on August 17, 1948. Exactly one week later he made his last. In May 1959, Eleanor and young William joined other families in Berlin for the memorial services. She ultimately moved to Valdosta, Georgia where her husband is interred and in 1992 published *A Time of Love,* a stirring memoir of her courtship with Bill and their three short years of married life.

October 2, 1948. The first of two fatal American ground accidents occurred on this date at Rhein-Main airfield when a fire truck driven by Private First Class **Johnnie Thomas Orms** collided with a C-54 taxiing onto the active runway. Johnnie was killed instantly by one of the Skymaster's whirling propellers. No one in the aircraft was injured. The accident was the first in which an enlisted man was killed and was also the first involving an army soldier. Johnnie was assigned to the 61st Installation Squadron at Rhein-Main.

Johnnie was born in Coffeyville, Kansas on November 23, 1919, the son of Nellie and Harry Orms. His father was a fireman at a local brick-making plant, a factor that may account for his son's ultimate army assignment as a fire truck driver. Johnnie was drafted in October 1942, and his first assignment following basic training was to England where he met and married an English woman in 1943.

The couple had three daughters. From England, Johnnie was assigned to Rhein-Main shortly after the airlift commenced. After the accident, at his mother's request and his widow's consent, Johnnie was returned to Coffeyville for burial next to his father, who also died in 1948. His widow, Qwendline, continued to live in their home in Foxton, England.

So little is known about Johnnie's youth, his education, and even his army life, that it seems appropriate to write what was once said about a famous American, "Johnnie, we hardly knew ye!"

October 18, 1948. On this date occurred the first fatal aerial crash of a C-54 as a Skymaster ripped through tree tops in the Taunus mountains, only three minutes flying time from its destination at Rhein-Main air base. The aircraft was returning empty from Berlin and crashed at approximately 5:45 a.m. with the loss of all three crew members. "Early investigation indicated that the C-54 was descending for a landing when the right wing of the plane tore into the trees," stated the accident report. "Shredded tree tops and twisted bits of fuselage and wings traced the plane's last seconds in the air." Killed in the crash were:

First Lieutenant Eugene S. Erickson

Captain James A. Vaughan

Sergeant Richard Winter

It is believed that Captain Vaughan was at the controls on the return flight, but this was never firmly established. In airlift flight operations, however, it was not unusual for pilots and copilots to alternate in the left seat going to, and returning from, Berlin.

Eugene Samuel Erickson, son of Marie and Samuel D. Erickson, was born in Marinette, Wisconsin on October 26, 1918. During their high school years, Eugene and his brother Walter learned the trade of their father, who owned Erickson Co., dealers and contractors in tiles, asphalts, and linoleum. Eugene graduated from Marinette High School in 1936. Four years later he enlisted in the army air corps, spent two years at Scott Field, Illinois, then entered officer candidate school in Miami, Florida. At Jefferson Barracks, Missouri, his new station upon being commissioned a second lieutenant, he married Margaret Archer of Collinsville, Illinois.

By May 1943, Gene was in aviation cadet training in California where he advanced through primary and basic flying school, took advanced training at Stockton, and won his wings in March 1944. For the rest of the war he served in the Ferry Command. Discharged in 1945, he returned to active duty within a year and eventually was assigned to flying duty with the 19th Troop Carrier Squadron at Hickam Field, Hawaii. "At the onset of the airlift," wrote Gene's good friend at Hickam, Ray Rogers, "our 19th TCS was sent TDY to Westover AFB, Massachusetts, and from there we were reassigned to TDY at Rhein-Main. Some weeks we flew into Tempelhof on a high fatigue, maximum utilization schedule of eight hours on and eight hours off. On occasion we could not be seen by the tower operator as we taxied past."

When Margaret returned with her daughter, Diane, to Berlin in 1959 for the memorial services, she was overwhelmed. "The red carpet was laid out for us all," she reported. "What is so dear to our hearts is that the people of Berlin dropped their coins in cans, like we do for Red Cross, polio, etc., to pay for all the families going to the tenth reunion of the Berlin airlift. They were as proud as we were."

Gene was returned to Collinsville where he was buried with full military honors in January 1949. Margaret remarried, and Diane grew up to marry and have two children. Grandpa Erickson would have been very proud.

James Arthur Vaughan. "A Davidson County veteran of nearly nine years service with the U.S. Air Force was one of three airlift fliers killed in the crash of a C-54 Skymaster Monday near Frankfurt, Germany," so read the obituary in the Nashville *Tennessean* of October 21, 1948. He was Capt. James A. Vaughan, 26, the son of Mr. and Mrs. Arthur B. Vaughan and the husband of Helene Meyer Vaughan." She was living in New Haven, Connecticut, her hometown, at the time of his death. "I had a feeling he had been killed when I read about the Frankfurt accident," she said. A graduate of Bellevue High School, James enlisted as a private in July 1940 and ultimately earned a commission as second lieutenant at Yale University where he had been enrolled in an officer training program.

During World War II, Jim, as he was known, was shot down over Hungary on December 11, 1944 when his Italy-based B-24 on which he was serving as radar observer was returning from a raid on Austria. Forced to bail out, he was captured and held for seven months in a German prisoner of war camp. After the war's end, he enrolled in the aviation cadets and graduated with pilot wings from Barksdale Field, Louisiana. Ordered to Germany for airlift duty, he had a total of 1,000 hours flying time, and in the 30 days prior to the accident he had flown 129 hours.

When Helene and her twelve-year-old son, James, Jr., visited Berlin in May 1959 as guests of the city government, she stated to the press, "Capt. Vaughan's family and I are very, very proud of the fact that he died saving lives and not killing—that has given me the greatest peace of all the many things that have been said to me in past years. Capt. Vaughan was a prisoner who suffered under them and then went back and lost his life helping them. Now they want to say thank you." For many years Captain Vaughan's sister, **Bess Etter** of Brandon, Mississippi, has honored his memory through her membership in the Berlin Airlift Veterans Association and through faithful attendance at BAVA annual reunions.

Richard Winter. The first air force enlisted casualty of the airlift was Richard Winter, the son of Ruth and Bert Winter, who was born in Seattle, Washington on September 30, 1924. He attended Washington and Whittier grammar schools, then graduated in January 1943 from Garfield High School. Two months later he enlisted in the army air corps, then reenlisted in October 1947 in order to continue flying. He had trained to be an aircraft engineer; status as a flight engineer was something special, so he was eager to continue.

Richard married during his early air corps years, and he and his wife had a daughter, Beverly. At the time of his death, he was separated from his wife; hence, his daughter, who was only three, had little personal recollection of her father. She did, however, attend the May 12, 1959 ceremonies in Berlin with Richard's sister-in-law, Mrs. Onalee Wolfe. Beverly was fourteen at the time.

Richard's love for flying ultimately led to his death, for he was the flight engineer of the ill-fated C-54 on that early morning of October 18. Four days later the Rhein-Main newspaper, *The Gateway*, memorialized him and his two crew members as follows: "We may measure the results of the airlift with facts and figures and the cost in dollars, but there is no way to gauge the human sacrifice necessary to sustain a city of 2.3 million people. We salute those who gave their lives that others might live."

Postscript: Sergeant Winter's daughter, Beverly, informed me in February, 2002, that her grandson, Cody Dirkschneider, from Dodge, Nebraska, was proudly writing a school essay about his great grandfather.

October 29, 1948. For many years the total number of American airlift casualties stood at 31: 28 air force, one navy, one army, and one army civilian. But in 1998 air force historian Roger Miller pursued the circumstances of **Corporal George S. Burns'** death at Tegel airfield on October 29, 1948. Following a tip from a friend of Burns, Miller learned that the corporal was on the runway construction project, driving a bulldozer late at night. Noticing his absence after a period of time, fellow workers searched and found his body crushed into the ground. They surmised that

Burns had stood up to warm himself in the bulldozer exhaust, fell onto the track, and was crushed.

George was a native of Granite Falls, North Carolina and was assigned to Company C, First Engineer Combat Battalion, whose teams were busily engaged in the construction of the new Tegel airfield in the French sector of occupation. A strange notation about George's death is that while for so long his name was not on the official casualty tally, it was among those inscribed on the Tempelhof airlift memorial, dedicated in 1951.

December 5, 1948. In late November and early December, 1948, Europe was enveloped by dense fog. Airlift deliveries to Berlin reached a new low, and in the 24-hour period ending on November 30, only ten flights, British and American combined, arrived in the blockaded city. Whenever a slight break occurred in the weather, air crews were rushed to duty in urgent efforts to make up for the times when so many flights were cancelled. On December 5, a C-54 heavily laden with coal departed Fassberg on a late night mission to Gatow airfield in Berlin. The weather was marginal—a 200 foot ceiling and one mile visibility in light drizzle and fog. A few minutes after lifting off, the Skymaster banked sharply, fell into a sideslip, and crashed four kilometers from the airfield. All three crew members, named below, were killed instantly:

Captain Billy E. Phelps

First Lieutenant Willis F. Hargis

Technical Sergeant Lloyd G. Wells

The crash was the first of two that occurred at Fassberg during the airlift, both of them in the winter months. A specific cause of the crash was never officially determined, but it was widely believed that air crew fatigue and a sense of urgency to keep flying were contributing factors. This accident, above all the others, British and American, remains burned into my memory, for on December 3, two nights before he died, I flew copilot with Billy Phelps on two Berlin missions.

Billy Eugene Phelps earned money for his first flying lessons and made his first solo flight at age fifteen, without his parents' knowledge, let alone permission. Born in McKinney, Texas on January 16, 1922, he graduated from local schools and enlisted the day after Pearl Harbor. Subsequently, he entered the aviation cadet program, progressed through its training stages in Florida, Georgia, and Mississippi, and was awarded pilot wings and a commission as second lieutenant on June 30, 1943.

In World War II Billy, as pilot of a B-17 at an English base, flew many bombing missions over Germany and Czechoslovakia, including three raids on Berlin, for which he was awarded the Distinguished Flying Cross. On his last mission, his ship was destroyed by flak, his crew was forced to bail out, and Billy spent almost exactly one year in a prisoner of war camp. From the end of the war until the airlift commenced, Billy was stationed in Vera Cruz, Mexico, serving as control officer for aircraft being ferried to South America. At the time of his death, Billy had completed 85 trips to Berlin as copilot and 82 as pilot. He had flown over 120 hours at night and

36 hours on instruments in the previous thirty days. He had also flown over six hours in the 24 hours preceding his crash. From Fassberg, six hours meant three roundtrips. He had to be tired. His wife was expecting Billy home soon after Christmas, as soon as a replacement might arrive.

Willis Francis Hargis was also born in Texas, in Nacogdoches, on December 20, 1920. He graduated from high school in 1938, then enrolled in the Stephen F. Austin state teachers college, but shortly before graduation, in October 1942, he enlisted as an aviation cadet. Moving through the flying training phases at Santa Ana, California and Phoenix, Arizona, he completed the cadet program at Chandler, Arizona where he was awarded a commission and pilot wings.

When the airlift commenced in June 1948, Willis was in Germany on occupation duty at Erding air depot, north of Munich. Many flying officers with administrative duties were hastily pressed into action at that time to meet the immediate need for pilots, and Willis quickly found himself on TDY at Fassberg RAF station in northern Germany, far from his Bavarian post at Erding. There, he transitioned to the C-54 Skymaster, with its faster speed and greater load-carrying capacity than the C-47. The crash that took his life on December 5 occurred as air and ground crews scurried to make up for a huge tonnage deficit caused by dense fog during the previous two weeks. Willis was unmarried. His mother, Euzelia, was his only immediately family survivor, and in 1959 she was present at the tenth anniversary ceremonies at the airlift memorial in Tempelhof.

Lloyd George Wells was the only child of Edith and Morgan Wells, and he was born in Liberty, Missouri on September 24, 1919, a prophetic city name, given the cause for which he died. When he was eight years old, the family moved to Winnwood, where he went through elementary schools, later graduating from North Kansas City High School as a football star. Following graduation he worked for six months for Trans World Airlines as a mechanic, then enlisted in the army air corps. Training commenced at Lackland air base in San Antonio, then continued in Douglas, Arizona. It was there that he married his school sweetheart, Anna Lee Hadix, in August 1942. In November 1943, a son, Clifford, was born to the couple.

During World War II, Lloyd spent time in Topeka, Kansas and Kelly Field in San Antonio, ultimately reporting in 1948 to Germany for airlift duty. At Fassberg he was a well-trained and well-experienced flight engineer who knew the C-54 thoroughly but also knew, as Captain Phelps had stated earlier, that some of them were flying wrecks. Lloyd's widow and her fifteen-year-old son traveled to Berlin in 1959 as guests of the city government to take part in the tenth anniversary ceremonies.

December 11, 1948. At one minute after midnight on this date, a navy R5D crashed near Königstein, about 16 kilometers northeast of Rhein-Main air base. The aircraft was returning from a routine supply mission to Berlin and was only minutes from touchdown when it hit the ground and skidded about 335 meters along an upslope spotted with rows of apple trees.

There were six persons on board the R5D:
  Lieut. Joseph L. Norris, USN
  Ens. George Blackwood, USN
  First Lieut. Frank T. Heffernan, USAF, passenger
  Diane Day, Special Services civilian
  Unnamed passenger
  AMM3 Harry R. Crites, Jr., USN

Harry Crites, Jr., the flight engineer, was the single fatality of the crash. Lieutenant Norris, the pilot, lost an eye, and Ensign Blackwood suffered a broken leg; the others had bruises, cuts, and other minor injuries. Lieutenant Heffernan, who was only shaken up, reported, "The plane seemed to be cruising fine, and the crew was preparing to swing into Rhein-Main for a landing. It was foggy. Suddenly we hit the ground. After a few seconds, I crawled out through the broken windshield. The pilot was pinned down, and I chopped him out. Then we got the seriously injured officer out. The plane started to burn, but some Germans arrived to help us get it [the fire] out." Crites was taken by ambulance to the 97th General Hospital in Frankfurt but was pronounced dead on arrival. For his role in extricating the injured from the airplane's wreckage, Lieutenant Heffernan was later awarded the Soldier's Medal. He died in 1983.

Harry Russel Crites, Jr. enlisted in the U.S. Navy on November 14, 1945 at Indianapolis. A native of Lafayette, Indiana, he was seventeen at the time. Following technical school training, he was assigned to the flag administrative unit of the Pacific air commander, then he moved to a utility squadron and was promoted on February 1, 1947 to Aviation Machinist Mate Third Class, with duty as a flight engineer.

Harry was born on October 13, 1928 in Lafayette, one of three children. He spent all his childhood years in his hometown, graduating from elementary and high schools there. Very much interested in military service, the young man was quick to enlist in the navy after his birthday, and he applied himself vigorously during his basic and technical training.

Still on duty as a flight engineer when the airlift commenced, Harry moved with his navy squadron on a 180-day TDY assignment to Rhein-Main on November 1. Less than six weeks later, he lost his life in the Königstein crash, the only fatality among the six on board.

In 1950 Harry's parents visited Lindsey air station in Wiesbaden to view and photograph the street named in his memory. Nine years later they were also among the group of American guests visiting Berlin for the tenth anniversary ceremonies marking the end of the blockade. But his story doesn't end here. A photo of Harry was donated to the Indiana military museum in Vincennes where it is now displayed with photos of Herbert Heinig, Bernard Watkins, and Robert Weaver, all sons of Indiana who died in airlift accidents. In 1999 and 2000, Harry's and Bernard Watkins' short lives were researched by students at Jefferson High School in Lafayette; detail of their efforts is cited in the next segment.

January 7, 1949. The most severe airlift loss of American lives resulted from a tragic accident over England on January 7, 1949, as a C-54 en route from Rhein-Main to RAF Burtonwood crashed about thirty miles from its destination. On board were six airmen; there were no survivors.

With First Lieutenant Richard Wurgel, an instructor pilot, at the controls, the Skymaster departed Rhein-Main on what was expected to be a routine two-and-three-quarter hour flight to the huge maintenance depot at Burtonwood. Weather conditions were good with six miles of visibility in a light drizzle. Wurgel, flying under visual flight rules, established radio contact with Burtonwood tower and received approach and landing instructions. An official cause of the crash was never determined, but quite possibly the pilot suddenly encountered instrument weather conditions since the search party had to make its way through driving rain and mist before reaching the wreckage. Those killed in the crash were:

> First Lieutenant Richard M. Wurgel, Pilot
>
> First Lieutenant Lowell A. Wheaton, Copilot
>
> Sergeant Bernard J. Watkins, Flight Engineer
>
> Corporal Norbert H. Theis, Radio Operator
>
> Captain William A. Rathgeber, Passenger
>
> Private First Class Ronald E. Stone, Passenger

Richard Melvin Wurgel was a 1939 honors graduate of Woodrow Wilson High School in Weehawken, New Jersey. Born on July 18, 1922 in Weehawken, his scholastic interest in school was chemical engineering which he continued to pursue during his short time in college. With World War II on, he enlisted in the aviation cadet program and graduated from Turner Field, Georgia in March 1944 with pilot wings and a commission. Richard had no actual combat time during the war, but at the time of his death he had logged more than 2,400 hours. Details are skimpy, yet his total time would suggest that he was either an instructor or a ferry pilot.

When the airlift commenced, Richard was stationed at Bergstrom AFB, Texas with the 313th Troop Carrier Group. He moved to Rhein-Main with his group as airlift units built up, and he remained there as an instructor when the 313th moved to Fassberg.

Richard's widow remarried but even ten years later, in 1959, it was too painful for her to make the trip to Berlin for the anniversary ceremonies.

Lowell Adair Wheaton, Jr. was born on January 21, 1923 in Galveston, Texas and lived in Corpus Christi during his youth. When he boarded the ill-fated C-54 on January 7, 1949 for its flight to Burtonwood, he was 25 years old. On that mission he flew as copilot after having been recalled to active duty in October, and after having completed the three-week airlift prep course at Great Falls AFB, Montana.

During World War II Lowell attended Texas A & M, then moved through the aviation cadet program and graduated at Lubbock army air field in April 1943 where he was awarded pilot wings and a commission as second lieutenant. From Lubbock he entered B-17 crew training, eventually flying 180 combat hours from a B-17 base in southern Italy.

At the time of Lowell's death, his wife, Dorothy, was preparing to join her husband in Europe. In 1959, however, it was Lowell's mother who attended the tenth anniversary ceremonies in Berlin.

Bernard Jerard Watkins, born August 27, 1922 in Lafayette, Indiana, attended Longlois Elementary School, then in June 1940 graduated from Jefferson High School where he was an excellent student and majored in numerous subjects—English, mathematics, social studies, and science. He also played quarterback on the football team and pitched on the high school baseball team. And he loved cars. Despite such youthful joy, his young life also knew sadness. When only twelve years old, he discovered his mother's body; she had shot herself. His only brother, Robert, was killed in World War II. Following graduation, Bernard worked in Lafayette in the electrical furnace business, following, after a fashion, his father's skills as a mechanic.

In 1942 Bernard enlisted in the army air corps and served in Europe as an airplane mechanic. He returned home at war's end and was discharged in November 1945. Still searching for what he really might do in life, he worked as an auto mechanic but pondered the future. Then, in March 1948, apparently feeling that military life was his best option, he reenlisted. From that point on, he was a part of the 313th Troop Carrier Group at Bergstrom AFB, Texas that moved to Germany in October 1948 to provide airlift support. A few short months later, Bernard lost his life in the Burtonwood crash. After his death, Bernard's father moved from Lafayette; hence, air force officials were unable to locate him in 1959 when invitations were mailed for the Berlin ceremonies.

In 1999, Don Fitzgerald, a history teacher at Jefferson High, recruited two students, Joanna Smelser and Katherine Shafer, for a research project on the two men from Tippecanoe County, Indiana who lost their lives on the airlift. The two men were Harry Crites and Bernard Watkins. The two students were assisted by a third researcher, Lisa Becker, and together they mounted a massive research effort that turned up previously unknown information on the two men. Their efforts also resulted in the men's names being inscribed on plaques in Lafayette's Columbian Park.

Norbert V. Theis, the crew's radio operator, was born near Dodge City, Kansas, one of nine children. In his early years, the family moved to Cunningham, Kansas, where Norbert attended high school, but only for a year and a half. He then found work as an auto mechanic in order to help support his family.

Before he was even eighteen, the young man enlisted for three years in the army air corps and went immediately into basic training. There followed a 32-week radio operator and mechanic course at Scott Field, Illinois, specialized training consistent with young Norbert's keen fascination with radios. Graduating in October 1947, he then moved to his next station at Bergstrom AFB, Texas and the 313th Troop Carrier Group.

Three days after the official beginning of the airlift, Norbert was on the first C-54 to arrive at Rhein-Main from the states. From that time on, he was actively engaged in radio operation and maintenance, and flying airlift missions as often as he was needed. Radio operators were used on C-54s for international and overwater flights but not necessarily on Vittles missions.

Norbert's mother did not remember ever receiving an invitation to attend the tenth anniversary ceremonies in Berlin, so she therefore never knew about the city's generosity in inviting family members of those killed to attend.

William A. Rathgeber was born in Spokane, Washington, attended North Central High School, then Gonzaga High and finally graduated from Rogers High School. His brother Albert summarized his life: "He was eighteen months older than I, and we were always together. He was the leader of the Rathgeber boys, as we were called in those days. He did some boxing, we both did, me in self-defense, mostly. Bill was a good friend, and I was proud of him. We were as close as brothers could be."

Bill enlisted in the army early on, went to Hawaii and served a three-year enlistment in a military police company. Upon returning home after discharge, he had difficulty finding work and so enlisted in a national guard observation squadron at Fort Lewis, Washington. While there, he applied for aviation cadet training, went through the program and received pilot wings and a commission in 1940. Years later Bill was stationed at Clark Field in the Philippines where he served as air provost marshal. Shortly after his return home from this assignment, he was transferred to Rhein-Main for airlift duty as a C-54 pilot. It was presumed that he was on a liaison mission from Rhein-Main to Burtonwood when he died as a passenger in the January 7 crash.

In May 1959, Bill's son, Billy, Jr., and Bill's father, Albert, were guests of the Berlin city government at the tenth anniversary ceremonies. Bill's wife had died from an accidental gunshot wound shortly before he returned from the Philippines. In Berlin, the elder Rathgeber was chosen from among the 37 relatives of those killed in airlift accidents to represent the fathers of all those who had fallen.

Once more, brother Albert summed up his feelings. "I'm not sure what those memories will do to the history of the airlift," he pointed out, "but if they just help to confirm that Bill was a real good guy to have around, then I am happy."

Ronald E. Stone enlisted in the air force on January 7, 1948. Exactly one year later to the day, he died as a passenger in the C-54 crash near Burtonwood. Thirty-four years later a display was dedicated in Ron's memory at a new leadership school for noncommissioned officers on Stone Street at Lindsey air station in Wiesbaden.

The third of four sons of Sidney and Mayme Stone, Ronald was born on December 6, 1929 in Mount Sterling, Kentucky, in the bluegrass country. During World War II one of his brothers served in the Aleutian

Islands and another in Japan. Ron was too young at the time for military service, and he felt badly that he wasn't old enough to fight.

On the day of the accident, Ron was returning to Burtonwood, his assigned station, from a trip to Rhein-Main where, according to his nephew, Gary Stone, he served as a witness in a court-martial proceeding. "He wanted to get back to Burtonwood," wrote Gary, "because he was in love with an English girl." A friend at Rhein-Main helped to secure passage for Ron on the ill-fated C-54.

At the 1959 Tempelhof ceremonies, Ron's mother Mayme was selected to represent the mothers of all those who had died in airlift accidents. In speaking later about her son, she stated, "He always wanted to do things for others. Some of his friends told me that he planned to come home and study for the ministry. I should have known, just by the way that he lived. But I just didn't know."

January 12, 1949. At five minutes past midnight on this date, three airlift flyers died when their C-54 crashed and burned about four kilometers east of Rhein-Main. The crew was returning from a routine mission to Berlin. Weather conditions were poor–dark, overcast skies with a 1,500 foot ceiling, visibility three miles in snow, and a fairly strong southwest wind. Two American officers who witnessed the crash from the nearby autobahn ran to the wreckage and pulled clear the bodies of three crew members. There were no survivors. Those killed in the crash were:

> First Lieutenant Ralph H. Boyd, Pilot
>
> First Lieutenant Craig B. Ladd, Copilot
>
> Technical Sergeant Charles L. Putnam, Flight Engineer

Ralph Hopkins Boyd, the pilot on the ill-fated January 12 flight, was a natural athlete. He played baseball and football in high school, then played first base on the University of Oklahoma Sooners baseball team. He studied also at the University of Texas but never graduated from either institution.

Ralph was born in Henrietta, Texas on April 2, 1916, the son of Mary B. Curry and James V. Boyd. His father was a veteran of the Spanish-American war, and his grandfather rode as a confederate with Nathan Bedford Forrest's cavalry during the Civil War. Despite such a military legacy, the family were all farmers and as Ralph's brother said, "solid, pastoral, God-fearing, church-going Methodists." Early on, Ralph picked up the unusual nickname of "Ecca," and it stuck with him.

During World War II, Ecca went through aviation cadet training and graduated at Pampa, Texas in August 1943 with pilot wings and a commission. He went into B-26 medium bomber transition training, then flew combat missions from England over Germany, was shot down in 1944, taken prisoner, escaped after two weeks, and returned to the United States. Discharged in 1945, Ecca flew for American Airlines for a few short years until recalled in October 1948 for airlift service, including prep school training at Great Falls AFB. By November he was at Rhein-Main, commencing Vittles missions to Berlin. Then came January 12, 1949. Ecca was survived by his wife, Wanda, and two small children, James and Patty.

Craig Burton Ladd wanted to become a forest ranger, but his draft board had other plans. Called to service in 1941 and trained in the infantry, he decided that the wild blue was for him and applied for flight training. Moving through the aviation cadet program, he graduated from advanced training at Altus, Oklahoma in July 1943 with pilot wings and a commission. During World War II he flew an amazing 240 hours of actual combat in 52 missions over Germany, and was awarded both the Distinguished Flying Cross and the Air Medal with five oak leaf clusters.

Craig was born in Bayfield, Wisconsin on May 30, 1918, graduated from Lincoln High School in May 1936, worked for a year, then enrolled at the University of Wisconsin at Madison where he majored in forestry for three years. Nothing is known about his later life following World War II until June 1948 when he was back on active duty and receiving an instrument check at Wold-Chamberlain field in Minneapolis. By November the airlift was picking up speed, and Craig was transferred to Great Falls AFB for the three week airlift training course, following which he was assigned to the 61st Troop Carrier Group at Rhein-Main. By that time his log book showed over 1,600 hours of flying time but only sixteen in the C-54.

Shortly after Christmas he commenced flying Vittles missions only to have his life cut short on January 12. Craig was survived by his wife, Eleanor, whom he married in May 1947. The couple had no children. Unfortunate family circumstances prevented Eleanor and Craig's mother from attending the Berlin ceremonies in May 1959, but he is not forgotten. His name, along with others killed in airlift operations, is inscribed in the memorial window in the Rhein-Main chapel.

Charles Lee Putnam was the flight engineer on the C-54 that crashed on January 12, 1949. Nicknamed "Lee" by his friends, he always wanted to fly. Color blindness, however, disqualified him from aviation cadet training, and he pursued instead training to become a flight engineer.

Born in Colorado Springs, Colorado on April 26, 1924, Lee graduated from Main High School in 1942. In school he was a strong athlete and played on the basketball team. Following graduation, both Lee and his brother enlisted in the army air corps. After basic training and technical schools, Lee was assigned overseas and became a B-24 crew member with the 15th Air Force in Italy. On only his ninth mission, his bomber was attacked on a raid over Friedrichshafen on Lake Constance in southernmost Germany. Severely disabled, the Liberator limped over the border into Switzerland where the crew bailed out. There they were interned until the end of the war.

Lee returned to Colorado after discharge and enrolled at the University of Colorado at Boulder, majoring in civil engineering. He never lost the bug for flying, however, even after his war experiences, and before graduating from college, in December 1947, he reenlisted. By the following July, he was on his way to Frankfurt with assignment as flight engineer with the 61st Troop Carrier Group at Rhein-Main. From that base, he flew Vittles missions for five months, but on January 12 his missions and his life came to an end.

In 1959 Lee's mother, Irene, traveled to Berlin at the city's invitation and took part in the tenth anniversary ceremonies. Her detailed diary of her trip reported on the numerous receptions and kindnesses shown by the German people not only in Berlin but also at events in Wiesbaden and Frankfurt.

January 18, 1949. January was a tragic month in terms of airlift casualties: three American and two British crashes, with a total loss of fourteen lives. On January 18 at about 1:30 p.m., an empty C-54 returning from a Vittles mission to Berlin crashed and burned approximately ten kilometers east of Fassberg RAF station as it commenced its final approach. **First Lieutenant Robert Porter Weaver**, the pilot, received severe burns that resulted in his death shortly thereafter. The other two crew members suffered minor injuries.

Born on January 25, 1918 in Fort Wayne, Indiana, Robert was the ninth child of Dr. and Mrs. Ben Weaver. At the time of his death he was only one week shy of his 31st birthday. Robert attended elementary and high school in Fort Wayne and later enrolled in Louisiana State University at Baton Rouge. During World War II, he received his flight training at Fort Bragg, North Carolina, then served more than three years as a civilian flight instructor and multi-engine pilot. In late 1947 he was recalled to active duty, this time in uniform, and was stationed for five months at Clark Field in the Philippines before being transferred TDY to Germany for airlift duty.

Robert was married during the war, and he and his wife, Mabel, had a son, Robert, Jr., who was born in 1947. In May 1959, Mrs. Weaver and twelve-year-old Robert, Jr. traveled to Berlin for the tenth anniversary ceremonies. On this occasion Robert, Jr. was selected to represent all sons of those men who died in airlift accidents.

March 4, 1949. During a routine Vittles mission on this date, a C-54 from Rhein-Main crashed 163 kilometers northeast of Frankfurt, close to the tiny Soviet zone village of Heroldishausen. Those citizens and those of nearby Grossengottern have honored Lieutenant Royce Stephens, who died in the crash, with a memorial at the accident site. According to official documents, the accident was caused by an engine oil leak that resulted in a fire. In the rush to escape the burning aircraft, two crew members were thrown out of the emergency door while others bailed out normally. Lieutenant Royce Stephens, the pilot, was last seen attempting to turn on the autopilot so as to stabilize the aircraft and escape to the rear, but he failed to get clear as the aircraft hit the ground in a steep dive. His body was found in the cargo compartment where he apparently sought to reach the emergency door to bail out.

Those on the aircraft were:

First Lieutenant Royce C. Stephens, Pilot

First Lieutenant Donald W. Keating, Copilot

Staff Sergeant John L. Hanlon, Flight Engineer

Sergeant William J. Sakkinen, Passenger

Sergeant William A. Kinzalow, Passenger

A brief account of how the surviving crew members returned to American custody is set forth in chapter four.

Royce Coy Stephens was born August 30, 1921 in Burkburnett, Texas, the son of Johnnie and Dennis Dee Stephens. He was one of five children, was known to his young friends as "Buster," and was a popular local youth. He grew up in Shamrock, Texas, where he graduated from high school, then attended the Southwest School of Aeronautics in Dallas.

During World War II Royce completed the aviation cadet program, and won his pilot wings and commission in 1942 at Waco, Texas. From there he moved to B-17 transition training, flew 25 combat missions from England with the 8th Air Force, and was awarded the Distinguished Flying Cross. Later he flew as an Air Transport Command pilot in the Pacific area. At the end of the war in 1945, Steve, as he preferred to be called, enrolled in the University of Texas but remained in the reserve forces. Then, in November 1948, he was recalled to active duty for the Berlin airlift. On the fateful day of the crash, he was flying his third trip of the day and his 36th mission to Berlin.

In seeking to control the stricken aircraft so that the crew members could safely bail out, Steve performed a true act of heroism. For his bravery, he was posthumously awarded an oak leaf cluster to his Distinguished Flying Cross, the only DFC awarded for airlift service. He was brought home following the fatal accident, and on April 15, 1949 he was buried with full military honors in the Fort Sam Houston national cemetery in San Antonio.

July 12, 1949. The only fatal American crash following the lifting of the blockade occurred exactly two months thereafter. On an early morning takeoff from Celle, a Skymaster hauling ten tons of coal to Tegel crashed nineteen kilometers west of Rathenow in the Soviet zone, only a few kilometers northwest of its destination, Berlin. The crew radioed that they had feathered number three engine due to a malfunction and that the propeller on number four engine was running wild. The C-54, extremely difficult to control with two engines out on the same side, was steadily losing altitude. Five minutes later it struck the ground and was destroyed. There were no survivors among the three man crew, nor was there any indication of an attempt to bail out of the stricken aircraft. They had apparently been engrossed in trying to keep the severely disabled C-54 flying.

The three crew members who died were:
>   First Lieutenant Robert C. von Luehrte, Pilot
>   Second Lieutenant Donald J. Leemon, Copilot
>   Technical Sergeant Herbert E. Heinig, Flight Engineer

Robert Charles von Luehrte was a Kentuckian, born in Covington on April 28, 1923. Following graduation from Covington Catholic High school in 1940, young Robert worked with his father for about a year and a half as an assistant lithographer in a Covington firm. He then enlisted in the aviation cadet program and successfully progressed through the pre-flight, primary, basic, and advanced phases, winning pilot wings and a commission as second lieutenant at Roswell, New Mexico on October 10, 1943.

Next followed transition training in the B-17 Flying Fortress, with later assignment to a heavy bomber group in Italy. From his base he flew fifty combat missions in the Mediterranean and southern Europe area. On July 24, 1947, two years after war's end, Robert was discharged at Davis-Monthan air base in Tucson and returned to Covington to take up civilian life as a salesman in restaurant supply.

Still in the air reserve, Robert was recalled to active duty in January 1949 and assigned to the three-week airlift prep course at Great Falls AFB, Montana, following which he moved to the 45th Troop Carrier Squadron at Celle RAF station. On April 12 he wrote to his family: "Dear Mom, Dad, and boys, I'm fine and dandy. Hauling lots of coal into Berlin these days and getting plenty black doing it. I have been to Berlin about 90 times now. Let's see, that's about 1.8 million pounds of that black stuff. How would you like to have all that in the coal bin, Dad?"

Robert was survived by his parents, his wife, Virginia, and a baby daughter. Virginia later remarried, but for reasons unknown she never received an invitation to the 1959 Berlin ceremonies.

Donald J. Leemon "was born on a farm on August 29, 1924 in the town of Chase, in Oconto County, Wisconsin," so reads his autobiography. "My early life was spent on the farm, getting into mischief, and doing what an ordinary child would do." By the time that Donald was thirteen, the family had moved to Pulaski, situated a bit further south and closer to Green Bay. Young Donald graduated from elementary and high school in Pulaski, where he played basketball, participated in the band, and was active in the Future Farmers of America.

Following high school graduation, Donald worked in Milwaukee in a defense job, but upon reaching age eighteen in 1942, he enlisted in the army air corps, studied radio mechanics, then applied for aviation cadet training. He completed the program successfully and won pilot wings and a commission as second lieutenant on June 27, 1944 at Stockton, California.

After Stockton, Don went through B-17 transition training at Kingman, Arizona and crew training at Lincoln, Nebraska, moved to the 398th Bomb Group in England, and flew twenty missions, the last against

Pilsen, Czechoslovakia on April 25, 1945. He was discharged in October and went through a series of unsatisfactory civilian jobs as well as a brief attendance at the University of Wisconsin. In January 1947 he reenlisted as a staff sergeant with assignment to Scott Field, Illinois where he met and married Marilyn Ragsdale of St. Louis.

As a reserve officer, Don was recalled to airlift duty in his rank as second lieutenant, assigned to Great Falls for the airlift training program, with further assignment to the 40th Troop Carrier Squadron at Celle. Marilyn joined him in Germany at Easter time in 1949, and the couple had approximately three months together before his fatal accident. Don was returned to Green Bay in August 1949 for burial with full military honors. Ten years later his father and mother attended the airlift remembrance ceremonies in Berlin.

Herbert Frederick Heinig, the son of Flora Pester and Robert Heinig, was born on March 16, 1915 in Fort Wayne, Indiana. He was the youngest of six children. His sister-in-law provided some details of his early life. "Herbert's parents and grandparents emigrated to the United States from Germany. His parents were only sixteen and eighteen years of age at the time. Herbert attended Lincoln School in Washington Township and graduated from the eighth grade. He continued his education at Northside High for three years but left to join the Civilian Conservation Corps, fighting forest fires out west. After a year he returned to Fort Wayne and pursued various jobs for four years."

By early 1941 young Herb was anxious for military life, but because he had not finished high school he had to complete a three-month technical course at Chanute Field, Illinois before he could enlist in April. After various assignments in Arizona and California, he was transferred to Hawaii in November 1944 and spent the war in the Pacific theater as an airplane engine mechanic. Following discharge a year later as a master sergeant, he returned to Fort Wayne where he worked at International Harvester and Phelps Dodge until 1947 when he reenlisted in the rank of technical sergeant.

By 1949 Herb was with the 40th Troop Carrier Squadron at RAF Celle, flying Vittles missions to Berlin. On the night of July 12, Skymasters were loaded and made ready for departure. The flight engineer scheduled for one C-54, however, could not be located. While a discussion was going on as to who would take the flight, "Sergeant Heinig, my roommate who had been on leave," recalls Bill Michaels, "came into the flight-line office and said that since he had slept all day and needed the flight time, he would take the flight." The rest of the tragic story unfolded as related above.

A week later, a memorial service for Herb and his two fallen comrades was conducted at the Celle station, and a month later Herb was brought home for burial in the family plot at Lindenwood Cemetery in Fort Wayne. In 1959 Herb's brother Albert and his wife, Alice, because both of his parents had died when he was very young, represented the Heinig family at the Berlin ceremonies, during which they attended the opera, enjoyed dinner at the Hotel Berlin, and went on a shopping and sightseeing tour of East Berlin.

Ж

"Courage is the price that life exacts for granting peace," wrote the noted aviatrix Amelia Earhart Putnam. And it was the courage and bravery of those veterans who lost their lives in airlift operations that helped to preserve the peace in those dark, uncertain days and nights of 1948 and 1949.

Nine

Airlift Veteran Groups and Reunions

What you airlift veterans did for Berlin was good, but what was better was that you did it despite what went on before.

Unnamed Berlin youth to RAF veteran David Hines during fiftieth anniversary reunion

THOSE UNITED LONG AGO in common bond find it only natural to reunite years later in memory, and in recognition of, the cause which originally brought them together. The men and women who took part in the Berlin airlift of 1948-1949 are no exception. During the many years and decades from 1949 until 1979, dozens, perhaps hundreds, of airlift veterans, British, Commonwealth, and American alike, returned to Germany to visit the air bases that were their homes throughout the long months of the Berlin blockade, and to dwell upon the rich memories of that fifteen-month period in which they gave their all to preserve not only Berlin but also West Germany, and conceivably all of Europe, from falling into the hands of the Soviet Union.

Yet those pilgrimages of the early years were clearly individual in nature, or carried out in small, informal groups; no official veterans' organizations existed at the time. It was not until 1990, in the aftermath of the fortieth anniversary observance of the airlift's end, that an effort was made to formalize a union of airlift veterans. Those groups that emerged, and a casual record of their activities that followed, are presented in the following pages.

The Thirtieth Anniversary

In perhaps the first instance of airlift veterans reuniting in groups, Americans and Britons arrived in Germany in 1979 to observe the thirtieth anniversary of the formal end of the airlift. No veterans' organizations had yet been formed, but those attending were organized by various tour groups, with strong, excellent support from the Airlift Gratitude Foundation in Berlin. **Jack A.V. Short**, who as a young RAF flying officer served as an air traffic controller and watch leader at Wunstorf, reports that he and his wife traveled with many other airlift veterans to Berlin for the ceremonies. Air Marshal Baker, who commanded Transport Command during the airlift, was also in attendance. American vets were well represented, too, and the U.S. Air Force flew a giant C-5 airlifter to Tempelhof for a static display.

"During the three-day weekend," Jack remembers, "there was an official reception at the Charlottenburg Palace and an afternoon outdoor service and dedication at the airlift memorial attended by all dignitaries and guests. In the evening we had an informal party at a hotel venue. The whole event was well-covered by German TV and radio." The USAF band also provided great music from the 1940s and 1950s. Following the airlift, Jack went on to serve 31 years in air traffic control, reaching the rank of group captain. He now lives in Dersingham, Norfolk.

The Fortieth Anniversary

In 1989 the mayor of Fassberg was one August Bruns, a jolly, plumpish, outgoing fellow, known around the community as "Mr. Fassberg." I had met him in 1986 during an earlier visit to the town and air base. Bruns was the owner of a local card, book, and gift shop and often conducted town business on its premises, since his office was officially part-time in nature yet required his 24-hour attention. A veteran of World War II, he served his military duty at Fassberg air base as a Luftwaffe corporal, or in the German parlance, a leading aircraftsman, and at the end of the war he decided to make Fassberg his home.

At the fortieth anniversary airlift reunion in 1989, Bruns took the returning veterans and their spouses under his wing and personally escorted them through the town hall and to various sites of historical significance. On one occasion he led the group several kilometers out of town and up a rise to a point where the beautiful, waving wild flowers of the Lüneberger Heath, a riot of color stretching far into the horizon, entranced the onlooker. At one point the mayor stopped, invited his visitors out of their vehicles, and pointed to a circle of large stones where water was bubbling from a spring. "Here is the origin of the name Fassberg," he exclaimed, pointing out that a *Faß* means a keg, tub, or container, and that everyone was standing at the peak of a *Berg*, the highest point in the area, although the elevation was a mere 100 meters above sea level. Almost all of northern Germany is lowland, gradually sloping down to the North Sea; hence, a *Berg* rising 30-35 meters over the surrounding terrain was about the highest mountain one could expect to see in this region.

A genuine bond between airlift veterans and Fassberg townies was very much in evidence during the reunion days. As a small farming community, Fassberg retains many social characteristics of rural towns everywhere—a sense of caring and a feeling of closeness among the citizenry. Such characteristics carried over to the American and British airmen who in 1948 and 1949 literally overwhelmed this small village by their close, crushing presence.

The air base, rather than being situated ten to fifteen kilometers outside of town, as is the case with so many military installations, has its main gate located immediately at the end of the town's main street. Although the historic village antedates the air base, modern Fassberg's proximity to the main gate was so planned and developed as the base was constructed in the 1930s. In 1948 and 1949, therefore, an ideal climate for the development of close town-military relations was nurtured by such proximity. This factor apparently did much for the development of close friendships between town citizens and USAF and British airmen, for many such friendships were maintained during the forty years between 1948 and 1988, and during the fortieth anniversary reunion in 1989, they manifested themselves in a memorable show of affection between the townspeople and returning veterans.

At the 1989 reunion, townspeople welcomed American veterans on the street, and in village shops and cafes, exuding the same warmth and openheartedness as did their mayor. During a formal address to the reunion group, Herr Bruns, reminiscing about airlift activities forty years earlier, suddenly grinned and mused, "If you veterans are still wondering what happened to all of the Fassberg fräuleins, don't worry, they're all grandmothers now." Later, in an emotional event typical of small-town society, a memorial service was conducted in the town's St. Michael's church, attended to the overflowing by both Fassberg citizens and returning airlift veterans, as well as their spouses. The church service was then followed, again in characteristic small-town fashion, by a lavish buffet dinner prepared by the women of the community in the classic dish-to-pass style.

During the 1989 reunion, Fassberg air base hospitality was also very much in evidence. Base officials hosted at the officers club a typical army luncheon whereby the meal was served family style in large bowls passed around the table. And on the final evening of the Fassberg visit, airlift veterans and their spouses, dressed in their finest, were guests at an official reception, cocktail hour, and a "dining in."

The Fassberg fortieth anniversary ceremonies were highlighted by the dedication of an airlift memorial, a large *Gedenkstein* (memorial stone) placed on a specially prepared site across the main street from the town hall. Mayor Bruns officiated, assisted by representatives of airlift veterans ved at Celle and Fassberg (there was no formal airlift associa-time), and a member of the Berlin *Senat*, the upper house of Berlin city and state governments. For this emotional event, ,undred Fassberg citizens were in attendance, further demon-strau.._ the bond between them and the airlift veterans. As a fitting climax to the ceremonies, Fassberg school children planted young linden trees on each side of the *Gedenskstein*. Ten years later, by the time of the fiftieth anniversary, they had grown strong and tall.

Following arrival in Frankfurt for the reunion, Celle and Fassberg veterans rode a special train to Hannover, courtesy of the German government, then transferred to buses for the short journey northward to their respective former air bases. Later, from Celle and Fassberg, the groups traveled to Berlin for several days of receptions, city tours, and ceremonies, including an emotional service at the Tempelhof airlift memorial, with the laying of wreaths and a welcome by governing mayor Walter Momper. One of the most memorable experiences for veterans returning to Berlin in 1989 was an invitation to the homes of individual Berliners, through a matching of guests and hosts. Following the drawing of names at *Rathaus Schöneberg*, the city hall, participating veterans and their spouses waved their match-up cards in the assembled crowd, met their respective hosts, and were whisked to their homes for an unforgetta-ble evening of dinner, good conversation, and much reminiscing about the blockade and airlift. This event was truly Berlin at its best.

After the Berlin ceremonies, most of the returning veterans traveled to the Frankfurt-Wiesbaden area for two days of further reunion events at Rhein-Main, and Lindsey air station in Wiesbaden. On September 25, the *Paulskirche* in Frankfurt was the site of a memorable commemorative ceremony recognizing the fortieth anniversary of the airlift. Hosted by Dr. Volker Hauff, the lord mayor, and officers of the *Luftbrücke* chapter of the Airlift Association, the event was followed the next day by a tour of the Berlin airlift memorial at Rhein-Main, an exact replica of the memorial in Berlin-Tempelhof. Dedicated in July 1985, the Rhein-Main memorial is flanked by a C-47 and C-54, the two American aircraft that did the heavy lifting in 1948-1949. That evening, returning veterans, their spouses, local German dignitaries, and Americans in the Frankfurt area came together at the Frankfurt Marriott for an unforgettable "Frankfurter Night," highlighted by German music, light speeches, and dancing, topped off by a sumptuous Hessian specialty buffet.

Lindsey air station was the scene on September 27 of a rededication of its streets named for those Americans killed in airlift operations. Originally dedicated in 1949, the street signs were dedicated again in 1982 with new black letters on a white enamel background. They have stood promi-nently as a vivid reminder that the airlift did not come without cost. As the ceremony proceeded, the names of the deceased airlift veterans were read aloud, followed by a special parade and review of air force troops on the parade ground.

The Fiftieth Anniversary

Many airlift veterans and aviation enthusiasts converged on Berlin in 1998 to observe the fiftieth anniversary of the airlift's onset. They came from many lands and were treated by Berlin citizens and officials to numerous welcoming receptions and ceremonies. On May 5 the Berlin Airlift Historical Foundation's *Spirit of Freedom,* a former navy R5D that actually saw service on the airlift, now piloted by BAHF president Tim Chopp and crewed by a mix of aging airlift veterans and younger volunteer airmen, lifted off from Floyd Bennett field, Long Island and commenced its lengthy journey to Europe to assume a prominent role in the many scheduled anniversary events. Making its first stop at Westover Air Reserve Base, Massachusetts, *Spirit* crew members were greeted by air base commander Brigadier General James Bankers; Dr. P.C. Hauswedell, German consul general in Boston; numerous on-duty reservists; and local school children who turned out for the occasion.

Winging its way north to Goose Bay, Labrador, the *Spirit* continued on to Keflavik, Iceland for refueling, then to Prestwick, Scotland and London, with media welcomes and static displays at each site. During May and June the *Spirit* thrilled assembled crowds as it made numerous scheduled stops in England, France, Luxembourg, and at Rhein-Main, Wiesbaden, and eventually Tempelhof and Schönefeld airports in Berlin. On May 12, 13, and 14 in Berlin, the central ceremonies of the 1998 reunion took place at Tempelhof air base, highlighted by the presence on May 14 of Chancellor Helmut Kohl and President William Clinton. Clearly, the *Spirit* and its crew were the crowd pleasers of the 1998 anniversary, and this beautifully restored flying airlift museum, as it rested majestically at Tempelhof, nose to nose with a giant USAF C-17 cargo airlifter, brought tears to the eyes of many Berliners who have never forgotten the dark days and nights of the Russian blockade.

Aircraftsman First Class Joe Raper, from Plymouth, remembers clearly the 1998 Berlin reunion. "We were entertained at the *Rathaus* [city hall] in Berlin, then at the British embassy," writes Joe, who was eighteen when he arrived in Germany for airlift duty. "We spent some time at the airlift museum, then proceeded on to Gatow airfield where I served for eleven months working in the aircraft spares section and keeping aviation fuel records." His tour group of about 35 RAF veterans and their spouses also enjoyed a memorable evening barbecue at the old Malcolm Club, with later entertainment by senior Luftwaffe officers. Group members also renewed their memories of fifty years earlier with a historic tour of Berlin. In later life, Joe returned to his hometown, completed a successful civilian career as chief buyer at the Royal Naval Dockyard, and served on the Plymouth city council.

The following year, in May, hundreds of airlift veterans from many corners of the world met once again in Berlin, the now united capital city of Germany, but which in 1948 and 1949 lay under siege by the Russian blockade of its western sectors. The veterans, with their spouses, arrived from England, France, Canada, South Africa, New Zealand, Australia, and the United States, this time to observe the fiftieth anniversary of the blockade's end and to live once again those dark days when the fate of the free world became dependent upon a steady stream of life-giving supplies to the blockaded city. Veterans of the blockade, too, Berliners who lived through its eleven months of cold, hunger, and deprivation and who toiled long, hard hours building runways and unloading airplanes, were also present at the anniversary ceremonies marking the lifting of the gates on the autobahn and the return of surface access to the city. And lest they be forgotten, family members of those who lost their lives on the airlift were also present to pay homage, as did all those in attendance, to the memory of their lost loved ones.

Most representatives of each nation involved in the airlift arrived in Berlin as members of an organized tour group, each group scheduled for its own tour activities while visiting airlift bases in western Germany and housed in its own hotels there and in Berlin. One such group of American veterans, organized by a tour company, arrived in Frankfurt, then moved on to Celle where they lodged for four days while touring both Celle and Fassberg before proceeding to Berlin for the major reunion festivities. During their visit to the 700 year old town of Celle, rich in history and tradition and largely undamaged in World War II, the group, composed of about eighty veterans and their spouses, was heartily welcomed in the *Rathaus* by the lord mayor, Dr. Herbert Severin. Following welcoming speeches at the town hall and the laying of wreaths at the town's airlift memorial, the group was hosted at the Celle air base in Immelman Hall, named after the famed World War I ace, Max Immelman, for whom the well-known aerobatic maneuver, the Immelman turn, was also named. As the returning veterans were briefed by the deputy base commander and his staff, several prominent World War I German aces, including Immelman and Baron Manfred von Richtofen, as well as Werner Mölders of World War II fame, looked down at them from their portraits on the far wall. Later, at a typical soldiers' mess in the officers club, the meal was passed around each table in huge bowls.

Group members next visited the flight line where units of the army helicopter regiment were positioned. Excellent briefings by English-speaking staff officers, using scale models of the air base, then and now, highlighted the flight line tour against a display backdrop of painstakingly prepared large-scale airlift photos, performance charts, and other memorabilia from a half century ago.

While staying in Celle, many returning veterans visited the nearby former Bergen-Belsen concentration camp, an ugly reminder of Nazis atrocities committed during their reign of terror from 1933 to 1945. Established in 1943 and administered by the SS, the camp housed approximately 55,000 Jews, political prisoners, and other presumed enemies of the state who were put to death or left to starve to death there during World War II. The site has now been preserved as a memorial with grassy mounds rising above the terrain level, under which are buried in mass graves hundreds, and at some sites thousands, of the dead.

One veteran in the returning group, **First Lieutenant Francis H. Potter**, from Spokane, Washington, had been a Skymaster pilot and supply officer at Celle, then remained on active duty, retiring as a colonel. In 1999 he brought his son Doug, who had heard about the airlift all his life, who in turn brought his son Travis, about twelve years old. The boy was playing hooky from school, to be sure, but he had been given a firm assignment from his teacher to prepare an oral report for his class upon return, and also to turn in a written essay. Adults in the group simply loved him; he became their mascot for the journey's duration. From time to time, everyone fed him information for his report. On the Celle air base flight line, one of the German helicopter pilots lifted Travis into a chopper cockpit and let the boy dream away.

Travis thoroughly enjoyed meeting the airlift veterans and their wives during the trip. "I felt like I was the grandson of all the veterans there, and all of them had a picture to show or a pin to give me," he writes. He is grateful to, among many others, Hans Baume, tour guide, for putting up with a teenager on his tour; **Bess Etter**, faithful BAVA member and sister of airlift casualty **Capt. James Vaughan**, for a game of scum; **Dan Forlenza**, Navy VR-6, Rhein-Main, for teaching him how to have a good handshake; **Bill Michaels**, flight engineer, Celle, for explaining why a radial engine cannot have an even number of cylinders; **Norman Melvin**, maintenance specialist, for his stories about Roswell, New Mexico; **Virginia Reissaus**, Special Services, Berlin, for her good conversations; and **Robert VanDervort**, avionics specialist, Celle, for his advice on life.

What Travis said in reflecting upon his dream journey to Germany will reassure and comfort those who may raise questions about today's youth. "I would also like to thank every veteran," he writes, "for your fight to make way for my generation's future, and for everyone on the trip for the conversations, advice on life, and a window into the past."

At Fassberg, the veterans learned that Mayor Bruns, their host in 1989, had passed on two years previously. His son, Eike, however, was present to welcome and speak with those who remembered his father, following which they were greeted at the town hall by Bruns' successor, Mayor Klaus Radlanski and town manager Horst Salzmann. The town's ceremonies observing the end of the blockade were scheduled, however, for May 12, on which date the group would be in Berlin with many others. Hence, the welcoming ceremony in Fassberg was brief. Air base officials did, however, arrange a nostalgic bus tour of the former airlift base, now the home of the Luftwaffe technical school. A visit to the newly renovated airlift museum, hosted by curator Rainer Kruppik, and a look-see at an ancient C-47, the well-known Fassberg Flyer, parked in its permanent resting place outside the museum, completed the group's Fassberg visit. One of the museum's most distinctive displays features the German Civil Labor Organization (GCLO), whose hundreds of members, housed in 1948-1949 in a specially built camp at Trauen, on the air base perimeter, performed the strenuous, unsung jobs of packing and loading coal for airlifting to Berlin.

From Celle and Fassberg, the group moved on to Berlin, driving the autobahn that before and after the blockade until 1989 was the only permissible highway passage to the city. Tour guides rode the buses and made the days pleasant with their knowledge of local history and their rare good humor. The Iron Curtain is gone, as are the watch towers, yet some landmarks of that time remain, such as the old guard stations at Helmstedt, the border checkpoint that for many years lay at the demarcation point between eastern and western Germany.

At the Hotel Berlin, home to many anniversary participants for the next several days, airlift veterans arriving from Celle and Fassberg were joined by about 200 more veterans and their spouses who had traveled directly from Frankfurt and Wiesbaden, where they had been stationed during the airlift days. Bus tours of the city took the returning Americans and Englishmen over the Glienicker bridge, famous for the exchange of spies in the cold war days; to Potsdam, a luxurious suburban town and site of Frederick the Great's Sans Souci Palace and the noted Cecilienhof, site of the 1945 Potsdam conference where Churchill, Truman, and Stalin made their momentous decisions about postwar Germany; and to the Allied Museum in the former American sector of Berlin where oodles of mementos of the occupation years and the airlift are housed, including a section of the Berlin Wall, brightly painted by local artists, and an old East German guard tower, as dismal as ever.

The big day, May 12, the actual fiftieth anniversary day of the blockade's end, started with a morning bus trip to Tempelhof and the airlift memorial. Many of the approximately 800 veterans in attendance wore miniaturized medals and ribbons on their caps and lapels; British vets were prominent in white caps, the Americans in light blue. All were dressed in their best. Over 1,500 people—veterans, spouses, dignitaries, young soldiers, Berliners who lived and worked through the blockade— were gathered at the memorial, which was originally dedicated in 1951. Bleachers had been constructed for a large assemblage of veterans and their families from Great Britain, France, Canada, Australia, New Zealand, South Africa, and the United States.

Taps was played. Then a prominent Catholic priest, the Reverend Georg Klar, chief chaplain and military dean of Berlin and Brandenburg, offered a prayer, invoking an ancient Chinese proverb about a conquering warrior turning his enemies into friends. The national anthems of Germany, France, Great Britain, and the United States were played by bands of their respective nations. Eberhard Diepgen, governing mayor of Berlin, gave a short speech to the assembled crowd, which included most of the diplomatic corps in Berlin. British defense minister George Robertson offered short remarks. Wreaths honoring airmen who lost their lives in airlift operations were laid at the base of the memorial by representatives of seven airlift organizations. Then it was over. There was not a dry eye anywhere.

At noon the International Congress Centrum (ICC) in the city's western reaches was the site of a massive, yet elegant buffet luncheon sponsored by the *Stiftung Luftbrückendank*, the Airlift Gratitude Foundation, an organization established in 1959 as a means by which Berliners could recognize those who took part in the great humanitarian enterprise of 1948-1949 by providing financial support and educational opportunities to the widows and children of those who lost their lives. At the ICC, people from all involved nations mixed freely at the luncheon tables, renewing old friendships and forging new ones. A few brief speeches were the order of the day. Nothing long or boring.

Later in the afternoon, still riding buses, veterans and their spouses, dignitaries, and Berliners who had built and repaired runways and unloaded airplanes arrived at the historic Olympic Stadium, where in 1936 Hitler refused to shake Jesse Owens' hand after his gold medal Olympic games victories. Guests were ushered into a vast VIP tent—a holding tank, of sorts, as it turned out—for beer, wine, champagne, and a light dinner as a prelude to the forthcoming evening's activities. The somber mood of the morning quickly turned to gaiety as airlift veterans marched, nation by nation, into the stadium to the tune of martial music, an overfly of German, British, and American aircraft, and the cheers of 30,000 Berliners. No sooner were the marching veterans seated next to their spouses in the stadium when the Royal Air Force Falcons parachute team and jumpers from the German army thrilled the assembled crowd with their precision spot landings in the center of the stadium.

Military bands from around Europe delivered exciting programs of march music and playful formations, followed by the Berlin Police Orchestra, a memorable performance by noted songstress Cornelia Froboess, more singing by the Berlin Children's' Choir (awesome), and entertainment by the Queen's Colour Squadron of the Royal Air Force, a precision drill team—all of this over a four-hour period extending into the late evening. The entire stadium program was capped by a ferocious (as the newspapers reported) thirty-minute fireworks display, thus bringing to a close the yearlong celebration in Berlin of the beginning and end of the blockade fifty long years ago.

While many veterans departed directly from Berlin for the United States, a post tour took those who had been stationed at Rhein-Main and Y-80 to Frankfurt and Wiesbaden for special reunion ceremonies. Traveling by chartered bus through the tranquil German countryside, they arrived in Frankfurt late on May 14, made the Frankfurt Forum hotel their headquarters, took a short tour of the city, were welcomed at a mayoral reception in city hall, and enjoyed a special welcoming dinner that evening. On the next day, the group was welcomed at the Berlin airlift museum at Rhein-Main by American historian John Provan. Veterans took part in a wreath-laying ceremony at the Berlin airlift memorial and visited the chapel and memorial window. On the following day, the group traveled to Wiesbaden to visit Lindsey air station and the airlift memorial there. Members rounded out their stay with a memorable farewell dinner at the Forum Hotel.

Airlift Gratitude Foundation

If anyone doubts the deep appreciation felt by Berliners for the airlift, rest easy. In 1949, a mere four years since the war's end, all of Germany, Berlin included, suffered severe economic hardship. Ten years later, however, the nation was getting back on its feet; its citizens were working, enjoying a rising standard of living, and they had money in their pockets. Time for payback, some were thinking. In that year, 1959, the *Stiftung Luftbrückendank,* the Airlift Gratitude Foundation, was established, with mayor Willie Brandt as a driving force, as a vehicle for registering the Berliners' thanks for the miracle of the airlift. With donations from business, industry, and private citizens, the foundation's leaders set up financial aid programs for widows and children of those killed in airlift operations.

"During the first ten years of its existence," reported the late Arthur Pearcy, "the foundation almost exclusively devoted its efforts to supporting dependents of the victims."

By 1997 four airlift widows had been fully supported by the Foundation. In all, 88 persons were through 1995 granted financial support, with more than DM 2 million expended. Over the years the Foundation has also broadened its mission to include awards of more than 200 fellowships for university studies and the support of artists, students, and scholars, expending DM 3.2 million for these educational purposes. Additionally, it has hosted numerous airlift veteran groups on return visits to Berlin and western airlift bases, most notably in 1999 as hundreds of veterans converged in Berlin for the fiftieth anniversary ceremonies. Managing director of the foundation is Heinz-Gerd Reese, a popular figure frequently seen at British and American airlift veteran reunions.

Berlin Airlift Historical Foundation

Tim Chopp's dream as a young man was to create a museum of the Berlin airlift in a restored, flying C-54. "I carried this idea for many years," he remembers. "When my mother passed away in 1988 at a relatively early age, this was a wake up call for me that time is marching on, and if I ever wanted my idea to come to fruition, I'd better get started."

Coming from a large family, many of whom had served in the army and navy during World War II, Tim was inspired by his love of history and old transport aircraft to search for some way of expressing his patriotism. Having listened to his dad, who was severely wounded in the Battle of the Bulge, he became intrigued with the Berlin airlift and the fact that the

United States, Great Britain, and France came to the aid of Germany, a nation that was their enemy only three years previously.

"As I grew older," Tim recalls, "I noticed that most Americans were not aware of the airlift. They simply didn't know what it was all about." A flying classroom/museum that could be used for educational and historical purposes seemed to him the perfect means by which the legacy of this momentous humanitarian endeavor could be perpetuated in the minds of people everywhere.

By November 1988, Tim was a corporate jet lease pilot. Behind him were three years of army service as an aircraft mechanic, thirteen months of which were spent in Vietnam. He then tackled college and in 1978 earned a B.S. degree in aeronautical technology. Now he could commence his quest for a flyable C-54 with which to pursue his dream and, equally important, for financial support for his intended project. It was not an easy task. "From November 1988 until October 1990, my efforts were consumed in searching for people to support the project and also to locate a Skymaster," reports Tim. "The going was slow and much more difficult than I realized. As a start, I contacted local artists who painted Berlin airlift scenes for sale to interested persons."

These efforts raised enough money for a down payment on an R5D, the navy version of the C-54, that he had located in storage in Toronto, Canada. In the end, it all turned out nicely. In December 1992, he signed a purchase agreement for the Skymaster, which actually saw service on the airlift, and with the purchase papers in his possession and a photograph, he was able to secure further financial support. Then, after taking delivery of the aircraft in July 1993, he had the actual bird in hand and within two years secured further funding for final payments, restoring the aircraft, and maintaining its flight operations.

During his early search for a flyable C-54, Tim was also busy setting up the Berlin Airlift Historical Foundation, incorporated in October 1990 as a nonprofit, tax-exempt, publicly supported charity, with the primary aim of preserving the memory of the Berlin airlift and those who served on it. Foundation officers and a board of directors, with Tim as president, are elected in accordance with the bylaws and articles of incorporation. With almost 500 supporting members from around the world, BAHF now enjoys a better financial status than earlier when Tim first began his quest for funds. Yet funding is an ongoing concern, and continued operations are always contingent upon sufficient funds becoming available. In 1998, when the C-54, now known as the *Spirit of Freedom,* flew to Europe for anniversary ceremonies, a small chapter of the foundation was thereafter established in Berlin, under the leadership of Dieter Ramthun, who is busy planning for the aircraft's return in 2004.

The *Spirit* is now wholly owned by the foundation, and with its interior elegantly furnished to exhibit the airlift's history in facts, figures, displays, and attractive photos, it flies on a regular annual schedule of events throughout the United States and foreign countries so that the general public may learn more about the airlift and its crucial cold war role. In recent years, the *Spirit's* role has been expanded to include airborne reenlistment oaths for air force and navy members, the dispersion of ashes of deceased veterans over designated areas, an on-board marriage proposal, and an actual wedding aloft. A second aircraft, a Boeing C-97 named the *Angel of Deliverance,* has now been acquired and will soon join the *Spirit* in seeking to perpetuate the story of the airlift and the cold war. BAHF's colorful, informative website may be viewed at: www.spiritoffreedom.org.

Airlift/Tanker Association

The Airlift/Tanker Association is numerically the largest group that memorializes the Berlin airlift and the pioneering effort of the airlift in establishing airlift and tanker operations as standard air force procedures. Although there are many association chapters in the United States, the *Luftbrücke* chapter, located at Rhein-Main air base in Frankfurt, is perhaps the best known to airlift veterans. Without the dedicated, thorough preparatory efforts of its members, many of whom were Americans living in the area, the fortieth anniversary reunion in 1989 would not have been so successful.

Soon after the reunion activities had concluded, chapter members continued their assistance by helping to organize the Berlin Airlift Veterans Association. The association membership was also extensively involved in financing and establishing the Berlin airlift memorial at Rhein-Main, a carbon copy of the memorial at Tempelhof. The Rhein-Main memorial is flanked by a static C-47 and C-54, each of which saw airlift service. Two German citizens who have worked tirelessly in the *Luftbrücke* chapter are Heinz and Gerdi Rausch of Frankfurt, a popular couple who have endeared themselves to airlift veterans with frequent attendance at their annual reunions.

Berlin Airlift Veterans Association

Approximately one year after airlift veterans convened in Germany to observe the fortieth anniversary of the airlift's end, Americans established their own association. With considerable encouragement and assistance from members of the *Luftbrücke* chapter of the Airlift Association at Rhein-Main, especially Colonel Tom Hansen, BAVA was founded in Las Vegas, Nevada in September 1990. Its members, numbering approximately 600, have met annually since inception, and every five years, in 1994 and 1999, the veterans have returned to Berlin for reunion ceremonies.

Under BAVA's bylaws, **Kenneth Herman**, who retired from active duty in the grade of colonel many years after airlift duty as a Skymaster pilot, served as the association's first president, and he continued in this office until 2000, when **Earl Moore**, an airlift navy pilot, was elected to succeed Herman upon his retirement. Association members come from all corners of the United States and several foreign nations, and at annual reunions they are a lively bunch, deeply dedicated to preserving memories of a time when the future of the free world depended so very much on the success of the Berlin airlift. Those who lost their lives in airlift operations have never been forgotten by BAVA members; each year a memorial wreath to their memories is dedicated at an air base or other military installation nearby the BAVA reunion site. BAVA publishes a quarterly newsletter, *The Legacy,* long under the editorship of **Fred Hall**, who also continues as reunion director *par excellence.*

Other BAVA officers are vice-president **Lewis Dale Whipple**, secretary **W.C. "Dub" Southers**, and treasurer **Fred Hall.** Dale and Fred now carry out duties formerly very well performed by secretary-treasurer **Bill Gross**, who supervised the unloading of C-54s at Tempelhof and who held the BAVA combined post for several years. **Sarah Garnett**, of Fort Stockton, Texas, serves loyally as association chaplain. Airlift flight engineer **Willie Jones**, of Hurst, Texas, is now the new historian. **Joe Studak**, from Austin, Texas, airlift navigator and ramp control officer, is ever busy as membership director, while Celle crew chief and "blockade buster" **Johnny Macia**, from Hayward, California, serves as public relations director. A website tirelessly maintained by Mark Vaughn, who was stationed in Berlin, promotes BAVA and its mission over the Internet at: www.konnections.com/airlift/main.htm.

British Berlin Airlift Association

In 1994 the western allies ended 49 years of occupation in Germany, and the occasion was marked by numerous closing ceremonies at army posts and air bases throughout the former zones of occupation and Berlin. One such ceremony, conducted at Berlin's Gatow airfield, once administered by the RAF, moved some participants to press thereafter for the creation of a British airlift veterans group. In due course, the British Berlin Airlift Association was founded during the same year, and it has since grown into a large, lively, and active organization, with a membership of 600, many of whom normally meet twice a year and on occasion, more frequently when a return trip to Germany is scheduled.

BBAA's first president was Air Chief Marshal **Sir Nigel Maynard**, KCB CBE DFC AFC, who during the airlift was the commander of No. 242 Squadron. He was succeeded recently by Air Marshal **Sir John Curtiss**, KCB KBE FRAes CBIM, who was a navigator with No. 59 York Squadron during the airlift. One of BBAA's leading personalities was its chairman, Captain **Alan D. B. Smith,** MRAes, a flight lieutenant and flight engineer with Transport Command Development Unit (TCDU) in the airlift time, and generally credited as founder of the association. BBAA members and all who knew him, personally or by reputation, were saddened to learn of his death on March 5, 2002. Other BBAA stalwarts are the vice-president, Air Vice Marshal **G.C. Lamb,** an airlift pilot with No. 47 Hastings Squadron; **Frank Stillwell**, a navigator with No. 30 Dakota Squadron at Wunstorf, now chairman; *Newsletter* editor **Geoff Smith,** who served as an electrician at RAF Gatow; and supplies officer **Peter Izard,** RAFVR, who was with No. 51 York Squadron.

On May 12, 2001, the 52nd anniversary of the lifting of the Berlin blockade, BBAA members took part in a memorable event at the National Memorial Arboretum in Alrewas, Staffordshire. On this occasion, 150 airlift veterans, together with their families, dedicated a memorial and a grove of trees in memory of the 39 RAF and civilian airmen who lost their lives in airlift-related operations. The memorial, a miniature replica of the airlift memorial in Berlin/Tempelhof, is further enhanced by a carved wooden eagle mounted at the top. The entire project was funded by donations from BBAA members, the general public, and the Airlift Gratitude Foundation in Berlin.

Geoff Smith creates the well-organized, well-written, enjoyable *BBAA Newsletter*, which is published twice yearly and contains news of past events, notices of forthcoming events, personal experience stories from airlift days, and notes on BBAA items for sale. The association now also boasts a colorful, detailed, and informative Internet website. It was launched on October 23, 2001 at: www-bbaa-airlift.org.uk.

South African Air Force Berlin Airlift Reunion Committee

It was a distinct pleasure for my wife and me to lunch with airlift veterans from South Africa at the Berlin ICC luncheon and reception on May 12, 1999. We had not known one another during the airlift time, but fifty years later, in a powerful mood of nostalgia, the bond was close. The South African Air Force contributed ten air crews to the airlift, a considerable effort. Arriving at Lübeck in late October 1948, they promptly went to work flying Dakotas provided by the RAF and, commanded by **Lieutenant Duncan Ralston,** they carved out a distinguished and accident-free record of airlift service. Duncan completed his military career as a major general and now serves as chairman of his country's Airlift Reunion Committee, which meets annually in October. Committee members also meet periodically on a local basis in Cape Town, Pretoria, and Johannesburg. In addition, the German Embassy annually hosts a Reunification of Germany event, with numerous South African airlift veterans in attendance.

Ж

Men, machines, memories. All converge in a remarkable mix of veteran associations that are nurtured in turn by regular and frequent group reunions, thereby seeking to perpetuate the legacy of noble deeds accomplished long ago. The Royal British Legion, Royal Air Force Association, American Legion, Veterans of Foreign Wars, Daughters of the American Revolution, and similar organizations benefit from ongoing infusions of new members and are thereby extended in time. Veterans of the Berlin blockade and airlift, however, stand today at a crossroads. Their ranks are thinning daily, and despite the addition of sons, daughters, and grandchildren to the membership rosters of BAVA, BBAA, and other airlift groups, to perpetuate the memory of 1948-1949 remains a difficult challenge. Will the opening battle of the cold war and the greatest humanitarian enterprise in modern times be relegated to the dustbins of history, or will their legacy continue, sustained by the determination of those who care?

Ten

Perspectives

What was at stake in Berlin was not a contest over legal rights, although our position was entirely sound in international law, but a struggle over Germany and, in a larger sense, over Europe.

Harry S. Truman, Years of Trial and Hope

Berlin, July 19, 1949

DUSK AND A LOW HANGING SKY, wild and untamed in appearance, winds blow fiercely, moving the weather mass as an endless conveyor belt. At Gatow, as Yorks take off they dip their wings in a determined attempt to fight the strong gusts and remain stable. At Tempelhof, Skymasters fight the same strong gusts. The winds whistle again in an equally strong effort to grasp the flying machines and slam them to earth as they struggle to remain airborne. Pilots of ships being unloaded loiter at the rolling snack bar, munching on sandwiches and sipping coffee. Some look off towards the active runway, watching their comrades approaching and departing. Now they check with the weather dispatcher making the rounds of each aircraft in an olive-green jeep. Pilots once more search the darkening skies as the clouds form jagged edges, whipped into unusual forms by the ever-increasing tempo of the wind.

Now a few drops of rain fall on the tarmac. The drops quickly become a torrent. How long will it last? Impatiently, the pilots clamber back into their ships, while the German unloaders hustle to complete their work. As the last sack of coal is lifted from a Skymaster, the engineer slams shut the cargo door; a whine is heard as number three engine turns over. In two minutes all four engines are running, and the huge craft moves slowly along the taxiway toward the takeoff line. Let the skies darken, let the ceiling lower to the ground. In a few hours the front will have passed, leaving behind a fresh, new wind, and a clear, bright sky. It's the final trip of the day.

The blockade was lifted over two months ago. Yet the airlift continues, albeit at a slower pace. There is need to build a stockpile, should the Soviets decide once again to lower the bar. Life in Berlin is slowly returning to a semblance of normalcy. Berliners go about their day with a renewed spring in their step. More and more food and consumer goods are appearing in the markets and shops. The currency reform introduced thirteen months ago is having a positive effect on the citizens. They are more confident about the future, more self-assured. The Russian bear has been tamed, and Berliners feel that they did their part in bringing it about. But will it last?

July 19, 1950. What Was Gained?

With the lifting of the blockade, life appeared to return to normal for Berliners and allied military forces in the city's western sectors. Trainloads of coal, mail, food, and passengers moved once more from Marienborn, in the west, to the Bahnhof Zoo and other West Berlin railroad stations. Barges loaded with supplies renewed their journeys from Hamburg, easing along the Havel into the city's network of waterways. Trucks by the hundreds chugged along the autobahn from Helmstedt to Drewitz, the check station at Berlin's southwest point of entry. Britons, Americans, and Germans alike proclaimed the end of the blockade a resounding victory for the western allies. To them, it was the first decisive win of the cold war, with not a shot having been fired.

In reality, the western allies, in their eagerness to bring the blockade to an end, settled for exactly that, when they might have renewed, during the negotiations with the Soviet Union, their insistence on free and unfettered two-way access to Berlin. "During the entire period of the blockade," wrote Robert Murphy, "the Russians denied the Western powers the use of ground and water routes to Berlin, and *access was made no more secure by the terms of the settlement than before the blockade.*" No more secure, indeed! The Soviets continued to halt traffic at the autobahn checkpoints, to examine individual papers, and to impose artificially trumped up traffic delays at any time, many lasting hours and hours. Western military travelers were normally exempt from such delays, but they were nonetheless made subject to a check of their papers, itself a time-consuming process. Trucks from the west, however, many of them transporting perishable meats, fruits, and vegetables, were often unreasonably delayed for 24 hours or more, with inevitable rotting of the trucks' contents as they stood detained at the Helmstedt checkpoint. Such harassment became the norm in the post-blockade months and continued for many years into the occupation. In reality, the western allies, in terms of their right of free access to Berlin, were back at the starting block. In effect, they apparently had settled for half a loaf.

That the western allies settled for half a loaf with the lifting of the blockade should not overshadow their momentous victory in defeating it. To stand fast in Berlin and beat Stalin's cruel isolation of 2.24 million West Berliners was the goal, and through hardship, dedication, accidents, casualties, and the long winter came the ultimate win. That the blockade was lifted, whether from the airlift's effectiveness or Stalin's feeling that he had better cut his losses, or both, served to highlight the gigantic political chess game in which the western allies were engaged with the Soviets over the future of Germany and beyond. Years after the blockade had been lifted and those who mounted the airlift had gone home, a Russian general observed that "The Soviet leadership...had not been prepared to commit suicide over Berlin." Stalin was forced, however, to swallow his pride; lifting the blockade was his most embarrassing political defeat.

The political chess game was one face of the blockade and airlift. At the same time, the airlift has been frequently characterized as the greatest humanitarian undertaking in history. Perhaps the ancient Chinese warlord, to whom Reverend Klar, the Berlin clergyman, alluded in his May 12, 1999 invocation, performed a greater humanitarian act by turning his conquered enemies into friends. If so, then the airlift was the greatest humanitarian feat in *modern* history. This serves as a reminder that the airlift was carried out to support Germans who only three years earlier were locked in mortal combat with the allies; those airlift veterans who previously flew combat missions against the German heartland need no prompting. And let it also not be forgotten, as Chuck Powell recently pointed out, that fifty years after the airlift, in 1999, Berliners were still saying *Thank You*. When, in ancient or modern history, did a single city ever before that time say *Thank You* to another nation, or to several nations?

Another thought. Many airlift veterans, British, American, and Commonwealth, whose military lives spanned a career or at least several years, declared that their airlift duty was the most meaningful and most satisfying to them of all their military experiences. Whereas many station assignments were humdrum and boring, airlift duty made them feel that they had made a distinct contribution to the betterment of the world. **Leading Aircraftsman David N. Carsey**, a teleprinter operator at Gatow, put it this way: "In 1947, at the age of eighteen, I was conscripted to serve in the RAF. Although I enjoyed most of the experience, it seemed in many ways to be a senseless exercise. But the airlift changed things; we felt that we were now doing something worthwhile." David echoed the feelings of so many, many others.

July 19, 2002

Now, more than a half century after the last bag of coal was delivered to Berlin by air, the world has witnessed many dramatic changes in Germany, Berlin, and all of Europe. Most propeller-driven military and commercial aircraft have faded into obscurity, and it was long ago estimated that if the airlift were again needed, a mere seventeen giant C-5 jet transports could easily support Berlin.

Germany's *Wirtschaft Wunder*, its economic miracle, has transformed the nation once more, almost unbelievably, into a major European power. But this time, the Federal Republic of Germany, created in 1949, is not only strong and prosperous, but also democratic. The nation now encompasses geographically not just its original borders but since 1989, the former German Democratic Republic—East Germany—as well. The nation's historic capital, Berlin, is once more the capital of a united people.

In that year, 1989, the world shook and its citizens looked on in amazement as the barbed wire and machine gun emplacements of the Iron Curtain disappeared virtually overnight. As walls and frontiers crumbled—most notably the infamous Berlin wall that stood for 28 years—people streamed from east to west in a flight from tyranny and dictatorial rule not previously seen in modern times. But equally important, those who for so many years imposed the tyranny disappeared, too, as the USSR and other east bloc nations collapsed, their political systems in shambles.

In that same year, 1989, for the fortieth anniversary ceremonies marking the end of the airlift, the USAF Military Airlift Command Band produced an album entitled *One Moment In Time,* in commemoration of the stirring events of the years 1948-1949. As we look back upon that memorable period, few among us will disagree that the blockade and airlift were indeed one moment in time, and that the airlift was unmistakably a bridge over troubled waters. If the Berlin airlift had failed, if the blockade inflicted by the Soviets had succeeded, and the western allies had been pushed out of Berlin, how far west might they have retreated, and would they have ceded all of Germany, perhaps all of Europe? What would Europe look like today had the airlift not broken the blockade?

Events occur in each of our lives when the journey is seen as important as the goal. In 1948 and 1949, the goal of the western allies was to defeat the ugly, brutal blockade imposed by Stalin on Berlin's western sectors. Thousands of good people, most particularly the unsung British and American enlisted ground troops, noncommissioned air crew members, and German and displaced person civilian laborers whose noble contributions lie at the heart of this book, all of them proud of their roles in the dramatic journey called the airlift, traveled on that pilgrimage to the final victory. In their proud, disciplined determination that the west not be pushed out of Berlin, they gave their very best efforts, day and night, unceasingly, over the long, uncertain months. In their selflessness, they caused the journey to become as important as the goal. They were the unheralded.

Appendix

Veteran Respondents

THE FOLLOWING AMERICAN, BRITISH, and Commonwealth veterans responded to my questionnaire or answered with information by letter, telephone, and e-mail. All are listed by name, current address, and airlift assignment, and unless otherwise noted, branch of service is USAF or RAF. Many of their eyewitness stories are included in, and form the basis of, this book. Unfortunately, it was not possible to include everyone's story, but to each of these gallant men and women of the blockade and airlift, I am deeply grateful.

American Veterans

Herman G. Benton	Rio Rancho, New Mexico	Line Chief, Rhein-Main
Sterling P. Bettinger	Colorado Springs, Colorado	Deputy Chief, CALTF
Rudy F. Bors	Palm Coast, Florida	Flight Engineer, Celle
Judson Boyce	Zeeland, Michigan	Line Mechanic, Rhein-Main
Gilbert Carlson	Carver, Massachusetts	Army Constabulary Trooper, Berlin
Charles K. Church	Rainelle, West Virginia	Line Mechanic, Rhein-Main
Johnny Clark	Papillion, Nebraska	Pilot, Wiesbaden, Fassberg
James P. Clark	Hendersonville, North Carolina	Flight Surgeon, Tempelhof, Wiesbaden
Roger R. Clift	Post Falls, Idaho	Army Constabulary Trooper, Berlin

James P. Colburn	Mulberry, Florida	Radio Technician, Rhein-Main
Kinzie K. Cole	Berwyn Heights, Maryland	Navy Line Supervisor, Rhein-Main
Larry R. Colegrove	Fort Lupton, Colorado	Line Mechanic, Rhein-Main
James E. Cunningham	Houston, Texas	Pilot, Rhein-Main, Wiesbaden
Paul S. Curtis	Fort Worth, Texas	Line Mechanic, Rhein-Main
Robert N. Cyzmore	San Antonio, Texas	Pilot, Wiesbaden, Celle
William A. Davis	St. Pauls, North Carolina	Pilot, Rhein-Main
Leighton Diehm	Sacramento, California	Line Mechanic, Rhein-Main
Ralph G. Dionne	Dracut, Massachusetts	Flight Engineer, Rhein-Main
Clarence W. Durbin	Pensacola, Florida	Line Mechanic, Burtonwood
Bess Etter	Brandon, Mississippi	Sister of Captain James Vaughan
Jack D. Fellman	Shelton, Washington	Control Tower Operator, Tempelhof
Eugene W. Garges	Manhasset, New York	Pilot, Rhein-Main
Sara Garnett	Fort Stockton, Texas	BAVA Chaplain
Jack L. Gilbert, Sr.	Summerville, South Carolina	Flight Engineer, Celle
Edwin L. Glazener	San Diego, California	Flight Surgeon, Wiesbaden
Orville C. Grams	El Centro, California	Flight Engineer, Wiesbaden
William Gross	Converse, Texas	Unloading Supervisor, Tempelhof
Fred A. Hall	Baltimore, Maryland	Flight Engineer, Rhein-Main
Gail Halvorsen	Provo, Utah	Pilot, Rhein-Main
John L. Hanlon	Weslaco, Texas	Flight Engineer, Wiesbaden
Calvin R. Haynes	Biloxi, Mississippi	Line Mechanic, Fassberg
Harold Hendler	Riverside, California	Pilot, Wiesbaden
Ronald M. A. Hirst	Wiesbaden, Germany	Army Counter Intelligence
Wendell H. Houck	Herald, California	Control Tower Chief, Rhein-Main
Ralph H. Hudson	North Charleston, South Carolina	Air Policeman, Oberpfaffenhofen
Melvin Jenner	Orlando, Florida	Engine Shop Mechanic, Celle

William K. Jones	Hurst, Texas	Flight Engineer, Fassberg
Donald W. Keating	Norman, Oklahoma	Pilot, Wiesbaden
Paul S. Levie	Martinsburg, West Virginia	Army Constabulary Intelligence, Germany
Raymond L. Lott	Austin, Texas	Motor Pool Dispatcher, Rhein-Main
Albert Lowe	Charleston, South Carolina	Pilot, Fassberg
Louis A. Lynn	Normal, Illinois	Army Constabulary Trooper, Berlin
Fred A. Manderioli	Fountain Hills, Arizona	Navy Pilot, Rhein-Main
Malcolm A. McBride	Olympia, Washington	Army Truck Driver, Berlin
George McClarity	Palatine, Illinois	Air Policeman, Rhein-Main
Richard McMahan	Parkersburg, West Virginia	Crew Chief, Wiesbaden, Fassberg
Charles Meadows	Laguna Niguel, California	Radio Technician, Rhein-Main
Donald W. Measley	Santa Barbara, California	Pilot, Rhein-Main, Fassberg
Frank A. Melton (deceased)	San Antonio, Texas	Army Postal Supervisor, Frankfurt
George M. Meyer	Columbus, Ohio	Army Engineer, Berlin
William R. Michaels	Wichita Falls, Texas	Flight Engineer, Celle
William F. Middaugh	Ventura, California	Navy Pilot, Rhein-Main
Robert Monasmith	Hemet, California	Army Constabulary Trooper, Berlin
Robert C. Moore	Live Oak, Texas	Office of Special Investigations, Wiesbaden
Earl Morrison	Broken Arrow, Oklahoma	Flight Engineer, Wiesbaden
William E. Morrissey	Danville, Indiana	Control Tower Operator, Celle
Gerald L. Munn	Bradenton, Florida	Pilot, Wiesbaden
Fred I. Murtishaw	Auburn, Washington	Line Mechanic, Oberpfaffenhofen
Howard S. Myers	Riverside, California	Pilot, Wiesbaden
Edward R. Nacey	Atwater, California	Operations Officer, Tempelhof
Donald R. Neild	St. Petersburg, Florida	Public Information Specialist, Celle
Phillip B. O'Brien	Orlando, Florida	Air Policeman, Tempelhof
Robert S. O'Brien	Redwood City, California	Public Information Specialist, Burtonwood

Elizabeth O'Neal (Dwinell) (deceased)	Granby, Massachusetts	Secretary, CALTF
William Perkins	Hollywood, California	Weather Forecaster, Fassberg
Cloyde C. Pinson, Sr.	Irving, Texas	Maintenance and Supply Specialist, Fassberg
Francis H. Potter	Spokane, Washington	Pilot and Supply Officer, Fassberg
Chuck Powell	Omaha, Nebraska	Navy Pilot, Rhein-Main
John J. Rahll	Pittsburgh, Pennsylvania	Pilot, Celle
Virginia Reissaus	Rockford, Illinois	Special Services, Tempelhof
John E. Ross	Little Rock, Arkansas	Line Mechanic, Gatow
Nicholas Rucci	Brick Township, New Jersey	Army Constabulary Trooper, Berlin
Robert Sattem	Centerville, Ohio	Personnel Officer, Wiesbaden
Daniel J. Schulte	Address Unknown	Army Constabulary Trooper, Berlin
Louis R. Schuerholz (deceased)	Dundee, New York	Army Ranger, Berlin
Kenneth K. Skoog	Wahpeton, North Dakota	Radio Operator, Rhein-Main
Kenneth H. Slaker	Olympia, Washington	Pilot, Wiesbaden
John Sorenson	Valdosta, Georgia	Pilot, Rhein-Main
W. C. Dub Southers	Duncanville, Texas	Flight Engineer, Celle
James R. Spatafora	Albuquerque, New Mexico	Hydraulics Specialist, Rhein-Main
William Sproul	Blawnox, Pennsylvania	Special Services, Tempelhof
Donald L. Stensrud	Colorado Springs, Colorado	Control Tower Operator, Tempelhof
William C. Strub	Briarcliff Manor, New York	Army Constabulary Trooper, Berlin
Joseph W. Studak	Austin, Texas	Ramp Control Officer, Fassberg
Thomas S. Talty	Rio Rancho, New Mexico	Finance Clerk, Rhein-Main
Dean W. Terlinden	Long Beach, California	Weather Forecaster, Burtonwood
Albert G. Tindall	Orlando, Florida	Truck Driver, Fassberg, Celle
Hugh M. Tosone	Gladstone, Missouri	Electrical Mechanic, Rhein-Main
Dorothy Towne	Colorado Springs, Colorado	CALTF Headquarters, Wiesbaden

William Trackler (deceased)	Aurora, Colorado	Air Policeman, Fassberg, Wiesbaden
Robert W. VanDervort	Murfreesboro, Tennessee	Avionics Supervisor, Celle
Louis N. Wagner	Bethune, South Carolina	Dispatcher, Tempelhof
Lewis D. Whipple	Benton, Louisiana	Supply Clerk, Celle
Jack Whitfield	Citrus Heights, California	Navy Pilot, Rhein-Main
Harry B. Winger	Portland, Maine	Pilot, Rhein-Main
Samuel Young	Salt Lake City, Utah	Army Constabulary Trooper, Berlin
John Zazzera	Kittery, Maine	Dispatcher, Rhein-Main

British and Commonwealth Veterans

Robert M. Aitken	Spalding, Lincolnshire	Medical Officer, Wunstorf
R. R. Bill Bailey	Virginia Water, Surrey	Civil Navigator, Hamburg
E. W. C. Bale	Milton Keynes, Northampton	Radio Fitter, Lüneberg
W. W. Ball	Thorne, South Yorkshire	Engine Fitter, Wunstorf, Celle,
Geoffrey Bere (deceased)	Address Unknown	Navigator, Lübeck
Ian LeC. Bergh	George East, South Africa	Navigator, Finkenwerder
Dennis Bishop	Sidford, Devon	Army Engineer, Minden
Maurice C. M. Blackburn	Thames Ditton, Surrey	Civil Pilot, Finkenwerder
Geoffrey Boston	Balsham, Cambridge	Pilot, Schleswigland
J. Burton	Dulverton, Somerset	Fitter, Fassberg
Graeme Bushell	Bury St. Edmunds, Suffolk	Pilot, Wunstorf
John L. Bushell	Chesham, Buckinghamshire	Army Engineer, Fühlsbüttel
William Campbell	Monmouth	Army Load Controller, Wunstorf
David N. Carsey	Aberdeen, Scotland	Wireless Operator, Gatow
Noel Robert Clark	Beaconsfield	Civil Pilot, British Airways
Brian Cooper	Sheffield, South Yorkshire	Army Infantryman, Gatow
Maurice B. Cooper	Southwold, Suffolk	Pilot, Wunstorf
Bert G. Cramp	Crawley, West Sussex	Civil Radio Engineer, Wunstorf
Terence Crowley	Coggeshall, Essex	Engine Fitter, Hamburg

Sir John Curtis	London	Navigator, Wunstorf
Raymond Darvall	Slough, Berkshire	Aircraft Mechanic, Lübeck
B. D. Davies	London	Pilot, Wunstorf
Desmond Dawe	Levin, New Zealand	Aircraft Mechanic, Wunstorf
J. P. Docherty	Hebburn-on-Tyne, Durham	Pilot, Wunstorf
Walter Dougan	Topsham, Devon	Pilot, Fassberg, Lübeck
Michael Downes	Southend-on-Sea, Essex	Navigator, Lübeck
Edward W. Duck	Southampton, Hampshire	Radar Operator, Wunstorf
John Dury	Bristol, Avon	Aircraft Mechanic, Wunstorf
David Edwards	St. Albans, Hertfordshire	Teleprinter Operator, Berlin
E. F. Edwards	Whangarei, New Zealand	Pilot, Wunstorf
Douglas S. Evans	Swansea, West Glamorgan, Wales	Army Dispatcher, Berlin
A. Garretts	Woodbridge, Suffolk	Pilot, Wunstorf
Ernest E. Gathercole	Hunstanton, Norfolk	Army Keyboard Operator, Berlin
Graham R. George	Bristol, Avon	Draftsman and Surveyor, Gatow
R. J. Goode	Northwich, Cheshire	Flight Engineer, Schleswigland
William H. Gordon	Salisbury, Wiltshire	Pilot, Wunstorf
A. Harper	Trowbridge, Wiltshire	Pilot, Wunstorf
Derek W. Hermiston-Hooper	Ryde, Isle of Wight	Civil Pilot, Schleswigland
Robert A. Hide	Hamilton, Ontario, Canada	Signaller, Lübeck
David T. Hines	Eaton, Cambridgeshire	Radar Operator, Tremsbüttel
Brian Hill	Bromham, Bedfordshire	Navigation Specialist, Gatow
A. E. Hough	Moruya, Australia	Signaller, Lübeck
Peter Izard	West Wickham, Kent	Loadmaster, Wunstorf
Kenneth Kessler	Spalding, Lincolnshire	Airfield Security, Fassberg
John Kilburn	Thornton Cleveleys, Lancashire	Civil Radio Officer, Schleswigland
Kenneth W. King	Witham, Essex	Army Loadmaster, Wunstorf
John B. Kite	Wokingham, Berkshire	Instrument Mechanic, Lübeck

Courtenay A. Latimer	Woodbridge, Suffolk	Army Water Base Officer, Gatow
David Lawrence	Delray Beach, Florida, U.S.	Civil Flight Engineer, Schleswigland
George F. Mahony	Uxbridge, Middlesex	Civil Pilot, Schleswigland
James F. Manning	Blandford Forum, Dorset	Pilot, Lübeck
James F. McCorkle	Brampton, Ontario, Canada	Pilot, Lübeck
L. Mills	New Milton	Airfield Security, Gatow
D. A. Mitchell	Beverley, East Yorkshire	Signals Section, Gatow
Ray Morris	High Wycombe, Buckinghamshire	Radio Observer, Medmenham, England
Ken Nichol	Sandhurst, Berkshire	Civil Flight Engineer, Wunstorf, Hamburg
George F. Morton	Birmingham	Teleprinter Operator, Bushy Park, London
John Overington	Doylestown, Pennsylvania, U.S.	Army Line Mechanic, Buckeberg
Sidney Parsonage	Ruthin, Denbighshire, Wales	Wireless Operator, Lübeck
Eric L. Pascal	Watford, Hertfordshire	Radar Fitter, Fassberg, Schleswigland
Joyce L. Peachey (Hargrave-Wright)	Tintagel, Cornwall	Air Traffic Controller, Bad Eilsen
James W. Peat	Don Mills, Ontario, Canada	Pilot, Lübeck
Stuart Perrin	Gt. Missenden, Buckinghamshire	Pilot, Lübeck
Alan Quinton	Paignton, Devon	Civil Pilot, Wunstorf
Duncan M. Ralston	Clubview, South Africa	Navigator-Pilot, Lübeck
Joseph Raper	Plymouth, Devon	Equipment Supervisor, Gatow
Douglas Raw	Crawley, Sussex	Radar Operator, Fassberg, Lübeck
Reginald L. G. Ray	Chipping Norton, Oxford	Signaller, Lübeck
Tony Ridge	Murphy, Texas, U.S.	Pilot, Wunstorf
Eric Robinson	Wirral, Cheshire	Pilot, Wunstorf
Leslie Senior (deceased)	Reading, Berkshire	Navigator, Fassberg, Lübeck
V. G. Sherwin	Slough, Berkshire	Civil Radio Operator, Wunstorf
Jack A. V. Short	Dersingham, Norfolk	Air Traffic Controller, Wunstorf
Stan Sickelmore	Wimborne, Dorset	Civil Pilot, Wunstorf

Alan D. B. Smith (deceased)	Port St. Mary, Isle of Man	Flight Engineer,Wunstorf
F. H. Smith	Lymington, Hampshire	Radar Operator, Bad Winterburg
Steve Stevens	Worthing, West Sussex	Pilot, Lübeck
Eric A. Stevenson	Ferndown, Dorset	Army Records Specialist, Celle
Frank Stillwell	Marlow, Buckinghamshire	Navigator, Lübeck
Alfred H. Sumner	Stretford, Manchester	Army Signals, Schleswigland
Victor J. Taylor	Girton, Cambridge	Engine Fitter, Oakington, Lübeck
Ronald E. Travell	Gooderham, Ontario, Canada	Aircraft Electrician, Wunstorf, Lübeck
Don A. Ward	Cheltenham, Gloucestershire	Air Movements Supervisor, Gatow
Russell R. Wauchman	Kenilworth, Warwickshire	Pilot, Training Officer, Fassberg, Lübeck
Peter D. White	Chiswick, London	Flight Mechanic, Schleswigland
W. S. Wilkinson	Edinburgh, Scotland	Radio Maintenance, Gatow
S. M. Williams	Forest Row, East Sussex	Headquarters Administration, Gatow
Ian Witter	Birkenhead, Merseyside	Pilot, Finkenwerder
William F. Young	Edmonton, Alberta, Canada	Pilot, Wunstorf

German Veterans

Most Germans listed here completed a special questionnaire and answered additional questions during personal interviews. Others provided information through direct correspondence. To each of these unheralded veterans I am very much indebted. They are listed by name, current address, and status during the blockade from June 1948 to May 1949.

Ursula Alker	Berlin-Staaken	Cargo Controller, Gatow
Rainer Baronsky	Berlin-Charlottenburg	Schoolboy
Eva Beeskow	Berlin-Friedenau, St. Louis, Missouri	U.S. Army Civilian Employee
Werner Dargatz	Berlin-Reinickendorf	Unloader, Gatow
Werner Demitrowitz	Berlin-Spandau	Siemens Mechanic, Unloader, Gatow
Wera Erdmann	Berlin-Reinickendorf	Schoolgirl

Werner Erdmann	Berlin-Reinickendorf	Unloader, Tempelhof
Michael Foppe-Vorpahl	Berlin-Wedding	Schoolboy
Alexander Gunkel	Leavenworth, Kansas, U.S.	Schoolboy
Suzanne Joks (Riedi-Joks)	Lucerne, Switzerland	Schoolgirl
Dietmar Kurnoth	Berlin-Tempelhof	Schoolboy
Dorothea Meier (Kühne), (deceased)	Unterluß, West Germany	Chambermaid, Fassberg
Horst Molkenbuhr	Berlin-Wilmersdorf	Schoolboy and Unloader, Tempelhof
Ilse Moschberger (Barbara Fairall)	London, England	Secretary, British Control Commission
Louis von Egloff	Acton, California, U.S.	Runway Builder, Tempelhof
Karl Pohmer	Berlin-Neukölln	Unloader, Tempelhof
Gisela Marianne Scholz (Irene Stevenson)	Burnettsville, Indiana, U.S.	Schoolgirl
Christian Seifert	Belleview, Washington, U.S.	Schoolboy
Inge Stanneck (Gross)	Eastsound, Washington, U.S.	Schoolgirl
Herta Tiede	Berlin-Tempelhof	Secretary, Fassberg Air Base

Abbreviations

AACS	Airways and Air Communications Service
ACC	Allied Control Council
AFC	Air Force Cross
BAFO	British Air Forces of Occupation
BAHF	Berlin Airlift Historical Foundation
BAVA	Berlin Airlift Veterans Association
BBAA	British Berlin Airlift Association
CALTF	Combined Airlift Task Force
CBE	Commander of the Order of the British Empire
CFM	Council of Foreign Ministers
CINCEUR	Commander-in-Chief, Europe
DFM	Distinguished Flying Medal
EAC	European Advisory Commission
FRAeS	Fellow of the Royal Aeronautical Society
GCA	Ground Controlled Approach
GCLO	German Civil Labor Organization
IFR	Instrument Flight Rules
JCS	Joint Chiefs of Staffs
KBE	Knight Commander of the Order of the British Empire
KCB	Knight Commander of the Order of the Bath
MATS	Military Air Transport Service
MRAeS	Member of the Royal Aeronautical Society, Institute of British Management
NSC	National Security Council
NCO	Noncommissioned Officer
OMGUS	Office of Military Government, United States
PCS	Permanent Change of Station

PSP	Pierced Steel Planking
RAAF	Royal Australian Air Force
RAF	Royal Air Force
RAFVR	Royal Air Force Volunteer Reserve
RASC	Royal Army Service Corps
RNZAF	Royal New Zealand Air Force
SAAF	South African Air Force
SAC	Strategic Air Command
S-Bahn	Street Railway
SHAEF	Supreme Headquarters, Allied Expeditionary Forces
SMA	Soviet Military Administration
TDY	Temporary Duty
USAF	United States Air Force
USAFE	United States Air Forces in Europe
VFR	Visual Flight Rules
VIP	Very Important Person(s)
WAAF	Women's Auxiliary Air Force
WAC	Women's Army Corps
WRAF	Women's Royal Air Force

Acknowledgments and Sources

MANY PERSONS HAVE contributed to this account of the Berlin blockade and ensuing airlift. Close to ninety British airlift veterans, most of them members of the British Berlin Airlift Association (BBAA), but also South Africans, New Zealanders, and Australians, responded to my questionnaire about their airlift experiences. An approximate equal number of Americans from the Berlin Airlift Veterans Association (BAVA) completed the same questionnaire. Returned questionnaires are not cited in the notes, but interviews forming the heart of a personal story, are cited.

Many, but not all, veterans reviewed a draft of the segment describing their experiences. During a two-week trip to Germany in March 2000, I interviewed as many Berliners as possible, some of whom were children during the blockade, while others were adults who endured the long, bitter winter of 1948-1949. Completed questionnaires and blockade memoirs were received from several other Berliners, most of whom now live in the United States.

Unfortunately, not all personal stories received could be included in this book; selection became a matter of available space and the need to strike a balance among individual experiences, job skills, and station assignments in an effort to achieve a representative sampling. Each person, however, who returned the questionnaire is listed in the Appendix, and to each one I am deeply grateful.

In addition to the American, British, Commonwealth, and German veterans who provided the raw material for this book, many other persons were instrumental in its preparation. Chuck Powell, Professor of Political Science at the University of Nebraska at Omaha, one of only four enlisted navy airlift pilots, offered me warm, regular comfort and encouragement throughout. He read the entire draft with a critical eye and took time to write the Foreword. Dan Harrington, USAFE historian at Ramstein air base in Germany, super airlift expert, author, and cold war scholar, read the first several chapters, saving me from some big errors of fact, and he also supplied me with numerous research materials. He, too, constantly offered strong words of encouragement.

Others read portions or chapters of the manuscript, particularly Courtenay Latimer, a Royal Army Service Corps airlift veteran, who read chapter five; Inge Stanneck Gross, a little girl in Berlin during the blockade, who read chapter six; and numerous airlift veterans who read their draft segments. My deep thanks to all of you.

Son David, grammarian *par excellence,* cleaned up the punctuation marks and otherwise made the manuscript readable. Daughter-in-law Claudia Gere, my editor-in-chief, read the entire manuscript many times over, vigorously researched publication options, offered numerous suggestions on grammatical correctness and stylistic appearance, and painstakingly formatted the entire manuscript for publication. Son Richard and daughter-in-law Dayna Thacker, each a superb artist, designed the cover and helped in many ways with stylistic suggestions. Brother Ludlow gave me valuable advice on literary style. Son Jonathan accompanied me on my 2000 journey to Germany and Berlin, did all the driving, was a great traveling companion, and charmed all of my interviewees. Thanks to all of you dear family members for your invaluable support, encouragement, and assistance.

My dear friend, Herta Tiede, a *Berlinerin,* who relates her airlift experiences in chapter three, helped me immeasurably from her vantage post in Berlin. She kept me supplied with airlift books, booklets, monographs, bibliographies, and articles, all of which have proved invaluable to the project; she made numerous telephone calls to other Berliners for various blockade details; she kept me up-to-date about goings on in Berlin; and she offered strong encouragement along the way with letters and telephone calls. *Vielen herzlichen Dank, Herta.*

Others who helped immensely are Ronald "Scotty" Hirst, a much decorated D-Day veteran, living in Wiesbaden, with whom Jon and I spent a pleasant afternoon, and who generously made available his lifetime writings on American airlift casualties; Heinz-Gerd Reese, managing director of the Airlift Gratitude Foundation in Berlin, who arranged contact with Berliners to be interviewed and provided detail on the Foundation; Bill Morrissey, my dear BAVA friend who was so very helpful with many aspects of my writing, especially detail on the Airways and Air Communications System; Squadron Leader Frank Stillwell, BBAA chairman, who has been wonderfully kind and helpful, acting as a link to the BBAA membership, and who painstakingly searched out biographical information on British and Commonwealth casualties; retired Master Sergeant David Menard, of the Air Force Museum at Wright-Patterson AFB, who made available, and assisted with, the Research Division's airlift files; and Tim Chopp, president of the Berlin Airlift Historical Foundation, who has been most supportive and encouraging of my writing project. To each of you, for your thoughtfulness, encouragement, and assistance, I am deeply grateful.

In researching airlift literature, I relied heavily on my own splendid University of Massachusetts library with its magnificent collection of public documents, books and papers ideal for my purposes. My good friend Bill Thompson, chief of the documents section, provided generous assistance, as he did during the many years I was actively teaching, in suggesting and locating numerous sources for my writing. Thank you once again, Bill.

For reference as primary sources, I turned to personal memoirs—those of Dean Acheson, Charles "Chip" Bohlen, Lucius Clay, Frank Howley, Curtis LeMay, Robert Murphy, Harry Truman, and William Tunner. These and other sources are cited below.

Documents

Air Force Museum, Wright-Patterson AFB, Research Division, *Berlin Airlift files.*

Office of Air Force History. Lt. Gen. Joseph Smith *Oral History Interview.*

Rosenman, Sam. *The Public Papers and Addresses of FDR,* vol.13. New York: Russell & Russell, 1969.

Smith, Jean Edward, ed. *The Papers of General Lucius D. Clay.* 2 vols. Bloomington: Indiana University Press, 1974.

U.S. Department of State. *Foreign Relations of the United States, 1945-1948,* various volumes, Washington, D.C., 1960.

_____ *Germany:1947-1949: The Story in Documents,* 1950.

Books

Acheson, Dean. *Present at the Creation.* New York: Norton, 1969.

Bohlen, Charles E. *Witness to History: 1929-1969.* New York: Norton, 1973.

Christienne, Charles and Lissarague, Pierre. *A History of French Military Aviation.* Washington: Smithsonian, 1986.

Churchill, Winston E. *The Grand Alliance.* Boston: Houghton Mifflin, 1950.

Clay, Lucius D. *Decision in Germany.* New York: Doubleday, 1950.

Collier, Richard. *Bridge Across the Sky.* New York: McGraw-Hill, 1978.

Color Collection GMBH International. *Berlin: Color Collection Städte.* Herrsching, 1981.

Djilas, Milovan. *Conversations with Stalin.* Rupert Hart Davis, 1962.

Donovan, Frank. *Bridge in the Sky.* New York: McKay, 1968.

Everett, Susanne. *Das War Berlin.* London: Bison Books, 1979.

Feis, Herbert. *Between War and Peace—The Potsdam Conference.* Princeton: Princeton University Press, 1957.

Förster, Uwe et al, eds. *Auftrag Luftbrücke: Der Himmel über Berlin 1948-1949.* Berlin: Nicolai, 1998.

Gaddis, John L. *We Now Know.* Oxford: Clarendon, 1997.

Giangreco, D.M. and Griffin, Robert. *Airbridge to Berlin.* Novata (Calif.): Presidio, 1988.

Halvorsen, Gail S. *The Berlin Candy Bomber.* Bountiful (Utah): Horizon, 1997.

Harmon, E. N. with MacKaye, Milton and MacKaye, Ross. *Combat Commander: Autobiography of a Soldier.* Englewood Cliffs: Prentice-Hall, 1970.

Harrington, Daniel F. *The Air Force Can Deliver Anything: A History of the Berlin Airlift.* Germany: USAFE Office of History, 1998.

Haydock, Michael D. *City Under Siege: The Berlin Blockade and Airlift, 1948-1949.* Washington: Brassey's, 1999.

Howley, Frank. *Berlin Command.* New York: Putnam, 1950.

Huschke, Wolfgang J. *The Candy Bombers: The Berlin Airlift 1948/1949.* Berlin: Metropol Verlag, 1999.

Jackson, Robert. *The Berlin Airlift.* Northamptonshire: Patrick Stephens, 1988.

Launius, Roger D. and Cross, Coy F. II. *MAC and the Legacy of the Berlin Airlift.* Scott AFB, Illinois: Military Airlift Command, 1989.

LeMay, Curtis, with Kantor, MacKinlay. *Mission with LeMay.* Garden City: Doubleday, 1965.

Merrill, Dennis, gen. ed. *Documentary History of the Truman Presidency.* Bethesda (Md.): University Publications of America, 1997.

Miller, Roger. *To Save a City: The Berlin Airlift: 1948-1949.* Air Force History and Museums Program: USGPO, 1998.

Murphy, David E., Kondrashev, Sergei A., and Bailey, George. *Battleground Berlin: CIA v. KGB in the Cold War.* New Haven: Yale, 1997.

Murphy, Robert. *Diplomat among Warriors.* Garden City: Doubleday, 1964.

Naimark, Norman. *The Russians in Germany.* Belknap: Harvard, 1995.

Nelson, Walter Henry. *The Berliners: Their Saga and Their City.* New York: McKay, 1969.

The Official World War II Guide to the Army Air Forces. Bonanza, 1988.

Parrish, Thomas. *Berlin in the Balance: 1945-1949.* Reading (Mass.): Addison-Wesley, 1998.

Pearcy, Arthur. *Berlin Airlift.* Shrewsbury: Airlife Publishing Ltd., 1997.

Read, Anthony and Fisher, David. *Berlin: The Biography of a City*. London: Pimlico, 1994.

Shirer, William L. *Berlin Diary*. New York: Alfred A. Knopf, 1940.

_____. *The Rise and Fall of the Third Reich*. London: Pan Books, Ltd., 1960.

Shlaim, Avi. *The United States and the Berlin Blockade, 1948-1949*. Berkeley: University of California Press, 1983.

Smith, Jean Edward. *Lucius D. Clay: An American Life*. New York: Henry Holt, 1990.

_____. *The Defense of Berlin*. Johns Hopkins, 1963.

Smith, Walter Bedell. *Moscow Mission: 1946-1949*. London: William Heinemann, Ltd., 1950.

Stärk, Hans. *Fassberg*. Selbstverlag des Verfassers, 1971.

Truman, Harry S. *Memoirs*. (2 vols.) Garden City: Doubleday, 1956.

Tunner, William H. *Over the Hump*. Washington: Office of Air Force History, 1964.

Tusa, Ann and John. *The Berlin Blockade*. London: Hodder & Stoughton, 1988.

Von Witten, Ulrich et al. *Celle: Porträt einer Stadt und eines Kreises*. Schloß Bleckede/Elbe: Otto Meisners Verlag, 1974.

Zubok, Vladislav and Pleshakov, Constantine. *Inside the Kremlin's Cold War: From Stalin to Krushchev*. Cambridge: Harvard, 1996.

Monographs

Das Offizielle Journal: 50 Jahre Luftbrücke. Berlin: Nishen, 1998.

Deutsches Technikmuseum. *Auftrag Luftbrücke, 1998*.

Foreign and Commonwealth Office. *Die Berliner Luftbrücke. Der Britische Beitrag*. London, 1998.

Gross, Inge Stanneck. *Memories of World War II by a Little Girl Growing up in Berlin*. 1999.

Heisig, Matthias and Thiele, Michael, eds. *Landing on Tempelhof*. Berlin: Bezirksamt Tempelhof von Berlin, n.d.

Michaels, W. R. *A Love Story*. Aurora (Colorado): Defense Printing Service, 1995.

Pioneers of the Airlift. Berlin: Nishen, 1998.

Reese, Heinz-Gerd; Schröder, Michael; and Schwarzkopf, Manfred; eds. *Blockade and Airlift*. Berlin: Stiftung Luftbrückendank, 1988.

Reichert, Dieter und Tintemann, Siegbert, eds. *Erinnerungstätte Luftbrücke Berlin*. Technische Schule der Luftwaffe 3, n.d.

Sievers, Helmut. *Fassberg und die Luftbrücke Berlin aus der Sicht des Bauingenieurs*. Fassberg: n.d.

Slaker, Kenneth. *Personal Diary*. 1949.

Whipple, Lewis Dale. *317th Troop Carrier Wing: The Mission, 1948-1949, Berlin Airlift, 2000.* Privately published.

Periodicals

"A Special Study of Operation Vittles," *Aviation Operations,* April 1949, 1-120.

Fisher, Paul. "The Berlin Airlift," *The Bee Hive* (United Aircraft Corporation), vol. 23, No. 4, Fall 1948.

Grose, Peter, ed. "The Berlin Airlift and the Future of the City," *Foreign Affairs,* July/August, 1998.

Harrington, Daniel F. "Philip Mosely and Access to Berlin," *The SHARF Newsletter,* September 1999, 1-9.

Morrissey, Bill. "The Tree Grew," *Phi Delta Kappa Magazine,* August 1978, 6-9.

Moser, Roger W., Jr. "Recollections of the Berlin Airlift," *The Journal of Air Traffic Control,* January-March 1999, 26-31.

Myers, Howard S., Jr. "Operation Vittles: Flying the Berlin Airlift in a C-47," *Airpower,* March 1994, 36-45.

Powell, Stewart M. "The Berlin Airlift," *Air Force,* June 1998, 1-15.

"The Forgotten Heroes of the Berlin Airlift," *Sergeants,* May 1998, 10-12.

Wernick, Robert. "Yalta: Witness to History," *Smithsonian,* January 2000, 101-114.

White, Stan. "The Berlin Airlift," *Mart,* July-September 1998, 12, 13.

Notes

3 "We must be prepared"....Clay. *Decision in German,* 239.

4 One must give trust....Charles E. Bohlen. *Witness to History,* 222.

4 "Within a few months"....*Ibid.*

4 Without warning....Ann and John Tusa. *The Berlin Blockade,* 47.

5 "After addressing"....Robert Murphy. *Diplomat Among Warriors,* 262.

5 "It was agreed"....Clay. *Decision in Germany,* 26.

5 no official record....Jean Edward Smith, ed. *The Papers of General Lucius D. Clay,* vol. *1,* 27–35 Hereafter cited as *Clay Papers.* Smith records herein notes of the meeting kept by Gen. Floyd C. Parks. He states that these notes comprise the only record of the verbal agreements made. Clay, however, kept his own minutes as indicated above, but in a less complete fashion than Park's notes. Historian Daniel Harrington also found summaries of the meeting in the British Public Record Office.

6 He then went on....Clay. *Decision in Germany,* 26.

6 Colonel Frank Howley....Frank Howley. *Berlin Command.* The account of Howley's journey into Berlin is adapted and summarized from pp. 26–38.

7 After a delay of....U.S. Department of State. *Foreign Relations of the United States,* vol. *1, 1945,* 123. Hereafter cited as *FRUS.*

7 In Berlin itself....Tusa. *The Berlin Blockade,* 31.

8 Howley was directed....Howley. *Berlin Command,* 42, 43.

8 At one point in....*Ibid.,* 43.

8 The drive came....Walter Henry Nelson. *The Berliners,* 127.

8 Defending German troops....Anthony Read and David Fisher. *Berlin: The Biography of a City,* 240.

9 Seventy-six per cent....Jean Edward Smith. *The Defense of Berlin,* 67.

9   Since no motorized....Clay. *Decision in Germany*, 32.

9   Medical services....*Ibid.*

9   His chief of staff....William D. Leahy. *I Was There*, 355, 356.

9   It was only then....*Ibid.*

10   "No, not until"....Herbert Feis. *Between War and Peace—The Potsdam Conference*, 141.

10   Zhukov was insistent....*Ibid.*

10   Stalin's reins on....Thomas Parrish. *Berlin in the Balance*, 27.

10   It was Andrei Y. Vishinsky ....Murphy. *Diplomat Among Warriors*, 28.

11   The Soviet Command....Parrish. *Berlin in the Balance,* 79.

12   "to take revenge"....Norman N. Naimark. *The Russians in Germany*, 74.

12   In some cases....*Ibid.*, 80.

12   Many victims could not recall....Anthony Read and David Fisher. *Berlin: The Biography of a City,* 258.

12   Even the armies....Clay. *Decision in Germany*, 64.

12   A rationale for....Milovan Djilas. *Conversations with Stalin.*

12   "The Red Army lost"....Tusa. *The Berlin Blockade*, 24.

13   The number of daily....*Ibid.*, 47.

13   "The Russians seldom"....*Ibid.*, 48.

14   The agreement....*Ibid.*, 48, 49.

14   "Give us the tools"....Winston S. Churchill. *The Grand Alliance*, 128.

14   "former naval person".... *Ibid.*

15   "a conference between us"....*Ibid.*, 427.

15   "the very maximum"....*Ibid.,* 444. Roosevelt adhered to the principles pf the Atlantic Charter, using them as a guide for conducting the war effort. See The Public Papers of Franklin D. Roosevelt, volume 13, 1944–45. New York:Russell & Russell, 564 (post-Yalta press conference aboard the U.S.S. *Quincy,* February 23, 1945): and 579 (address to the Congress on the Yalta conference, March 1, 1945).

16   "American industrial"....Bohlen, *Witness to History,* 150.

16   "Allow me to express"....Murphy, *Diplomat Among Warriors,* 163.

17   Limited recognition of....*Ibid.,* 184.

17   "He foresaw in the"....*Ibid.,* 139, 140.

18   Churchill stayed at....*Ibid.*, 135.

19   The Russians had....*Ibid.*, 171–174.

19   "Roosevelt weather"....*FRUS*, 1945, vol. 1, 558, 559.

20   France, after considerable....Murphy, *Diplomat Among Warriors*, 237.

20   A compromise....Rosenman, *The Public Papers of FDR*, vol. *13*, 535, 536.

21   "We will meet again"....Murphy, *Diplomat Among Warriors,* 264.

21   Hopkins, with whom....Truman, *Memoirs, vol. 1*, 262, 263.

21   "I decided to make"....*Ibid.*, 333.

22 Since his predecessor....Murphy, *Diplomat Among Warriors,* 269.

22 In classic Truman fashion....Bohlen, *Witness to History,* 226.

22 Through the final months....*Ibid.*

22 "No, I don't need one"....Truman, *Memoirs, vol. 1,* 340.

23 In the final weeks....Tusa, *The Berlin Blockade,* 28, 29.

23 "a decision of such"....Murphy, *Diplomat Among Warriors,* 229

23 Brightened by new paint....Bohlen, *Witness to History,* 227.

25 "Stalin and his group....Murphy, *Diplomat Among Warriors,* 279.

26 Although Ulbricht and....Read and Fisher, *Berlin,* 249.

26 Ulbricht, who one day....*Ibid.,* 248, 249.

26 One document innocently....Howley, *Berlin Command,* 61.

30 At the second Quebec....Rosenman, *The Public Papers of FDR,* 269.

30 "No one wants to"....*Ibid.,* 269, 270.

30 "I made it clear"....Truman, *Memoirs, vol. 1,* 235.

30 "That was the end"....*Ibid.,* 237.

31 "[Lewis and I] were shocked"....Clay, *Decision in Germany,* 18.

31 "This thing was assembled"....Murphy, *Diplomat Among Warriors,* 251.

31 The document had been....*Ibid.*

31 Not wishing to become....*Ibid.,* 285.

33 "The British occupiers"....Tusa, *The Berlin Blockade,* 52.

33 By comparison, there were....*Ibid.*

34 In the Allied Control Council....Clay, *Decision in Germany,* 105.

34 As an American....*Ibid.,* 78.

34 "As long as an occupation"....*Ibid.,* 79.

34 General Clay had expressed....Smith, *Lucius D.Clay: An American Life,* 388. Hereafter cited as *Clay.*

35 Germany's financial condition....Clay, *Decision in Germany,* 209.

36 Following ten weeks of....*Ibid.,* 209–211.

36 Clay remained opposed....Smith, ed., *Clay Papers, vol. 1,* 303.

36 By early December....Clay, *Decision in Germany,* 209.

36 "In fact, we are trying"....Smith, ed., *Clay Papers, vol. 1,* 512.

38 Unless the Russian....Bohlen, *Witness to History,* 262, 263.

39 "a large scale attempt"....Zubek and Pleshakov, *Inside the Kremlin's Cold War,* 50.

40 Matters of Germany and....Smith, *Clay,* 446.

40 Throughout seventeen....*FRUS, vol. 12, 1947,* 676–829.

41 At the same time....Murphy et al, *Battleground Berlin,* 55.

41 Then, on December 22....*Ibid.,* 52.

41 Behavior on informal....Clay, *Decision in Germany,* 159.

41   Sensing the Soviet mood....Shlaim, *The United States and the Berlin Blockade*, 111.

41   Much later, in July....Miller, *To Save A City,* 110.

41   "By late 1947"....Bohlen, *Witness to History*, 275.

42   They also moved ahead....*Ibid.*

42   During the remainder of....Förster et al, eds , *Auftrag Luftbrücke*, 110, 113.

43   General Clay reported....Clay, *Decision in Germany*, 136.

43   Field Marshal Sir Bernard....*Ibid.*

43   At the January 20 ACC....Smith, *Clay,* 465.

43   At the council's next....*Ibid.*

43   "which repeated all of the"....Clay, Decision in Germany, 356.

44   "I certainly did not expect"....Smith, *Clay,* 471.

44   Air Commodore Reginald....Account of the five British agents was adapted from "Conversations with RNW," privately published in the early 1970s and furnished to me by the Waite family.

44   USAFE C-47s hauled 327 tons....Giangreco and Griffin, *Airbridge to Berlin,* 78, 79; Harrington, *The Air Force Can Deliver Anything,* 8, 9.

45   He told his officers and men....Clay, *Decision in Germany,* 360.

45   Bradley was happy, but....Smith, *Clay,* 475.

46   In his view, the blockade....*Ibid.,* 480.

47   Secretary of the Army....Murphy, *Diplomat Among Warriors*, 316.

48   President Truman, however....*Ibid.*

48   On June 26 he dispatched....*FRUS*, vol. 12, 1948, 919.

48   "If we docilely withdraw"....*Ibid.*

48   "The U.S. position in Europe....*Ibid.,* 920.

48   Ambassador Murphy conjectured....*Ibid.*

48   "Moreover," continued Caffery....*Ibid.,* 916, 917.

49   "We could sustain"....Clay, *Decision in Germany,* 365.

49   These veteran workhorses....Harrington, *The Air Force Can Deliver Anything,* 17.

49   A 47-year-old flying boat....Letter from Romilly Waite (daughter), February 26, 2002.

49   In fact, he had already....Smith, *Clay,* 500.

50   If it turned out....LeMay, *Mission with LeMay,* 413.

50   "If you do that"....Collier, *Bridge Across the Sky*, 55.

50   "I am still convinced"....Smith, ed., *Clay Papers,* 697.

50   "All you can haul".... LeMay, *Mission with LeMay,* 415.

50   "I want you to take every"....Smith, *Clay,* 501.

51   By the end of the month...."A Special Study of Operation Vittles, 8.

51   "No matter what we may do"....Smith, *Clay,* 501.

51 "General, I can assure you"....*Ibid.*

52 "I never asked"....*Ibid.*, 502, 503.

52 "It is my duty not to carry us"....*New York Times*, July 24, 1948, 2.

52 "On June 26, the day after I"....Truman, *Memoirs*, vol. 2, 123

52 "demanded the biggest possible"....Tusa, *The Berlin Blockade*, 152.

52 The next day Bevin issued....*Ibid.*

53 He called on Brigadier General....Launius and Cross, *MAC and the Legacy of the Berlin Airlift,* 10

53 On June 26, C-47s flying out of....*Ibid.*, 11.

53 Thirty days later....*Landing on Tempelhof*, 92-95.

53 Too slow and capable of....Brig. Gen. Sterling P. Bettinger, Telephone Interview, December 1999.

54 "It must be admitted that"....Christienne and Lissarague, *A History of French Military Aviation*, 436.

54 "But this was not combat"....Tunner, *Over The Hump,* 160.

54 "So I was relieved"....Lt. Gen. Joseph Smith Oral History Interview, 230.

54 "I am frank to say"....*Ibid.*, 234.

54 "He [Tunner] didn't create"....*Ibid.*, 235.

55 Warming to an idea....Harrington, *The Air Force Can Deliver Anything*, 52; Gen. Smith Oral History Interview, 231.

55 "Two planes based at Fassberg"....Tunner, *Over The Hump,* 186.

58 "The three week course provided....Miller, *To Save a City,* 80.

58 Needless to say, they had not....*Ibid.*

58 Upon arrival in Germany....*The Task Force Times,* April 14, 1949.

58 A little airlift within....*The Times* (London), November 24, 1948, 2.

58 In August 1948....Tusa, *The Berlin Blockade*, 178.

59 They took a quick look....Halvorsen, *The Berlin Candy Bomber*, 42-44.

61 "We urge you to make"....Merrill, gen. ed., *Documentary History of the Truman Presidency,* 20, 21.

61 Representatives of the labor....*Ibid.*, 14, 26, 62, 86, 87.

61 Throughout Germany in particular....*New York Times*, July 26, 1948, 2.

61 "Dear President Truman"....Merrill, gen. ed., *Documentary History*, 593, 594.

61 "The so-called Berlin Crisis"....*Ibid.*

61 In Philadelphia at the....*New York Times,* July 26, 1948, 1.

65 "The National Security Council....Clay, *Decision in Germany*, 385.

65 Other wrecks occurred....*The Times* (London), November 29, 1948, 4.

66 The winter of 1948-1949....*New York Times,* November 30, 1948, 4, 12.

66 By Tuesday, November 30, 1948....*Ibid.*, December 2, 1948, 8.

66 Despite such doubts....Interview, St. Louis, September 28, 1999.

67 "the general certainly earned"....*Ibid.*

67   Discovered by movie magnate....*New York Times,* July 26, 1965, 23: 1.

68   Cal, who was assigned....Interview, St. Louis, September 27, 1999.

69   When Connie arrived in Fassberg....Letter from Herta Tiede, August 2, 2000.

69   The few wives present....Interview, September 28, 1999.

70   Hope and his group....Letter from Jeffrey Dwinell (son), February 15, 2001.

70   "Soup I can take"....As cited in Haydock, *City Under Siege,* 257.

71   Another Fassberg group....*The Task Force Times,* December 20, 1948.

73   Captain Flynn worked aggressively....*Ibid.,* May 14, 1949.

73   The former secretariat officer....Murphy, Kondrashev, and Bailey, *Battleground Berlin,* 67.

73   Although secrecy surrounded....Morrison interview.

74   Kingsbury Smith, an American....Bohlen, *Witness to History,* 283-285.

74   "Truman and [Secretary of State]....*Ibid.,* 285.

84   On February 12, 1921....*The Official Guide to the Army Air Forces,* 16, 35, 194, 241.

85   "During the Berlin airlift"....Telephone Interview, October 18, 2001.

85   "Although much of the technology"....Ginagreco and Griffin, *Airbridge to Berlin,* 199, 200.

86   "Train trips to Hannover"....Morrissey, *The Tree Grew,* 7.

87   "act of brutality against"....*New York Times,* December 17, 1948, 1:4.

97   "For exceptionally meritorious service"....USAFE Release No. A329, July 11, 1949.

99   Harmon, you are going to head"....Harmon, *Combat Commander: Autobiography Of A Soldier,* 280.

104 Elizabeth "Libby" O'Neal....Libby's son, Jeffrey, completed a questionnaire about his late mother. His father, Cliff, died January 6, 2002.

110 Some flight engineers suffered....Hanlon and Keating *Memoirs* and Newspaper Clips.

111 Technical Sergeant William R. Michaels....Much of the segment on Bill Michaels is adapted from his memoirs, *A Love Story.*

117 Other pilots achieved fame....Slaker, *Memoirs.*

136 Yes, there were British women....Portions of Joyce's story were furnished by questionnaire and also adapted from the December 1999 BBAA Newsletter.

138 Nineteen-year-old Brian Cooper....Portions of Brian's story were furnished by questionnaire and also adapted from the BBAA Newsletter.

139 In October 1947, Ted Duck....Portions of Ted's story were furnished by questionnaire and also adapted from the June 2000 BBAA Newsletter.

162 In the accompanying culture....Read and Fisher, *Berlin: The Biography of a City,* 169.

162 "The people in Berlin, I must say"....Shirer, *Berlin Diary,* 333.

162 "Berliners were a rather special breed"....Donovan, *Bridge in The Sky,* 27.

163 "on six great wagons"....Read and Fisher, *Berlin: The Biography of a City*, 63, 64.

163 Destroyed in World War II....Color Collection GmbH International, *Berlin: Color Collection Städte*, 21.

163 Allied bombing between 1943 and 1945....Everett, *Das War Berlin*, 8.

164 "[It] is bigger than all of Chicago"....*The Berliners: Their Saga and Their City*, 19.

164 Berliners take great pride....Everett, *Das War Berlin*, 8.

166 "There seems to be a great"....Letter, January 21, 2000.

169 For Gisela, her early childhood years....Portions of Gisela's story are adapted from "A Berliner's Memories of Berlin," *Friends Journal*, Summer 1998, 103. By permission and from memoirs furnished me by Mrs. Stevenson.

178 Inge and I met in September 1999....Portions of Inge's story are adapted by permission from her *Memories of World War II by a Little Girl Growing up in Berlin*, September 1999.

180 In September 2000, Christian....Adapted by permission from the text of Christian's speech.

191 A local resident, F. Green....*The Times* (London), November 23, 1948, 4.

196 Daniel Harrington's careful....*The Air Force Can Deliver Anything*, 114.

196 and Wolfgang Huschke's detail....*The Candy Bombers*, 271–274.

234 "During the first ten years"....*Berlin Airlift*, 134.

234 "By 1997 four airlift widows"....*Ibid.*

242 "During the entire period"....Murphy, *Diplomat Among Warriors*, 321. Italics mine.

243 "The Soviet leadership...had not been"....Gaddis, *We Now Know*, 48.

244 In that same year, 1989....Recorded January 1989 at Universal Recording Corp., Chicago.

Index

317th Troop Carrier Wing
  documented airlift role, 106
AACS (Airways and Air
  Communications Service). *See also*
  GCA
  airlift demands, 85
  origin, 84
  personal stories, 84–88
ACC (Allied Control Council)
  convening, 11
  installing, 10
  member relationships, 43
  Soviet walkout, 43
air corridors
  establishing, 13
  governance, 14
Air Force, U.S.
  participating personnel, 81
Air Police
  origin, 82
  personal stories, 82–84
airlift. *See also* Operation Vittles,
  See also Operation Plainfare
  calculating logistics, 49
  commencing, 50
  humanitarian undertaking, 243
  implementing decision, 53
  official announcement, 50
  perfecting procedures, 73
  perspective, 242
  public support, 61
  Soviet interference, 135
airlift anniversary. *See* fiftieth
  anniversary, *See* fortieth
  anniversary, *See* thirtieth
  anniversary

Airlift Gratitude Foundation
  broadened mission, 234
  supporting veteran dependents,
  234
airlift memorial. *See also*
  Luftbrückendenkmal
  at Alrewas, Staffordshire, 238
  at Gatow, 187
  at Rhein-Main, 228, 236
  dedicated at Dover, 187
  dedicated at Fassberg, 227
  rededicated at Tempelhof, 232
airlift museum. *See also* Allied
  Museum
  at Fassberg, 231
Airlift/Tanker Association
  activities, 236
Airways and Air Communications
  Service. *See* AACS
Alker, Ursula
  unloader at Gatow, 175
Allied Control Council. *See* ACC
Allied Museum
  airlift mementos, 232
American forces. *See also*
  Noncommissioned aircrews
  (American), *See also*
  Commissioned aircrews
  (American)
  casualties, 202–24
  housing arrangements for
  dependents, 71
  statistics for airlift accidents, 202
American veterans
  welcomed at Celle, 230
American zone

in 1946, 33
Atlantic Charter
  background, 15
  Soviet Union and, 15
Bachman, F. L., Capt.
  finance officer at Rhein-Main, 103
Ball, W. L., Aircraftsman First Class
  engine fitter at Wunstorf, 143
Barlow, Leslie, Signaller 1
  wireless operator at Wunstorf,
    Fassberg, Lübeck, 151
Baronsky, Rainer
  parachute candy drop, Tempelhof,
    174
base support specialists
  personal stories, 102–10
Batteas, J. D., Cpl.
  presented Legion of Merit, 97
  radio mechanic, Rhein-Main, 96
BAVA (Berlin Airlift Veterans
  Association)
  activities, 236
Beeskow, Eva
  ordnance supply specialist,
    Steglitz, 172
Bennett, Constance
  morale builder, 67
Bennett, Donald, Capt.
  World War II Pathfinder fame,
    154
Bergen-Belsen concentration camp
  reminder of Nazi atrocities, 230
Bergh, Ian, Flying Officer
  flying Sunderlands, 63
Berlin
  1948, 163
  2002, 244
  after more than fifty years, 244
  communist control, 25
  devastation, 9
  electing city officials, 35
  establishing communist control,
    26
  final siege, 8
  geography, 164
  historic, 162
  unofficial access agreement, 5
Berlin Airlift Historical Foundation
  setting up, 234
Berlin Airlift Veterans Association.
  See BAVA
Berliners
  1918-1945, 161

1948-1949, 165
  personal stories, 165–84
  personality, 164
  propagandizing, 11
Berman, S., Sgt.
  military pay section, Rhein-Main,
    103
Bettinger, Sterling P., Maj.
  retirement rank, 123
Big Lift, The
  movie with Montgomery Clift, 103
Blackwood, George, Ens.
  injured in aircrash near
    Königstein, 214
blockade
  ending, 74
  implemented, 46
  settlement terms, 242
  two months after end, 242
  western response, 47
Bohlen, Charles (Chip)
  on getting along with Russians, 4
Boyd, Ralph Hopkins, 1st Lt.
  aircrash fatality near Rhein-Main,
    218
Bradley, Omar, Gen.
  reassigning son-in-law, 45
British Berlin Airlift Association
  activities, 237
British forces. See also
  Commissioned forces (British), See
    also Noncommissioned forces
    (British)
  airlift complexities, 129
  airlift personalities, 129
  casualties, 188–95
  home leave, 130
  occupation approach, 33
  statistics for airlift accidents, 195
British Royal Air Force
  detained at Gatow airfield, 7
British zone
  in 1946, 33
Brodie, Lt.
  Sudbahnhof party, 69
Bruns, August, mayor of Fassberg
  escorting veterans at 1989
    reunion, 226
Burns, George S., Cpl.
  ground fatality at Tegel, 211
Bushell, Graeme, Flight Lt.
  York pilot at Wunstorf, 149
Bushell, John L., Sgt.

army engineer at Fühlsbuttel, 132
Byrnes, James F., Secretary of State
  achievements, 37
  on American occupation, 34
C-47 airplane
  background, 57
C-54 Skymaster
  aircrew training, 58
C-74 Globemaster
  transporting engines to States, 97
Cannon, John K., Lt. Gen.
  USAFE command, 55
Carsey, David N., Leading
  Aircraftsman
  on meaningful airlift experience,
    243
Casablanca conference
  Stalin and, 16
Celle air base
  community features, 116
  housing problem, 60
CFM (Council of Foreign Ministers)
  disunity, 40
  failure, 40
  formation, 39
Chopp, Tim
  setting up Berlin Airlift Historical
    Foundation, 234
Church, Charles K., Staff Sgt.
  on French occupation, 32
Churchill, Winston. See also Poland,
  establishing borders
  Atlantic Charter, 15
  Casablanca conference, 16
  Iron Curtain speech, 38
  meets Roosevelt, 15
  Soviet postwar intentions, 22
  Teheran conference, 17
civilian (German)
  airlift casualties, 196–97
civilian contract flyers
  access to navigation aids, 156
  age and career service, 158
  personal stories, 153–58
  statistics, 154
Clark, Charley
  gifts for Berlin children, 71
Clark, Johnny, 1st Lt.
  pilot at Wiesbaden, Fassberg,
    Berlin, 117
Clay, Lucius D., Gen.
  appointed Command-in-Chief
    Europe, 37

  at Karlshorst meeting, 5
  at NSC meeting, 3
  early years in Germany, 4
  JCS 1067 and, 29
  on JCS 1067 restrictions, 30
  support for airlift, 52
Clift, Roger, PFC
  at Templehof, 99
Colburn, James P., Sgt.
  radio operator at Rhein-Main, 115
Cole, Kinzie K., Aviation Electronics
  Technician Second Class
  at Rhein-Main, 95
Colegrove, Larry (Corky), Sgt.
  crew chief at Rhein-Main, 97
Collett, Bill, Sgt.
  in military pay section, Rhein-
    Main, 103
Commissioned aircrews (American)
  age and career service, 122
  personal stories, 117–22
Commissioned forces (British)
  age and career service, 157
  personal stories, 149–53
Commissioned forces
  (Commonwealth)
  age and career service, 157
  personal stories, 149–53
Commonwealth forces. See also
  Commissioned forces
  (Commonwealth), See also
  Noncommissioned forces
  (Commonwealth)
  airlift personalities, 129
  casualties, 188–95
  statistics for airlift accidents, 195
Condon, Tom, Lt.
  awarded Air Force Cross, 149
Constabulary forces
  establishing, 99
  personal stories, 98–101
Cooper, Brian, Pvt.
  army infantryman at Kladow, 138
Coulter, Theron (Jack), Col.
  base commander, Fassberg, 67
Council of Foreign Ministers. See
  CFM
Cramp, Bert G.
  radio engineer at Wunstorf,
    Schleswigland, 154
Crisp-Jones, Ken, Maj.
  at Wunstorf, 141
Crites, Harry Russel, Jr., AMM3

aircrash fatality near Königstein,
88, 214
Crowley, Terence O'Neil, Leading
Aircraftsman
engine fitter at Hamburg, 140
currency reform
implementing, 35, 42, 45
reason for the blockade, 74
Soviets and, 36
Curtis, Paul, Sgt.
senior aircraft mechanic at Rhein-
Main, 98
Cyzmoure, Robert N., 1st Lt.
pilot at Wiesbaden and Celle, 120
Czamata, Ed, Tech. Sgt.
military pay section, Rhein-Main,
103
Dakota airplane
airlift service, 57
overloading, 152
Dargatz, Werner
unloader at Gatow, 181
Davies, B. D., Flight Lt.
pilot at Wunstorf, 149
Davis, C. C., 1st Lt.
deputy finance officer, Rhein-
Main, 103
Dawe, Desmond, Leading
Aircraftsman
Fitter IIA Airframes, Wunstorf,
131
Day, Diane
Special Services at Tempelhof, 88
de Gaulle, Charles
French Committee of National
Liberation, 17
ordering American departure, 32
Demitrowitz, Werner
crafting airlift models, 167
unloader at Gatow, 166
DeVolentine, Joel Monroe, Capt.
aircraft collision fatality over
Ravolzhausen, 206
background, 207
Diltz, Edwin Cary, Maj.
aircraft collision fatality over
Ravolzhausen, 207
background, 208
Dionne, Ralph G., Sgt.
flight engineer, Rhein-Main, 113
Dodge, Joseph, Dr.
planning currency reform, 36

Dougan, Walter (Dickie), Master
Pilot
at Fassberg and Lübeck, 146
Douglas, Lewis W.
on JCS 1067 restrictions, 30
Dowling, Frank, Sgt.
aircrash fatality in Soviet zone,
191
Downes, Michael, Flight Lt.
airlift service, 58
Duck, Edward W., Aircraftsman
radar operator at Wunstorf, 139
Durbin, Clarence W., Tech. Sgt.
line mechanic at Burtonwood, 73
Dwinell, Clifford, Capt.. See also
O'Neal, Elizabeth (Libby)
flying Bob Hope, 70
EAC (European Advisory
Commission)
forming occupation zones, 19
Eade, Flight Sgt.
navigator at Wunstorf, 153
Eagle Aviation
contractor, 155
Eakins, Merle, Cpl.
military pay section, Rhein-Main,
103
Edwards, David, Aircraftsman First
Class
on airlift calculations, 49
Edwards, E. F. (Ted), Flight Lt.
pilot at Wunstorf, 152
Erdmann, Wera
young girl during airlift, 180
Erdmann, Werner
laborer at Tegel, 179
unloader at Tempelhof, 179
Erickson, Eugene Samuel, 1st Lt.
aircrash fatality near Rhein-Main,
210
European Advisory Commission. See
EAC
Fairall, Barbara. See Moschberger,
Ilse
Fassberg air base
housing problems, 59
proximity to town, 227
touring in 1999, 231
USAF assumes command, 58
Fellman, Jack D., Cpl.
control tower operator and air
traffic controller at Templehof,
87

fiftieth anniversary
  of airlift end, 230
  of airlift's onset, 229
flight engineers
  job responsibilities, 110
  personal stories, 110–16
flying boat. *See also* Sunderland
  flying boat, *See also* Hythe flying
  boat
  unloading, 62
Flynn, N. C., Capt.
  requisitioning dependent housing,
  72
Flynn's Inn
  American dependents and
  housing, 71
fog
  impact, 65
Foppe-Vorpahl, Michael
  beneficiary of airlift medicine, 167
Forrest, Mary
  gifts for Berlin children, 71
fortieth anniversary
  at Berlin, 228
  at Fassberg, 226
  at Frankfurt, 228
French participation
  limited, 53
French policy
  ACC vetoes, 34
Fuller, David, Staff Sgt.
  cashier at Rhein-Main, 103
Gathercole, Ernest E., Signalman
  army keyboard operator, Berlin,
  133
Gatow airfield
  rebuilding the runway, 142
GCA (Ground Controlled Approach)
  assuring airlift success, 85
George, Robert G., Cpl.
  draftsman and surveyor at Gatow,
  142
German Civil Labor Organization
  loaders memorialized, 231
Gibbs, Roy Reginald, Engineer II
  aircrash fatality at Tegel, 195
Gibson, Katie
  civilian, 54
Glazener, Edwin L., Capt.
  flight surgeon at Wiesbaden, 119
Goot, Al, pilot
  baseball coach at Celle, 102
Grams, Orville C. (Sarge), Staff Sgt.

flight engineer at Wiesbaden, 114
Green, John
  gifts for Berlin children, 71
Gross, Bill
  unloading supervisor at
  Tempelhof, 116
Gross, Inge Stannek
  on remembering experiences, 166
Ground Controlled Approach. *See*
  GCA
ground support forces (American)
  age and career service, 122
Grout, John E., Signaller I
  aircrash fatality in Soviet zone,
  193
Gunkel, Alexander
  schoolboy during airlift, 175
Hagen, Karl Victor
  aircrash fatality near Königstein,
  204
Hall, Frederick A. (Joe), PFC
  line mechanic and flight engineer
  at Rhein-Main, 90
Halvorsen, Gail S., 1st Lt.
  parachute candy drops, 117
Hamilton, James, Radio Officer
  aircrash survivor, Schleswigland,
  193
Hamilton, Jock
  at Flynn's Inn, 72
Hanlon, John L., Staff Sgt.
  bailing out over Soviet zone, 110
Hargis, Willis Francis, 1st Lt.
  aircrash fatality at Fassberg, 213
Hargrave-Wright, Jack. *See also*
  Peachey, Joyce, Aircraftwoman
  Class I
  wireless operator at Bad Eilsen,
  136
Harmon, Ernest N., Gen.
  heading the constabulary, 99
Haynes, Calvin R., Staff Sgt.
  remembering Connie Bennett, 68
Heffernan, Frank T., 1st Lt.
  aircrash survivor at Königstein,
  214
Heinig, Herbert Frederick, Tech. Sgt.
  aircrash fatality in Soviet zone,
  112, 223
Heinig, Karl-Heinz, foreman
  unloading flying boats, 62
Hermiston-Hooper, Derek W., Capt.
  youngest contract flier, 154

Hide, Robert A., Master Signaller
 at Fassberg and Lübeck, 144
 shot down over northwest
 Germany, 144
Hines, David T., Aircraftsman First
 Class
 radar operator at Tremsbüttel,
 145
Hirst, Ronald M. A.
 on American casualties, 201
Hitler
 Berliners' view of, 164
Hope, Bob
 entertaining troops, 70
 rescheduling for airlift personnel,
 70
Hopkins, Harry
 personal advisor to Roosevelt, 10,
 21
Howard, William Riley, Capt.
 aircraft collision fatality over
 Ravolzhausen, 207
 background, 208
Howland, Richard I., Cpl.
 truck driver at Fassberg, 108
Howley, Frank, Col., deputy
 commandant
 detained at Babelsberg, 7
 entering Berlin, 9
 incident in transit to Berlin, 8
Hudson, Ralph H., Cpl.
 air policeman at
 Oberpfaffenhofen, 83
Hythe flying boat
 delivering salt, 62
Immel, Harry D., Jr., Capt.
 number of missions, 117
Izard, Peter, Cpl.
 loadmaster at Wunstorf, 141
JCS 1067
 British and, 31
 French and, 31
 instructions for day-to-day
 occupation, 30
 interpreted, 31
 origin, 29
 Roosevelt and, 30
 Soviets and, 31
 Truman and, 30
Jessup, Philip, UN Ambassador, 74
Karlshorst meeting
 addressing occupation details, 5
Keating, Thomas W., Lt.

bailing out over Soviet zone, 110
Kemp, Larry, Lt.
 arriving at Fassberg, 60
Kilburn, John
 radio officer at Gatow, 154
King, Charles Howard, 1st Lt.
 aircrash fatality at Tempelhof,
 205
King, Kenneth W., Sgt.
 army loadmaster at Wunstorf, 135
Kinzalow, William A., Sgt.
 bailing out over Soviet zone, 110
Kite, John B., Aircraftsman Second
 Class
 instrument mechanic at Lübeck,
 137
Konev, Ivan S., Marshal
 advancing on Berlin, 8
Korndorfer, Bill, Sgt.
 dancing with Connie Bennett, 69
Kurnoth, Dietmar
 Berliner's outlook, 64
Lacakes, Kathy
 gifts for Berlin children, 71
Ladd, Craig Burton, 1st Lt.
 aircrash fatality near Rhein-Main,
 219
Lancashire Aircraft Corporation
 liquid-fuel carrying operations,
 155
Latimer, Courtenay A., 2nd Lt.
 unloading flying boats, 62
Lawrence, David
 flight engineer at Fühlsbuttel, 156
Leemon, Donald J., 2nd Lt.
 aircrash fatality in Soviet zone,
 222
LeMay, Curtis, Gen.. See also airlift,
 commencing
 commander USAFE, 50
lend-lease program
 Soviet participation, 14, 15
Lewis, Paddy
 signaller at Wunstorf, 153
Licata, Joe, Staff Sgt.
 cashier at Rhein-Main, 103
Lindsay air station
 rededication of street names, 228
line mechanics (American)
 personal stories, 88–98
 working conditions, 88
London, Jack F.
 at Flynn's Inn, 72

Louch, Philip Arthur, Signaller III
  aircrash fatality in Soviet zone,
    190
Lowe, Albert, 1st Lt.
  airlift service, 55
Lübeck airfield
  accommodations for ground crews,
    137
Lucas, William T., Jr., 1st Lt.
  aircraft collision fatality over
    Ravolzhausen, 206
  background, 207
Luftbrückendenkmal
  airlift memorial, 165
  nickname, 165
Luftwaffe airplane mechanics
  line mechanics, Oberpfaffenhofen,
    91
  line mechanics, Rhein-Main, 90
Malik, Jacob, UN Ambassador, 74
Malone, Mike
  flight engineer at Wunstorf, 153
Manning, James F., Flight Lt.
  pilot at Wunstorf, Fassberg,
    Lübeck, 151
Marshall Plan
  enacted into law, 38
  Stalin's view, 38
Marshall, George C., Gen.
  establishing new foreign policy, 38
McBride, Malcolm A., PFC
  truck driver at Berlin, 109
McClarity, George, PFC air
  policeman, Rhein-Main, 82
Measley, Donald W., 1st Lt.
  pilot at Rhein-Main and Fassberg,
    121
  presented flowers by barefoot
    child, 121
Meier, Dorothea
  chambermaid at Fassberg, 183
Meyer, George M., Cpl.
  Army engineer at Berlin, 107
Michaels, William R., Tech. Sgt.
  flight engineer at Celle, 111
Molkenbuhr, Horst
  unloader at Tempelhof, 168
Monasmith, Robert, PFC
  moving to Berlin, 9
Morgenthau, Henry, Treasury
  Secretary
  JCS 1067 and, 29
Morrison, Earl, Tech. Sgt.

flying in dense fog, 66
Morrissey, William E., PFC
  control tower operator at Celle, 85
Morton, George F., Aircraftsman
  First Class
  teleprinter operator at Bushy
    Park, 132
Moschberger, Ilse
  leaving in Plainfare aircraft, 177
Munn, Gerald L., 1st Lt.
  pilot at Wiesbaden, 119
Murtishaw, Fred I., Cpl.
  line mechanic at Oberpfaffenhofen
    and Burtonwood, 91
Navy, U.S.
  airlift role, 57
  participating personnel, 81
Neild, Donald R., Cpl.
  information specialist, Celle, 102
Neumann, Richard K. O.
  truck collision fatality at
    Schleswigland, 196
Nichol, Ken
  flight engineer at Wunstorf and
    Hamburg, 155
Noncommissioned aircrews
  (American)
  age and career service, 122
Noncommissioned forces (British)
  age and career service, 157
  personal stories, 131–49
Noncommissioned forces
  (Commonwealth)
  age and career service, 157
  personal stories, 131–49
Norris, Joseph L., Lt.
  injured in aircrash near
    Königstein, 214
Oberpfaffenhofen air base
  maintenance depot, 83
occupation zones
  Eisenhower and, 23
O'Neal, Elizabeth (Libby)
  civilian secretary, Wiesbaden, 70,
    104
Operation Plainfare
  British name for airlift, 53
  memorial, 187
Operation Santa Claus
  for Berlin children, 70
Operation Vittles
  memorial, 187
  named by Gen. Smith, 53

Orms, Johnnie Thomas, PFC
   ground fatality at Rhein-Main,
      209
Overington, John, Sgt.
   army line mechanic, Bückeburg,
      147
Peachey, Joyce, Aircraftswoman
   Class I. *See also* Hargrave-Wright,
   Jack
   air traffic controller at Bad Eilsen,
      136
Peat, James W., PII
   pilot at Lübeck, 134
Phelps, Billy Eugene, Capt.
   aircrash fatality at Fassberg, 212
pilot certifications
   authorized load and, 149
Pinson, Cloyde C., Tech. Sgt.
   maintenance and supply sergeant
      major at Fassberg, 92
Plumber Flight
   purpose, 58
Pohmer, Karl
   unloader at Tempelhof, 171
Poland
   establishing borders, 18, 20
Polish guards
   guarding Fassberg, 83
Potsdam conference, 20–25
   agreements, 24
   Churchill and, 22
   events leading to, 14
   Truman and, 20
Potter, Francis H., 1st Lt.
   at 1999 reunion, 231
Putnam, Charles Lee, Tech. Sgt.
   aircrash fatality near Rhein-Main,
      219
Quebec conference
   impact on Soviet relations, 17
Quinn, Mel Joseph, Flight Lt.
   aircrash fatality at Lübeck, 193
radio operators (American)
   personal stories, 110–16
   scarcity, 110
Ralston, Duncan, Lt.
   SAAF pilot-navigator, 149
Raper, Joe, Aircraftsman First Class
   at 1998 Berlin reunion, 229
Rathgeber, William A., Capt.
   aircrash fatality near
      Burtonwood, 217
Reese, Heinz-Gerd

Airlift Gratitude Foundation, 234
Reeves, Kenneth, Flying Officer
   aircrash fatality at Lübeck, 194
Reissaus, Virginia
   Special Services at Tempelhof, 88
reparations
   Soviet's share, 24
Reuter, Ernst
   support and, 51
Robertson, Brian, Gen. Sir
   British support for airlift, 52
Roblejo, Rolando, PFC
   at Fassberg, 93
Ross, John E., Cpl.
   line mechanic, Gatow, 89
Sakkinen, W. J., Sgt.
   bailing out over Soviet zone, 110
Schiele, Harry, Capt.
   arriving at Fassberg, 60
Schnabel, Rudolph
   escorting downed pilot, 117
Scholtz, Gisela Irene Marianne
   war bride, 169
Schuerholz, Louis R., Cpl.
   relationship with Soviets, 39
Seifert, Christian, schoolboy,
   Pankow, 180
Sherwin, V. G., radio officer
   British civilian, 130
Short, Jack A.V., flying officer
   reporting on 1979 reunion, 226
Sickelmore, Stan, Capt.
   on contribution of civil carriers,
      153
Skoog, Kenneth, Cpl.
   radio operator, Rhein-Main, 112
Slaker, Kenneth, Capt.
   bailing out over Soviet zone, 117
Smith, Geoff, RAF airman
   halted by Soviets, 42
Smith, George Bates, 1st Lt.
   aircrash fatality near Königstein,
      204
Smith, Joe, Gen.
   airlift commander, 53, *See also*
      Operation Vittles.
Smith, Walter B., Gen.
   at NSC meeting, 3
South African Air Force
   airlift contribution, 238
South African Air Force Berlin
   Airlift
   Reunion Committee

events, 238
Southers, W. C. (Dub), Staff Sgt.
  BAVA secretary, 116
  flight engineer, Celle, 116
Soviet army
  unconscionable behavior, 12
Soviet Military Administration
  established ordinances, 26
Soviet soldier
  character and personality, 7
Soviet zone
  in 1946, 34
Soviets
  campaign to remove allies, 40
  halting surface traffic, 42, 44
  plundering Berlin, 11
  relationship with western allies in
    1945, 26
Spatafora, James R. (Spat), PFC
  hydraulics specialist, Rhein-Main,
    93
Spirit of Freedom (R5D)
  acquiring, 235
  en route to fiftieth anniversary,
    229
  perpetuating airlift story, 235
Stalin, Joseph V., Marshal
  assuring access to Berlin, 5
Stanley, Vincent, Radio Officer
  survivor of Thurxton aircrash, 192
Stanneck, Inge
  school girl during airlift, 178
Steber, Clarence, Lt.
  bailing out over Soviet zone, 117
Stensrud, Donald L., Sgt.
  control tower operator, Tempelhof,
    86
Stephens, Royce Coe, 1st Lt.
  aircrash fatality in Soviet zone,
    110, 220
Stevens, Steve, Lt. DFC
  SAAF pilot at Lübeck, 151
Stevenson, Irene. *See* Scholtz, Gisela
  Irene Marianne
Stiftung Luftbrückendank. See Airlift
  Gratitude Foundation
Stillwell, Frank, Flying Officer
  navigator at Wunstorf, Fassberg,
    Lübeck, 150
Stone, Ronald E., PFC
  aircrash fatality near
    Burtonwood, 217
Strub, William C., Staff Sgt.

constabulary trooper, Berlin, 99
Stuber, Robert Wallace, 1st Lt.
  aircrash fatality, Tempelhof, 206
Sunderland flying boat
  delivering salt, 62
Supernat, Theodore, Ground
  Engineer
  struck by plane at Schleswigland,
    192
Talty, Thomas S., Sgt.
  finance clerk, Rhein-Main, 103
Taylor, Cyril, Capt.
  aircrash fatality at Thruxton, 191
Taylor, Victor J., Sgt.
  flight line supervisor, Lübeck, 148
technicians (American)
  personal stories, 88–98
  working conditions, 88
Tegel airfield
  building, 107
Teheran conference, 17–18
  results, 18
Terlinden, Dean W., 1st Lt.
  at Potsdam, 23
  weather forecaster, Burtonwood,
    106
Theis, Norbert, Cpl.
  aircrash fatality near
    Burtonwood, 216
thirtieth anniversary
  at Berlin, 226
Thompson, Hugh Wallace, Flight Lt.
  aircrash fatality at Gatow, 189
Tiede, Herta
  remembering Connie Bennett, 69
Tindall, Albert G., Cpl.
  truck driver, Fassberg, Celle, 108
Tobin, Eliot, Major
  arriving at Fassberg, 60
tonnage deliveries
  significant increase, 73
Tosone, Hugh, Sgt.
  airplane electrical mechanic at
    Rhein-Main, 98
Trackler, William, Cpl.
  air policeman, Fassberg,
    Wiesbaden, 83
trains
  delayed by Russians, 13
Travell, Ronald E., Aircraftsman
  First Class
  aircraft electrician, Wunstorf,
    Lübeck, 145

Truman, Harry S., President
specifying access to Berlin, 5
Tunner, William H., Gen.
assuming airlift taskforce
command, 54
flying in dense fog, 66
people skills, 119
Ulbricht, Walter
seizing Berlin, 25
Utting, Clement W., Capt.
struck by lorry, Gatow, 154, 192
VanDervort, Robert W., Sgt.
avionics supervisor at Celle, 96
Vaughan, James Arthur, Capt.
aircrash fatality near Rhein-Main,
210
Victory Quadriga
history, 163
Villas, Capt.
civilian pilot, 156
Vishinsky, Andrei Y., vice-minister
for foreign affairs
authority in Germany, 10
Volkssturm home guard
defending Berlin, 8
von Egloff, Louis
laborer at Tempelhof, 172
von Luehrte, Robert Charles, 1st Lt.
aircrash fatality in Soviet zone,
222
Waite, Reginald N., Air Commodore
calculating logistics, 49
Wallace, Bob, Staff Sgt.
at Fassberg, 93
water transport
access problems, 13
Watkins, Bernard Jerard, Sgt.
aircrash fatality near
Burtonwood, 216
Weaver, Robert Porter, Lt.
aircrash fatality near Fassberg,
220
Wehrmacht Pioneers
engineers at Fühlsbuttel, 132
Wells, Lloyd George, Tech. Sgt.
aircrash fatality, Fassberg, 213
West Germans
employed at military installations,
183
western allies
combining occupation zones, 41
Wheaton, Lowell Adair, Jr., 1st Lt.

aircrash fatality near
Burtonwood, 215
Whipple, Lewis Dale, Cpl.
supply clerk at Celle, 105
Wilkins, John Graham, Flight Lt.
aircraft casualty in Soviet zone,
190
Williams, Leland Vee, 1st Lt.
aircrash fatality near Königstein,
203
Williams, S. Michael, Aircraftsman
Sunderland ride, 62
Williams, Thomas A., Capt.
airlift service, 58
Winter, Richard, Sgt.
aircrash fatality near Rhein-Main,
211
Wurgel, Richard Melvin, 1st Lt.
aircrash fatality near
Burtonwood, 215
Yalta conference
establishing postwar strategy, 19
York (Avro)
takeoff crash at Wunstorf, 136
Young, Samuel, PFC
constabulary trooper, Berlin, 101
Zamboni, Frank, Lt.
airlift service, 56
arriving at Fassberg, 60
Zarkowsky, John, MSgt.
mascot namesake, 97
Zazzera, John L., Sgt.
aircraft dispatcher, Rhein-Main,
104
Zhukov, Georgi K., Marshal
advancing on Berlin, 8
authority in Germany, 10
seizing Berlin, 8
Zülsdorf, Kurt, German Policeman
fatality at Gatow, 196